MAJOR LEAGUE BASEBALL
★ A MILE HIGH ★
THE FIRST QUARTER CENTURY OF THE
Colorado Rockies

EDITED BY BILL NOWLIN AND PAUL T. PARKER
ASSOCIATE EDITORS: LEN LEVIN AND CARL RIECHERS

Society for American Baseball Research, Inc.
Phoenix, AZ

Major League Baseball A Mile High -- The First Quarter Century of the Colorado Rockies

Edited by Bill Nowlin and Paul T. Parker
Associate Editors: Len Levin and Carl Riechers

Front cover photograph:
Top of the ninth, Game Four of the NLCS, October 15, 2007. Before the NLCS began, Arizona's Eric Byrnes
said in an interview that the Diamondbacks were simply a better team than the Rockies. Colorado had won 14
of their last 15 games, including a tiebreaker with the Padres, then swept the Phillies in the Division Series. They
took the first three games from Arizona and completed the sweep in this game, Byrnes lying face down, having
made the last out as first baseman Todd Helton exults at the Rockies having—against all odds—coming from
fourth place on September 16 to earn a berth in the World Series. Photograph courtesy of John Leyba.

Photographs courtesy of the Colorado Rockies Baseball Club and the National Baseball Hall of Fame.
Courtesy of the Colorado Rockies Baseball Club: 8, 27, 31, 71, 76, 80, 89, 94, 108, 118, 123, 128, 140, 160, 179, 180, 194, 251.
Courtesy of the National Baseball Hall of Fame: 19, 38, 45, 56, 66, 85, 99, 146, 151, 167, 174, 209.

ISBN 978-1-943816-77-4
(Ebook ISBN 978-1-943816-76-7)

Book design: Gilly Rosenthol
Society for American Baseball Research
Cronkite School at ASU
555 N. Central Ave. #416
Phoenix, AZ 85004
Phone: (602) 496-1460
Web: www.sabr.org
Facebook: Society for American Baseball Research
Twitter: @SABR

CONTENTS

Nolen Arenado / Charlie Blackmon / Jorge de la Rosa / Dexter Fowler / Carlos Gonzalez / Matt Holliday / Ubaldo Jimenez / Trevor Story / Troy Tulowitzki

THE BALLPARKS

MEMORABLE GAMES

FOREWORD

BY THOMAS HARDING

WE REPORTERS ROOT, JUST NOT LIKE the fans. We tell each other that we root for the story so often that the statement is on the border of crossing from truth to cliché. But sometimes we root for something even more trivial. We root for ourselves to make deadline. It's not that we are machines, and it's not that we so high and mighty that we can't share feelings with the fans. It's a job, and somebody's gotta do it when the stadium is shaking.

But writing is often about sharing feelings. When you reach that point, it's beautiful.

On October 1, 2007, after shamelessly and selfishly rooting for myself, I took time to feel the Coors Field tremble and just enjoy it.

I have covered the Colorado Rockies since December 1999, for two seasons with *The Gazette* in Colorado Springs and since 2002 for MLB.com, when newly hired general manager Dan O'Dowd was frantically trading everyone he could while trying to stop the Rockies' inevitable decline from success early in their days as an expansion club. By '07, I had covered exactly one better-than-.500 season — the first.

In September 2007, it wasn't so much that the Rockies turned hot while going 12-1 to finish the 162-game schedule and force the October 1 National League Wild Card tiebreaker with the San Diego Padres. It was how it was done. A team worth rooting for and a story worth rooting for became one in the same.

There were tremendous feats along the way. Matt Holliday's finish should have earned him NL Most Valuable Player honors and Troy Tulowitzki's performance should have been worthy of NL Rookie of the Year (baseball writers didn't deem those good enough for the honors, but many of them still haven't taken the time to understand baseball in Denver … here's a book for ya). However, it was the kind of baseball my dad preached and my youth coaches tried to teach. When a runner needed to be moved, it happened. If a fielder got to a ball, it was an out. Runners ran when

prudent. Throws went to the right base. Cutoffs and relays were sharp.

Of course, Game 163 was fraught with wild twists and turns, but somehow you got the feeling it would turn out right for the Rockies. The folks at Coors sure did. After Scott Hairston's home run in the top of the 13th quieted the house and gave the Padres an 8-6 lead, the fans broke into a wild ovation as the Rockies trudged to the dugout for what turned out to be not their last chance but a new beginning to a wild postseason.

And the Rockies won the game the right way.

Tie score, Matt Holliday at third after his triple. Jamey Carroll up against future Hall of Famer Trevor Hoffman. Sure it would have been nice if Carroll had homered and made it all easy. But Carroll did his thing — a fly ball to right fielder Brian Giles. Holliday's slide into home plate — no matter what Padres fans or stop-action replay says, he was safe — sent the Rockies to the playoffs in fitting fashion, for it was Carroll's sixth sacrifice fly. Nothing like fundamental baseball.

But that wasn't why I pounded my fist and screamed, "Yes!" as the celebration began. I wish I could say that's why I let out the cheer. It would have been unprofessional

The reason for my elation was simple.

MLB.com is for the speedy writer. As soon as something happens, fans are refreshing their smartphones and hitting F8 on their browser. They expect detailed, accurate, and readable information *right now.*

So, while the Padres were ahead and anticipating a postseason trip and the Rockies fans were trying to will them into a comeback, I quickly completed a story on the Padres winning and advancing to the NL Division Series against the Phillies. (If this book falls into the hands of a San Diego fan, just know this: It was a well-written piece of sports journalism).

Had Hoffman locked down the save, I was set.

But the second I turned that story in, I began crafting a story on a Rockies comeback. I can't say I knew it was going to happen, but A) I had seen this team pull off unexpected feats night after night, and B) I didn't want to be caught unready should it actually happen. So even before Kazuo Matsui doubled on Hoffman's 2-2 pitch, I was ready for a Mile High miracle.

For me, the sound of the crowd faded and I was locked. See Troy Tulowitzki double in Matsui, add to my "Rockies win" story; save that detail for my "Padres win" story in case the nothing else happens. See Holliday, who had gone 1-for-5, drive one off the right-field wall, just over the leaping Giles, to tie the game; really get cracking on the comeback story. I'm in tune with the game as I'm dealing with these details, so I know the Padres will walk Todd Helton and I'll have time.

Now, even if you're on a deadline, you don't cheat and write a detail before it occurs. You don't want to forget you wrote it and end up with a mistake. But I looked at Carroll in the box, and even before he lifted that first pitch into short right field I could feel my fingers typing "sacrifice fly."

As quickly as it all happened, somehow within seconds of the "safe" call, I e-mailed in my story. It was my walkoff, and I broke into a little celebration at my spot in the press box.

At that moment, it hit me: My outburst violated all social press box norms. I looked around and actually announced to a more-veteran reporter, who was staring at me, "This is because I made deadline. Not because I'm cheering."

He looked back, more concerned with his story, and said, "I don't care."

Fine.

But at that moment, I stopped myself.

Suddenly, I could feel the thunder and see the jubilation. It was wilder than I thought. Later I was told total strangers were hugging and kissing. I didn't smooch anyone. Hey, the curmudgeonly reporter was not an option. But instead of running down to position myself for interviews during the celebration, I simply stopped, took a deep breath and sat, and

just took in the moment. Maybe at some point, there will be a World Series-clinching moment. But right then, right there, this was as good as it could get. Players were all over the field, grasping their heads in disbelief. Holliday, after colliding with Padres catcher Michael Barrett's shin guards, was dazed, with head athletic trainer Keith Dugger making sure he was OK — and possibly telling him he's going to the playoffs.

The story I was rooting for, and the fact I met deadline, faded. I took the time to forget all that, take in the jubilation, hear the crowd's roar — which was louder than the fireworks set off beyond the right-field wall.

Elsewhere, the moment is remembered for the controversy over whether Holliday actually touched the plate. If anything, that's what makes Holliday's daring slide a fitting Rockies moment.

This book is full of great performers and performances that might have gone unseen by a national audience, largely because the Rockies play in a time zone that usually isn't even acknowledged when networks announce their schedules. So many of the bios of stars contained here have references to players being discredited for playing at Coors Field, even though many of the discrediting media members haven't truly assessed the effects of playing at 5,280 feet. That's partly because even the mathematicians and stat analysts often leave out factors, or have stopped short of true accuracy.

Well, that and nationally televised Rockies games have been rare. Catcher Brent Mayne's pitching win in a crazy extra-innings game against the Atlanta Braves (page 216), Ubaldo Jimenez's no-hitter at Atlanta (page 235), and Nolan Arenado's cycle with a walkoff homer against the San Francisco Giants (page 243) were at best brief late highlights on the networks.

To much of the baseball world, the Rockies winning 21 of 22 games in '07 was rendered meaningless by the sweep at the hands of the Boston Red Sox in the World Series.

But that's fine. We're used to it, and it doesn't dissuade us. The Rockies fans who willed a team to Denver when many believed the market was too small and the time zone was too hard to remember have these many moments that can't be taken away.

And, like that glorious October night, I will continue to take a few moments from deadlines to enjoy them with you.

When you need to remember, *Major League Baseball A Mile High — The First Quarter-Century of the Colorado Rockies* will be here for you.

—February 2018

MAJOR LEAGUE BASEBALL A MILE HIGH — THE FIRST QUARTER CENTURY OF THE COLORADO ROCKIES

ALTHOUGH THE HISTORY OF THE Colorado Rockies is only 25 years old at this writing, the game's presence in Colorado and Denver's long pursuit of a major-league baseball franchise stretches back considerably longer.

Most local historians agree the first mention of Base Ball appeared as an advertisement in the *Rocky Mountain News* in 1862. This was only four years after the discovery of gold in the Rocky Mountains, when Denver was a small settlement along the banks of the South Platte River, containing as many teepees of the Arapahoe and Sioux tribes as wooden structures built by white settlers migrating from the East and Midwest in pursuit of metallic riches.

The advertisement called for interested parties to assemble by the river on a Sunday afternoon for the purpose of participating in the first organized game of ball in the area. It was not long before base ball was flourishing in mining towns throughout the Colorado Territory.

Statehood arrived in 1876, and by 1886 the first openly professional baseball team was representing Denver in intercity competitions. That Denver team was first referred to as the "Bears" during the 1900 season, and they competed in various configurations of the Western League during much of the first half of the twentieth century.

Due to socioeconomic factors influenced by the Great Depression and World War II, professional baseball took a hiatus from Denver from 1933 until 1947. The Denver Bears returned to action in 1948 and that summer moved into their new home, Bears Stadium, which was later renamed Mile High Stadium.

Colorado's first flirtation with major-league baseball came in 1959, when Branch Rickey and others explored the possibility of creating the Continental League, a new major league to challenge the long established American and National Leagues. Denver was used as a leveraged pawn in the ultimately unsuccessful effort to launch the new league.

The 1960s and 1970s saw Denver become one of the stronger-Triple-A markets in America, often drawing attendance in major-league-like numbers.

Another big-league tease for Denver unfolded after the 1977 season. The unconventional and often controversial owner of the Oakland Athletics, Charles O. Finley, decided to sell the A's to Denver oil billionaire Marvin Davis. A deal was struck, and everything was in place to move the Athletics to Denver and begin play there in 1978 … until Finley changed his mind and made an eleventh-hour pullout on the agreement. The Denver major-league bride was left standing at the altar.

There were other proposals involving the Chicago White Sox and San Francisco Giants using Denver as a bargaining chip to win better stadium deals in those cities, but none came as close to fruition as the Oakland experience.

Baseball had gone through a series of labor conflicts throughout the years, and the National League declared it would turn its attention to expansion following a labor peace accord in 1990. Just before Christmas of 1990 the six finalist cities for two National League expansion franchises were announced: Miami, Tampa Bay/St. Petersburg, and Orlando in Florida, plus Washington, Buffalo, and Denver.

On July 5, 1991, Denver's major-league dream was finally and officially fulfilled. The other new team was awarded to Miami.

This book endeavors to pursue an in-depth exploration of the first quarter-century of that major-league team in Denver, the Colorado Rockies.

Included in that exploration are biographies of 24 of the most important players, managers, and club executives as selected by a panel of members of the Rocky Mountain chapter of SABR. In addition, 18 memorable and historic games were chosen for detailed examination.

We hope this presentation provides the readers, both the casual Rockies fans and the more serious baseball historians among us, with insightful knowledge of the first 25 years of Rockies history, as well as pleasurable and entertaining reading.

Paul T. Parker
Denver, Colorado

BIRTH OF THE COLORADO
ROCKIES BASEBALL CLUB

BY ROGER L. KINNEY

THE YEAR 1959 WAS A GOOD ONE— a very important year for baseball in Colorado. It was the first time a formidable, well-assembled plan was presented for bringing major-league baseball to Denver.

During the late '50s, the Denver Bears were the Triple-A farm team of the New York Yankees. The team was loaded with future major-leaguers including Bobby Richardson, Tony Kubek, Ryne Duren, Mark Freeman, and Marv Throneberry. Ralph Houk was the manager. Denver fans loved their baseball and they supported the team with record attendance among minor-league cities.

Denver was emerging as a major transportation hub as well as a leading financial center in the Rocky Mountain area. Enthusiastic fans in the Denver area were eager to welcome and support major-league professional sports. The Denver Broncos began play in the American Football League in 1960 and the fans hoped a major-league baseball team would soon follow.

Bob Howsam, president of Rocky Mountain Sports, and US Senator Edwin "Big Ed" Johnson, his father-in-law, created a plan to bring major-league baseball to Colorado. Actually, they began to formulate the plan in the early '50s while the Howsam family was building a successful leadership team, both on and off the field. They met with Branch Rickey, who agreed that there was a need throughout the country for more major-league teams. While Howsam discussed plans with representatives of other major- and minor-league cities, Senator Johnson met with colleagues and friends in Congress. They made lasting friendships and paved the way for future alliances.

In 1958, the city of New York lost the Dodgers and Giants when they moved to California. New York Mayor Robert Wagner and Bill Shea formed a committee to attract another team for the city. They were unable to attract an existing franchise to move to New York. Once they considered an expansion team, they joined forces with Howsam and potential candidates from seven other cities for gaining major-league status. Thereafter, with extensive study and faced with rejection from the existing major-league teams, the eight cities gave their support to the formation of a new major league.

The Continental League was officially organized on July 27, 1959.[1] The original members of the league were: Denver, Houston, New York, Buffalo, Dallas-Fort Worth, Toronto, Minneapolis-St. Paul, and Atlanta. The new league appeared to be formidable, especially with some wealthy and determined owners and the abundance of talented players in the minor leagues who were capable of playing at the major-league level. But the announcement of the new league was met with strong opposition from the existing major-league teams. National League and American League owners united in opposition and directed Commissioner Ford Frick to appeal to Congress for support. With a negative vote from the Senate, the new league was derailed and eventually terminated. However, with the threat of the new league, the existing major-league teams responded with a promise that eventually all of the cities from the Continental League would someday have major-league baseball.[2]

Denver's presentation was important because it set the stage. From then on, Denver became a player in the ongoing game whenever a new city was considered for a major-league franchise. Although it took 33 years, Denver became the seventh city of the original Continental League to have major-league baseball when the Colorado Rockies began play in 1993. What happened during those 33 years of knocking on the door and waiting for a team is a fascinating story, filled with great expectations, some sad and disappointing setbacks, and wild jubilation when the team finally arrived.

The Early Years

The first recorded game of "base ball" in Denver was played on April 26, 1862, when the McNeils Side defeated the Hulls Side, 20-7.[3] After the Civil War, as settlers moved west, baseball grew in popularity throughout the mining towns, the farming communities, and Denver, the Queen City of the Plains. Common rivalries grew in popularity as baseball outings became the social and family entertainment throughout the summer. George "Patsy" Tebeau (December 26, 1861- February 4, 1923) and David Rowe (October 9, 1854 - December 9, 1930), who both played major-league baseball, are referred to as the "fathers of Colorado baseball."[4] They were instrumental in developing amateur teams and bringing barnstorming teams to play in Denver. The first professional team was the Denver Browns in 1879 and the first team to play in the Western Baseball League was the Denvers in 1886.[5]

As Denver's population increased and the economy grew stronger, youth baseball programs flourished throughout the state. As baseball grew in popularity, there were many sandlot fields and ballparks where the games were played. In Denver, Merchants Park was built in 1922 and provided the site for Denver Post Tournaments and exhibition games involving barnstorming teams. Babe Ruth and Lou Gehrig played in Denver in 1927 on a barnstorming tour. Baseball in Denver gradually developed a strong grass-roots following and a reputation as a good baseball town as local players developed and the visiting players, who had favorable experiences in Denver, traveled about the country.

Professional Baseball

After World War II, the Western League was reorganized and began play with eight teams: Denver (farm team of the New York Yankees), Pueblo (Brooklyn Dodgers), Omaha (St. Louis Cardinals), Des Moines (Chicago Cubs), Sioux City (New York Giants), and Lincoln (Philadelphia A's). The country was in a rebuilding period; the success and the fortunes of all the professional baseball teams rested heavily with the ownership of the local minor-league teams.

The owner of the Denver Bears was a group headed by former Mayor Will Nicholson, his brother Eddie Nicholson, and Colorado financial magnate Charles Boettcher.[6] In 1948, Bob Howsam and his family purchased the Bears and moved to a new location in central Denver where they built Bears Stadium.[7] Howsam proved to be a knowledgeable baseball entrepreneur as well as a popular and successful businessman. He made friends and loyal supporters throughout the country, and he never lost his zeal or support for Denver's bid for a major-league team. After the demise of the Continental League, on May 26, 1961, Howsam sold the Denver Bears to Rocky Mountain Sports, Inc., headed by Gerald and Allan Phipps. Shortly thereafter, Howsam moved to St. Louis and later, to Cincinnati, where he was the general manager of the Cardinals and then the Reds. His teams won four World Series before he returned with his family to Colorado.

Gerald "Jerry" Phipps, a legend in his own right, had a genuine love for baseball, the Denver Bears, the Denver Broncos, and his beloved state of Colorado. He hired Jim Burris, former general secretary of the American Association, to be the general manager of the Bears. Burris, a baseball loyalist, became the leader of Denver's ongoing campaign to attain a major-league team. Whenever an opportunity occurred, he would trumpet the favorable attributes of Colorado for a big-league team. Burris attended major-league baseball meetings every year. While other prospective cities were often represented with elaborate displays and well-organized promotional teams, Denver's presence was sometimes a lonely affair. Burris, who had a charming sense of humor, used to tell friends that he held the meetings for the Denver delegation in a telephone booth.

Over time, Denver's presence began to change, and in 1974, the Denver Chamber of Commerce sent four members, Jim Burris, Larry Varnell, Rex

Jennings, and Dale Mitchell (a former player with the Cleveland Indians), to New Orleans with a model of Mile High Stadium (formerly Bears Stadium) and a presentation promoting the attractions of Denver.[8] For 21 years, Burris continued to "carry the torch" for Denver at the major-league meetings, often escorting supporting members of the Denver delegation.

Destination Denver

In the early 1970s, a formal bid was made to hold the Winter Olympics in Colorado. The International Olympic Committee approved the bid and the Winter Olympics were scheduled to be held in Colorado in 1976. But there was strong opposition to the organizers' plan. After a heated campaign, the voters rejected the plan and the Colorado Olympics were canceled. (The 1976 Winter Games were instead held in Innsbruck, Austria.)

Keli McGregor, Dick Monfort, and Charlie Monfort.

The Colorado sports scene was shaken for several years. Some people called it a black eye for the state. Promoters were hesitant to submit bids to attract other sporting events. Some hostelries said tourism suffered with Denver becoming known as an airport city on the way to the mountains. In time, the city rebounded and its desire to attract major sporting events was renewed. Denver Convention and Visitors Bureau president Roger Smith vowed to attract major events, including national conventions and sporting events. This eventually led to a successful vote to finance a new Denver Convention Center. Presidents Rex Jennings and Shelby Harper of the Denver Chamber of Commerce created the Denver Metro Sports Committee. This eventually led to support for the Denver Nuggets of the NBA and for the NBA All-Star Game, which was held in Denver in 1984. This in turn led to the NCAA Final Four basketball tournament. held in Denver in 1990. With these successes and the improving economy, sports fans again set their sights on a major-league baseball franchise.

High Hopes — Disappointing Results

When Marvin Davis, a wealthy oil investor, expressed an interest in owning a big-league team and bringing it to Denver, the fans were hopeful for success. There were reports that Davis tried to purchase the Chicago White Sox in 1976 and the Baltimore Orioles in 1977.[9] Larry Varnell, past president of the Colorado Sports Hall of Fame, became the public spokesman for Davis as he made numerous attempts to purchase a team. Varnell said, "One year when I went to the winter (baseball) meetings, Davis said, you find the team, I'll write the check."[10] In 1985, there were reports that the San Francisco Giants might make a temporary move to Denver to facilitate the construction of a new stadium in San Francisco. There were other rumors involving the Pittsburgh Pirates, the Cleveland Indians, and the Minnesota Twins.

Perhaps the closest possibility for a sale came in two stages. First, in 1977-78 when Marvin Davis was negotiating with Charlie Finley to move the Oakland A's to Denver, Varnell reported that the American

League owners were agreeable to a sale to Davis if a settlement could be made with the Oakland Coliseum Authority. After extensive negotiations, the parties could not reach a settlement and the sale was canceled. The second proposal come in 1979-80 when "an official of the Oakland Coliseum made a public disclosure that the Oakland Coliseum would consider a cash offer to allow Finley to break his lease and sell the team to Davis."[11] Rumors circulated that a deal was close to completion. But Marvin Davis denied the rumors and a sale was never completed.

The Denver Baseball Commission, created by Mayor Federico Pena and led by executive director Steve Katich and City Attorney Steve Kaplan, worked in support of Marvin Davis. To gain fans' support, the commission held a Baseball Symposium and sponsored exhibition games played by visiting major-league teams. In 1984, the commission hosted a display booth at the winter baseball meetings and distributed a daily newspaper extolling Denver's worthiness for a major-league team.

Marvin Davis eventually lost interest in bringing a team to Denver, and the Denver Baseball Commission shifted support to John Dikeou and his family. The Dikeous had purchased the Denver Bears from Gerald and Allan Phipps in 1984 and renamed the team the Zephyrs. A popular Denver native and a successful businessman, Dikeou assembled a strong management team led by Robert Howsam Jr. and Tom Maloney. The team won the Triple-A championship in 1991. The fans responded, and as the Zephyrs prospered, the momentum for a major-league team gained strength. John Dikeou became the likely and assumed new owner of an expansion team.

Congress and the Commissioner

In 1985, Peter Ueberroth became commissioner of baseball, succeeding Bowie Kuhn. At that time, baseball owners were dealing with a wide range of financial problems involving the players' salaries, free agency, and the wide disparity of economic interests among the owners. In 1986 Tim Wirth of Colorado was elected to the US Senate. In the spring of 1987, Wirth suggested to Ueberroth that, "Major League Baseball and the Senate could talk to each other about expansion."[12] Extolling the attractions of Denver for a new franchise, Wirth continued to attempt to convince Ueberroth that expansion would be good for baseball and the country. Wirth gained support from other members of Congress, and on November 4, 1987, they formed a Senate Task Force on Expansion of Major League Baseball. Their goal was to have six new major-league teams by 2000.[13]

For the next two years, Wirth and his colleagues made a persistent campaign for expansion. Commissioner Ueberroth resisted any public commitments to expansion and continued to deal primarily with the financial concerns of the major-league owners, the players, and their union. But in the summer of 1988, while announcing that he planned to step down, he indicated that "expansion was coming in the not too distant future."[14]

A. Bartlett Giamatti was selected to succeed Ueberroth in the spring of 1989. Giamatti was popular, dedicated, and a forceful advocate for the traditional values associated with the national pastime. In the summer of 1989, at the owners' quarterly meeting, they agreed to expand by two teams in the National League.[15] Giamatti died of a heart attack on September 1, 1989, just five months after becoming commissioner. Fay Vincent succeeded him.

The Invitation

Shortly after a contract agreement was signed with the Players Association on June 16, 1990, Vincent presented a timeline for all prospective new owners.[16] The owners' Expansion Committee would receive presentations from the applicants by September 30, and the finalists would be announced by the end of the year. The committee would make its recommendation to the major-league owners and the final selection would be made by September 30, 1991.

It soon became apparent that the application would have four major requirements. First, the owners of a new franchise (preferably local people) must be acceptable to the current owners. "This is the fundamental thing to remember in expansion.

Cities are never awarded franchises. Owners are rewarded franchises."[17] Second, there must be a new, baseball-only stadium that is first class in all respects. Third, there must be sufficient support from the fans and general public. This meant a support base of at least 20,000 season-ticket holders. Fourth, the entry fee would be $95 million. The applicants needed to agree to all the accompanying conditions regarding the expansion process, including the draft of eligible players, the finance schedule, and the nonparticipation in television revenue for the initial season.

Colorado's Response — House Bill 1351

In 1988, Pat Grant, a Colorado legislator, had been instrumental in creating a successful district taxing authority to support the cultural arts in the Denver area. Faced with a stalemate over the financing of a new ballpark, Neil Macey, a Denver real-estate entrepreneur and avid baseball fan, envisioned a similar plan as a practical way to finance the planning and construction. Macey envisioned the creation of a five-county authority that would expand the tax base, oversee the project, and impose a 0.01 percent sales tax. Macey took his plan to John Dikeou and Kathi Williams, a member of the Colorado House of Representatives from Adams County. They took the plan to Governor Roy Romer, and after considerable negotiating, they presented Colorado House Bill 1351. With an appeal to all the state legislators who supported major-league baseball, the bill passed the Colorado legislature and sent the measure to the electorate in August 1990.[18]

The bill created a Colorado Baseball Stadium Authority with a seven-member board responsible for site selection, financial planning, construction, and the ongoing operation of the ballpark. The bill also created an 18-member Colorado Baseball Commission tasked to conduct the election campaign and any activities necessary to support the prospective owners and meet the requirements set by the major leagues' expansion committee. The commission would go out of existence once its mission was completed.

The Colorado Baseball Stadium Authority

After House Bill 1351 was passed, Governor Romer, with input from Neil Macey and Kathi Williams, began to make appointments to the Stadium Authority and the Baseball Commission.[19] All appointments were subject to approval by a committee of the Colorado Senate. Senator Claire Taylor conducted many of the appointment hearings and passed along the recommendations to the governor. Once the seven members were selected and approved, the Stadium Authority began meeting on a regular basis.

At the first meeting, John McHale Jr. was elected chairman. Shortly thereafter, Jack Sperling and Craig Umbaugh of the legal firm Fairfield and Woods were named legal counsel. Lee White, an investment banker, was chosen to be the financial adviser. Since there were minimal funds available for the operations of the authority, in-kind contributions were solicited. Many supporters responded, including Dave Herlinger, president of the Colorado Housing Authority, who provided office and meeting space for the authority.

Under McHale and Ray Baker (who succeeded McHale as chairman), the board began seeking a site for the new stadium. Many sites were considered. With recognition of the large amount of land along the Amtrak rail lines, the site at 20th and Blake was selected on March 13, 1991.[20] In addition to the availability of the land for parking, the site had other attractive features: The site was above the flood plain, which would facilitate building the playing field at the lower level, and it was within walking distance of the downtown area and Union Station, the transportation center for the metropolitan area. Shortly thereafter, HOK Sports was selected to be the architectural firm for the stadium.

Once the site was selected and the election neared, the Stadium Authority created an ambitious schedule, making public presentations to all five of the counties in the voting district. The presentations included a display of the plans for the stadium, followed by a "no holds barred" question-and-answer session with the board members. The response throughout the five-county area from those attending was positive and they were asked to seek the support of their neighbors and friends, especially those who would vote in the election slated for August 1990.

As the time neared for the National League expansion committee to visit Denver, the Stadium Authority Board turned its attention to the lease of the new stadium to the owners. John McHale, as chairman of the MLB Stadium District and Steve Ehrhart, then president of the Colorado Baseball Partnership, signed a memorandum of agreement for the lease of the new stadium on March 14, 1991.[21] The lease caught the immediate attention of major-league owners and the expansion committee. Carl Barger, president of the Florida Marlins, said, "It's a great lease. I gotta hand it to those people who negotiated it."[22] With the site and the lease in place, the Stadium Authority prepared to meet with the expansion committee, who were planning to be in Denver in March 1991.

The Colorado Baseball Commission

The Colorado Baseball Commission was created with 15 members representing all of the five counties in the district. John Dikeou was named chairman and Neil Macey was the executive director. After a difficult start to raise money for its operational needs, cable magnate Bill Daniels and the Greater Denver Chamber of Commerce made substantial contributions to set the campaign on a winning track. United Airlines made a generous contribution to facilitate goodwill visits to six National League teams, the Dodgers, Padres, Giants, Cardinals, Reds, and Cubs. Many supporting companies and loyal fans made monetary and in-kind contributions. A record number of volunteers donated their time and talents to the campaign.

The commission had a wide range of projects to address. One of the first was to create a plan for the sale of season tickets. With help from the accounting firm of Deloitte Touche and the legal firm of Holme, Roberts and Owen, who donated office space and telephone service, they began the season-ticket

drive in early May 1990. The conditions for a commitment were well publicized by the media, including a deposit for obtaining a priority number on a first-come (via a telephone call), first-served basis. Priority would be given to season-ticket holders of the Denver Zephyrs, the Triple-A farm team. A team of volunteers would man the telephones, ready to take orders. When the switchboard opened, the telephone calls (including those for the law firm) overwhelmed the system. Callers were desperate in their attempts to make a deposit and obtain a low priority number. Carolyn "Skinny" Writer, a supervisor for the event, said, "It was the most frantic, and the most gratifying experience I could possibly imagine."[23] It took several days to properly record the initial ticket requests and return the telephone system to normal operation. The season-ticket campaign was off to a great start.

At that time, the Denver Broncos had a huge following in the area and dominated the sports pages. Some avid baseball fans were concerned that the Broncos not support the drive for a baseball team. Just the opposite was true. The Broncos were very supportive, and when the season-ticket drive was close to reaching its goal, Rod Buscher, president of John Elway Motors, committed to purchase enough season tickets to surpass the goal of 20,000, putting the drive over the top. Eventually, the sale of season tickets reached 28,250. The success of the drive had a positive impact as the election for the stadium bond issue approached.

The vote was scheduled for August 14, 1990. The campaign theme was simple: The cost of the ballpark would be "a penny on a purchase of ten dollars." The bonds would be paid off within 20 years. (Actually they were paid off in about eight years.) With the leadership of co-chairmen Larry Varnell and Sam Suplizio, the Colorado Baseball Commission campaigned with public appearances, media coverage, and personal calls to sports fans in the area. The early polls were discouraging because they predicted defeat. Since the election would be held as a primary, not a general election, a smaller than average turnout was expected. Rick Reiter, the campaign adviser, developed a selective plan to target key areas.

As the voting results came in, the celebration party at the downtown Radisson Hotel grew with optimism and excitement as it became apparent that the bond issue would pass. The votes in favor were 187,539, about 54 percent, and the opposing votes were 157,954, about 46 percent.[24]

The votes in Arapahoe and Jefferson Counties were so overwhelmingly favorable that they overshadowed the negative votes in Denver and Adams County. The election was a big step forward. It meant that if Colorado were awarded a franchise, the plan was in place, approved by the electorate, to build a new, first-class ballpark.

The next step was to solidify the ownership and support their presentation to the expansion committee. When John Dikeou withdrew his ownership interest, there was widespread uncertainty about finding a new owner. Several potential ownership groups expressed an interest. The Colorado Baseball Commission informed Governor Romer of the potential problems. He quickly responded, drawing on business leaders, involving Dick Robinson, Jim Baldwin, and Tryg Myhren, to conduct a search and identify the best qualified ownership group. Romer identified the "Ehrhart-Nicklaus" group as the local ownership official leaders on August 23, 1990.[25]

Paul Jacobs, a Denver lawyer and sports enthusiast, became the driving force to assemble the new ownership group. As potential owners moved in and out of the picture, Jacobs worked night and day to assemble an ownership group with sufficient investment to pay the franchise fee of $95 million and the initial startup costs. The ownership group gained strength and momentum when Peter Coors, representing the Coors Brewery, made a major commitment of $25 million, part of which would be allocated to the naming rights of the new stadium. Several very important commitments followed, including those from Cary Teraji, Linda Alvarado, Bill Fletcher, representing the *Rocky Mountain News,* Lee Larson, representing radio station KOA, and the Beverage Distributing Company.

Jacobs established a good relationship with National League President Bill White and members of the expansion committee, Doug Danforth, Fred Wilpon, and Bill Giles. Jacobs later became executive vice president and general counsel of the Rockies, instrumental in creating the partnership agreements, the leases, and other initial legal documents.

The Visit

The National League expansion committee visited Denver on March 26, 1991.[26] It was billed as "the biggest day in Denver's baseball history."[27] Before making the trip, the committee had requested that there be no elaborate displays, wining, or dining. They simply wanted it to be a business trip. But the CBC, with the agreement of business leaders, disagreed. This was Denver's biggest chance and they were going to make the most of it.

Shortly after the arrival at Stapleton Airport, the eight members of the expansion committee were taken on a helicopter tour of the Denver area with a landing on the outfield grass at Mile High Stadium. It was anticipated that the new team would play one or two years at Mile High while the new ballpark was being built. Next the committee went to the governor's mansion for a festive lunch and a visit with the governor and other dignitaries. As the committee traveled throughout the city, baseball fans, all volunteers, lined the streets with welcome signs and a mile-long petition supporting the campaign for a big-league team.

After lunch, the committee went to the United Bank Center, where about 5,000 baseball fans had gathered to welcome them. As scheduled by Don Hinchey, director of the event, when the committee arrived, the crowd sang "Take Me Out to the Ball Game," followed by cheers and applause for the visitors. Sportscaster Norm Jones gave a short welcoming address, several of the guests responded, and the crowd continued to sing and cheer for the distinguished visitors. The committee was visibly moved by the enthusiastic reception. "That visit, highlighted by the forbidden rally, sealed the deal."[28] On the way to the business meeting, Doug Danforth of the Pittsburgh Pirates said, "I never get an ovation like this back in Pittsburgh."[29]

While the warm reception set a positive stage, the committee still wanted to know the financial condition of the owners. Jerry McMorris, Steve Ehrhart, and Paul Jacobs led their presentations, providing updated information about the ownership and their ability to meet the required financial investment. The meeting lasted about 2½ hours. At the press conference after the meeting, the mood was upbeat with favorable comments from the committee about the owners' presentation. The expansion committee would continue to evaluate the applicants and a decision would be anticipated later in the spring.

The Announcement

Bill White, president of the National League, came to Denver on July 5, 1991. A crowd of fans, dignitaries and the media gathered at the Denver Hyatt Hotel. White spoke directly: "I am here to tell you that at 10:40 A.M., you officially became a member of the National League."[30] The audience reacted with a boisterous standing ovation. When the celebration calmed, White continued his remarks, indicating that Miami and Denver would be the new franchises, and that he anticipated both teams would be competitive much sooner than expansion teams in the past. Players from the National and American Leagues would be available to the expansion teams and both leagues would participate in the distribution of the funds from the expansion fees. White spoke with confidence that Denver and Miami had the potential to be very successful franchises for the long term.

Shortly after the announcement, John Antonucci, the chairman of the new team, and Steve Ehrhart, the president, set up offices in the United Bank Center and began to hire key personnel for the business operations. Michael Kent, formerly with the Philadelphia Phillies, and Sue Ann McClaren, formerly with the St. Louis Cardinals, joined the organization. Paul Egins, from the Atlanta Braves, was named assistant director of scouting and player development. They announced that purple would be one of the colors for the team, with reference to "the purple mountain majesties" as written by Katharine Lee Bates in the song "America the Beautiful."

With an effort to reach out to the entire state and the Rocky Mountain areas, they introduced the logo and announced that the team would be called the Colorado Rockies.[31] Governor Romer gave special recognition to the governors of Wyoming, New Mexico, Nebraska, Oklahoma, and Kansas for their support in bringing major-league baseball to the region, at that time America's only time zone without a team.

The first Rockies banquet, billed as "Colorado Welcomes Major League Baseball," was held on September 25, 1991, at the Denver Marriott Hotel.[32] Jim Wilkins was the general chairman and Commissioner Fay Vincent and Bill White were the honored guests.

In September, Bob Gebhard was selected to be the general manager for the Rockies. At the time, Gebhard was working for the soon-to-be American League champion Minnesota Twins, and it was agreed that he would not come to Denver until after the World Series. The Twins won the World Series and Gebhard arrived one day later, ready to begin a new career in Denver. It did not take long for everyone in the organization to recognize his devotion and commitment to building a championship organization.

New Leadership

Jerry McMorris became the chairman, president, and CEO of the Colorado Rockies on January 26, 1992.[33] He assumed the leadership position after he, Oren Benton, and Charlie Monfort purchased the stock in a buyout agreement from Steven Kurtz and Paul Jacobs. Confronted with extensive legal problems, Michael "Mickey" Monus and Antonucci left the team after Monus was charged with embezzlement and fraud at Phar Mor. Kurtz and Jacobs purchased the stock from Monus and Antonucci, and held it during the interim period.

As the transition of ownership moved forward, McMorris set his sights on selecting key personnel, commencing business operations, and making preparations for the selection of coaches and players. General manager Bob Gebhard hired Pat Daugherty to head the scouting department and veterans Larry Bearnarth and Dick Balderson joined the staff.

Gebhard drew up elaborate plans for himself and his scouting staff to cover the entire country in preparation for the draft of players and the formation of the Rockies' farm teams. It was reported that "Pat Daugherty's 15 scouts traveled 198,105 miles by car and watched 2,250 high school and college games in the continental 48 states and Puerto Rico."[34]

In February, KOA Radio was selected to be the flagship station for the Rockies. Jeff Kingery and Wayne Hagin would cover the play-by play. KWGN Channel 2 was chosen to be the television station with veteran announcer Charley Jones. Alan Roach was selected to be the public-address announcer. Frank Haraway, with over 50 years' experience, was selected to be the official scorer.

In March, the Rockies announced that they would hold spring training in Tucson, Arizona. Their home field there would be Hi Corbett Field, former home of the Cleveland Indians. The Pima County Sports Authority agreed to make major improvements to the field and the supporting facilities.

In the June major-league draft, the Rockies chose John Burke, a Colorado native and pitcher for the University of Florida, to be their number-one draft selection.[35] He would eventually join the other Rockies rookies to play for the Bend Rockies in the first organized game, June 16, against the Boise Hawks in the Class-A Northwest League. The Bend Rockies won the game, 6-4, with a grand slam by catcher Will Scalzitti.

In June, the Rockies held a tryout camp at the University of Denver. With the Rockies coaches and staff participating, the tryout camp was very popular with the local fans and participants. On July 4 the Rockies introduced their home and away uniforms. With purple pinstripes, the home uniforms were distinctive. The away uniforms were gray and black.

On October 27, Gebhard named Don Baylor to be the Rockies' first manager. Baylor was quickly put to work preparing for the expansion draft. The draft was held on November 17. Denver's Currigan Hall, site of many conventions and public events, was packed with an estimated 10,000 fans who came to watch the event, taking place in New York, Miami, and Denver. Alan Bossart of the Rockies staff created an elaborate venue, complete with a stage, numerous TV screens, and Rockies decorations throughout the hall. Secrecy and security surrounded the preparations before the announcement of the player selections.

Denver won the coin-flip and would select first. General manager Bob Gebhard selected David Nied, pitcher from the Atlanta Braves.[36] Marlins general manager Dave Dombrowski selected Nigel Wilson from the Toronto Blue Jays. Gebhard also announced the signing of Andres Galarraga as a free agent. In a surprise announcement, Galarraga and Nied, who were kept in hiding prior to the announcement, appeared on stage for their introductions. The crowd went wild and shouted for joy as the players were surrounded by fans and members of the media. Throughout the evening, as additional players were selected, the fans continued to welcome the new team with wild enthusiasm.[37]

Spring Training

After the players, coaches, and managers were selected, Gebhard and the staff turned their attention to spring training. Major improvements at Hi Corbett field were underway, including additional seating, improved clubhouse facilities, extended practice fields, and improved media facilities.

Several weeks before spring training, manager Don Baylor and players David Nied and Eric Wedge went on the first Caravan trip throughout the Mountain Time zone. They visited Wyoming, Utah, New Mexico, and many cities in Colorado. It was a promotional trip for the coming season and a time to thank the fans for their support in attracting a franchise. Many people had moved to the region from throughout the country where they had previously enjoyed major-league baseball. They knew what they were missing. Now it was time for them to change their allegiance and become fans of the Rockies. The annual Caravans proved to be a big success and have continued over the years.

The pitchers reported to Tucson about February 22 and the position players reported by February 27. The players needed to become acquainted with their teammates and coaches. To add a little levity to the situation, pitcher Bryn Smith handed out name tags to his teammates. The players responded with clever additions and exchanges, which confused some unsuspecting fans and media writers.

Once the team began practicing, the focus turned to preparation for the coming exhibition games. Veteran Don Zimmer was hired as bench coach and veteran Larry Bearnarth became the pitching coach, giving the team confidence that they would be ready to play at the major-league level.

The first exhibition game was played on March 6 against the San Francisco Giants. The opening game ceremony began with a flyby performed by the Davis-Monthan Air Force Base aerial team. The Sons of the Pioneers sang the national anthem. A crowd of 7,726 was on hand to see the Rockies win, 7-2.

The first regular-season game was played on April 5 in New York against the New York Mets. The first home game followed on April 9 at Mile High Stadium against the Montreal Expos before a record crowd of 80,227.[38]

The founding of the Colorado Rockies is a unique story involving many people from all walks of life, uniting and working together to enrich the quality of life with the major-league baseball experience. Colorado Rockies baseball is a game for all ages, all nationalities, and all creeds. It is a reflection of our national heritage, the bedrock of our common values, and involves the constant struggle to play the game, win or lose, to the best of one's ability. And now, throughout the Rocky Mountain area, it is a cherished part of our history - and our future lives, to be shared throughout the ages.

NOTES

1   Robert Lee Howsam, *My Life In Sports* (Denver: Bob Jones, 1999), 44.

2   Howsam, 46.

3   Jay Sanford, *Before the Rockies* (Denver: KEM Publishing, 2016), introduction page.

4   Sanford, 1.

5   Matthew Kasper Repplinger II, *Baseball in Denver* (Charleston, South Carolina: Arcadia Publishing, 2013), 7.

6   Alan Gottlieb, *In the Shadow of the Rockies* (Niwot, Colorado: Roberts, Rinehart Publishing, 1994), 12.

7   Gottlieb, 13.

8   Mary Kay Connor, *Dick Connor Remembered* (Golden, Colorado: Fulcrum Publishing, 1995), 122.

9   David Whitford, *Playing Hardball* (New York: Doubleday Press, 1993), 26.

10   Whitford, 26.

11   Irv Moss and Mark Foster, *Home Run in the Rockies, The History of Baseball in Colorado* (Denver: Publication Design, Inc., 1995), 26.

12   Whitford, 58.

13   Whitford, 59.

14   Whitford, 70.

15   Moss, 41.

16   Whitford, 77.

17   Whitford, 84.

18   Whitford, 51.

19   See Appendix for a full list of appointments.

20   "Rockies Timeline," Rockies.com, accessed April 23, 2017, colorado.rockies.mlb.com/col/history/timeline2jsp.

21   Whitford, 124.

22   Whitford, 87.

23   Personal interview with Carolyn Writer, June 12, 1990.

24   Moss, 49.

25   Moss, 51.

26   Norm Clarke, *High Hard Ones* (Denver: Phoenix Press, 1993), 151.

27   Clark, 151.

28   Gottlieb, 23.

29   Clarke, 154.

30   Moss, 62.

31   Benjamin M. Leroy, *Colorado Rockies* (Madison, Wisconsin: Quiz Master Books, 2008), 8.

32   Carolyn Writer, *Colorado Welcomes Major League Baseball, Banquet Program* (Denver: Hirschfeld Press, 1991), 1.

33   *Colorado Rockies Inaugural Media Guide*, 1993, 3.

34   Moss, 70.

35   Leroy, 8.

36   Leroy, 12.

37   Leroy, 13.

38   Leroy, 13.

BIRTH OF THE ROCKIES

Appendix

Metropolitan Stadium Authority
Board Members
(who served prior to April 1, 1993)

Ray Baker, Chairman

John McHale, Past Chairman

Debra Brody	Jack Shapiro
Steve DelCastillo	Joe Talarico
Edmundo Gonzales	Penfield Tate
Josie Heath	Dean Quamme
Roger Kinney	Max Wiley
Dan Muse	

Colorado Baseball Commission
Board Members

Sam Suplizio, Co-Chairman

Larry Varnell, Co-Chairman

Neil Macey, Past Director

Roger Kinney, Director

Helen Anderson	Bob Howsam,
Gary Antonoff	Robert Howsam Jr.
Odell Barry	James Murray
John Benitez	Trygve Myhren
Joe Blake	Sue O'Brien
Robert Bows	Chris Paulson
Irv Brown	Jim Turner
Chris Christiansen	Gil Whiteley
John Dikeou	Kathi Williams
Jim Harrington	Zee Ferrufino
Don Hinchey	

Denver Baseball Commission Members

Federico Pena, Mayor

Steve Katich, Chairman

Dean Bonham, Vice Chairman

Jerry Arca	Bob Litchard
Jim Burris|	Eloy Mares
Forrest Cason	John McHale
Don Carlsen	Bill Michaels
Craig Caukin	Sherm Miller
Deb Dowling	Dan Muse
Richard Fleming	Mike Raabe
John Gawaluck	Bob Russo
Tom Grimshaw	Elwyn Schaefer
Bruce Hellerstein	Carl Scheer
Dave Herlinger	Rob Simon
Don Hinchey	Steve Stern
Neil Hinchman	Irv Sternberg
Steve Kaplan	Ruben Valdez
Willie Kellum	Larry Varnell
Elena Metro Kroll	Steve Welchert
Dan Kubby	

MLB Visitation Team Members

Don Hinchey, Chairman

Carolyn Writer, Vice Chairman

Alan Bossart	Nancy Holst
Lew Cady	Robert Howsam Jr.
Tom Clark	Chuck Javernick
Butch Cosby	Doug Kinney
Mike Flaherty	Ken Reed
Lana Fry	Roger Smith
Kevin Hannon	Michelle Strauss
Linda Hantman	Joe Talty
Ed Henderson	Howard Weese

PEDRO ASTACIO

BY GREGORY H. WOLF

RIGHT-HANDER PEDRO ASTACIO made national news by tossing a shutout and fanning 10 in his major-league debut and proceeded to record four shutouts in just 11 starts as a midseason call-up for the Los Angeles Dodgers in 1992. Never the superstar his meteoric rise might have suggested, Astacio eventually developed into a sturdy, and sometimes spectacular, innings-eater. Traded to the Colorado Rockies in late 1997, Astacio proved a pitcher could have success hurling half his games in the mile-high hitters' paradise Coors Field. "I didn't put doubts in my mind (about pitching in Coors)," said Astacio, who twice led the league in home runs allowed with the Rockies. "Just get the ball, go to the mound, make some good pitches and see what happens."[1] In parts of five seasons in Denver, Astacio won 53 games (which ranked sixth in franchise history as of 2017) despite a 5.43 ERA, and his 17-win, 210-strikeout campaign in 1999 still ranks among the best single seasons in Rockies' history. "He's the pitcher who mentally has not been affected by pitching in Colorado," said one GM. "Pedro has always tended to throw strikes. He's aggressive with his stuff and trusts his stuff is good enough."[2] Astacio's teammates were equally impressed with his dogged determination. "He was a battler," said teammate Todd Helton. "He wouldn't back down. He could give up three early runs and you'd never know it."[3]

Pedro Julio (Pura) Astacio was born on November 28, 1968, in Hato Mayor, in the eastern Dominican Republic. He grew up on a rural farm between Hato Mayor and coastal San Pedro de Macoris, where his father, Fulgencio, planted crops and tended to livestock on about 100 acres. Astacio's mother died when he was 8, leaving his father the sole provider for his six children (three boys and three girls). Like almost all boys on the baseball-crazed island, Pedro loved baseball. According to one story, he learned to pitch by using an old tractor tire as a strike zone.[4] By the time Astacio was a student at Pilar Rondon High School, he was on the radar of big-league scouts. On November 21, 1987, 19-year-old Astacio signed with legendary Los Angeles Dodgers scout Ralph Avila and Elvio Jimenez.

Astacio's first taste of professional baseball came a few months later when he donned the uniform of the Tigres de Licey in Santo Domingo in the Dominican Winter League. Though he hurled only one game, he'd return to that club to pitch occasionally for the next eight seasons (through 1995-1996), compiling a 13-10 record.[5] In the spring of 1988 Astacio arrived in Campo Las Palmas, at the Dodgers visionary baseball academy Avila founded the year before.[6] That camp would serve as a model for almost all other big-league teams and produced dozens of major leaguers, among them Pedro and Ramon Martinez, Raul Mondesi, and Jose Offerman, but Pedro was the first protégé to reach the majors. Astacio's 4-2 record with 2.08 ERA in the Dominican Summer League earned him a promotion to the Dodgers farm system in 1989.

Over the next three years Astacio progressed through the Dodgers system. He earned All-Star honors in the Rookie Gulf Coast League in 1989 and two years later had advanced to the Double-A San Antonio Missions in the Texas League. Though he struggled (4-11, 4.78 ERA) facing more experienced hitters in the Texas League, the Dodgers were impressed enough to invite him to spring training in 1992.

The 23-year-old Astacio surprised the coaching staff by going 2-2 with a 1.42 ERA in the Grapefruit League.[7] Nonetheless, he began the 1992 season with Triple-A Albuquerque, where he was converted into a reliever. Astacio struggled in his new role, yet a series of events conspired to lead to his unexpected promotion to the Dodgers. Following the riots that had engulfed Los Angeles from April 29 to May 4 after four police officers were acquitted of using excessive force against Rodney King, the Dodgers were forced to play four doubleheaders in six days in early July. Desperately needing pitching, the club called up Astacio as an emergency starter. In what was described as the "finest debut in franchise history," Astacio tossed a five-hit shutout and fanned 10 (a new team record for debuts) to beat the Philadelphia Phillies, 2-0, in the second game of a twin bill on July 3.[8] "It was hard to believe what I was seeing," said teammate Brett Butler. "[H]e's toying with major-league hitters.[9] Astacio exhibited the kind of enthusiasm and raw emotion that would define his career—on and off the diamond—by jumping around after strikeouts and openly celebrating.

Astacio's roller-coaster ride was in its infancy. He was returned to Albuquerque after his next start, five days later, then recalled a month later to replace the injured Tom Candiotti. He tossed another shutout in three starts, and despite an eye-popping 1.42 ERA (six earned runs in 38 innings) was demoted again. Back with the Dodgers in September, Astacio was the feel-good story in the Dodgers' otherwise forgettable season and worst record in the majors. Astacio finished with a 5-5 slate, including four shutouts in 11 starts, and a 1.98 ERA in 82 innings.

Standing 6-feet-2 and weighing about 175 pounds, Astacio had a "good, lean power pitcher's body with a long trunk," according to one scout.[10] Indeed, Astacio was primarily a fastball pitcher with a bullwhip-like delivery that created late ball movement. Astacio struggled with mechanics his entire career. One scout described them as "poor [because] he hyperextends his elbow which throws off his command" and added "[h]e also arches his head, tightening his back, further contributing to his inconsistent command."[11] Astacio also had a big overhand curve and a changeup, and was never shy to challenge pitchers inside as evidenced by twice leading the league in hit batsmen.

Astacio's rookie success surprised everyone, yet the Dodgers were careful to temper their expectations in 1993. Slated for the fifth spot in the rotation after a productive spring, Astacio struggled early in the campaign. "It's his command," said skipper Tom Lasorda. "He's not getting the ball where he wants to or where he's supposed to."[12] By the end of July Astacio's 4.74 ERA (easily the highest on the staff) threatened his role in the starting rotation. In almost a repeat performance from a year earlier, Astacio caught fire, going 7-3 and posting a 1.82 ERA in 74⅓ innings over the last two months of the season. "He's not flying off the handle anymore and making dumb pitches," said catcher Mike Piazza of Astacio's transformation. "He realizes that every pitch has a purpose."[13] Called the "ace of the staff" by sportswriter Gordon Verrell, Astacio fashioned consecutive shutouts in September as part of a career-best 21⅓ scoreless innings. While the Dodgers split their 162 games to finish in fourth place in the NL West, Astacio led the steam with 14 victories and was the only starter with a winning record, while his 186⅓ innings were just short of the 200-inning barrier his mound mates Orel Hershiser, Ramon Martinez, Candiotti, and Kevin Gross all surpassed.

During Astacio's remaining tenure with the Dodgers, the right-hander flashed the brilliance that many experts had expected; however, he often struggled mightily, and rarely found a middle ground. Frustrations—by both the pitcher and the organization—grew as Astacio's inconsistencies baffled his managers. One scout called Astacio "probably the most inconsistent 60-grade pitcher in the game."[14]

Astacio had a scare in spring training in 1994, when team physicians detected a heart murmur. Although the diagnosis was ultimately determined to be insignificant, Astacio was sidelined for much of camp. Nonetheless he was ready to start the season and fanned 11 in his debut, a 6-0 loss to Atlanta on April 8. Astacio seemed to catch his stride during a six-start stretch beginning June 14, going 3-1 with a 1.88 ERA and holding batters to a .175 average, and leading sportswriter Tim Kawakami of the *Los Angeles Times* to declare, "There's no doubt Pedro has established himself as one of the top pitchers in the division."[15] Such a comment typified glowing perceptions of Astacio. In stark contrast were those voiced just weeks later when he failed to make it through the third inning in consecutive starts. Pitching coach Ron Perranoski said that Astacio's lack of English made it "difficult to make adjustments" during the game, suggesting that his struggles would continue because of a language barrier.[16] The Dodgers were in first place in the NL West when the players union began its strike on August 12, resulting in the cancellation of the rest of the regular season and postseason. Astacio finished with a 6-8 record and 4.29 ERA (highest among the club's starters) in 149 innings.

While baseball executives and union representatives haggled in the offseason over the future of baseball, Dodgers brass wondered what to do with the erratic, streaky Astacio, whose potential seemed as limitless as his flameout as a starter was likely. One report described Astacio as "teetering *this* close to mental disaster all the time" during the 1994 campaign, leading many to wonder if the high-strung flinger might be better suited as a reliever.[17] Calls for Astacio's banishment to the bullpen intensified when he went winless in his first five starts of the 1995 campaign before blanking the New York Mets on six hits on May 24, thereby recording his first victory since June 25 of the previous year. Losses in his next five consecutive starts resulted in his demotion. Beat reporter Bob Nightengale of the *Los Angeles Times* suggested that Astacio's "emotional fluctuations" and not his ability were the root cause of his "mystery struggles."[18] Used primarily in mop-up and low-leverage situations, Astacio fared better in the bullpen (3.40 ERA vs. 4.82 as a starter), or as team VP Fred Claire said, "had better focus."[19] The Dodgers captured their first division crown since they won the World Series in 1988. Astacio pitched in relief in each contest of the three-game sweep by the Cincinnati Reds, yielding just a hit in 3⅓ scoreless innings.

Astacio arrived at camp skeptical about the Dodgers' claim that he had a chance to regain a spot in the starting rotation. "They said it's my job to lose, but that doesn't mean anything," he said. "[L]ast year they told me I'd be back in the rotation."[20] After blowing up in his debut, Astacio produced his best and most consistent season in Dodgers blue. Though he didn't complete any of his 32 starts, he proved to be a dependable workhorse, logging 211⅔ innings with a sturdy 3.44 ERA (including a 2.95 clip over the last three months). Poor run support

contributed to his misleading 9-8 record. According to the *Los Angeles Times*, three factors led to Astacio's success: He quickened his pace on the mound (he had been one of the NL's slowest workers), he relied much more on his fastball, and he seemed less demonstrative.[21] Astacio joined Hideo Nomo (16-11), Ismael Valdez (15-7), and Ramon Martinez (15-6) to anchor the NL's best staff (a major-league-low 3.46 ERA) as the Dodgers finished in second place and captured a wild-card berth in Lasorda's final season in the dugout. The team was once again swept in the NLCS, this time by the Atlanta Braves. In his only appearance, Astacio hurled 1⅔ scoreless innings in Game Two.

The now 28-year-old Astacio arrived in camp in 1997 after yet another offseason filled with trade rumors, and also a new skipper, Bill Russell, who replaced the legendary Lasorda after 21 seasons. Astacio got off to a hot start, winning his first three decisions, while producing a 2.00 ERA a month into the season. In one of those victories, he tossed seven hitless innings against the Mets at Shea Stadium before yielding a leadoff double in the eighth. "He's one of the most underrated guys in this league," gushed pitching coach Dave Wallace.[22] Astacio then lost his next seven decisions, during which time he had an ugly altercation. Yanked after surrendering five runs in four dismal innings against the Cardinals in Los Angeles on national television, a visibly angered

Astacio confronted Russell in the dugout and had to be restrained by third-base coach Joe Amaltifano after a shoving match.[23] (Three days earlier Valdes and Russell had a similar dugout confrontation.) Astacio immediately apologized in the press, but his fate was sealed. "When something like that happens in the dugout with the cameras there, you have to pay the consequences," said VP Claire, who fined Astacio an undisclosed amount.[24] Normally a quiet player in the clubhouse, Astacio was considered by some as too emotionally volatile to be consistently successful; on the other hand, some reporters sympathized with the pitcher, suggesting that the Dodgers never helped him settle into a rhythm as a starter and put too much pressure on him to conform to the "Dodger Way." On August 19, the Dodgers shipped Astacio to the Colorado Rockies for All-Star second baseman Eric Young. "[Astacio] has great ability, character and work ethic," said Claire about the transaction. "He pitched some outstanding games, (but never with consistency.)"[25]

Astacio wasted no time proving his worth to Rockies manager Don Baylor following the loss of the fan favorite Young. After fanning eight in a 6⅔-inning no-decision in his debut against the Houston Astros, in the Astrodome, Astacio won five consecutive decisions. Those victories included a career-high 12-strikeout performance in eight scoreless innings against Atlanta and an emotional six-inning outing with nine punchouts versus his former team in Los Angeles. After just six starts, pitching coach Frank Funk pronounced Astacio the best pitcher ever to wear a Rockies uniform.[26] The Rockies went 23-14 after acquiring Astacio to finish with a winning record (83-79; third place NL West) for the third consecutive season since they entered the league as an expansion team in 1993. "He came in and really took charge," said Funk of Astacio (5-1, 4.25 ERA in seven starts), and really fired up our ball club."[27]

A hot free-agent commodity in the offseason, Astacio signed a four-year deal worth more than $24 million with the Rockies. "He's one of our leaders," said Funk when spring training opened. "He has that aggressive, I-love-to-play attitude. He's got the work ethic of a high-school kid in his first major-league camp."[28] The Rockies, with the signing of free-agent pitcher Darryl Kile, were expected to challenge the San Francisco Giants and the Dodgers for the West crown in 1998. And then the season started. Astacio struggled mightily, yielding 27 earned runs in his first 20 innings (12.15 ERA). He's fighting with his control," said skipper Don Baylor. "He's up in the (strike) zone, and behind in the counts. You can't pitch like that."[29] While the Rockies limped to a 77-85 record, Astacio took a beating, producing the highest ERA in the majors among starters (6.23), tied for the major-league lead with 39 gopher balls, and led the NL by hitting 17 batters; still, he went 13-14, made 34 starts, set a new team record with 170 punchouts, and exceeded the 200-inning mark for the third straight season. Nonetheless, rumors swirled that Astacio's arm was injured—it wasn't. "[Astacio] bears no resemblance from the nasty right-hander" from 1997, wrote Denver sportswriter Ray McNulty.[30] Beat reporter Mike Klis noted that Astacio relied more on breaking balls instead of his heater.[31] Like all hurlers, Astacio had to adjust his pitching in Coors Field, with its thin air, where balls flew out of the park at a record pace in an era of home-run records. And that process wasn't easy, as the split in Astacio's home and away ERA indicated (7.39 to 4.90).

Astacio reached the heights and depths of his career in 1999, but for vastly different reasons. On the field he enjoyed his best season, consistently pitching deep into ballgames despite yielding a league-leading 38 home runs. His victory against the Milwaukee Brewers on June 6 might best capture Astacio's career at Coors Field. In 7⅔ innings, he surrendered four round-trippers and five runs while fanning 10 and emerged the victor when the Rockies exploded for eight runs (and also smashed four home runs) in the seventh. On July 6, he took revenge against the Dodgers, tossing a complete game with 10 punchouts and drove in the go-ahead run in a 5-2 victory at Coors Field. Not known as good hitter (.133 career average), Astacio had his most productive season at the plate, collecting 20 hits.

Just as Astacio seemed to realize the potential many had predicted for him, he was arrested on August 12 after a violent altercation with his estranged, pregnant wife, Ana, allegedly striking her in the face.[32] (It was his second marriage. His first, to Dorca Garcia Thomas, ended in divorce in 1995.)

Neither suspended nor fined by either the Rockies or Major League Baseball, Astacio took the mound three days after the incident and tossed eight innings, fanning 11 in a 12-4 victory over the Montreal Expos in Denver, where the initial chorus of boos gradually turned to cheers for the pitcher. While the Rockies plunged to a last-place finish, Astacio completed a career year despite his legal distractions. He won 17 games (tying Kevin Ritz from 1996 for the franchise record), and set new club records in innings (232), complete games (7), and strikeouts (210, third best in the NL).

Astacio's charge of domestic abuse cast a dark shadow over his best season and raised questions about his future. On January 28, Astacio pleaded guilty to third-degree assault and received two years deferred judgment, thereby avoiding jail.[33] Soon thereafter the Department of Immigration and Naturalization Services (INS) informed Astacio that a felony or misdemeanor involving domestic violence was a deportable offense. (Astacio was a citizen of the Dominican Republic and had since reconciled with Ana.) Apparently unaware of the legal ramification of his plea, Astacio left the Rockies spring training in March and was granted permission to withdraw his guilty plea in an effort to remain in the United States with the formal trial set for early July. (The trial was subsequently deferred to November.) Despite his legal troubles, Astacio was the Rockies' Opening Day starter. After losing his first two starts, he won his next six decisions. Included was a four-start stretch with at least 10 strikeouts. He fanned 10 or more seven times during the season, and matched his career high of 12 punchouts in seven overpowering innings, yielding just two hits and one run in a 2-1 victory over the Chicago Cubs at Wrigley Feld on August 1. Seemingly headed to matching his totals from the previous season, Astacio injured his

left oblique on September 1, making only three very brief starts thereafter before he was shelved the last two weeks of the season. He concluded the campaign with a 12-9 slate (5.27 ERA in 196⅓ innings) and racked up 193 strikeouts. Weeks after the season, he underwent arthroscopic surgery on his left knee to remove damaged cartilage that had bothered him for two years.

Astacio's legal woes were far from over. On November 13, he pleaded guilty to lesser charges, a single count of spousal harassment, and was sentenced to six months' probation; however, his residency status was still unclear.[34] INS eventually abandoned deportation procedures by the beginning of spring training. Astacio opened his 10th big-league season red-hot. On April 22, he tossed two-hit ball over eight innings to beat the Arizona Diamondbacks in Phoenix, 2-1, to improve his record to 3-1 and lower his ERA to 1.93 after four starts. And then the bottom dropped out. He won only three of his next 15 decisions with an ERA well north of 6.00, prompting trade rumors as the Rockies were headed to their second straight last-place finish in the NL West in three years. Despite Astacio's horrendous numbers, contenders still sought his services. In a cost-cutting move, the Rockies shipped Astacio, due to be a free agent at season's end, to the Houston Astros for pitcher Scott Elarton. Astacio had a renaissance of sorts (2-1, 3.14 ERA) before shoulder pain ended his season after just four starts.

Astacio was diagnosed with a torn labrum in the offseason, but decided to forgo possible season-ending surgery given his status as a free agent. The Mets took a chance a chance on the 33-year-old hurler, signing him to a two-year contract in January. Reunited with former Dodgers teammate Mike Piazza, Astacio emerged as one of the surprises of the season, winning his first three starts. On April 27, he threw 7⅓ hitless frames against the Brewers at Shea Stadium, ultimately tossing eight innings in a 2-1 victory. Mets beat writer Rafael Hermoso reported that the team was impressed with Astacio's "maturity" and "preparation" and how he mentored young hurlers on the club.[35] Teammates gave him the moniker Mule for his ability to carry them late into innings. On August 6, he tossed a complete-game three-hitter and fanned 10 (the 20th and final time he reached double digits in strikeouts) to beat the Brewers in Milwaukee, improving his record to 11-4 and lowering his ERA to 2.95 before the clock stuck midnight in his fairy-tale season. As the pain in his shoulder intensified, Astacio collapsed in his final nine starts, yielding 54 earned runs in 45 innings (10.80 ERA) while losing seven of eight decisions. Through it all, Astacio still took the mound every five days and never became a distraction for the last-place Mets. On the contrary, Hermoso described Astacio as "one of most jubilant members of the Mets' clubhouse, joking about almost everything and dismissing poor performances as if he had a bad hair day."[36]

Astacio spent four more seasons in the big leagues, battling an array of arm and shoulder injuries, chasing a dream. Occasionally he found lightning in a bottle. He made only seven appearances for the Mets in 2003, signed in the middle of the 2004 season with the Boston Red Sox, making five appearances in September during their historic run to the World Series (he was not on the postseason roster), and made 22 combined starts for the Texas Rangers and San Diego Padres in 2005. His 4-2 slate and 3.17 ERA for San Diego earned him his first and only postseason start. In Game Two of the NLCS he lasted only four innings yielding four runs (two earned) and was collared with the loss, 6-2, to the Cardinals in St. Louis. The 37-year-old Astacio finished his 15-year big-league career with the Washington Nationals in 2006, splitting 10 decisions in 17 starts, one of which was his second two-hitter for his 12th and final shutout, blanking the Braves, 5-0, on August 15 in the nation's capital.

The typically modest, media-shy Astacio was never an All-Star but he retired as one of the most productive pitchers from the Dominican Republic. At the time of his retirement following the 2006 season, his 129 victories (124 losses) ranked fourth behind Juan Marichal (243) and brothers Pedro Martinez (206)[37] and Ramon Martinez (135). (Astacio's total has since been passed by Bartolo Colon's 235 and Ervin

Santana's 144, both as of 2017.) Astacio also became just the fourth Dominican hurler to log at least 2,000 innings, joining Marichal, Pedro Martinez, and Joaquin Andujar.

After his active playing days Astacio returned to his longtime residence and ranch in San Pedro Macoris, near where he grew up. In 2013, he donned a big-league uniform for the first time in seven years when he returned to the Rockies as a special assistant coach during spring training. As of 2017 Astacio still resided primarily in the Dominican Republic.

SOURCES

In addition to the sources cited in the Notes, the author also accessed Retrosheet.org, Baseball-Reference.com, the SABR Minor Leagues Database, accessed online at Baseball-Reference.com, SABR.org, and *The Sporting News* archive via Paper of Record.

NOTES

1   Owen Perkins, "In Camp With Rox as Coach, Astacio Thrilled to Help," MLB.com, February 28, 2013. m.mlb.com/news/article/42093506/in-camp-with-colorado-rockies-as-coach-pedro-astacio-thrilled-to-help/.

2   Quote by New York Mets GM Steve Phillips in Tyler Kepner, "Astacio's Health Is a Key Issue," *New York Times*, January 18, 2002: D2.

3   Perkins.

4   Randy Franz, "Performance Does the Talking," *Orange County Register* (Anaheim, California), March 26 1993: C1.

5   Pedro Astacio page, *WinterBall Data*, winterballdata.com/.

6   Ken Baxter, "Avila Led the Charge in MLB's Latin Revolution," ESPN, October 2, 2006. espn.com/espn/hispanichistory/news/story?id=2607258.

7   Allan Malamud, "(Notes) on a Scorecard," *Los Angeles Times*, July 6, 1992: C3.

8   Gordon Verrell, "LA Dodgers. Fly on the Wall," *The Sporting News*, July 13, 1992: 21.

9   Ibid.

10 "Scouting Report: Pedro Astacio," *The Sporting News*, August 13, 2001: 35.

11 Ibid.

12 Steve Dilbeck, "Astacio's Having Problems," *San Bernardino* (California) *Sun*, May 11, 1993: C2.

13 Associated Press, "Astacio, Dodgers blank Marlins," *San Bernardino* (California) *Sun*, September 13, 1993: C2.

14 "Scouting Report: Pedro Astacio."

15   Tim Kawakami, "Baseball Daily Report," *Los Angeles Times*, July 6, 1994: C9.

16   Maryann Hudson, "Baseball Daily Report," *Los Angeles Times*, July 24, 1994: C7.

17   "Caught on the Fly," *The Sporting News*, March 25, 1996: 5.

18   Bob Nightengale, "Dodgers Reconsidering Astacio's Starting Role," *Los Angeles Times*, June 16, 1995: C5.

19   Gordon Verrell, "Los Angeles Dodgers," *The Sporting News*, February 19 1996: 23.

20   Bob Nightengale, "(Baseball) Daily Report," *Los Angeles Times*, February 24, 1996: C6.

21   Bob Nightengale, "He Gets By With Help From Friends," *Los Angeles Times*, July 26, 1996: C1.

22   Bob Nightengale, "Los Angeles Dodgers," *The Sporting News*, April 28, 1997: 27.

23   Chris Baker, "Call It Dodger Blew — As in a Fuse," *Los Angeles Times*, June 9, 1997: C1.

24   Steve Springer, "Dodger Report," *Los Angeles Times*, June 10, 1997: C6.

25   Ross Newhan, "Baylor Looks for a Change From Astacio," *Los Angeles Times*, August 24, 1997: C9.

26   Mike Klis, "'Dodger Way' Isn't Working Well," *Gazette* (Colorado Springs, Colorado), September 21, 1997: SP 11.

27   Ray McNulty, "A Rockies' Attitude Adjustment," *Gazette* (Colorado Springs, Colorado), February 26, 1997: SP1.

28   Rob McNulty, "Preview," *Gazette* (Colorado Springs, Colorado), February 26, 1998: SP2.

29   Tony DeMarco, "Colorado Rockies," *The Sporting News*, April 27, 1999: 37.

30   Ray McNulty, "Rockies Better Batters in Beer-League Title," *Gazette* (Colorado Springs, Colorado), September 8, 1998: SP4.

31   Mike Klis, "Colorado," *The Sporting News*, May 22, 2000: 48.

32   "Rockies' Astacio Arrested," *CBS News*, August 12, 1999. cbsnews.com/news/rockies-astacio-arrested/.

33   "Rockies P Astacio Avoids Prison," CBS News, January 28, 2000. cbsnews.com/news/rockies-p-astacio-avoids-prison/.

34   Associated Press, "Astacio Sentenced to Supervised Probation," ESPN, November 13, 2000. a.espncdn.com/mlb/news/2000/1113/876164.html.

35   Rafael Hermoso, "It's Astacio's Turn to Take a Run at a No-Hitter," *New York Times*, April 28, 2002: G4.

36   Rafael Hermoso, "With Astacio Hurt, Mets Look to Cone," *New York Times*, March 21, 2003: S3.

37   Pedro Martinez was still active at time and had 206 victories; he finished with 219.

GARRETT ATKINS

BY PAUL HOFMANN

WHEN GARRETT ATKINS MADE HIS major-league debut with the Colorado Rockies on August 3, 2003, the sky appeared to be the limit. The young corner infielder had progressed through the Rockies' minor-league system in three years and appeared to be Colorado's heir-apparent to third baseman and fan favorite Vinny Castilla. The unassuming Atkins rose to the challenge and let his big bat do his talking for him. By the end of his second full major-league season, Atkins had quietly become one of the best hitters in baseball.

Garrett Bernard Atkins was born on December 12, 1979, in Orange, California. He was the older of two children born to Ron and Diana Atkins. Garrett grew up in both a nurturing and disciplined environment. His father was a marketing manager with a schedule that permitted him to spend a great deal of time with his son, much of it as Garrett's private hitting coach. By contrast, his mother was a no-nonsense assistant high-school principal with a low tolerance for excuses.[1]

As a young child, Garrett loved baseball and early on his father recognized he had a talent for hitting. He continually reminded Garrett this was a gift to be cherished and developed. When other kids were goofing around and playing video games, Garrett and his father could be found on a baseball diamond honing his swing. During these "coaching" sessions, Garrett's father emphasized hitting through the middle and driving the ball the other way just like the Padres' Tony Gwynn, one of Garrett's favorite players.[2]

Atkins attended University High School in Irvine, California, from 1993 to 1997. Located adjacent to the campus of the University of California Irvine, University High School is consistently ranked among the top public high schools in the United States, offering a curriculum with a strong emphasis in performing arts.[3] In addition to producing a number of actors and entertainers, the institution also produced a number of world-class athletes including former major-league All-Star third baseman Tim Wallach.

Atkins pitched and played outfield and third base in high school. He earned all-league honors in each of his three varsity seasons and helped lead the school's baseball team to two state championships. During his senior season, he positioned himself as one of the nation's top high-school prospects when he hit .557 with a school record 13 home runs.[4] After his senior season, the New York Mets selected him in the 10th round of the June amateur draft.

At the same time, Atkins was being recruited by baseball powerhouses UCLA, USC, Cal State Fullerton, and Oklahoma State and had a difficult decision to make. Reflecting back on the decision, Atkins said, "My parents were big supporters of me going to college. It was the right thing for me to do. But it was the toughest decision I had to make."[5]

Atkins signed a national letter of intent to play baseball at UCLA, where he majored in sociology.[6] He and fellow five-star recruit Chase Utley formed the foundation of one of the strongest recruiting classes in the nation. It was also the start of a lifelong friendship when UCLA coach Gary Adams had the two freshmen standouts room together.[7] The relationship fueled the two friends to get better. "If he can do it, I know I can do it," Atkins said. "And it's the same way with him." With the two prized recruits pushing each other and the return of seniors Eric Byrnes and Eric Valent, great things were expected of the Bruins.

UCLA had a disappointing 1998 season and finished in fifth place in the Pac 10 conference with a 24-33 record. Atkins, however, was one of the team's bright spots. After Adams installed him as the starting third baseman, Atkins manufactured a school-record 33-game hitting streak and finished the season with a team-leading .383 average, the ninth highest single-season average in UCLA history. He also set freshmen records for hits (85) and doubles (22).[8]

UCLA steadily improved over the next two seasons, earning bids to the NCAA Regionals both years and advancing to the Super Regionals in 2000. Atkins was a mainstay in the Bruins lineup, starting every game during his three seasons, and became the Bruins' first-ever three-time All-Pac-10 performer and All-American. Atkins finished his three-year Bruins career with a .369 average (fourth best in school history) and 276 hits, second only to Byrnes' 326.[9] Adams characterized Atkins as a natural hitter: "I coached at UCLA for 30 years and he's at the top of the list for fluid swings. He's a guy who could fall out of bed and hit."[10]

After his junior season, Atkins was selected in the fifth round of the June 2000 amateur draft by the Colorado Rockies. Rockies scouting director Bill Schmidt looked at Atkins and saw another UCLA player, 1992 NL Rookie of the Year Eric Karros, who had a long and successful major-league career because of his bat.[11] Schmidt believed that Atkins, like Karros, needed to work on his defense.

Atkins opted to forgo his senior year and signed with the Rockies. He was farmed out to the low Class-A Portland Rockies of the short-season Northwest League. In 69 games Atkins, who played both first base and third, finished with a team-leading .303 average, 7 home runs, and 47 RBIs, earning league MVP honors. Despite playing on a team with a roster that included Clint Barmes, Brad Hawpe, and 11 other future major leaguers, the Rockies finished with a 32-44 record in last place in the circuit's western division.

Atkins spent the 2001 season with the Salem Avalanche of the Class-A Carolina League. The sweet-swinging right-handed hitter was used almost exclusively at first base and hit .325, second in the league to Victor Martinez (.329). He had 5 home runs, 67 RBIs, a league-leading 43 doubles, and a .421 on-base percentage. He was named both a mid- and postseason all-star, tabbed as the Rockies' third-best prospect by *Baseball America*, and honored by the Rockies as the organization's Player of the Year.

Promoted to Carolina Mudcats of the Double-A Southern League in 2002, Atkins moved across the

diamond to third base, where he appeared in 119 of his 128 games. The move to the hot corner may have partially explained his drop-off in average. For the year, he hit .271 with 12 home runs and 61 RBIs. As he was rising through the Rockies' minor-league system, Atkins was most often compared with Sean Casey and projected as a prospect who could develop into a major-league hitter with 15-home-run power.[12]

Atkins started the 2003 season with the Colorado SkySox, the Rockies' Triple-A Pacific Coast League affiliate. He continued to play third base and enjoyed a solid season with the bat and earned two promotions to Denver. The third baseman hit .319 with 13 home runs and 67 RBIs with the SkySox.

Atkins made his major-league debut on Sunday, August 3, 2003, against the Pittsburgh Pirates at Pittsburgh's PNC Park. Starting at third base and batting seventh, Atkins took little time to record his first major-league hit. With the Rockies already ahead 4-0 in the top of the first inning, he shot a groundball double down the left-field line off Jeff D'Amico to plate right fielder Rene Reyes with the fifth run of the inning. Atkins drove in a second run in the seventh when he grounded out to shortstop to score Preston Wilson with the Rockies' 15th and final run of the game. Atkins finished 1-for-6 with a pair of RBIs.

But Atkins struggled to hit major-league pitching, and was returned to the SkySox. He was recalled when major-league rosters expanded in September. However, it was clear that he was not yet ready to play every day at the major-league level. During his two brief stints with the Rockies, he hit just .159 with 2 doubles and 4 RBIs. After the season he was invited to play for Team USA, which was participating the Arizona Fall League in preparation for the 2004 Olympic Games.

Atkins returned to the SkySox for the 2004 season. Despite missing 15 games in July with an acute viral infection of his lower intestine, Atkins hit a league-leading .366 with 15 home runs and 94 RBIs. He hit a team-high 43 doubles and had a career-high 23-game hitting streak on his way to being named to the PCL All-Star team. Atkins was now viewed as a complete hitter.

Atkins was once again called up to the Rockies when the rosters expanded in early September and enjoyed more success at the plate than he had a year earlier. On September 11, 2004, he hit his first major-league home run, against the San Diego Padres at Coors field. Pinch hitting for Castilla in the top of the seventh inning, Atkins hit a two-run shot off right-hander Steve Watkins in the Padres' 13-2 blowout loss to the Rockies. During the month with the parent club, Atkins gave the Rockies a glimpse into the future. In 15 September games he hit .357 with two doubles, a homer, and eight RBIs.

After the 2004 season, Castilla signed a $3 million contract with the Washington Nationals clearing the way for Atkins to become the Rockies' everyday third baseman. However, two days before the start of the 2005 season, Atkins strained his right hamstring during the team's final exhibition game and landed on the disabled list. Atkins missed the first 18 games of the season before coming back to have an outstanding rookie season. He played in 138 games (136 at third base) and hit .287 with 13 home runs and a team-leading 89 RBIs. While his RBI total led all NL rookies by 26, Atkins finished a surprising (if not disappointing) distant fourth in NL Rookie of the Year voting behind Ryan Howard, Willy Taveras, and Jeff Francoeur.

In his second full season, Atkins became the centerpiece of a strong Rockies offense. In 2006 he played 157 games at third base and hit .329 with career highs in home runs (29), runs (117), and RBIs (120). He was one of only four players in the majors who hit better than .320 with at least 20 home runs, 100 RBIs, and 100 runs scored. The others were Albert Pujols, Miguel Cabrera, and teammate Matt Holliday.[13] Atkins' breakout season had many wondering what the future had in store. Rockies manager Clint Hurdle thought there were no limits. "I would not put a ceiling on what kind of hitter this kid is going to be," Hurdle said.[14]

Atkins' consistency during the 2006 season was also noteworthy. His batting average climbed over

.300 in the season's third game and never dropped below that level the rest of the year. Despite the spectacular season, the Rockies third baseman was not named to the NL All-Star team and was again overlooked in postseason award voting. Atkins finished 15th in NL MVP voting. In the end, the season proved to be not only a breakout year for the 26-year-old, it was also his career peak.

Atkins had another solid year in 2007 as the Rockies captured the NL wild card. He started slowly and hit only .223 in the first two months of the season. However, he eventually found his stroke and finished with a .301 average, 25 home runs, and 111 RBIs, while matching the career-high 157 games he played in the year before. During the Rockies' magical 15-game run in which they went 14-1 to close out the season, Atkins hit .414 with 3 home runs and 9 RBIs. Unfortunately, he went into a postseason slump.

The 2007 NLDS between Colorado and Philadelphia offered the interesting subplot of two good friends trying to keep each other from advancing in the playoffs as Atkins and the Rockies squared off against Utley and the Phillies.[15] The series was anti-climactic as the Rockies swept the Phillies in three straight. Atkins went 3-for-13 in the series with three runs scored and a lone Game One RBI, a second-inning double that scored the first run of the series. Utley managed to go just 2-for-11.

Atkins' offensive struggles continued in the NLCS against the Arizona Diamondbacks. The third baseman batted a pedestrian .143 (2-for-14) as the Rockies swept the Diamondbacks to advance to the World Series against the American League champion Boston Red Sox. With the sweep, the Rockies increased their winning streak to 10 games and had won an improbable 21 of their last 22.

The World Series brought with it a change of fortune for Colorado as the Red Sox swept the Rockies in four straight. Atkins went 2-for 13 in the Series. He had double and scored the Rockies' only run in Game One and homered off Hideki Okajima in Game Four. Atkins, however, was not the only member of the Rockies to struggle. The Red Sox pitching staff limited the Rockies to 10 runs and a collective .218 average in the four games.

Atkins' offensive production continued to slightly decline in 2008. In 155 games split between third base and first, he hit .286 with 32 doubles, 21 home runs, and 99 RBIs—perfectly acceptable numbers for a middle-of-the-order hitter. However, the precipitous drop in his OPS (on-base percentage plus slugging percentage) from two years prior was a clear indication that he was in decline. Atkins' career-high .965 OPS in 2006 had fallen to .853 in 2007 and dropped even further to .780 in 2008.

After the 2008 season, the Rockies and Atkins became involved in an arbitration battle. Jeff Blank, his agent, felt the Rockies' corner infielder's numbers compared favorably to the Twins' Justin Morneau.[16] Atkins requested a salary of $7.95 million, while the Rockies offered $6.65 million. The two sides avoided arbitration by settling on a $7.05 million contract for the 2009 season.[17]

The 2009 season was a struggle for Atkins from start to finish. He started the season with an 0-for-12 skid before breaking out of it with a two-run home run off the Phillies' Cole Hamels in the Rockies' fourth game of the season. From May 13 to June 10 he was below the Mendoza line[18] and finished the season with .226 average, 12 doubles, 9 homers, and 48 RBIs. As the season progressed, Ian Stewart, who hit a career-high 25 home runs in 2009, saw an increasing amount of time at third base.

Despite Atkins's disappointing statistics, the Rockies earned their second playoff berth in three years. He was the starting third baseman all four games of the NLDS rematch with Utley and the Phillies. He went 3-for-13 in the series with a pair of RBIs in Game Three. Utley hit .429 for the series with a Game Three homer as the Phillies avenged their 2007 NLDS loss by beating the Rockies in four.

On December 12, 2009, Atkins' 30th birthday, the Rockies told him they wouldn't be offering him a contract for 2010. Though an unpleasant message to receive on his birthday, the move was not unexpected. Within a period of 12 months, Atkins had become an underperforming, overpriced veteran. He was the only arbitration-eligible Rockies player not to get a contract offer from the club.[19]

Ten days later the Baltimore Orioles signed Atkins to a one-year guaranteed $4 million contract with the hope that he could fill a gap they had at first base and return to the 20-homer, 100-RBI form of seasons past. However, Atkins' stint with the Orioles proved short-lived. After hitting safely in his first five games with the Orioles, Atkins managed to hit only .192 in his final 39 major-league appearances. He batted .214 with one home run and nine RBIs before being designated for assignment on June 26, 2010. The Orioles president for baseball operations, Andy MacPhail, summarized the situation by stating, "We gambled that we could resurrect a bat, and it just wasn't happening."[20] Atkins was released by the Orioles on July 6 when he refused to accept a minor-league assignment.

Manager Juan Samuel praised Atkins for being a consummate professional in the Orioles clubhouse

under difficult circumstances. "He's a great guy," Samuel said. "He was professional throughout this whole process and understands why he wasn't playing. He was very quiet, didn't cause any issues in the clubhouse. He was just a veteran professional."[21]

Not yet ready to call it a career, Atkins signed a minor-league contract with the Pittsburgh Pirates on January 5, 2011. The now 31-year-old veteran was brought into the Pirates camp to compete with Andy Marte, Steve Pearce, and Josh Fields for the team's backup corner-infield position. The Pirates released Atkins on March 21, 2011, after he hit .129 in 33 plate appearances in 17 Grapefruit League games.[22] Rather than continue to pursue the goal of making it back to the major leagues, Atkins retired and started a new chapter in his life.

In an eight-year major-league career, Atkins hit .285 with 169 doubles, 99 home runs, and 488 RBIs. From 2005 to 2008, he hit .301 and averaged 22 home runs and 105 RBIs per year. Amazingly, he hit only .223 with 10 home runs and 57 RBIs during his final two major-league seasons. While he enjoyed a significantly higher average (.327) and OPS (.892) at Coors Field, Atkins actually hit more home runs on the road (50) than he did at home (48) while playing for the Rockies.

As of 2017 Atkins resided with his wife and son in Castle Pines, Colorado, a suburban oasis about 20 miles southeast of Denver. He said he enjoyed reading, watching TV, skiing, and playing golf—identifying himself as the "Worst Club Champion in the US" for 2017.[23]

SOURCES

In addition to the Sources cited in the Notes, the author also consulted Baseball-Reference.com.

NOTES

1 Troy Renck, "With This Sweet Swing, Hits Just Keep Comin'," *Denver Post.* March 17, 2007.

2 "Garrett Atkins—Bio," jockbio.com/Bios/GAtkins/GAtkins_bio.html.

3 Actor Will Ferrell and many other notable entertainers are among University High School's alumni.

4 "Garrett Atkins—Bio."

5 "Garrett Atkins—My Say," jockbio.com/Bios/GAtkins/GAtkins_mysay.html.

6 Thomas Harding, "Q & A with Garrett Atkins," Retrieved from mlb.com.

7 Gerry Fraley, "The Friendship Baseball Made: Utley, Atkins Now Aren't Rooting for Each Other Much," *Rocky Mountain News* (Denver), October 5, 2007.

8 "2017 UCLA Baseball Information Guide," uclabruins.com.

9 Ibid.

10 Troy Renck.

11 Gerry Fraley.

12 Troy Renck.

13 Ibid.

14 "Garrett Atkins—They Say," jockbio.com/Bios/GAtkins/GAtkins_theysay.html.

15 Atkins was the best man in Utley's wedding in January 2007.

16 Mark Townsend, "Rockslide: Tracking The Decline of Slugger Garrett Atkins," March 21, 2011. sports.yahoo.com/mlb/blog/big_league_stew/post/rockslide-tracking-the-decline-of-colorados-garrett-atkins?urn=mlb,wp1023.

17 David Martin, "Colorado Rockies and Garrett Atkins Strike a Deal and Avoid Arbitration," bleacherreport.com/articles/119437-colorado-rockies-and-garrett-atkins-strike-a-deal-avoid-arbitration.

18 The "mendoza line" is a baseball term for batting around or below .200, mediocrity. The term was coined by George Brett after Mario Mendoza. The term has also crossed over into America's pop-culture lexicon and is frequently used to describe almost any type of subpar performance, from the performance of stocks and mutual funds to bad grades, and to quotas for salespeople.

19 Thomas Harding, "Rockies Part Ways With Atkins," mlb.com, December 13, 2009.

20 Brittany Ghiroli, "Orioles Designate Atkins for Assignment," mlb.com, June 27, 2010.

21 Ibid.

22 Tim Dierkes, "Pirates Release Garrett Atkins," March 21, 2011. mlbtraderumors.com/garrett-atkins.

23 "Garrett Atkins (@GAtkins32)," Twitter.com

CLINT BARMES

BY KURT WELLS

AFTER SPENDING FIVE SEASONS IN the minor leagues, in addition to a late-season call-up in 2004, rookie Clint Barmes was thrilled to be named the Colorado Rockies' starting shortstop on Opening Day 2005. With the sold-out Coors Field crowd on their feet and the score tied 10-10 in the bottom of the ninth, Barmes launched a Trevor Hoffman first-pitch fastball into the left-field seats for a walk-off two-run homer, capping a four-hit day.

Six weeks later, on May 13, Barmes went 3-for-6, hitting two home runs with five RBIs, raising his batting average back to .400, where it had been hovering since Opening Day. Barmes' sensational stretch carried into June and was one the best starts to a season any rookie has ever experienced. Although this was one of the major highlights of his 13-year career, teammates, coaches, and managers continuously claim his biggest impact came from the intangible qualities he brought to the ballpark on a daily basis. His legacy in major-league baseball is epitomized by his passion for the game, dedication and hard work, playing the game right, and being an exemplary teammate.

Clint Hurdle, who managed Barmes with the Colorado Rockies and later with the Pittsburgh Pirates, had the ultimate respect for those intangibles and said, "We went our separate ways and were able to reconnect in Pittsburgh. I shared with our GM, Neal Huntington, Clint would be a perfect fit to bring cohesion and collaboration to our club on the field and in the clubhouse. He was an integral part of the Renaissance of Baseball on the North Shore and the Pirates' return to prominence in major-league baseball."[1]

Clint Harold Barmes was born in Vincennes, Indiana, on March 6, 1979, the older of two sons of Barry and Erma Barmes. He was named after his mother's favorite actor, Clint Eastwood. The Barmes family farmed in Beal, Indiana, outside Vincennes

in the southwest corner of the state, until Clint was in the third grade, when the family left the farm and moved into town.[2]

Clint spent "a lot" of time playing baseball and basketball on the farm with his father. When they moved to town, Barry built a pitcher's mound in the backyard and Clint spent many hours pitching to his dad. "Dad worked with me all the time," Clint said. "He was the most impactful person in my life. He coached my teams all the way into high school." Barry had been a good athlete, having played two years of junior-college baseball and basketball at Wabash Valley College in Mount Carmel, Illinois.[3] Clint also had an uncle, Bruce Barmes, who hit .318 in 1,439 minor-league games and had a cup of coffee with the Washington Senators in 1953.

Clint started playing organized baseball in a machine-pitch league at the age of 7. When he was 12, playing in the Bambino League, his team qualified for the Bambino World Series in Pueblo, Colorado. "It was the first time I was ever on an airplane," Clint said. He pitched and played shortstop and center field for the team, which finished fourth in the tournament. Clint played in the league from age 9 through 12 and made the all-star team all four years.

Jumping the fence at Lincoln High School to hit in the cage was a regular occurrence for Barmes when the field was closed. Throughout high school, he excelled at the plate, in the field as a center fielder and shortstop, and as a pitcher. During an intrasquad scrimmage in college, after walking four straight batters, his coach walked to the mound and advised, "Why don't you stick with playing the field?" Thus, his pitching career came to an abrupt end.

Barmes also starred on the basketball court. A friend of his had a basketball court in his backyard, where they spent a lot of time honing their skills. "Being from Indiana, basketball was the big sport," Clint said, "but even though I loved both sports, baseball was actually my number one love." At

Lincoln High School, Barmes made the varsity as a sophomore shooting guard. In the state tournament, his team made the round of 16 in both his junior and senior years.[4]

After high school, Barmes attended Olney (Illinois) Central College, a junior college 32 miles from Vincennes, on basketball and baseball scholarships. He played both basketball and baseball during his first year, but in his second year Barmes elected to focus solely on baseball and quit the basketball team.[5]

Playing mostly in left field as a freshman and at shortstop as a sophomore,[6] Barmes finished his two-year junior-college career with a .426 batting average, boosted by a .445 sophomore season.[7] He graduated from Olney holding eight offensive records[8] and as of 2018 still had the single-season record of 105 hits and 81 runs scored in 1999, along with career marks for hits with 172 and triples with 14.[9] After his second season he was named a junior-college All-American.[10] According to Olney's baseball coach, Dennis Conley, Barmes had a 35-game hit streak, went hitless in one game, then hit in another 17 straight. "Not only was he the best player, but he was also the best teammate and the hardest worker," Conley said. "When you wrap that all up you get a pretty special player and person. I have always said if he didn't go into baseball he would have been very successful at anything he did and that is a direct result of his upbringing."[11]

Barmes had a similar respect for coach Conley, praising him for the major influence he had on his career. "I learned more about how to play the game during those two years from him than any other time up to that point," Barmes said.

Barmes' record at Olney earned him a scholarship to Indiana State in the Missouri Valley Conference, where in 2000 he batted .375 with 10 home runs and struck out only eight times in 248 at-bats. He tied the Indiana State record by hitting in 30 consecutive games.[12] Barmes commented, "The 30-game hitting streak at Indiana State got me drafted."[13]

Barmes, a right-handed batter and thrower, was selected after his junior year at Indiana State in the 10th round on June 5, 2000, by the Colorado Rockies. He signed four days later, receiving a $45,000 signing

bonus. He used the majority of his bonus to purchase a 1999 Chevy pickup.[14]

The 21-year-old shortstop was sent to the Portland Rockies, in the short-season rookie Northwest League. Barmey, as teammates and fans called him throughout his career, and two other players shared a studio apartment and slept on air mattresses. The three lived in this modest arrangement until Barmes was called up to Asheville in the low Class-A South Atlantic League later in the season. He got a base hit in his first professional game, in Boise, Idaho.[15]

Barmes returned to Asheville for the 2001 season. He broke the hamate bone in his hand and missed three weeks of spring training and the first three weeks of the season, before settling in to the starting shortstop position. After 74 games with the Tourists, he was promoted to Salem of the high-A Carolina League.[16] For the two teams, Barmes hit a modest .256, but had only 57 strikeouts in 457 plate appearances. That season, Barmes played with a very tight-knit group of teammates he would eventually spend a major part of his big-league career with as members of the Rockies, including Matt Holliday, Garrett Atkins, Aaron Cook, Brad Hawpe, Cory Sullivan, and Jason Young.[17]

Promoted again in 2002, Barmes played ball for the Carolina Mudcats (Raleigh, North Carolina). He batted .272 and led the team with 15 home runs despite missing three weeks with a broken hand after getting hit by a pitch.[18] He was named to the Southern League postseason all-star team. After the season he played for the Mesa Solar Sox in the Arizona Fall League. During the winter he was named to the Rockies' 40-man roster for the first time.

The 2003 season brought another promotion, to the Triple-A Colorado Springs Sky Sox. Barmes hit .276 and led the league in doubles with 35. At the end of the season he got his first major-league call-up. When he arrived at his locker, uniform number 12 was awaiting and that stuck with him throughout his career, other than in 2007, when Steve Finley took number 12 and Barmes flipped to 21. On September 5, in the second at-bat of his first major-league game, he got a hit in front of the home crowd at Coors Field in

Denver.[19] Barmes recalled it: "a single up the middle off (Kazuhisa) Ishii of the Dodgers."

The 6-foot-1 Barmes, with clean-shaven head, reported to spring training each year at about 215 pounds and came home at the end of the season around 200. His typical playing weight was 205. Reporting to spring training in 2004, he had his first hopes of sticking with the big-league club.[20] Despite a good spring, he began the 2004 season in Triple-A with the Sky Sox and had a fine season, hitting .328 with 16 homers and leading the league with 175 hits. He was named to the Pacific Coast League's postseason all-star team. His achievements over the two years in Colorado Springs earned him the nod for starting shortstop on the Sky Sox team of the decade announced in 2010.[21]

In August, Barmey was again called up to the Rockies. In his second game after being recalled, he hit his first major-league home run, off the Florida Marlins' Carl Pavano in Miami. One important learning experience that came out of his month with the big club resulted from splitting time with Royce Clayton, who taught him life lessons he would pass

on in future years about positively affecting the career of a person in direct competition for his position. "He taught me a lot of things and took me under his wing. He's a great guy that I've always respected," Barmes said.

After spring training in 2005, Barmes was the Opening Day shortstop. For Barmes, spring training was productive in more ways than one. On St. Patrick's Day in Tucson, his manager while with the Carolina Mudcats, PJ Carey, and his wife, Katherine, introduced Barmes to the woman he would marry, Summer Dennison. Summer was from Platteville, Colorado, and had played college softball at Lamar Community College, finishing her degree at the University of Northern Colorado.[22]

Hitting a walk-off home run off Trevor Hoffman on 2005's Opening Day made Barmes an instant fan favorite in Denver. "I remember running the bases thinking this can't be real," he said. "The next game I was still on cloud nine, but the game slowed down for me after the home run."[23] Barmes finished April hitting .410 with 4 home runs and 14 RBIs and was named the National League Rookie of the Month.[24]

He was only the third rookie to hit .400 in April with a qualifying amount of plate appearances. By mid-May, Barmes was still leading the major leagues in batting.[25]

By June, Barmes was not only the front-runner for Rookie of the Year, but was being mentioned as a leading candidate to make the All-Star team. Then the magical start to the season came to a crashing halt on Sunday, June 5, when he had a freak accident, falling while climbing the stairs to his apartment. He broke his collarbone on the fall, which garnered national attention because he was carrying deer meat that teammate Todd Helton had given him after Barmes had spent time on Helton's ranch riding an ATV.[26]

The injury placed Barmes on the disabled list until September 2. His batting average at the time of the injury was .327, with 8 home runs and 34 RBIs. After the injury, Barmes said, his swing was affected for the remainder of his career. Before the injury, he would swing and release the bat with his right hand, finishing his swing with the left hand elevated. Afterward he was unable to repeat his swing and his follow-through included both hands on the bat.[27]

Barmes still finished the season with a respectable .289 batting average, 10 homers, 46 RBIs, and only one strikeout per 10.5 plate appearances. He finished eighth in the National League Rookie of the Year voting. Clint Hurdle remembers the start Barmes had in '05. "We started our journey together in Colorado where I witnessed him have one of the best starts ever for a rookie."[28]

After the season, Barmes played winter ball in the Dominican Republic.[29] He was the first American everyday shortstop to play in the Dominican. This experience had a major impact on improving his defense. He watched the players' footwork and started playing with quicker hands. It was also a great opportunity for him to gain an appreciation of what the foreign players experience when they come to the United States to play ball. "It was good being in a different country and seeing what they go through when they come to the States," he said. "The Dominicans took

me in and accepted me. I remember what that felt like and I wanted to make sure I treated them the same."

Barmes started for the Rockies at shortstop for most of the 2006 season, recalling that "I spent most of the year trying to reinvent my swing, but it was my best defensive year up to that point." He finished second in the NL among all positions with a 3.2 defensive WAR, but he batted only .220 with seven home runs. Always a good bunter, Barmes finished second in the NL with 19 sacrifices. He also led the National League by hitting into only two double plays, the lowest rate in the league.

After the season, Clint and Summer were married in Maui on December 12 (12/12/06), a planned tribute to Barmes's uniform number 12. They made Denver their home that winter and remained Colorado residents as of 2018.[30]

The emergence of Troy Tulowitzki as the Rockies' new shortstop phenom in 2007 forced Barmes to start the year in Colorado Springs. He was moved up and down between Denver and Colorado Springs three times that year, sticking with the Rockies after his August 29 call-up, allowing him the opportunity to be part of the Rockies' remarkable run for the pennant that became known as Rocktober.

September 18, 2007, was one of the most historic days in Rockies history. In the bottom of the ninth inning of the second game of a doubleheader, with two outs and two strikes, Todd Helton hit a walk-off home run off Dodgers closer Takashi Saito to keep the Rockies in the pennant race. On that same day, Clint and Summer had their first child, a son they named Wyatt. "I remember watching the game from the hospital and holding Wyatt," Clint said. The day before, the Rockies had started a streak of winning 21 of 22 games, catapulting them to their first appearance in the World Series, in which they were swept by the Boston Red Sox.

Barmes had a good year at Colorado Springs and was hit by a pitch 22 times, which was another intangible part of his game that he excelled at throughout the years. "I always liked the ball inside so I'd crowd the plate, so I'd get hit a lot. I was willing to take the hit by pitch," Barmes said. He played in only 27 games for the Rockies that year, but played in the Triple-A all-star game. Although Barmes suited up and took batting practice throughout the playoffs and World Series, he was not activated.

Barmes broke camp with the Rockies in 2008 as a utility player, with Jayson Nix named as the starting second baseman. However, with Nix slumping, three weeks into the season Barmes took over the starting role at second base and remained there the rest of the season. He had a good season at the plate (.290, a career-high .790 OPS), but he also teamed with Tulowitzki to create a formidable double-play combo.

Barmes was the Rockies' everyday second baseman in 2009, playing in 154 games. That season he switched from a 33-30 bat to a 34-inch bat[31] and established career highs with 23 home runs, 32 doubles and 76 RBIs. However, his batting average dropped to .245 and he struck out 121 times, the most in his career. He tried at times later in his career to go back to the 33-inch bat he had always used before but was never comfortable with it again.[32]

The Rockies made the playoffs that season and Barmes had the opportunity to play in his first postseason games. He was hitless in four games as the Rockies lost the Division Series to the Phillies.

After his back-to-back solid seasons, the Rockies signed Barmes to a one-year, $3.325 million contract for 2010. He opened the season starting at second base, but Troy Tulowitzki injured his wrist and Barmes played shortstop during his extended absence. When Tulowitzki returned, Barmes moved back to second. After he went through a slump in August, Eric Young Jr. replaced Barmes as the starting second baseman to finish out the season. Even when not in the starting lineup, he was typically inserted for defensive purposes late in games. Barmes finished the season with a .235 batting average and 8 homers.

It had been a tough year: Barmes learned on June 15 that his father, Barry, had stage-four cancer.[33] Jim Tracy and the Rockies organization were understanding and allowed several breaks from the Rockies during the season to visit his father.[34] Three days after the end of the regular season, on October 6, Clint and

Summer had a baby daughter, Whitney. Seven days later, on October 13, the day of Barry's 56th birthday, Barry died of lung cancer.[35]

On November 18, 2010, Barmes was traded to the Houston Astros for Felipe Paulino. The Astros signed him for $3,925,000, another one-year contract. Late in spring training, Barmes broke his left hand when he was hit by a pitch from Ivan Nova of the Yankees.[36] The injury forced him to miss the first month of the 2011 season, but upon his return, Barmes took over the starting shortstop position for the remainder of the year. He hit .244 with 12 home runs and was solid in the field. For the second time in his career, Barmes finished second in the National League in defensive WAR for all positions. He enjoyed his season with the Astros. "I loved Houston," he recalls. "The fans and people were great."

After the season, Clint had his first opportunity to test free agency. The Pittsburgh Pirates, now managed by Clint Hurdle, Barmes' manager in Colorado from 2003 to 2009, signed him to a two-year, $10.5 million contract, based on Hurdle's recommendation.[37] He started at shortstop for the Pirates in 2012 and played solid defense. In 144 games, he hit .229. His eight home runs included his first career grand slam, against San Diego.

Barmes started the 2013 season as the everyday shortstop in 2013. By midseason he was splitting time with Jordy Mercer. "I loved working with Jordy," Barmes said. It reminded me of when I came up and had Royce Clayton working with me. I said to myself at that time, 'This is exactly how I'm going to treat whoever comes up behind me. Jordy and I ended up having a great relationship.'" The Pirates made it to the playoffs as a wild-card team and lost in five games to the St. Louis Cardinals in the NLDS. Barmes played in all six games of the wild card and NLDS and went 3-for-11.

When Barmes first came to the majors, the Rockies gave him Kenny Chesney's "Back Where I Come From" as his walkup song, which he kept for a few years. In 2013 he changed his song to "Don't Stop Believing" by Journey, which was his favorite band. His wedding song had been "Faithfully," by

Journey. The song was a hit with the players and fans and became the signature song of the Pirates. When Barmes approached the plate, fans sang along. Barmes also shared another memory, "The team would sing the song as they were landing the plane returning home from a road trip."[38]

Barmes was a free agent at the end of the season and re-signed with the Pirates for 2014, a one-year $2 million deal. He understood that his role was to back up Mercer; he seized the opportunity and spent a great deal of time mentoring him on playing short-stop.[39] Barmes spent the first half of the 2014 season as the backup shortstop, but pulled his groin just before the All-Star break and played in only seven games after returning late in the season. "I loved Pittsburgh," he said. "It was a fun environment. The teams were awesome and the fans came out and supported us. I remember how much fun it was to compete there. Everyone was there to win."[40]

Just before 2015 spring training, Barmes signed with the San Diego Padres. At age 36, he was still a valuable commodity for teams looking for a good glove in the infield, a strong clubhouse presence, and a good role model for the younger players. By now he had developed a reputation as one of the game's hard-est workers. "I was always early to the field. I'm a big routine guy and wanted to be as ready as I could be," he said. That season he was hitting .282 at the All-Star break and maintained an average above .250 until an 0-for-15 slump at the end of the season dropped his average to .232.

Barmes liked playing for Bud Black, but the Padres manager was fired a couple of months into the season. Cameron Maybin, who was the Asheville Tourists' batboy when Barmes played there, was a teammate during spring training, but was traded to the Atlanta Braves before Opening Day.[41]

A highlight of the season with the Padres came in Barmes' return to Pittsburgh. On July 7, as he approached the plate, the Pirates exhibited the paramount respect to an opposing player by play-ing his old walkup song, "Don't Stop Believing," a tribute that seldom occurs for the visiting team. The

Pittsburgh fans gave him a standing ovation and he responded with a 2-for-4 day.[42]

Going into the 2016 season, Barmes signed a mi-nor-league contract with the Kansas City Royals. "I had a solid spring and felt like I could help the club," he said, but he didn't make the Royals' roster. Clint played for a while before his body told him he was done.[43] He announced his retirement from baseball on May 23, 2016.[44] Through exceptional work ethic, dedication, and commitment, being a team player and a great teammate, the small-town kid who struggled to get a baseball scholarship out of high school had achieved 10 years and 122 days of major-league ser-vice time.

Barmes finished his career with 89 home runs and a .245 batting average. Asked who the tough-est pitcher he faced was, without hesitation he re-sponded, "Brandon Webb's sinker. At one point I was something like 1-for-15 against him. The one hit was a broken-bat single to shortstop that I beat out."

As for the pitchers Barmes had the most success against: "I actually had a lot of success against Clayton Kershaw and Zack Greinke. I also had some of my best stats against Paul Maholm and Noah Lowry." A deeper look into his stats revealed some lofty num-bers against a number of pitchers, including Odalis Perez (.556), Maholm (.417), and Greinke (.368).

Barmes spent his entire career in the National League, but put up some of his best stats facing American League pitching. He had a career OPS of over .900 against five AL teams. The only other team he had an OPS in excess of .900 against was his former Colorado Rockies team. "I always got excited to play against my old teammates and coach-es and to play in front of my friends," Barmes said. "I always felt comfortable at Coors Field. That was always home to me."

In retirement, Barmes remained a part of the Colorado Rockies family. He was chosen to announce the 2017 Rockies amateur draft picks in New Jersey and was part of a 2017 Rockies 25-year reunion over a three-day weekend in September.

Clint Hurdle, reflecting on the years he managed Barmes, said: "I watched him play a game that he loved and share that love with others to make them better. I watched him grow up, fall in love and get married. I watched Clint and Summer become parents. I am proud of him and happy for him. He made me better."[45]

As of 2018 Barmes and his family lived in Mead, Colorado. Taking a page from his father's book, he enjoyed coaching his children in sports.

SOURCES

In addition to the sources noted in this biography, the author consulted Barmes' Hall of Fame player file, Baseball-Reference.com, ESPN.com's game-by-game stats, Baseballamerica.com, the baseballcube.com, rotowire.com, and the Colorado Rockies official website for statistical data, as well as Foxsports.com for historical transactions.

NOTES

1   Clint Hurdle, email correspondence with author, May 8, 2017.

2   Clint Barmes, interview with author, March 8, 2017.

3   Ibid. All quotations attributed to Barmes are from this March 8 interview unless otherwise noted.

4   Barmes Interview.

5   Ibid.

6   Ibid.

7   Official Home of the Olney Central College Blue Knights Baseball Record Book: olneycentralathletics.com/sports/bsb/records.

8   Dennis Conley, telephone interview with author, July 29, 2017.

9   Craig Pearson, "From Terre Haute to the Majors: Former Sycamore Clint Barmes Calls It a Career," *Terre Haute Tribune-Star*, May 28, 2016.

10 Official Home of the Olney Central College Blue Knights Baseball Notable Knights: olneycentralathletics.com/sports/bsb/pictures.

11 Conley interview.

12 Pearson.

13 Barmes interview.

14 Barmes interview.

15 Ibid.

16 Ibid.

17 Ibid.

18 Ibid.

19 "Deals and Newcomers, Clint Barmes, SS," *USA Today Baseball Weekly*, October 1-7, 2003: 57.

20 Barmes interview.

21 "Clint Barmes Named Starting Shortstop to Colorado Springs' Team of the Decade," May 10, 2010, milb.com/milb/news/clint-barmes-named-starting-shortstop-to-colorado-springs-team-of-the-decade/c-9942936?tid=185364810.

22 Barmes interview.

23 Ibid.

24 Thomas Harding, "Barmes Is NL's Top Rookie," Colorado Rockies Official Site, May 2, 2005. m.rockies.mlb.com/news/article/1036172//

25 Vicki Michaelis, "Rockies Rookie Barmes Hitting It Off," *USA Today*, May 12, 2005.

26 Tracy Ringolsby, "It's a Different Story About Barmes' Fall," *Rocky Mountain News* (Denver), June 10, 2005.

27 Barmes interview.

28 Hurdle email correspondence.

29 "5 Colorado Rockies, Escaping the Cellar Will Depend on a Young Team's Rate of Maturity," *Sports Illustrated*, April 3, 2006. si.com/vault/2006/04/03/8373971/5-colorado-rockies#.

30 Barmes interview.

31 Ibid.

32 Ibid.

33 Troy Renck, "Rockies' Barmes Carries Burden for Cancer-Stricken Father," *Denver Post*, August 31, 2010.

34 Barmes interview.

35 Brian McTaggart, "Barmes finds Peace Thanks to Dad's Strength," m.astros.mlb.com/news/article/20485970//, June 15, 2011.

36 "Astros Barmes Breaks Left Hand," *Toronto Sun*, March 26, 2011.

37 Hurdle email correspondence.

38 Barmes interview.

39 Adam Berry, "Mentoring Newman, Mercer Pays It Forward/Veteran's Tutelage Can Be Traced Through Long Chain of Shortstops," MLB.com, February 24, 2017. mlb.com/news/article/216924114/jordy-mercer-mentoring-prospect-kevin-newman/.

40 Barmes interview.

41 Ibid.

42 Marty Leap, "Former Pirate Shortstop Clint Barmes Announced His Retirement After 13 Major League Seasons Yesterday," May 24, 2016, rumbunter.com/2016/05/24/paying-homage-to-clint-barmes/.

43 Barmes interview.

44 Charlie Wilmouth, "Former Pirate Clint Barmes Retires,"
May 24, 2016, bucsdugout.com/2016/5/24/11758684/clint-
barmes-retires.

45 Hurdle email correspondence.

DON BAYLOR

BY MALCOLM ALLEN AND ALFONSO L TUSA C

DON BAYLOR WAS A HUSTLING player who ran the bases aggressively and stood fearlessly close to home plate as if he were daring the pitcher to hit him. Quite often they did, as Baylor was plunked by more pitches (267) than any other player in the 20th century, leading the American League eight times in that department and retiring as the category's modern record-holder (though he's since been passed by Craig Biggio). Notoriously tough, Baylor wouldn't even acknowledge the pain of being hit, refusing to rub his bruises when he took his base. "Getting hit is my way of saying I'm not going to back off," he explained. "My first goal when I go to the plate is to get a hit. My second goal is to get hit."[1]

Baylor played for seven first-place teams in his 19 seasons and was a respected clubhouse leader, earning Manager-of-the-Year recognition in his post-playing career. The powerfully built 6-foot-1, 195-pounder hit 338 home runs and drove in 1,276 runs, and clicked on all cylinders when he claimed the AL Most Valuable Player award in 1979. Not only did he lead the California Angels to their first-ever playoff appearance by pacing both leagues in both runs scored and RBIs, he proved unafraid to kick 30 or so reporters out of the clubhouse. After a critical loss in Kansas City late in that season's pennant race, the press corps made the mistake of asking losing pitcher Chris Knapp about a "choke" within earshot of Baylor, who promptly ordered them to leave.

Baylor broke into the majors with the Baltimore Orioles when the Birds were in the midst of winning three straight pennants. The Baltimore players policed their own clubhouse with a "kangaroo court" that handed down a stinging but good-natured brand of justice for a variety of on- and off-field infractions. Before he'd even played in the majors, a 20-year-old Baylor ran afoul of the court by predicting—even though the Orioles had a trio of All-Star outfielders plus skilled reserve Merv Rettenmund—"If I get

into my groove, I'm gonna play every day." Court leader Frank Robinson read the quote aloud in the Baltimore clubhouse, and shortstop Mark Belanger warned Baylor, "That's going to stick for a long time." Indeed, Baylor was known as Groove in baseball circles even after he retired.[2]

Don Edward Baylor was born on June 28, 1949, in the Clarksville section of Austin, Texas. His father, George Baylor, worked as a baggage handler for the Missouri Pacific Railroad for 25 years, and his mother, Lillian, was a pastry cook at a local white high school. Don had two siblings, Doug and Connie, and going to church on Sundays was a must in the Baylor family.

Baylor was one of just three African-American students enrolled at O. Henry Junior High School when Austin's public schools integrated in 1962. One of the friends he made was Sharon Connally, the daughter of Governor John Connally, and Baylor would never forget hearing her screams from two classrooms away when Sharon learned over the school's public-address system that her father had been shot along with President John F. Kennedy on November 22, 1963.

At Stephen F. Austin High School, Baylor had to ask the football coach three times for a tryout, but by his senior year he had made honorable mention all-state and got a half-dozen scholarship offers, including ones from powerhouses like Texas and Oklahoma. Baylor also played baseball, as a sophomore becoming the first African-American to wear the school's uniform, and being named team captain for his senior season. After a tough first year under a coach who wasn't accustomed to dealing with blacks, Baylor benefited when a strict disciplinarian named Frank Seale, who believed in playing the game the right way, took over the program for his last two seasons. "Frank was not only my coach, but my friend," said Baylor. "He looked after me and made me feel like I was part of his family."[3] When Baylor finally

got to the World Series two decades later, Frank Seale was there.

After suffering a shoulder injury serious enough to inhibit his throwing for the rest of his career, Baylor decided to spurn the gridiron scholarship offers and pursue a career in professional baseball. Some teams, like the Houston Astros (who opted to draft John Mayberry instead), were scared off by Baylor's bum shoulder, but the Baltimore Orioles selected him with their second choice in the 1967 amateur draft. Scout Dee Phillips signed Baylor for $7,500.

Baylor reported immediately to Bluefield, West Virginia, where he wasted no time earning Appalachian League player-of-the-year honors after leading the circuit in hitting (.346), runs, stolen bases, and triples under manager Joe Altobelli. "Alto taught me the importance of good work habits," Baylor recalled. "He was a tireless worker himself, serving as manager, batting-practice pitcher, third-base coach, and, when you got right down to it, a baby sitter."[4]

The 1968 season started with a lot of promise. In 68 games for the Class-A Stockton Ports, Baylor smashed California League pitching at a .346 clip to earn a promotion to the Double-A Elmira Pioneers of the Eastern League. He stayed there only six games, batting .333, before moving up to the Triple-A Rochester Red Wings. In 15 games against International League pitchers, Baylor batted only .217 and was benched for the first time in his life by manager Billy DeMars. "I felt frustration for the first time in my career," Baylor admitted. "Maybe DeMars hated young players, period. I also noticed that his favorite targets were blacks like Chet Trail, Mickey McGuire, and a guy from Puerto Rico named Rick Delgado. I felt that DeMars did not have my best interests at heart. I was trying very hard to learn, but I got nothing from him."[5]

Nonetheless, the Orioles invited Baylor to his first big-league spring training in 1969, and he got to meet his role model, Frank Robinson. Soon, Baylor was even using the same R161 bat (taking its model number from Robinson's first MVP season in 1961) that the Orioles right fielder did so much damage with. With it, Baylor began the season by hitting .375 in 17 games for the Class A Florida Marlins of the Florida State League. He spent the bulk of the year with the Double-A Dallas-Fort Worth Spurs, hitting .300 in 109 games to earn a Texas League All-Star selection.

After a strong spring training with the Orioles in 1970, Baylor returned to Rochester to bat third and play center field every day. Midway through the season, he reluctantly moved to left field because manager Cal Ripken believed Baylor's weak arm would prevent him from handling center in the majors. Baltimore's Merv Rettenmund insisted that Baylor remained a triple threat. "He can hit, run, and lob," quipped the Orioles outfielder.[6] Pretty much everything else that happened that season, however, couldn't have been scripted more perfectly for Baylor. He was married before a summer doubleheader, and tore through the International League by leading all players in runs, doubles, triples, and total bases. *The Sporting News* recognized Baylor as its Minor League

Player of the Year. He batted .327 with 22 home runs and 107 RBIs, and was called up to the Orioles on September 8. Ten days later, Baylor made his major-league debut at Memorial Stadium in Baltimore, batting fifth and playing center field against the Cleveland Indians. The bases were loaded for his first at-bat, against right-hander Steve Hargan, and Baylor admitted feeling "scared to death."[7] He didn't show it, though, driving the first pitch into right field for a two-run single. In 17 at-bats over eight games, Baylor batted .235.

After the 1970 season Baylor went to Puerto Rico to play for the Santurce Crabbers in the winter league. The manager was Frank Robinson. "There I would get to know Frank even better because he was my manager and hitting guru," Baylor remembered. "Mostly he taught me to think while hitting. He would say, 'A guy pitches inside, hit that ball right down the line. Look for certain pitches on certain counts.' Frank also wanted me to start using my strength more. Frank knew there was a pull hitter buried somewhere inside me and fought to develop that power. In Santurce, Frank worked with me to strengthen my defense and throwing. I wound up hitting .290."[8]

With nothing left to prove in Triple-A but no room on the star-studded Orioles roster, Baylor returned to Rochester in 1971 and made another International League All-Star team. He put up strong all-around numbers, hitting .313 with 31 doubles, 10 triples, 20 homers, 95 RBIs, 104 runs scored, 79 walks, and 25 steals as the Red Wings won the Little World Series. The Triple-A playoffs went on so long that Baylor got into just one major-league game after they finished.

He returned to Santurce with the island still celebrating Roberto Clemente's MVP performance in the 1971 World Series, in which he helped the Pittsburgh Pirates dethrone the Orioles. "When Roberto played in Puerto Rico that winter I got a chance to witness up close what a great player he was," Baylor recalled. "In a game against Roberto's San Juan team, I tried to score from second base on a hit to right. I know I had the play beat. I ran the bases the right way; made

the proper turn, cut the corner well. But by the time I started my fadeaway slide catcher Manny Sanguillén had the ball. I couldn't believe it. I was out."[9]

Baylor wound up hitting .329 to win the Puerto Rican League batting title. He was confident that he'd be on some team's major-league roster in 1972, but was shocked when the Orioles cleared a spot for him by dealing away Frank Robinson before Baylor returned from Latin America. The Orioles effectively had four regular outfielders in 1971 (Robinson, Merv Rettenmund, Paul Blair, and Don Buford), so Baylor still had some competition in front of him.

Baylor got into 102 games with an Orioles team that missed the playoffs for the first time in four years. By hitting .253 with 11 home runs and 24 steals, he was named to the Topps Rookie Major League All-Star Team. He became a father when Don, Jr. was born shortly after the season ended. Baylor came back from Puerto Rico to get his son, before the family returned to the island together to help him get ready for the next season.

Much like the Orioles, Baylor started slowly in 1973, but heated up when it mattered most. Baltimore was in third place in mid-July, and Baylor was batting just .219 with four homers in 219 at-bats. Starting on July 17, though, he mashed at a .366 clip the rest of the way, contributing seven home runs and 30 RBIs as the Orioles played .658 ball and won the American League East title going away. Baylor batted .273 in his first taste of playoff action before sitting out a shutout loss to Catfish Hunter in the Series' decisive Game Five.

He played enough to qualify for the batting title for the first time in 1974, batting a solid .272 when the average American Leaguer hit 14 points less. The Orioles were eight games out on August 28, in fourth place, when Baylor and the team caught fire again for another furious finish. Baylor batted .381 as the Birds went 28-6 to finish two games ahead of the Yankees before getting swept by the Oakland A's in the American League Championship Series.

Baylor joined the Venezuelan League Magallanes Navigators that winter, displaying good patience and power with seven homers, 32 RBIs, and 29 walks in 56 games while batting .271. When major-league action got underway in 1975, Baylor's talents continued to blossom. He hammered three home runs in a game at Detroit on July 2, and smacked 25 overall. That made the league's top 10, and his .489 slugging percentage was also among the leaders. With 32 stolen bases, Baylor cracked the AL leader board for the fourth of what would eventually be six consecutive seasons. Though the Orioles finished second to the Red Sox, Baylor's name appeared towards the bottom of some writers' MVP ballots. He was only 26 and going places, just not where he imagined.

Just a week before Opening Day in 1976, Orioles manager Earl Weaver pulled Baylor out of an exhibition game unexpectedly. "When he told me to sit beside him I knew something was wrong, Baylor recalled. 'I hate to tell you this,' Earl said quietly, 'but we just traded you to Oakland for Reggie Jackson.' I looked at Earl but he couldn't look at me. I was stunned. I started to cry right there on the bench. 'Earl,' I sobbed. 'I don't want to go anywhere'."[10] Weaver believed Groove would one day be an MVP, but the Orioles sent him packing in a six-player deal to land a guy who'd already won the trophy. Other than a career-high four stolen bases on May 17, and his best season overall for swipes with 52, the highlights were few and far between for Baylor in 1976. He didn't hit well at the Oakland Coliseum, and batted just .247 with 15 homers overall. On November 1, Baylor became part of the first class of free agents after the arbitrator's landmark decision invalidated baseball's reserve clause.

Just over two weeks later, Baylor signed a six-year, $1.6 million deal with the California Angels, but he struggled to justify his salary for the first half of 1977. When manager Norm Sherry got the axe midway through the season, Baylor was hitting a paltry .223 with nine home runs and 30 RBIs. Dave Garcia took over as skipper, and hired Baylor's ex-teammate Frank Robinson as his hitting instructor. Under the Hall of Famer's tutelage, Baylor broke out to bat .281 with 16 homers and 75 RBIs the rest of the way. He never looked back.

Baylor finished seventh in American League MVP voting in 1978 after a breakout season that saw him smash 34 home runs, drive in 99 runs, and score 103. The surprising Angels logged their first winning season in eight years and remained in the West Division hunt until the final week, but Baylor will always remember that September for one of his saddest days as a ballplayer. Teammate Lyman Bostock made the last out of a critical one-run loss on September 23 in Chicago, then stormed by Baylor ranting and raving before exiting the clubhouse after a fast shower. "Veterans know enough to leave other veterans alone," Baylor said. "So when Lyman walked by, I didn't say a thing. I didn't know there would be no next time for him."[11] Bostock was shot to death that night in Gary, Indiana. The career .311 hitter was only 27.

Baylor propelled the Angels to their first playoff appearance in franchise history in 1979, batting cleanup in all 162 games and earning 20 of a possible 28 first-place votes to claim MVP honors. His totals of 139 RBIs and 120 runs scored led the major leagues, and he added career bests in home runs (36), on-base percentage (.371), slugging percentage (.530), and walks (71) while striking out just 51 times. He batted .330 with runners in scoring position. Baylor struggled while battling tendinitis in his left wrist in June, but sandwiched that down spell with player-of-the-month performances in May and July. He earned his only All-Star selection, starting in left field, batting third, and getting two hits with a pair of runs scored. In his first at-bat, he pulled a run-scoring double off Phillies southpaw Steve Carlton. On August 25 at Toronto, Baylor logged a personal-best eight RBIs in one game as the Angels romped, 24-2.

In the 1979 playoffs, Baylor and the Angels met the same Baltimore Orioles club that developed him, but a storybook ending was not in the cards. Though Baylor went deep against Dennis Martinez in California's Game Three victory, he batted just .188 as the Angels lost three games to one.

As wonderful as 1979 played out, the 1980 season was a nightmare. The Angels started slowly, and were buried by a 12-28 stretch during which Baylor missed nearly seven weeks with an injured left wrist. He struggled mightily when he returned, batted just .250 with five homers in 90 games, and missed most of the last month with an injured right foot. The Angels went from division champions to losers of 95 games. The next season, 1981, Baylor became almost exclusively a designated hitter, and remained one for the balance of his career. Though he batted a career low (to that point) .239, his totals of 17 homers and 66 RBIs each cracked the American League's top 10 in the strike-shortened season.

In 1982 Baylor homered 24 times and drove in 93 runs as the Angels made their second postseason appearance in what proved to be his last season with California. After beating the Brewers in the first two games of the best-of-five Championship Series, the Angels dropped three straight and were eliminated. It certainly wasn't Baylor's fault; he batted .294 and knocked in 10 runs in the series.

Baylor became a free agent for the second time in November 1982, and signed a lucrative deal to join the New York Yankees. In three seasons with the Bronx Bombers, he was twice named the designated hitter on *The Sporting News'* Silver Slugger team (1983 and 1985), and averaged 24 home runs and 88 RBIs. His batting average declined from a career-best .303 to .262 to .231, however, and they were not particularly happy years as Baylor feuded with Yankees owner George Steinbrenner. In 1985 Baylor was selected as the winner of the prestigious Roberto Clemente Award, presented annually to a major leaguer of exceptional character who contributes a lot to his community. He was recognized for his work with the Cystic Fibrosis Foundation and the 65 Roses (so-named for the way one child pronounced Cystic Fibrosis) club.

The Yankees traded Baylor to the Boston Red Sox shortly before Opening Day in 1986 for left-handed-hitting designated hitter Mike Easler. Though Baylor struck out a career-high 111 times and managed to bat just .238 in '86, his 31 home runs and 94 RBIs were his best since his MVP year. He also established a single-season record by getting hit by pitches 35 times. The Red Sox won 95 games to beat

out the New York for the American League East title, with Baylor operating a kangaroo court as his mentor Frank Robinson had done in Baltimore. On the night Roger Clemens set a major-league record by striking out 20 Seattle Mariners, Baylor fined him $5 for giving up a single to light-hitting Spike Owen on an 0-2 pitch. In the American League Championship Series, against the Angels, Boston was two outs from elimination in Game Five when Baylor smashed a game-tying, two-run home run off 18-game winner Mike Witt to spark an amazing comeback. Baylor batted .346 in the seven ALCS games, but started only three of seven World Series contests against the New York Mets as designated hitters were not used in the National League ballpark. This time the Red Sox let a Series clincher slip away, losing to New York in seven games.

Baylor turned 38 in 1987, and he posted the lowest power totals since his injury-plagued 1980 campaign, declining to 16 homers and 63 RBIs. He did reach a milestone on June 28, his 38th birthday, when he was hit by a pitch for a record 244th time. "Change-ups and slow curves feel like a butterfly, a light sting," he said. "Fastballs and sliders feel like piercing bullets, like they're going to come out the other side."[12] He added that getting hit in the wrist by a Nolan Ryan heater in 1973 was the worst feeling of all.

The Minnesota Twins, making a surprising playoff run, craved Baylor's right-handed bat and presence and acquired him from the Red Sox for the final month of the 1987 season. Baylor batted .286 to help Minnesota reach the postseason for the first time in 17 years, and his eighth-inning pinch-hit single drove in the go-ahead run in Game One of the ALCS against the Tigers. Baylor batted .385 in the World Series against the St. Louis Cardinals, including a game-tying two-run homer off John Tudor in Game Six, helping the Twins to a comeback victory en route to the title.

Baylor wrapped up his playing career with a return to the Oakland Athletics in 1988. Though he batted just .220 in 92 games, the club won 104 regular-season contests and became the third American League pennant winner in a row to feature Baylor on its roster.

Oakland defeated the Red Sox in the ALCS but lost the World Series to the Los Angeles Dodgers in an upset, and Baylor struck out against National League Cy Young winner Orel Hershiser in his only at-bat. In the offseason Baylor called it a career after 2,135 hits with a .260 batting average, 338 home runs, and 1,276 RBIs. He stole 285 bases and was hit by a pitch 267 times.

Baylor returned to the big leagues for a two-year stint as the Milwaukee Brewers' hitting coach beginning in 1990, and spent 1992 in the same role with the Cardinals. In 1993 he was named the inaugural manager of the expansion Colorado Rockies, and earned Manager-of-the-Year honors in 1995 when he led the third-year club to a playoff berth faster than any previous expansion club. Pitching coach Larry Bearnarth observed, "He doesn't lose his cool very often. On the other hand, he can be intolerant sometimes of people who don't give their best. He is very direct and he never varies from that, so players are never surprised. If he has something to say, he just says it like he's still a player, like players used to do to each other."[13]

Baylor's Rockies played winning baseball for two more years, but he was fired after the club fell under .500 and slipped to fourth place in the five-team division in 1998. He turned down an offer to become a club vice president, instead opting to become a hitting coach again with the Atlanta Braves. After earning rave reviews for helping Chipper Jones develop into an MVP candidate, Baylor got another chance to manage in 2000 with the Chicago Cubs. Despite 88 wins and a surprising third-place finish in his second year in Chicago, Baylor was fired after a Fourth of July loss in 2002 with a disappointing, highly-paid club sputtering in fifth place. Overall, he went 627-689 as a major-league manager.

Baylor resurfaced with the Mets the next two seasons, serving as a bench coach and hitting instructor under Art Howe, while battling a diagnosis of multiple myeloma. When the Mets changed managers, Baylor moved to Seattle in 2005 to work with Mariners batters. In 2007 he worked part time as an analyst on Washington Nationals telecasts. After three years out of a major-league uniform, Baylor returned to the Rockies in 2009 as their hitting coach, before moving on to hold the same role with the Arizona Diamondbacks (2011-12).

The Angels brought him back in 2014, but he suffered a freak fracture of his right femur on Opening Day catching the ceremonial first pitch from Vladimir Guerrero, at the time the only other Angels player to win a MVP award. Baylor came back to serve through the end of the 2015 season before settling into retirement with his second wife, Becky, who he'd married in 1987.

On August 7, 2017, Baylor died from complications in his 14-year battle with multiple myeloma. He was 68. Frank Robinson, Bobby Grich and writer Tracy Ringolsby spoke at his funeral before he was laid to rest at Texas State Cemetery in Austin.

SOURCES

In addition to the sources cited in the Notes, the author also consulted:

Daniel Gutiérrez, Efraim Alvarez, and Daniel Gutiérrez hijo, *La Enciclopedia del Béisbol en Venezuela* (Caracas, 2006).

Craig Neff, "His Honor, Don Baylor," *Sports Illustrated*, June 16, 1986.

NOTES

1   Jack Friedman, "For Don Baylor, Baseball Is a Hit or Be Hit Proposition," *People*, August 24, 1987.

2   Don Baylor, *Nothing But The Truth: A Baseball Life* (New York: St. Martins Press, 1990), 47.

3   Baylor, *Nothing But The Truth*, 32.

4   Baylor, *Nothing But The Truth*, 38-39.

5   Baylor, *Nothing But The Truth*, 44-45.

6   *Detroit Free Press*, March 4, 1980: 42.

7   Baylor, *Nothing But The Truth*, 52.

8   Baylor, *Nothing But The Truth*, 60.

9   Baylor, *Nothing But The Truth*, 68.

10 Baylor, *Nothing But The Truth*, 80.

11 Baylor, *Nothing But The Truth*, 125.

12 Friedman, "For Don Baylor."

13 Howard Blatt, "Ultimate Player's Manager Baylor is Tough But Fair With Rockies," *New York Daily News*, July 15, 1995.

DANTE BICHETTE

BY MANNY RANDHAWA

DANTE BICHETTE IS ONE OF THE most important figures in Rockies history. Though his major-league career began with the Angels, and included stints with the Brewers, Reds, and Red Sox, it was in Colorado that Bichette made a name for himself as one of the game's great sluggers in the mid-1990s.

Bichette holds a unique place in Rockies lore, having hit the first home run in franchise history and a game-ending home run in the first game at Coors Field, as well as becoming the first Rockies player to hit for the cycle.

What many don't know about Bichette, who was a four-time All-Star and hit 274 career home runs, is that he was unable to fulfill his full potential because of a knee injury that plagued him for much of his career. He was an avid student of the game, and there is much more to his story than the image of a free-swinging slugger in the hitter-friendly environment of Colorado.

———

Alphonse Dante Bichette was born on November 18, 1963, in West Palm Beach, Florida, to Maurice and Mary Bichette. He was named for his father's brother, who drowned in a storm as a child.

Bichette was one of seven children (three siblings from his father's first marriage, and three—two sisters and a brother—from the marriage of his mother and father) and grew up in Palm Beach Gardens. Bichette's father worked in construction, and his mother owned an antique shop.

Bichette first became enamored with baseball a month shy of his 10th birthday, when he watched on television as Reggie Jackson hit a two-run home run for the Athletics in Game Seven of the 1973 World Series against the Mets.

"For me, that was pretty much the goal after that," said Bichette. "To hit homers for a living."[1]

Bichette asked his parents if he could play baseball, and the next day his father took him to the local Little League field, where he signed up for the Juno Park Braves team. He pitched that very day.

The next year, Bichette was coached by Hondo Wilkes, who would become a lifelong influence, even after Bichette reached the major leagues.

When Bichette tried out for the baseball team at Jupiter High School as a sophomore, he didn't make it. He tried out again the next year, and made the team, though he mostly came off the bench. In his senior season, he played shortstop and hit four home runs in four games before being suspended for missing too many days of school.

After high school, Bichette, with Wilkes accompanying him, went to Palm Beach Community College to seek a tryout. Wilkes spoke with the head coach, Frank Cacciatore (who would later become a minor-league coach for several organizations). Tryouts had been completed, and Cacciatore said he needed only a catcher.

"So Hondo said, 'That's what he is, a catcher,'" recalled Bichette. "I'm 17 years old, and caught maybe twice in Little League. And this is a nationally ranked junior college."

Cacciatore told Bichette to show up at the field at 4 o'clock the following morning, during the team's "Hell Week," for two hours of running laps. Bichette did so, and Cacciatore allowed him to try out during a scrimmage later that day.

Bichette, as would have been expected, did not play well behind the plate. But in his two at-bats that afternoon, he lined out to left and homered. The home run is still spoken of at Palm Beach Community College; it hit the light standard in left field, landing on the adjacent racquetball courts. The prodigious power display landed Bichette a spot on the roster.

With Palm Beach Community College, among other smaller schools, competing against schools like the University of Miami and the University of Florida back then, major-league scouts began to take notice of Bichette's power.

First-year California Angels scout Preston Douglas was one of them, and being new to the area, he was given a list of players he didn't really know.

"He told me that when he got his list of players to see, I was 50th of 50 on the list," Bichette said. "I was just a real raw player at that point. I still hadn't played any serious baseball — Little League, high school, then junior college."

The Angels drafted Bichette in the 17th round of the June 1984 amateur draft, 424th overall. He reported to his first professional camp, which was held on the campus of California State University at Fullerton.

Bichette's first taste of professional baseball was at short-season Low-A Salem, Oregon. The jump from community-college baseball to the professional level was a big one.

"The game was just so fast, and it was every day," said Bichette. "I was sleeping on a basement floor, not even a bed that year. I was eating at Burger King every day. I didn't even have a ride to the ballpark. Those growing pains that a lot of young players go through aren't so much on the field, but how to live off the field."

In that first season, Bichette batted .232 with 4 home runs in 64 games. He played Class-A ball in 1985 at Quad Cities, Iowa, seeing an improvement in his performance at the plate: He batted .265 with 11 home runs in 137 games.

At Class-A Palm Springs in 1986, Bichette hit .272 with 10 home runs and 73 RBIs in 68 games.

"When I first started really understanding things was in Palm Springs," Bichette said. "I really found my niche as an offensive player: It was driving in tough runs. It was something I ended up doing my whole career.

"I played for a great coach, Tom Kotchman, who is also a Hall of Fame scout now. He was just good for me. I remember I was a week into that [1986] season, I had just swung at a bad pitch with the game on the line, and we lost the game. But I was hitting like .360,

and I didn't think much of it. And the hitting coach, Rick Downs, comes in the clubhouse and said, 'You're not moving any higher than right here until you learn to swing at strikes.'"

It was then that Kotchman saw a rare opportunity, and gave Bichette some homework: to read *The Science of Hitting*, by Ted Williams.

"For player development, you need 'good cop, bad cop,'" Kotchman said. "It's not often you get to be the good cop as a manager. It was a chance for me to do that, and it was a book that, it's not like it's some guy you don't know. It was freaking Ted Williams."[2]

To that point in his life, Bichette had only his raw talent to guide him, while many of his contemporaries had been exposed to such instruction far earlier in their baseball careers.

"That was the first time in my life that I really started to understand that there was more to hitting than just trying to hit this next pitch over that light over there, or over that scoreboard," Bichette said. "It's the first time I went to a two-strike approach, hunting pitches, reading pitchers, picking up release points."

Midway through the 1986 season, Bichette was promoted to Double-A Midland, where he put up even better numbers: .284 (.335 on-base average, .514 slugging average), with 12 homers in 62 games. By the start of the 1987 season, Bichette was at Triple-A Edmonton in the Pacific Coast League.

"When I got to Triple A, I scuffled a little bit because I was told my mechanics were off," Bichette said. "That's where it took me about two years to realize that I've got to coach myself, and there's gonna be too many opinions out there to listen to everybody."

Even with his early struggles in '87, Bichette managed to finish the season with a .300 batting average, with 13 home runs in 92 games. In '88, he hit .267, with 14 home runs in 132 games for Edmonton.

Then came September of that season.

"Tom Kotchman was my manager again at Triple A; he was kind of moving up the chain as well," Bichette said. "He called me in and told me. I'm glad he was the guy. He just said, 'Hey, you're going to the big leagues.' Just like that. I was stunned."

On September 5, Bichette made his major-league debut as the Angels played the Royals in Kansas City. He entered as a defensive replacement, going in at center field to start the bottom of the seventh inning.

"I remember going into the game, and the crowd was chanting, 'Roo-kie! Roo-kie!'" Bichette said. "I couldn't feel my body from the neck down, I was so nervous."

Bichette's first major-league plate appearance came in the top of the eighth. With a runner on second, two outs, and the Angels leading, 3-2, he stepped into the box against veteran left-hander Charlie Leibrandt. Leibrandt got Bichette into an 0-and-2 hole, and Bichette then flied out to Bo Jackson in deep right field.

Bichette got an opportunity in spring training the following year. With outfielders Chili Davis and Claudell Washington both hurt, he stepped in and hit .367 with four homers.[3] He impressed Angels manager Doug Rader enough that he wound up making the big-league club out of spring training.[4]

Bichette got off to a blistering start in the 1989 regular season, hitting .385 and slugging .731 in 29 plate appearances through April 22. But his performance then began to decline steadily, and he was hitting just .195 by June 14. He was sent down to Edmonton a few weeks later, and hit .243 with 11 homers in 61 games before being called back up in September.

Once Bichette returned to the Angels that September, his minor-league days were behind him. And once again, he got off to a hot start at the plate to start the 1990 campaign. Having put on about nine pounds of muscle over the offseason through a weight training regimen, he was hitting .302 with four home runs on May 11.

That day, the Angels traded for future Hall of Fame right fielder Dave Winfield.

"It was frustrating," Bichette said. "My year was pretty much part-time after that."

Bichette finished the 1990 season batting .255 with 15 home runs in 371 plate appearances.

"I think what it came down to was that, for Doug Rader, I wasn't his guy," Bichette said. "I was a little

too much of a free swinger. I'd try to throw behind runners, throw everybody out. And I think he wanted more of a polished player at the time. But sometimes that's what you get with the young guys."

That offseason, Bichette was traded to the Brewers for 39-year-old designated hitter Dave Parker. Bichette had proved he could hit at the big-league level, and Milwaukee needed to bolster its outfield defense, having committed 28 outfield errors in 1990.

In Milwaukee, Bichette put up similar numbers in 1991, though his average was down somewhat. He batted .238 with 15 home runs in 134 games.

"I made one of the biggest mistakes of my career in '91," said Bichette. "When [Brewers manager] Tom Trebelhorn came to me after spring training, he said, 'I don't care how many times you strike out. What I want from you is 20-25 homers and 75-80 RBIs. And you'll be good. I don't care what you hit for average.'

"So I made the mistake of getting off my two-strike approach and by the All-Star break, I was hitting like .230 [actually .236] with 12 homers and 40-something RBIs. Right on pace for what they wanted. And they took my job away. I wasn't mature enough at the time to question it. I just got pissed, as a young player would do, and wouldn't talk."

That offseason, something happened that would affect the rest of Bichette's career, perhaps precluding him from being regarded as one of the best all-around players in the game some years later.

"I was playing flag football, and I intercepted a ball and I was trying to make a cut," Bichette said. "And I went right and my knee went left, and it swelled up on me. I didn't think anything of it; I just thought it would heal, like a sprained ankle. About two months later, my knee's still about as big as my head."

Bichette called the Brewers, and they flew him in to have his left knee scoped by the team physician. After being evaluated, he was told he had torn the anterior cruciate ligament (ACL). The injury would hamper him for the next six seasons.

"The injury actually helped me offensively by shortening my stride so I didn't jump at the ball," Bichette said, "but slowly but surely it hurt me defensively."

To that point in his career, Bichette had not been an everyday player, and had few opportunities to demonstrate his defensive ability. But according to Kotchman, a major-league scout for three-plus decades, Bichette had the raw tools to be a great defensive outfielder.

"I'd have to sit down and go through my rosters over the past 30 or 35 years to see if I had anybody that had as much of a five-tool raw package as him," Kotchman said.

Kotchman described Bichette's raw range in the outfield as "solid-average to plus," noting that while he needed refinement on his routes, he had a rocket for an arm and the underlying tool set to potentially become a Gold Glove outfielder.

Bichette was never able to fully reach his potential defensively because of the weakened left knee; lateral movement wasn't as much of an issue for him, but his ability to make the necessary cuts to chase fly balls was diminished.

"The reason I didn't have it reconstructed that year is because I waited too long and would've had to miss a season, and I couldn't afford to miss a season then," said Bichette. "And I ended up playing seven years without an ACL."

In 1992, Bichette's batting average climbed, while his power declined. Once again a part-time player, he hit .287 for the Brewers, but with only 5 home runs in 387 at-bats.

"To hit homers, you have to play every day, and I never was the everyday player that season," said Bichette. "But I did get back to my two-strike approach. The .287 batting average was actually because I slumped at the end. I was around .315 most of the year."

Bichette's stint in Milwaukee lasted just two seasons, but a relationship he developed in that period proved to be perhaps the most important of his career, and one of the most important in his life off the field.

Don Baylor was the Brewers' hitting coach in 1990 and '91. And the 1979 American League Most Valuable Player saw potential in Bichette that Bichette didn't know was in him.

"Don Baylor pulled me over one day, and he said, 'You don't realize how good you are. When you figure this league out, you're gonna run this league,'" Bichette recalled. "I had never had anyone talk to me like that before."

Baylor was named the first manager of the Colorado Rockies, one of two expansion teams to debut in 1993, along with the Florida Marlins.

On November 17, 1992, the Rockies traded outfielder Kevin Reimer, whom Colorado had selected from the Rangers in the expansion draft the same day, to the Brewers in exchange for Bichette.

"I was the guy he wanted," Bichette said. "I didn't realize he believed in me that much."

On April 5, 1993, as the Rockies prepared to play the New York Mets at Shea Stadium in the franchise's first-ever regular-season game, Baylor penciled Bichette into the number-3 spot in Colorado's batting order. It would be only the second time in Bichette's career he had started a game batting third in the lineup.

While the Rockies were shut out by Dwight Gooden and the Mets on Opening Day, Bichette would make history in the next game. In the seventh inning, he belted a solo home run to left field off two-time Cy Young Award winner Bret Saberhagen. It was the Rockies' first home run and first run scored.

In a career-high 581 plate appearances during the 1993 season, Bichette posted the best offensive numbers of his career, batting .310 with 21 home runs, 14 stolen bases, and a 117 park-adjusted on-base plus slugging percentage (OPS+). With the league average OPS+ set to 100, Bichette was 17 percent above average at the plate even considering he played his home games in the thin air of Denver.

That year was monumental for Bichette off the field, as well. He married his wife, Mariana, in 1993 after they had dated for two years. Baylor was a central figure in bringing the two together.

When Baylor and Bichette were together with the Brewers in 1991, Milwaukee was in Boston to play the Red Sox for a three-game series in May. Bichette's routine while in Boston was to work out at a Gold's Gym across the street from Fenway Park, just behind the Green Monster. After taking early batting practice before one game, he walked over.

"I walk in, and this girl is walking away from me. And she turns around, and I'm thinking, 'Wow. I could marry this girl,' Bichette recalled. "I never said anything to her. I was too scared."

Bichette walked back to Fenway, where he saw Baylor.

"I said, 'Don, I just saw a girl I could marry.' And he said, 'Did you ask her out?'" Bichette remembered. "I told him I didn't, that I was too scared."

Baylor made Bichette walk back over to the gym and ask Mariana out. They celebrate their 25th wedding anniversary in 2018.

"God bless him. I owe Don Baylor a lot," said Bichette of his friend and former manager, who died on August 7, 2017. "He was put into my life for a reason."

That offseason, Bichette's salary more than tripled, from $230,000 to $735,000, as a settlement after Bichette filed for salary arbitration.

In 1994, Bichette turned in another strong campaign, albeit shortened by the strike that canceled the season in mid-August, as well as the postseason.

Bichette hit .304 (111 OPS+) with 27 homers and 21 steals in 116 games, earning his first career All-Star selection.

The Rockies combined to go 120-159 (.430) in their first two seasons, but set a single-season major-league attendance record in 1993 (4.48 million, which remains a record as of 2018) and drew another 3.28 million to Mile High Stadium in the strike-shortened '94 campaign.

Meanwhile, construction of a new ballpark was underway in Lower Downtown Denver. Coors Field was scheduled to open the following season, but only after the strike ended.

Bichette's contract had expired at the end of the '94 season, and he was a free agent. That November, the Rockies made Bichette a three-year, $10 million contract offer, which he declined. There were no further developments on contract negotiations that winter, and Bichette began weighing an offer to play in Japan.

The Rockies, meanwhile, signed free-agent right fielder Larry Walker, who was coming off a career year for the Expos (.322, with 19 home runs in 103 games). At that point, having been Colorado's everyday right fielder the previous two seasons, Bichette figured his time with the Rockies was at an end.

"It was really a frustrating time," Bichette said. "We were working on a multiyear deal, and they weren't serious about it. At the last second, the only reason I signed back with the Rockies was Don Baylor called me personally, and I owed Don Baylor. He gave me the opportunity to play. There was no way I wasn't coming back to play for him when he called."

The strike ended in late March of 1995, and the regular season began in late April. The mood at 20th and Blake Street, site of the Rockies' new ballpark, was celebratory when the gates officially opened on the evening of April 26.

That night, the Rockies hosted the Mets. At first pitch, 5:38 P.M. Mountain Time, the temperature was 42 degrees.

In a seesaw affair, the teams were tied, 7-7, going into extra innings. In the 13th, each team scored to push the contest into the 14th. In the top of the 14th, Joe Orsulak's RBI double put the Mets on top, 9-8, setting the stage for one of the greatest finishes in Rockies history.

Rockies catcher Joe Girardi singled to open the bottom of the 14th, with the game now well into its fifth hour. Walker came to the plate next, and struck out. First baseman Andres Galarraga followed with a groundball that Mets third baseman Tim Bogar misplayed. With runners at first and second and one out, Bichette strode to the plate.

He faced left-hander Mike Remlinger, and worked the count to two balls and a strike. The game was nationally televised by ESPN, with Jon Miller providing the play-by-play, and Joe Morgan providing color commentary.

"Two and one to the dangerous Dante Bichette," Miller said as Remlinger came set. The next pitch leaked out over the plate, and Bichette hammered it.

"A high drive, way back, and there's the storybook ending for the Rockies!" Miller exclaimed as Bichette's blast landed halfway up the bleachers in left-center field to send Colorado to an 11-9 victory.[5] Immediately after making contact, Bichette dropped his bat with a flourish, turned toward the home dugout and pumped his right fist as he began his trot around the bases.

"It could've been the World Series for me," said Bichette. "It probably was, for me. It was the most exciting homer I hit in my career. It was so exciting to open the new stadium like that."

The way Bichette dropped the bat after hitting the iconic homer became a signature move of his, but it wasn't premeditated.

"The name of that is 'the Shucky Ducky,'" said Bichette. "(Teammate) Marvin Freeman gave it that name. He'd say, 'OK, go and Shucky Ducky one for me here.'"

Bichette was an avid foosball player, beginning when as a boy he played at his older brother's fun and games shop at the mall. He even toured the country a notch below the professional level during the offseason of the strike year.[6]

"The signature shot is a move similar to my home-run swing," Bichette said. "The next time I picked up a bat, and hit a homer, I just reacted exactly like I did on a foosball table. It was the weirdest thing."

Opening Day in 1995 was a sign of things to come for the Rockies and, in particular, Bichette. That season became Bichette's finest, and he helped lead Colorado to its first postseason berth via the new wild-card position.

Bichette batted .340 with 40 home runs in 139 games, finishing second to Reds shortstop Barry Larkin in that season's National League MVP voting.

But by the middle of that season, many observers dismissed Bichette's surge as largely due to his home ballpark, and the mountain air that enables baseballs to travel farther.[7] Those detractors had plenty of ammunition: By July 24, all 17 of his home runs on the season had come at Coors Field.

"It was totally getting in my head," Bichette said. "I didn't even realize it until the media got ahold of it, and man, the next thing I know, Don Baylor wants me to talk to a sports psychologist. It was like, 'Oh man, I better figure this out.'"

From that point forward, nine of Bichette's remaining 23 homers in the season came on the road, beginning with a five-day binge on the very next road trip, during which he hit three.

"It's so easy to be good in Coors Field, and it's so difficult to make that adjustment to go on the road," Bichette said. "When you go on the road and see a good breaking ball for the first time in two weeks [because of how the elevation flattens breaking balls at Coors Field], by the time you start getting used to it, you go back home and it's a vicious cycle.

"And playing at altitude is a drain on the body, there's no doubt about it. You get dehydrated, and you can never get loose."

Like any other player who spends most of his career playing home games in the altitude of Denver, Bichette's offensive statistics can be deceiving. But that goes for both home numbers and road numbers.

"I'm not saying I'm as good as my Coors Field numbers. Heck, nobody's that good," said Bichette. "But I'm not as bad as my road numbers were, either.

I was somewhere in between. I felt like I was a .300 hitter, a 25-30 homer, 100-RBI guy. I didn't have the plate discipline to do more than that. If I had the plate discipline, I really could've been something with the power numbers."

With Bichette, Walker, Galarraga, and third baseman Vinny Castilla, the Rockies had four players in the middle of their lineup in 1995 who hit more than 30 homers, joining the 1977 Dodgers as the only major-league team with that distinction (Steve Garvey, Reggie Smith, Dusty Baker, and Ron Cey). Collectively, they came to be known as the Blake Street Bombers, a reference to the Blake Street address of Coors Field.

Bichette actually coined the term along with then-Rockies radio broadcaster Wayne Hagin. Hagin said it was really Bichette's brainchild.

"We got to Coors Field, and anytime the Rockies did anything late in a ballgame, I would use the phrase 'LoDo magic' (for Lower Downtown Denver)," Hagin said. "But I do recall in the clubhouse, talking with Dante, and I remember him saying, 'We need to come up with something.' And Dante was just a creative sort."[8]

The quartet of sluggers helped lead Colorado to a 77-67 record in the shortened season, earning the franchise's first postseason berth. Castilla remembered that time fondly, as well as the work ethic he saw in Bichette.

"He was in the cage every day for hours and hours," said Castilla. "He was always in the media room checking out all the pitchers. It's not easy to hit 40 home runs, man. I don't care if you're hitting in Little League or the majors. We did a couple of times. It was a lot of fun to celebrate that together and be teammates back then."[9]

The Rockies faced the Atlanta Braves in the 1995 NL Division Series, which meant facing the best starting rotation in baseball. It also meant facing a powerhouse that had reached the World Series twice in the previous three seasons (not counting '94, when there was no postseason), but had yet to win a championship.

In a best-of-five series, with a 2-3 format in which the lower-seeded Rockies hosted the first two games, Coors Field was electric for Game One on October 3, the first postseason game in franchise history. Colorado lost Game One, 5-4, and Game Two, 7-4.

As the scene shifted to Atlanta-Fulton County Stadium, Game Three was tied, 5-5, entering the 10th inning. With two outs and nobody on, Bichette doubled to left field off Braves reliever Mark Wohlers. Walker was intentionally walked, and Galarraga followed with a single to score Bichette. The Rockies won, 7-5, in 10 innings.

In Game Four, the Braves gave the ball to the best starting pitcher of the decade, right-hander Greg Maddux. The future Hall of Famer had won three consecutive NL Cy Young Awards, and was on the precipice of winning his fourth straight. Though the Rockies would lose that game, and the series, it was Maddux who was on the mound when Bichette's signature postseason moment took place.

With two on and one out in the third inning, Bichette stepped to the plate against Maddux in a scoreless game.

"The first pitch was a sinker inside that was a total ball that the umpire called a strike," Bichette recalled. "Most pitchers won't get that strike, but Greg Maddux gets that strike.

"I stepped out, and I'm thinking to myself, 'If he threw that pitch to get me out, I'm in trouble. But if he threw that pitch to set up the breaking ball away, I can hit that pitch. And I thought a little more: If Greg Maddux is gonna throw the breaking ball away, he's gonna hit the glove four to six inches off the plate and get the call."

The next pitch was a breaking ball just off the plate, away. Bichette lined it deep down the right field line and over the fence for a three-run homer.

Overall, Bichette hit .588 (10-for-17) with three doubles and that home run for the series. Four of the hits came off Maddux, and three apiece came against John Smoltz and Tom Glavine. The trio of Braves hurlers combined for seven career Cy Young Awards, and each is in the Hall of Fame.

Bichette referred to the at-bat against Maddux as "a Ted Williams at-bat." Ever since being presented with Williams's *The Science of Hitting* instructional for the first time in 1986, Bichette devoured the book every year, as he did with numerous other instructionals on hitting.

It was in February of 1996 that Bichette first met Williams, at the annual Ted Williams Hitters Hall of Fame dinner in Citrus Hills, Florida. Bichette was one of a handful of contemporary hitters invited to the event, which was held to honor new inductees Josh Gibson, Chuck Klein, Harmon Killebrew, Duke Snider, and Willie McCovey.

Williams quizzed Bichette, asking him questions about how to approach certain pitches and how to deal with slumps at the plate.

"He's only been around a few years," Williams told columnist Hal Bodley afterward. "He knows how he has to hit. I asked him a lot of questions. He answered them all. I've asked 500-home run hitters about inside-out hitting and they haven't answered as well."[10]

Williams invited Bichette to breakfast at his home the next day.

"I got to spend an hour with Ted in his kitchen, just me and him," Bichette said. "It was the neatest thing ever."

Following Bichette's big 1995 campaign, the Rockies signed him to a three-year, $11.1 million contract. When he arrived three hours late to the first full-squad workout in February of 1996, with shoulder-length hair that was in violation of Baylor's dress code, Bichette was viewed by some as having become smug after finishing runner-up in the MVP voting.[11]

Bichette had missed a flight to Arizona, resulting in the tardiness. And the haircut wasn't new, nor was the controversy over it.

"My haircut was always an issue when I came to spring training," Bichette said. "The long hair was a little taboo back then. Baylor wasn't about to put up with that. He asked me to cut it, and I cut it, no problem."

Bichette also struggled in that spring training, further emboldening his critics.

"I've gotta admit," Bichette said, "that spring training, I was absolutely burned out, because the year before, I absolutely grinded. I could never get up for the games in spring training [in '96]. And going into the regular season, a lot of people were pissed at me. It wasn't players or anything, but I had some people really kind of frustrated. And then by the All-Star break, I was hitting [.335]."

Bichette had a stellar first half in '96, even better than his first half during the prior season. By the All-Star break, he was batting .335 with 17 home runs and 14 steals. He was voted an All-Star for the third consecutive year, and for the first time as a starter.

Bichette not only put up big numbers at the plate in '96, he also stole 31 bases in 43 attempts to join the 30-home run/30-steal club. And he did so despite his left knee.

"I was still fairly fast straight on," Bichette said. "With an ACL tear, you can accelerate but you can't decelerate, and you can't cut left or right. But the reason I was able to steal bases was I had really strong legs to get a good jump. The first two or three steps were good, and I took pride in reading pitchers."

The Rockies finished the '96 season with a record of 83-79, third place in the NL West. That offseason, Bichette would finally have reconstructive surgery on his left knee.

Bichette's production at the plate dipped somewhat 1997; he posted a 103 OPS+, his lowest park-adjusted OPS since being traded to the Rockies. Colorado finished with an identical record and standing that season, at 83-79 and third place in the division.

Bichette bounced back in 1998, leading the majors with 219 hits and raising his OPS+ to 108, but his power numbers were down: his 22 homers were the fewest he had hit in a single season since 1993 (21).

"I got big that offseason (entering spring training at 263 pounds), but every bit of weight I put on was fat," Bichette said. "I got to camp and I realized I was way too fat. And by the time the season started,

I was at 244, which was pretty much around my usual weight."

By the end of April, Bichette was red-hot, hitting .415. But he had only homered once.

"I'm thinking, 'This ain't OK,'" Bichette recalled. "But then I started thinking, 'OK, what's going good? I'm hitting .387 [by May 4]. So I just beared down and decided to see how many hits I could get."

In August of 1998, *Denver Post* columnist Mark Kiszla had his Rockies credentials removed after he was seen taking a bottle of supplements out of Bichette's locker. The supplements were androstenedione, the same used by Cardinals slugger Mark McGwire as he broke Roger Maris's single-season home-run record of 61 with 70 homers that season.[12]

Kiszla saw the bottle in Bichette's locker a week after Associated Press reporter Steve Wilstein noticed a bottle of the supplement in McGwire's locker, sparking a national story over whether his pursuit of the record was tainted.

Though the fallout over the McGwire story really wouldn't come for several years, Bichette would come to a crossroads in his own career shortly after.

"I'm no saint. I would've done the steroids very quickly, with no hesitation," Bichette said. "Because so many people were doing it and they were making gazillions of dollars and putting up huge numbers. And it was getting to the point where something's gonna come to a head, and you're gonna have to do them if you're gonna play in this game.

"So I was looking for a way to compete, and tried the androstenedione. It was legal at the time, I got it at GNC. And it didn't help me any. I tried my best, but it was getting crazy. McGwire was freaky large. And Sammy Sosa, I'm not sure he plays any longer and then I saw him that spring and it's like, 'Whoa, this is crazy.'

"Someone actually gave me the steroids, and my wife said, 'Absolutely not. I'm not going to be married to a druggie.'"

Bichette finished the '98 campaign with a .331 batting average and a career-high 48 doubles. He earned his fourth All-Star selection in five years, and on June 10 against the Rangers at Coors Field, he became the first Rockies player to hit for the cycle. After starting the game 0-for-2, he doubled, homered, tripled, and hit a walk-off single in the 10th.

That September, Bichette signed a three-year, $21 million extension with the Rockies.

But the 1999 season would be Bichette's last in Colorado. He batted .298, hitting 34 home runs in 151 games. That September, Dan O'Dowd, who had been the assistant general manager for the Cleveland Indians, took over as Rockies GM.

O'Dowd said that offseason that he wanted the Rockies to become "more athletic and more versatile."[13] Bichette waived his no-trade clause and accepted a trade to the Cincinnati Reds on October 30. In exchange, the Rockies received right-hander Stan Belinda and outfielder Jeffrey Hammonds.

"The honeymoon was over," Bichette said of the situation in Colorado. "It was just a little different feel at that time. That was Don Baylor's final year, too. I had no reason to stick around."

Bichette was traded to Cincinnati at an exciting time for that franchise. The Reds would soon acquire one of the best all-around players of his generation in center fielder Ken Griffey Jr, whom the Mariners traded to Cincinnati the next February.

Hitting cleanup for Cincinnati, behind Griffey, Bichette batted .295 with a 103 OPS+, with 16 homers in 125 games. With the Reds out of postseason contention, they traded Bichette to the Red Sox on August 31, in exchange for minor-league pitchers John Curtice and Chris Reitsma.

Bichette put up those impressive numbers with Cincinnati despite a slow start: Through May 19 (40 games), he was hitting just .213. From May 20 through August 31, when he was traded, Bichette batted .331 with 11 homers.

Bichette produced in his lone month with Boston that season, batting .289 with seven homers in 30 games. The Red Sox finished 2½ games behind the Yankees in the AL East, and missed the postseason. In 2001, Bichette posted a 104 OPS+ with 12 home runs in 107 games for Boston.

With the Reds and Red Sox, Bichette played his home games closer to sea level. He didn't have to contend with the effects of leaving the thin air of Denver to play on the road, and the toll it took on his body.

Over those final two seasons, at age 36 and 37, Bichette hit .291. While some might argue that he was playing his home games in the hitter-friendly Cinergy Field and Fenway Park, his park-adjusted OPS was 104. During his seven seasons with the Rockies, Bichette's road OPS was .734. Over the final two seasons of his career, it was 37 points higher.

After the 2001 season, Bichette still felt, as evidenced by his production, that he had more in the tank. He signed a minor-league contract with an invitation to spring training with the Dodgers.

But just prior to the beginning of the regular season, Bichette made the decision to retire from professional baseball.

"I kind of saw that my time was gonna be reduced with the Dodgers, and I had just missed my oldest son's first home run in Little League," Bichette said. "I just pulled off to the side of the road on my way to a spring-training game one day, and said to myself, 'Why am I playing now?' I wanted to be with my boys. I didn't want to miss any more home runs."

Bichette became the coach for his oldest son Dante Jr.'s Little League team, guiding it all the way to the semifinal round of the Little League World Series in 2005.

"That was the coolest thing I have ever done in baseball, period," said Bichette.

Both of Bichette's sons, Dante Jr. and Bo, were in major-league farm systems in 2018. Dante Jr., a corner infielder, signed a minor-league contract with the Rockies in December 2017. Bo, a middle infielder, was the Blue Jays' number-2 prospect per MLB.com.[14]

Bichette served as the Rockies' hitting coach in 2013, but decided not to return the following season because he wanted to continue coaching his boys.

"It's been a blast, and it's allowed us to really develop our relationship even further," he said. "I can't tell you how precious it is to me that I have that relationship with them. I'm glad God blessed me with kids who love baseball, and I can pass that on to them."

Bichette passed to his sons a baseball legacy that is founded on a passion for the game.

"You know, I tried to model my game after my father," said Bichette, who never spent a day on the disabled list. "I never remember my dad missing a day's work. And he was always there when it counted. I felt like I was a clutch hitter, and came through with an at-bat when the team needed it."

The league batting average with two strikes during Bichette's career was .188. His average in that situation was 31 points higher. In "late and close" situations, defined by Baseball-Reference.com as seventh inning or later while tied, ahead by one or with the tying run on deck, Bichette batted .301.

Bichette was also at his best against the game's elite pitchers. He hit .478 (11-for-23) against Roger Clemens, .381 (8-for-21) against Trevor Hoffman, .327 (17-for-52) against Glavine, and .319 (15-for-47) against Maddux.

After a 14-year major-league career, Bichette passed the torch to his sons. But as one of the Blake Street Bombers, he is revered in Colorado for his place in Rockies history.

"I was blessed with a really quick bat and great hand/eye coordination," said Bichette. "I was never a five-tool player, but I had all five tools at some point in my career. I'm thankful that Colorado is where I got my opportunity. If I got my opportunity somewhere else, maybe it would've been different. But that's where I got my shot, and I had to make the most of it."

NOTES

1   Personal interview conducted with Dante Bichette, October 16, 2017. Unless otherwise indicated, all quotations attributed to Bichette are from that interview.

2   Personal interview conducted with Tom Kotchman, December 5, 2017. Unless otherwise indicated, all quotations attributed to Kotchman are from that interview.

3   *The Sporting News*, April 3, 1989: 21.

4   Tom Singer, "Bichette Gets Reprieve," *The Sporting News*, March 27, 1989.

5   youtube.com/watch?v=TVFO_BhUOHk.

6   Tim Kurkjian, "Mere Child's Play," *Sports Illustrated*, July 3, 1995.

7   Greg Guss, "Bichette Happens," *Sport Magazine*, June 1996

8   Personal interview conducted with Wayne Hagin, December 15, 2017.

9   Personal interview conducted with Vinny Castilla, June 20, 2017.

10 Hal Bodley, "Idol Talk: Bichette, Williams Hit It Off," *USA Today,* February 28, 1996.

11 Tracy Ringolsby, "Bichette Eager to Lighten Mood at Rockies' Camp," *Rocky Mountain News* (Denver), February 24, 1996.

12 Rod Beaton, "Columnist Caught Raiding Bichette's Locker," *USA Today,* August 12, 1998.

13 "Reds-Rockies Trade: Bichette Is Dealt to Cincinnati," Associated Press, October 31, 1999.

14 toronto.bluejays.mlb.com/mlb/news/prospects/index.jsp?c_id=tor.

ELLIS BURKS

BY ROBERT BRUSTAD

FEW PLAYERS IN THE HISTORY OF major-league baseball have displayed each of the prized "five tools," meaning the ability to hit for average and for power, to run, to field, and to throw. On that short list belongs the name of Ellis Burks, who began his major-league career as a 22-year-old rookie for the Boston Red Sox in 1987 and concluded it as a member of the 2004 Red Sox team that ended 86 years of frustration for the franchise with their World Series title. Burks had stops with four additional clubs, most notably with the Colorado Rockies, where he spent five seasons and where in 1996 he produced one of the greatest individual seasons in Rockies history.

Ellis Rena Burks was born in Vicksburg, Mississippi, on September 11, 1964. When he was 3 his family moved to the state capital, Jackson, where he completed elementary school and his father worked as an electrician. As a child in Jackson he had no real opportunities to play organized sports but he learned to love baseball by playing sandlot games with his cousins. He was not particularly skilled at the game as a child, however, and his cousins used to tease him because he batted cross-handed and they liked to inform him, "You don't know how to play, Ellis, you don't know how to play."[1]

At 10, the family moved to Fort Worth, Texas, and Ellis started to get serious about baseball, playing in a summer league after his freshman year at O.D. Wyatt High School. His varsity baseball coach, Bill Metcalf, would become an important influence upon him. As a sophomore, Burks was more than happy just to earn a varsity letter but Metcalf conveyed to the 15-year-old that he had uncommon instincts for the game and could become a special player.[2] As a senior, Burks transferred to nearby Everman High School, the local baseball powerhouse. He had an outstanding senior season at Everman, playing for coach Jim Dyer. It was at Everman that Burks adopted the batting stance of his favorite major leaguer, Jim Rice. "I tried to look

exactly like that in high school," he once said. "I had his number, 14. I adopted his stance. My feet were pretty much placed the same as his in high school, junior college, and the minor leagues."[3]

Despite a torrid senior season at the plate, college scholarship offers were slow to materialize. On one occasion his grandmother, Velma Burks, asked him about his college plans and Ellis informed her that he would be going to Ranger Junior College, although the coaches at Ranger had not yet contacted him with an offer to play baseball.[4] He also entertained the thought that he might be selected in the major-league draft, but he escaped the notice of scouts despite the fact that he capped his impressive senior season by being the first high-school player to hit a ball out of Arlington Stadium.[5] (He did it in a high-school all-star game.) His grandmother died in March of his senior year but Ellis honored his promise to her and committed to Ranger even after other schools began to show interest.

At Ranger Junior College, Burks played for coach Jack Allen. Allen was a master of homespun homilies delivered to full effect with a Texas drawl and he had quite the influence on the 18-year-old Burks. On one occasion, Burks hit a routine groundball to shortstop and was running to first at slightly less than full speed. Allen surprised Burks by inquiring if he was, perhaps, nursing an injury of some sort. When Burks informed him that he was fully healthy, Allen lectured him in no uncertain terms and stated, "By golly, I don't care if you can throw a strawberry through a battleship or run a hole in the wind … on this team we play at full speed!"[6] It was a lesson Burks would never forget and his hustle became a trademark of his professional career. The Ranger team was a real powerhouse during Burks's freshman year and he led the parade by tearing the proverbial cover off of the ball throughout the fall season. He was excited because a number of scouts planned to attend a coming game, and he was shocked when game day arrived and

Allen told him he wouldn't be in the lineup because the coach was afraid the scouts would see him and that Allen would lose Burks, his best player, in the coming January draft. Burks assured his coach that, even if drafted in January, he would not sign with a pro team until the end of the spring season and Allen relented and allowed Burks to play the game.

Indeed, the scouts had a very favorable opinion of Burks and on the advice of scout Danny Doyle, he was selected by the Red Sox with the 20th overall pick of the January 1983 draft. Five of Burks's teammates were also selected in that draft, including future major-league pitchers Mike Smith and Jim Morris. As Burks had promised Coach Allen, he did not sign with the Red Sox until the end of the spring college season.

Burks made his first stop in professional baseball with the Elmira (New York) Pioneers of the New York-Pennsylvania League as an 18-year-old playing short-season A ball in 1983. At the plate he hit just .241 that season with two home runs but demonstrated his range of abilities as he stole nine bases and contributed five outfield assists. He was promoted to high-A ball at Winter Haven in the Florida State League the following season where he was a full three years younger than the league average but displayed a mature set of skills. In 112 games for Winter Haven, he stole 29 bases and contributed 12 outfield assists. Burks had the good fortune of meeting his idol, Jim Rice, then still with the Red Sox. "I met him in spring training. I was in 'A' ball, and I got called up for a split-squad game. He was in the clubhouse. I said, 'Excuse me, Mr. Rice, my name is Ellis Burks. It's a pleasure to meet you.' He said, 'Yeah, I know who you are, kid.'" Burks added, "I was like, whoa, how does he know who I am?" I happened to sit beside him on the bench that day. I was pretty much in awe. I was too scared to ask him any questions. The next year, I was on the roster, and he told the spring-training clubhouse attendant to put my locker next to his. It was unbelievable to grow up idolizing a guy, and now he wanted my locker next to his."[7]

Burks spent the 1985 and 1986 seasons at New Britain in the Double-A Eastern League and it was here that he really caught the attention of the big club. Red Sox coach Johnny Pesky became an admirer and declared that Burks "can run, hit, throw, and catch the ball. He may be ready for the big leagues sooner than people may think."[8] Burks's ascent through the Red Sox system was slowed slightly by two right-shoulder injuries but his power began to blossom with 24 home runs over the course of the two seasons. It was the 31 stolen bases that he collected during the 1986 season in New Britain, however, that really caught the attention of the Boston front office. The Red Sox system had many promising young hitters in addition to Burks, including Mike Greenwell, Brady Anderson, Todd Benzinger, and Sam Horn, but it was the baserunning abilities Burks displayed that made him stand out from the other quality hitting prospects as the big-league club was sorely deficient in basestealing. (The 1986 Red Sox finished a distant last in the major leagues in stolen bases with just 41, of which six were by 36-year-old first baseman Billy Buckner.)

Burks made a strong impression on the Red Sox with an outstanding spring training in 1987. He was the team's last cut, optioned to Triple-A Pawtucket.

The Red Sox did not have a strong sense of urgency to bring up their younger players to start the 1987 season; the team was coming off of a tremendously successful and memorable 1986 season in which they won their first American League pennant since 1975, and a heartbreaking seven-game loss to the New York Mets in the World Series. Lofty expectations for the 1987 Red Sox were misplaced as the team floundered to open the season. In late April, they had a 9-12 record and were in fourth place, 9½ games behind the high-flying Milwaukee Brewers. The Red Sox suddenly looked like a team that was past its prime and needed contributions from some of its talented prospects.

Burks had played a mere 11 games at the Triple-A level for Pawtucket when he was summoned to the big-league club. On the night of April 30, 1987, Boston manager John McNamara inserted 22-year-old Burks into the starting lineup as the Red Sox center fielder. Burks was batting ninth as the Red

Sox faced pitcher Scott Bankhead and the Seattle Mariners in the Kingdome. Burks was hitless in three at-bats in a career that began with a weak groundball back to the mound, followed by a strikeout and a foul popup. He also dropped a line drive on which he had attempted to make a diving catch during the 11-2 Mariners victory. The game marked the first occasion that Burks had played on artificial turf,[9] a circumstance that contributed to a base hit skipping past him in the outfield. Burks reflected great dismay and determination. "I felt bad after that first game. Everything happened so fast and I was not happy at what happened. I just wanted to come right back in my next game and show it wasn't me," he told a sportswriter.[10] Skipper McNamara assured Burks that he would be in the starting lineup again the next game.[11] The next night in Anaheim brought out the "real" Burks as he collected his first major-league hit in the second inning, a double down the right-field line off Urbano Lugo that brought home two runs. He went 3-for-3 as he shook off the jitters. In that

series against the Angels, he showed a dazzling display of speed by sprinting from shallow center field to haul in a drive hit by Gary Pettis. Burks apparently liked Angels pitching because he connected for his first major-league home run, against future Hall of Famer Don Sutton, in the third inning of a game back in Boston on May 10. He later hit five home runs during a single road trip and brought his home-run total to 10 by June 18. When he hit a go-ahead home run off the Yankees' Bob Tewksbury on June 21 it was the third time the rookie had provided the Red Sox with a game-winning blast.

Burks's success fueled the Boston youth movement. In short order, Todd Benzinger, Sam Horn, and Jody Reed were promoted to the big-league club to join Burks and Greenwell and the look of the team began to change. Burks split time in center with Dave Henderson and they became close friends rather than rivals. In fact, Henderson provided great help to Burks in outfield positioning and in reading hitters and Burks later identified Henderson as one of his greatest influences and closest friends in the game.[12] The front office liked what it saw from Burks so much in center field that it traded Henderson to Oakland on September 1. General manager Lou Gorman said, "Henderson's home run put us into the World Series. He did everything we asked of him, but Burks just came along and took his job."[13] Don Baylor, who had provided enormous offensive and leadership contributions during the previous season, was also traded, to Minnesota. The 1987 Red Sox finished 78-84 but the infusion of young talent brought great excitement to Beantown.

Burks's 1987 batting line exceeded all expectations with 20 home runs and 27 stolen bases to accompany 59 runs batted in and a .272 batting average. He became only the third Red Sox player to total 20 home runs and 20 stolen bases in the same season. He had 15 outfield assists, which as of 2017 remain the most in a season for a Red Sox center fielder. But Burks stood out for his entire game and his unusually refined skills, such as the ability to correctly read the flight of the ball off the bat. These defensive skills caught the attention of Lou Gorman who stated that

Burks reminded him of a young Amos Otis.[14] Don Baylor was notably impressed by Burks' defensive prowess and paid him the highest of compliments by comparing him to Paul Blair.[15]

The young but talented Red Sox entered the 1988 season with high hopes. Burks set a personal goal of 40 stolen bases.[16] However, a bone chip in his ankle required offseason surgery and he was unable to open the season with the team. Upon returning, he compiled six multihit games in his first nine games. A jammed left wrist slowed him temporarily but he finished the 1988 campaign with a .294 average, 18 home runs, 92 runs batted in, and 25 stolen bases. On September 4, the Red Sox assumed a permanent hold on first place in the American League East on their way to an 89-73 record and the American League East title. Postseason play was less noteworthy as the Sox were swept in four games by the Oakland Athletics as former Red Sox pitcher Dennis Eckersley saved all four games and Dave Henderson threw some salt in Boston's wounds by going 6-for-16 with a home run. Burks was 4-for-17 in the series.

The 1989 season proved challenging for the team and for Burks. The team stumbled out of the blocks and was slow to recapture its form from the previous season. On April 30, the Red Sox faced the Texas Rangers in a game at Arlington as Nolan Ryan and Roger Clemens faced off on the mound. It was not much of a homecoming for Burks as a Ryan fastball in the first inning glanced off his shoulder and caught him behind the left ear. He was removed from the game and was not pleased with the situation. Burks said, "Why should I be when a guy who throws 100, throws one at my head?"[17] The same two pitchers were matched up in their next start, at Fenway Park on May 5. This time Burks exacted some revenge against Ryan and the Rangers by going 3-for-4 with a stolen base. In the seventh inning a Ryan fastball zipped under Burks's chin, causing Ellis to glare out at the mound and Ryan to take a step toward home plate. "I was making a statement," Burks commented.[18] In return, Ryan said, "Everyone was on edge because of what'd been said or written after the incident in Texas."[19] When order resumed, Burks fouled off a

couple of pitches and then singled home Jody Reed to give the Red Sox the lead for good in a 7-6 victory.

New Red Sox manager Joe Morgan was very impressed with Burks and considered him to be highly capable in every aspect of the game. "He's way above average in everything," Morgan said. "Hitting, hitting with power, throwing, running, catching the ball. Everything. And he's a good fellow. The other day I yelled out to him, 'Burks, I hope you never change,' and he said, 'I won't change.'"[20] The biggest challenge Burks faced seemed to be staying healthy. While attempting to make a diving catch in a game against Detroit on June 14, he tore cartilage in his left shoulder. He underwent surgery and missed the next 41 games. The season came to an abrupt end for Burks during a September 6 game in Oakland in which Burks had gone 3-for-3 before he suffered a shoulder separation in a collision with Mike Greenwell in the outfield and surgery became necessary. Burks was limited to 97 games in the 1989 season, batting .303 with 21 stolen bases.

Burks completed a strong 1990 season that led to some overdue recognition as one of the top players in the game. He batted .296 and contributed 21 home runs and 89 runs batted in as the Red Sox compiled an 88-74 record and won the AL East Division title. His clutch hitting was particularly important as 23 of his first 43 runs batted in were delivered with two out. Against Cleveland on August 27, he became the 25th major leaguer to hit two home runs in one inning. The team's stay in the postseason was again brief; they fell once again in four straight games to the Oakland Athletics in the ALCS. Burks went 4-for-15 in the series. Burks received a Silver Slugger Award as a recognition of his excellence over the 1990 season. He was the only 20-home-run hitter that season for a Red Sox franchise traditionally known for its power. He also earned his first Gold Glove Award, joining fellow outfielders Ken Griffey Jr. and Gary Pettis. He was selected for his first All-Star team although he did not play in the game due to injury. Burks finished 13th in the American League MVP voting.

The subsequent two seasons in Boston brought a steady diet of frustration. The 1991 season was seriously compromised by tendinitis in both knees and continual back pain. The tendinitis disrupted Burks's timing and power at the plate and he had only two home runs in his first 29 games. The back pain increased over the course of the year and kept him out of the lineup for 11 games during a key late-September stretch run. The back problems proved to be a persistent foe over the coming years and Burks was later diagnosed with a bulging disk. His totals for the season reflected the extent to which he played hurt as he had only a .251 average with 14 home runs and 56 RBIs. A better reflection of the effects of the injuries was his uncharacteristically poor success rate on the bases with only 6 stolen bases in 17 attempts.

Trade talk percolated after the 1991 season but new Red Sox manager Butch Hobson was committed to Burks and batted him primarily in the leadoff spot in 1992. The knee problems compromised Burks's speed and these issues were compounded when he played on artificial turf. The back problem did not respond to rest and medication and his season was limited to 66 games and 235 at-bats, which yielded an uncustomary .255 batting average with 8 home runs and 30 runs batted in. The Red Sox did not tender Burks a contract for 1993 and he was left off the team's original 15-man protected list for the expansion draft, only to be pulled back when the Rockies selected Jody Reed.[21] Nonetheless, the Red Sox made no effort to sign him.

The Chicago White Sox emerged as the club with the greatest interest in Burks and he signed with the team in early January of 1993. The White Sox had assembled a talented and experienced team, and in spring training, GM Ron Schueler commented, " ... Right now, Ellis looks as good as I've seen him look since I was scouting him years ago. If we can keep him going, he would give us a whole added dimension."[22] On April 16, and in his ninth game as a member of his new team, Burks made his return to Fenway Park. Facing Danny Darwin in his first at-bat of the game, Burks turned on a 3-and-2 pitch and launched a shot well over the left-field wall. As he rounded the bases, Burks received a standing ovation from the 26,536 fans. He commented, "It hasn't

been an easy transition. ... I gave it a lot of thought this winter how it would be in this game. In spring training it hit me—I was wearing different colored socks."[23] The 1993 season marked a strong return to form for Burks. He batted .275 with 17 home runs and 74 RBIs. More importantly, he was able to stay free of serious injury and played in 146 games. The White Sox realized expectations in winning 94 games against 68 defeats and claimed the American League West title. They met the Toronto Blue Jays in the American League Championship Series but fell, four games to two. Burks went 7-for-23 with a home run.

Burks became a free agent after the season and all indications were that he would re-sign with the White Sox, where he felt wanted and appreciated. "I'll take anything—three years, five years, ten years—whatever they want," he said. "It's been great here. One of the reasons I wanted to come here in the first place was a chance to win, and we're doing that."[24] But the White Sox offered only a two-year deal and wanted Burks to play right field[25] and so he was willing to consider other offers. The Colorado Rockies sorely needed a quality center fielder and offered Ellis a three-year, $9 million deal, which Burks accepted.

A new chapter in Burks's career began when he signed with the Rockies but the story had some familiar elements. In Colorado he was reunited with two teammates from his rookie year in Boston in manager Don Baylor and hitting coach Dwight Evans. Playing for the Rockies had an additional allure as the franchise had just set a major-league attendance record in their inaugural season by drawing nearly 4.5 million fans to Mile High Stadium. Playing there was a hitter's dream and a pitcher's nightmare as the altitude and reduced air resistance translated into additional carry on batted balls. Defense became a priority in this park, and particularly in the outfield, where outfielders needed speed and arm strength to handle the largest outfield in the majors. Playing 81 games a year in Denver also came with costs, including the physical demands of playing long games and chasing down a lot of batted balls yielded by a pitching staff that had the National League's highest ERA during the previous season.

The 1994 season was the second and final season for the Rockies at Mile High Stadium. They moved to Coors Field in 1995. Burks began the 1994 season just as he and the Rockies had hoped. He hit a home run off Curt Schilling of the Philadelphia Phillies in his first at-bat at Mile High Stadium and he was batting a lofty .354 with 12 home runs through his first 34 games. However, in a game against the Los Angeles Dodgers on May 17 he tore a ligament in his left wrist on a checked swing. He missed the next 70 games and when he returned to the club, every swing of the bat proved to be painful. He was limited to 42 games but still managed to hit .322 with 13 home runs. The 1994 season was shrouded by the specter of labor unrest and there was little movement in talks between owners and players as the season progressed. Indeed, the players union struck and the season concluded for the Rockies and all of the other major-league teams on August 11, and the 65,043 fans in attendance that night witnessed the last major-league baseball game to be played in Mile High Stadium, an otherwise forgettable 13-0 pasting of the home club by the Atlanta Braves. The Rockies finished 53-64 in their abbreviated season. Burks underwent surgery immediately after the season ended and his wrist remained in a cast for three full months following the surgery.

Resolution of the labor dispute was not reached until April 2, 1995, after a 232-day work stoppage that wiped out all 1994 postseason play. After an abbreviated spring training, the Rockies opened the 1995 season on April 26 in their brand-new ballpark, Coors Field. The 1995 lineup featured the "Blake Street Bombers," so named because Blake Street bordered the new ballpark on the east side and the lineup contained an assemblage of certifiable sluggers that included Burks, Andres Galarraga, Dante Bichette, and Larry Walker. Vinny Castilla proved to be an unexpected but formidable additional power source and became the fifth member of the brigade. On April 26, the Rockies baptized their new park in unforgettable fashion as Bichette hit a three-run walk-off home run in the 14th inning off Mike Remlinger of the New

York Mets to provide the 47,228 fans with an 11-9 victory. Burks was not able to join the fun until May 5 when he came off of the disabled list. The strong play of Mike Kingery in center field in his absence, and the presence of Bichette in left field and Walker in right field resulted in limited playing time for Burks for the rest of the season. His first home run of the season did not come until June 2 when he launched a walk-off pinch-hit three-run homer against Dan Miceli to beat the Pirates. Burks was able to play in only 103 games with 14 home runs and a .266 batting average to show for his injury-limited 1995 season. The team finished just one game behind the Los Angeles Dodgers in the National League West and they earned their first postseason berth courtesy of the wild-card spot. The Rockies lost three games to one in the first round of the postseason to the eventual champion Atlanta Braves as Burks went 2-for-6 in limited postseason playing time.

Burks arrived at spring training three days early in 1996 knowing that quality preparation and good health were going to be the keys to his success during the coming campaign. "For years I've just been trying to stay healthy and to get rid of that stereotype that I can't stay away from injuries," he said.[26] More than anything, he was determined to erase the memories of 1995 when he was relegated to a role as the Rockies' fourth outfielder. He was slotted to spend more time in left field during the season as manager Baylor wished to minimize the wear and tear on Burks and to see if center field might be a fit for the athletic Larry Walker. A full season of good health enabled Burks to have a remarkable turnaround in 1996 and he carried the Rockies offensively as injuries to Walker and Bichette severely affected the team's attack. Burks played in a career-high 156 games, and 129 of those games were spent in left field. His .344 batting average was second in the National League only to Tony Gwynn's .353 mark, and he led the league with 142 runs scored and also drove in 128 runs. Burks's 93 extra-base hits, 392 total bases, and .639 slugging average all led the league. Although some skeptics attributed his numbers to the "Coors Field Effect," his road statistics were more than sufficient to reject that notion. Away from home, Burks hit .291 with 17 home runs and had 49 runs batted in with a .903 OPS in 75 games. As Burks went, so went the Rockies in 1996. He batted .413 with 10 home runs when leading off an inning. He hit .362 with runners in scoring position and .369 with two outs and runners in scoring situations that year. Against the vaunted Atlanta Braves staff that featured three future Hall of Famers (Greg Maddux, Tom Glavine, and John Smoltz), Burks hit .380 (19-for-50). His 32 stolen bases were more than he had compiled in the previous five seasons combined. He joined Henry Aaron as the second player in history to record 40 home runs, 200 hits, and 30 stolen bases in a season. He finished third in the NL MVP voting behind Ken Caminiti and Mike Piazza and he received his second Silver Slugger Award. His WAR of 7.9 led the Rockies. Galarraga (47), Burks (40), and Castilla (40) became the first trio of teammates to reach 40 home runs in a season since Davey Johnson, Darrell Evans, and Henry Aaron accomplished the feat for the 1973 Atlanta Braves.

Burks became a free agent but was re-signed by the Rockies for the 1997 and 1998 seasons with an $8.8 million deal that included incentives. Burks had no regrets about re-signing and commented, "I signed early because I knew what I wanted. I'm sure I could have gotten a lot of money elsewhere. But money isn't the main issue with me."[27] Preseason expectations were high for the club in 1997 as Walker and Bichette were expected to make stronger contributions after their previous injury-plagued seasons. In fact, Walker contributed even more than expected with 49 home runs, 140 RBIs, and 33 stolen bases to accompany a .366 batting average that earned him the National League MVP Award. Burks began 1997 slowly but his first four hits were home runs. His biggest nemesis during the season was a groin injury that caused him to miss a full month and he reinjured the groin in his second game back. He also had wrist and ankle injuries that lingered throughout the season and limited him to 119 games. Nonetheless, he batted .290 with 32 home runs and 82 RBIs and had a .934 OPS. His season total of just seven stolen bases, however, was

evidence of the physical limitations he encountered during the year.

As the 1998 season opened, Burks said he felt he could not continue to play center field beyond the current season due to the effects of the hamstring, back, and knee problems that continued to limit his mobility.[28] One of the major highlights of his season occurred on April 2, when he connected off the Diamondbacks' Brian Anderson for his 100th home run in a Rockies uniform. The Rockies fell from contention early in the season and they made a move to fill their need for a younger center fielder capable of patrolling spacious center field at Coors. At the July 31 trading deadline, they sent Burks to the San Francisco Giants for center fielder Darryl Hamilton and minor-league pitcher James Stoops. They later received another minor leaguer, Jason Brester, to complete the deal. Burks concluded his time with the Rockies with a .306 batting average and 115 home runs in 520 games, and his 1996 season will be remembered as one of the greatest individual seasons in Rockies history.

Burks was a solid contributor to the Giants, batting .306 with 5 home runs and 8 stolen bases as the team went 31-23 following his arrival to conclude the 1998 season in second place in the National League West. Manager Dusty Baker planned to play him in right field during the 1999 season and to provide Burks with scheduled rest days to reduce his injury risk. Two offseason knee surgeries resulted in pain and soreness that compromised his power as he began the season. As the season progressed, Burks began to drive the ball into the gaps. Despite playing just 120 games in 1999, he concluded the year with 31 home runs and 96 runs batted to go with a .282 batting average and a .964 OPS. He nearly became the first National League player to drive in 100 runs in fewer than 400 at-bats as he fell just four short of 100 in 390 at-bats. The Giants once again finished second in the NL West.

The 2000 season marked a strong return to excellence for Burks despite two additional knee surgeries in the offseason. He batted .344, which equaled his best mark, set in 1996 with the Rockies, and he complemented the high average with 24 home runs and 96 RBIs. Burks's contributions in San Francisco were duly noted as the team had the best record in the National League with a 97-65 mark and won the NL West title by 11 games over the Dodgers. They fell in four games to the New York Mets in the National League Division Series, in which Burks was 3-for-13 with a home run.

Burks became a free agent after the season and the American League seemed like the logical destination: He could serve as a team's designated hitter and limit his time in the field to accommodate the knee issues. In only 284 games in a Giants uniform, Burks had hit .312 with 60 home runs and 214 runs driven in. Remarkably, Burks had a better OPS with the Giants (.971) than he had in his previous five seasons in Colorado (.957).

The Cleveland Indians signed the 36-year-old Burks to a three-year, $20 million offer in 2001 with the hope that he could play 100 to 120 games a year. Burks broke his right thumb in mid-July but still hit 28 home runs and drove in 74 runs with a .290 batting average. The Indians won their division with a 91-71 record and headed to the ALCS, where they faced a Seattle Mariners team that had compiled an all-time major league record of 116 wins. Burks went 6-for-19 in the series with a home run but the Mariners prevailed in five games.

Burks assumed the designated-hitter role for the Indians during the 2002 season and showed what he could do when provided a full season with the bat. He played 138 games and had 32 home runs and 91 runs batted in to accompany a .301 average. He completed his fourth consecutive season with an OPS above .900 (.903) with each coming after the age of 34. After the season, Burks required surgery on his left shoulder but he was in the Indians' starting lineup again on Opening Day in 2003. He began the season well and continued to drive the ball with authority through the early part of the year. However, right elbow pain hampered his swing and he was required to end his season on June 7 in order to undergo ulnar nerve reconstruction surgery. In his abbreviated third season with the Indians, Burks batted .263 with 6 home runs and 28 RBIs. The Indians released Burks after the season, but he was not yet ready to retire from the game.

Burks' career came full circle when he signed with the Red Sox as a free agent on February 6, 2004. At a press conference he said, "I can let you know that I will retire a Red Sox."[29] He was attracted to Boston by his wish to finish out his career where it had started and also felt that the team had a chance to reach the World Series. In turn, the Red Sox felt that Burks's leadership abilities provided an important contribution to a team hoping to finally end their World Series drought. Burks appeared in nine of the team's first 17 games but underwent additional knee surgery in late April. Although he was unable to resume playing for many months, Burks remained with the team and even accompanied the Red Sox on road trips as he recovered from his injury. His commitment to the team was duly noted and appreciated by his teammates and Burks later commented that he wanted to contribute in whatever way that he could to a team that he felt was destined to win the World Series.[30] After missing nearly five months with the injury, he returned to the lineup on September 23. In the season's next-to-last game, at Camden Yards in Baltimore on October 2, manager Terry Francona inserted Burks into the lineup for his 2,000th major-league game. Batting fifth and in the DH role, he singled in his first at-bat in the second inning of that game for his 2,107th and final career hit. In the bottom of the fourth inning he was replaced by rookie Kevin Youkilis. The Red Sox capped their dream season with their first World Series title since 1918 by sweeping the St. Louis Cardinals in the World Series although Burks was not on the roster for the playoffs.

The 2004 World Series title vanquished the bitter memories of previous seasons and will always be regarded as one of the greatest accomplishments in Boston sports history. A largely unknown part of the story involves the team's triumphant return home from St. Louis. As the plane approached Boston, Pedro Martinez asked for everyone's attention and delivered an impromptu speech in which he recognized the contributions of the players on the field in contributing to the historic accomplishment. As Martinez continued, he singled out "The Old Goat" in reference to Burks and provided special praise for the teammate who had remained with the club and who had contributed his knowledge and leadership over the five long months of his injury rehab. At the request of Martinez and his teammates, Burks led the team down the steps of the plane to the tarmac at Logan Airport carrying the World Series trophy overhead.[31]

Ellis Burks retired after the 2004 season with a .291 lifetime batting average to go with 352 home runs. He is one of just a few major league players to have hit 60 or more home runs with four separate teams. Injuries robbed Burks of the opportunity to put up even more impressive numbers and a possible berth in the Hall of Fame, but he looked back on his career with no regrets and said that he "loved every minute of it."[32] Burks received the respect of his peers for his professionalism and his willingness to play with pain. He remained in the game, working for the Cleveland Indians, Colorado Rockies, and San Francisco Giants.

The Ranger College baseball team now plays at Ellis Burks Field. As of 2017 Burks worked for the San Francisco Giants as an instructor, scout, and talent evaluator. He, his wife, Dori, and their daughters, Carissa, Elisha, and Breanna, resided in Chagrin Falls, Ohio. His son, Chris, began his own professional career in the Giants' minor-league system in the summer of 2017.

SOURCES

In addition to the sources noted in this biography, the author also consulted Baseball-Reference.com, Retrosheet.org, and the SABR Minor Leagues Database, accessed online at Baseball-Reference.com.

NOTES

1   Mel Antonen, "Red Sox Ellis Burks Steals Into the Spotlight: Fastest Player on the Team Learns by Survival," *USA Today*, April 8, 1991.

2   Author interview with Ellis Burks, November 20, 2017 (Hereafter cited as Burks insterview).

3   Ellis Burks, as told to Matt Crossman. "My Idol," *The Sporting News*, July 6, 2009.

4   Burks interview.

5   Ibid.

6   Ibid.

7   Ellis Burks, as told to Matt Crossman.

8   "Minor Leagues," *The Sporting News*, May 20, 1985.

9   Ibid.

10   Joe Giuliotti, "Burks Brings Raw Speed to Red Sox," *The Sporting News*, May 18, 1987.

11   Burks interview.

12   Ibid.

13   Joe Giuliotti, "In Boston, the Spotlight Shifts," *The Sporting News*, September 14, 1987.

14   Moss Klein, "AL Beat," *The Sporting News*, May 25, 1987.

15   Ibid.

16   "AL East: Red Sox," *The Sporting News*, February 22, 1988.

17   "AL East," *The Sporting News*, May 15, 1989.

18   Phil Rogers, "Ryan-Roger Rematch Not So Hot," *The Sporting News*, May 15, 1989.

19   Ibid.

20   Jerome Holtzman, "Red Sox's Burks Really on His Way," *Chicago Tribune*, May 4, 1989.

21   Joe Giuliotti, "Boston Red Sox," *The Sporting News*, November 30, 1992.

22   Peter Pascarelli, "Bo or No, White Sox Look Like Contenders," *The Sporting News*, March 9, 1993.

23   Joe Goddard, "Burks Homers in Homecoming," *The Sporting News*, April 26, 1993.

24   Joe Goddard, "Burks Should Be Back in '94," *The Sporting News*, September 20, 1993.

25   Joe Goddard, "Chicago White Sox," *The Sporting News*, November 29, 1993.

26   Tom Verducci, "The Best Years of Their Lives," *Sports Illustrated*, July 29, 1996.

27   Tony DeMarco, "Colorado Rockies," *The Sporting News*, December 30, 1996.

28   Tony DeMarco, "Rockies," *The Sporting News*, March 23, 1998.

29   David Heuschkel, "Burks' Return: It's Been Ages," *Hartford Courant*, February 6, 2004.

30   Burks interview.

31   Ibid.

32   Ibid.

VINNY CASTILLA

BY KYLE EATON

FERNANDO VALENZUELA IS PROBA-
bly the most famous Mexican-born player ever to
compete in major-league baseball, but that distinction is closer than one might expect. Or at least
there is a strong argument that Valenzuela deserves
company atop the Mexican ballplayer hierarchy.
Vinny Castilla ended his 16-year big-league career
as the all-time leader among Mexican-born players
in career home runs, RBIs, extra-base hits, and total
bases.[1]

Vinicio "Vinny" (Soria) Castilla, born on July 4,
1967, in Oaxaca, Mexico, was a right-handed-hitting shortstop and third baseman who played for
the Atlanta Braves, Colorado Rockies, Tampa Bay
Devil Rays, Houston Astros, Washington Nationals,
and San Diego Padres over his 16-year major-league
career. He is primarily known for his time with the
Rockies. The 6-foot-1, 175-pound infielder was a two-
time All-Star and three-time Silver Slugger recipient.

Typically, athletes in Mexico are drawn to playing
soccer rather than baseball, but Castilla cited his father's experience playing amateur baseball in Mexico
as a driving force influencing him and his brother to
choose baseball over soccer as their desired sport.[2]
In fact, most schools in the region did not even field
baseball teams, and for boys like the Castillas who
desired to play baseball, they would have to seek out
leagues outside the school system.[3]

Growing up in Oaxaca, Castilla attended high
school at Carlos Gracita Institute, and once he completed his education there, he attended Benito Suarez
University, also in Oaxaca. Castilla was the first, and
as of 2018 the only major-league baseball player to
attend the university.[4] (In fact, he and Geronimo
Gil are the only Oaxacans to make it to the major
leagues.[5])

In 1987 the 19-year-old Castilla began playing
for the Saltillo Saraperos in the Mexican League.
He played in the Mexican League for three seasons,
2½ with Saltillo and half of the 1988 season with

the Monclova Acereros. After his 1989 season with
Saltillo, the Atlanta Braves purchased his contract
from the Saraperos for $20,000, of which Castilla
got $17,000. The Dodgers, Reds, and Pirates had also
showed interest in Castilla. At the time, he was a
skinny shortstop with a wild swing and an uncanny
ability to hit a fastball. He was projected by most
scouts to be no more than a utility infielder rather
than the slugging third baseman most fans remember
from the 1990s and 2000s. Castilla took the criticism
in stride and sought to prove the naysayers wrong.
"No one gave me a chance," he said. "When they told
me I was nothing but a utility player, I said, 'Fine, I'll
be the best utility player in the league.'"[6]

The Braves assigned Castilla to the Class-A
Sumter (South Carolina) Braves for the 1990 season.
In 93 South Atlantic League games he showed
decent power, with 9 home runs and with 14 doubles.
Castilla's defensive acumen was still developing and
he made 23 errors. (He and seven teammates made
the major leagues (Ryan Klesko, Tyler Houston,
Melvin Nieves, Tony Tarasco, Eddie Perez, Ed
Giovanola, Mark Wohlers), all with the Braves in
the early to mid-1990s. Late in the season Castilla
was promoted to the Greenville Braves (Double-A
Southern Association), where his power tailed off a
bit, but his errors subsided a bit as well.

On a personal level, the 1990 season was tough
for Castilla. He was in a foreign country, away from
his family, riding a bus from town to town, with the
realization that this would be his life for the foreseeable future, even if he progressed quickly through the
minors. Castilla had his doubts about pursuing his
baseball dream and contemplated quitting and returning to Mexico. He was getting paid $800 a month
in the United States versus the $2,000 a month he
had made in Mexico. Castilla did not speak English
well enough to order a burger from McDonald's,
and he could not find any decent Mexican food in
Sumter.[7] Then a letter from his father reminded him

of his abilities and that the Braves had signed him based on his abilities. "I thought, 'This is my dream. If I go back, it will never happen,'" Castilla said.[8] He decided to stick it out and despite some struggles, he was able to sustain a successful major-league career.

Castilla began the 1991 season back in Greenville, where his offensive production was up from his previous season in Greenville, and his defensive production remained steady. He was not the highest-ranked prospect in Greenville, this honor going to Ryan Klesko, but Castilla did get promoted to the Triple-A Richmond Braves, while Klesko finished the season in Greenville. The The 23 pitchers who toiled for the squad all made it to the major leagues. Castilla's defense remained constant on defensive and he declined a bit on offense, but not enough to deter the Braves from calling him up at the end to season to receive his first taste of major-league action.

Castilla made his major-league debut on September 1, 1991, when he came into a home game at shortstop against the Philadelphia Phillies in the bottom of the ninth. His first at-bat came three days later in Montreal when he popped out to second in the ninth inning. Castilla's first start and first hit, a line-drive single, came against the Houston Astros on October 6, 1991, the last game of the regular season for the Braves.

Castilla opened the 1992 season back in Richmond, where he played until another late-season call-up. His home-run production fell off from 14 to 7 in nearly twice as many at-bats. Castilla's defense regressed; he made 31 errors. During his call-up he played third base as well as shortstop.

During the expansion draft after the season, the Braves left Castilla unprotected, and he was selected by the new Colorado Rockies. Years later he was philosophical about having been "cast aside" by the Braves: "It was a new opportunity. There weren't many chances for me to play in Atlanta."[9]

Castilla debuted for the Rockies at his natural position of shortstop in 1993, playing in 104 games while splitting time with Freddie Benavides. Reflecting on his career with the Rockies, he said many years later, "This team picked me in the expansion draft in 1992

and gave me my first real, honest opportunity to play at this level. I played for other organizations, but the purple stripes have always felt better on my body."[10] But in his first season, Castilla still had not developed into the power hitter many Rockies fans remember him to be, and finished with just nine home runs and .686 OPS. (He did hit a career-best seven triples.)

That year was one of transformation for Castilla off the field as well. While purchasing a cell phone, he was enticed to sign a contract with the promise of a date with the salesperson's sister, Samantha Owen. Despite some reservations about dating a baseball player ("I said, 'He's a baseball player? I don't think so.' I had heard stories") the pair eventually did go out on a date, which led to more dates, and they were married the following year.[11]

Castilla opened the 1994 season as the recently signed free agent Walt Weiss's backup at shortstop, hoping to build upon his previous season and earn more playing time. He played sporadically during the first month of the season, and was sent down to the Triple-A Colorado Springs Sky Sox, where he received consistent playing time and much-needed at-bats. Castilla returned to the Rockies in a utility role, seeing playing time at all four infield positions. In his return to the majors, Castilla flourished, and he batted .331/.357/.500 in the strike-shortened season.

When the 1995 season began, Castilla became the starting third baseman, replacing the departed Charlie Hayes.[12] The transition to third base did not intimidate Castilla; he felt that his time at shortstop would only help his ability to play third base. "If you can play shortstop, you can play any position in the infield," Castilla said later about his transition.[13] Castilla flourished at third base and became a charter member of the Blake Street Bombers, the quintet of sluggers also including Ellis Burks, Dante Bichette, Larry Walker, and Andres Galarraga.[14]

The 1995 season was one to remember for Castilla and the Rockies. They earned the first-ever National League wild card after winning 77 games in the truncated season, finishing second in the National League West. Castilla earned his first of two All-Star Game selections, and first of three Silver Slugger Awards.

The Rockies finished first in the National League in runs, hits, triples, home runs, batting average, and slugging, helped by Castilla's breakout season at the plate. He finished the season with an impressive slash line of .309/.347/.564, and 32 home runs, 34 doubles, and 90 RBIs. The Rockies lost to the Braves, three games to one, in the Division Series. Castilla performed well, batting .467 with three home runs and six RBIs. Castilla later cited the Rockies clinching a playoff berth in 1995 as his favorite baseball moment.[15]

Castilla was quick to thank Art Howe, the Rockies' hitting coach in 1995, for his emergence at the plate. "He really taught me a lot," Castilla said. "Before, I tried to pull everything; I'd hit either a home run to left or a weak ground ball to short. Art taught me to go the other way, and I learned how to hit for power to the opposite field."[16]

The 1995 season was the start of something special for the Rockies, and Castilla was a vital part of the impressive era of offense-minded baseball. "Man, I love the name Blake Street Bombers, it just sounds so good," he reflected during the celebrations of the 25th anniversary of the Rockies franchise. "That name stuck with the fans and the organization. I'm so proud that I was a part of it. What a great experience."[17]

After his strong 1995 season, Castilla continued his ascension to the top ranks of major-league third basemen. His 1996 and 1997 seasons were nearly identical, .304/.343/.548 in 1996 and .304/.356/.547 in 1997, with 40 home runs and 113 RBIs in each season. Despite those numbers, Castilla did not make an All-Star team either year, but he did take home his second Silver Slugger Award in 1997. Castilla's rise as a power hitter, whether fueled by the thin air of Denver or not, surprised talent evaluators in Atlanta. Chuck Lamar, assistant general manager of the Braves in the early to mid-1990s, said, "No one in the organization predicted [Castilla] would ever hit more than 15 home runs."[18] The uninspiring scouting reports for Castilla were not reserved for the Braves organization. One of his future managers, Clint Hurdle, predicted while managing the Triple-A Norfolk Tides, "Nothing special. ... Might make it as a utility player."[19]

Castilla and his Samantha's first son, Vinicio Jr., was born on March 12, 1996.[20]

The 1998 season was Castilla's best as a professional. It was the only one in which he played in all 162 games, and he had career highs in hits (206), runs (108), home runs (46), RBIs (144), batting average (.319), on-base percentage (.362), and slugging percentage (.589), as well as his second All-Star Game appearance and his third Silver Slugger Award. Even with his impressive stats in 1998, the results for the Rockies were beginning to decline. The team didn't fare as well, and despite a string of great offensive seasons by Castilla and other Rockies, the 1995 Division Series was the team's only postseason appearance during Castilla's nine-year tenure with the Rockies.

The Rockies and San Diego Padres opened the 1999 league in Monterrey, Mexico, the first time an opener had been played outside the United States. Back in front of his countrymen, Castilla shined by going 4-for-5 and helping the Rockies win, 8-2. After the game, he said, "I tried my last two at-bats to hit a home run. It didn't happen, but I'm happy for the win."[21]

That season was solid in many ways for Castilla, but it did not compare to the results he had enjoyed from 1995 to 1998. His numbers declined in almost every meaningful statistical category, and the team lost more games than in the previous year. After the season, Castilla was traded by the Rockies to the Tampa Bay Devil Rays for Rolando Arrojo and Aaron Ledesma. After a lackluster performance in 2000, he was released on May 10, 2001. He was still a desired commodity. The Cubs and Astros both pursued his services, and Castilla chose the Astros, who planned to play him on a regular basis. "The Cubs didn't want me as an everyday player," Castilla said. Castilla performed well for the Astros, clubbing 23 home runs and driving in 82 runs for the NL Central champions. Castilla enjoyed his second trip to the playoffs, but this trip again ended in defeat by the Braves in the NLDS. On a happier note, he and Samantha welcomed their second son, Dalton Samuel, on November 22.[22]

Castilla was a free agent after the season and signed a two-year, $8 million contract to return to the Braves. On paper, this union did not make sense as the Braves already employed a perennial All-Star playing third base in Chipper Jones, but Jones willingly moved to left field to strengthen the team. Jones said, "We've gone out and gotten a top-notch third baseman and I'll move." The idea was that the value Castilla provided was in line with a top-tier outfielder at a fraction of the cost.[23] And if Castilla had performed anywhere close to the way he had for the Rockies, or even for the Astros the previous season, the signing would have been beneficial for the Braves. Instead, Castilla managed only 12 home runs in a dismal 2002 season as well as his worst career slash line,.232/.268/.348. Castilla rebounded slightly in 2003, hitting 22 home runs and seeing improvements in virtually every offensive category.

But Castilla did have the chance to play in the postseason both seasons in Atlanta. Again, his team was unable to advance past the NLDS either time, and never again reached the postseason.

The 2004 season saw a reunion with the Rockies. It was preceded by the birth of Castilla's third son,

Cristian, on February 20.[24] His return to the Rockies apparently rejuvenated him, and along with 35 home runs, he had a league-leading 131 RBIs, even though the team's results were not that great. (They went 68-94.) It was as if Castilla was in the midst of his Blake Street Bombers Rockies teams once again. The offensive resurgence showed that Castilla still had some ability to hit a baseball, and earned him one more contract before he retired.

Castilla left the Rockies after the 2004 season, signing a free-agent contract with the Montreal Expos, who became the Washington Nationals a few weeks after he signed a two-year, $6.2 million contract. Castilla was the starting third baseman for the Nationals in 2005, but his production declined drastically from his 2004 renaissance. He finished the season with just 12 home runs and 66 RBIs. After the season, the Nationals traded Castilla to the San Diego Padres for Brian Lawrence and cash. The Padres released Castilla in July 2006, and the Rockies signed him for one last hurrah with the team. In his 15 games to close out the season, Castilla had only four hits. He was released after the season.

The 2006 season was not all disappointment for Castilla. He was elected the captain of Team Mexico in the inaugural World Baseball Classic in 2006. Team Mexico finished sixth in the tournament with a record of 3-3, and won Pool B by virtue of beating the United States head to head. Castilla cited his experience in the 2006 WBC as his impetus to stay involved with baseball as a manger and/or executive after retirement.[25]

Castilla announced his retirement in February 2007 after playing first base for Mexico in the Caribbean Series at Carolina, Puerto Rico. He retired as a hero to many players and fans in Mexico. "Vinny is a hero, there's no doubt about it," Mexican League manager Lorenzo Bundy said. "There's not going to be anybody that comes close to what he's done offensively."[26] Castilla retired as the all-time leader among Mexican-born players in career home runs, RBIs, extra-base hits, and total bases.[27] Castilla joined the Rockies' front office as a special assistant to

GM Dan O'Dowd, a position he still held as of 2018 despite a 2014 change in general managers.[28]

In addition to his front-office duties, Castilla also managed the Mexican national team in the 2007 Pan American Games, held in Brazil. O'Dowd said managing would be "another great experience for him. And it's good for us, too, to expose him to that and for him to see players from around the world a little bit. He'll do some scouting for us and I think that only benefits us."[29] Castilla also served as player-manager of the Hermosillo Naranjeros of the Mexican Pacific League from 2006 through 2010, and in 2008, it was announced that Castilla would be the manager for Team Mexico in the 2009 World Baseball Classic. "I like it. … I like it a lot," he said. "I love the game. It's my life … it's my passion. I want to be involved somehow with the game. I like managing. It's tough … it's not easy, but I enjoy it."[30]

In 2014, Castilla, along with Moises Alou, Bert Campaneris, Omar Moreno, and Ozzie Virgil Sr. was inducted into the Latino Hall of Fame.[31] In 2016, he was one of six athletes, and the only major-league baseball player, inducted into the Colorado Sports Hall of Fame.[32]

Castilla's longevity with the Rockies has been viewed as an asset for the team, both by the players and the front office. He drew on his successful career in the majors, specifically his time in Colorado and playing at the high altitude of Coors Field, and his Latin heritage to relate to and encourage players. Singing his praises, All-Star third baseman Nolan Arenado said, "Vinny brings energy every day and he brings happiness, if you want to put it that way. When you are down, he's always there for you. He always brings positive energy to the ballpark. I've never seen Vinny down or bummed out. I mean, he's great at trash talking, but it's all in fun. He's awesome."[33]

Castilla also began to give back to the community as an advocate for organ donation[34] and education.[35]

NOTES

1. "Vinny Castilla," IMDB.com. imdb.com/name/nm1758753/bio?ref_=nm_ov_bio_sm.

2. Owen Perkins, "Q and A With Vinny Castilla," Rockies.com, September 16, 2006. colorado.rockies.mlb.com/news/print.jsp?ymd=20060916&content_id=1666489&vkey=news_col&fext=.jsp&c_id=col'

3. Matt Krupnick, "A Baseball Academy in a Talent-Poor Part of Mexico," New York Times, May 23, 2013.

4. According to baseball-refence.com.

5. Krupnick.

6. Gerry Callahan, "Vinny, Vidi, Vici He Doesn't Get the Ink of a McGwire or a Griffey, But in Only Four Seasons Vinny Castilla of Colorado Has Gone From Utilityman to the Man," Sports Illustrated, May 11, 1998.

7. Ibid.

8. Chris Bolin, "Vinny Castilla, Mark Jackson Discuss Their Pasts at Friends of Baseball's Breakfast of Champions," Greeley (Colorado) Tribune, January 28, 2018.

9. Irv Moss, "Vinny Castilla's Ability to Hit Fastball Helped Him Into Colorado Sports Hall of Fame," Denver Post, April 22, 2016.

10. Patrick Saunders, "Vinny Castilla's High-Octane Energy Still Driving Rockies After 25 years," Denver Post, May 13, 2017.

11. Mike Klis, "Trade Talk Impacts Wife, Too," Denver Post, August 1, 1999.

12. Tony Almeyda, "Braves Rewind: Whatever Happened to …Vinny Castilla?" TalkingChop.com, April 18, 2016. talkingchop.com/2016/4/18/11447772/braves-rewind-whatever-happened-to-vinny-castilla

13. Moss.

14. Patrick Saunders, "Blake Street Bombers Left Unforgettable Impression in Rockies' First 25 years," Denver Post, July 22, 2017.

15. Patrick Saunders, "2016 Inductees," Colorado Sports Hall of Fame, April 19, 2016. coloradosports.org/index.php/2016-04-19-23-18-38/item/330-vinny-castilla

16. Callahan.

17. "Blake Street Bombers Left Unforgettable Impression."

18. Jonathan Weeks, Latino Stars in Major League Baseball: From Bobby Abreu to Carlos Zambrano (Lanham, Maryland: Rowman & Littlefield, 2017), 228.

19. Callahan.

20. IMDB.com.

21. Associated Press, "Bichette and Castilla Spark Rockies in Opener in Mexico," New York Times, April 5, 1999.

22. IMDB.com.

23. Morris News Service, "Chipper to move to left field," Augusta Chronicle, December 10, 2001.

24. IMDB.com.

25. Perkins.

26   CBC Sports, "Vinny Castilla Retires, Joins Rockies Front
      Office," cbc.ca/sports/baseball/vinny-castilla-retires-joins-rock-
      ies-front-office-1.690370, February 7, 2007.

27   IMDB.com

28   CBC Sports.

29   Associated Press, "Vinny Castilla to Manage Mexican National
      Team," ESPN.com, February 28, 2007. espn.com/mlb/news/
      story?id=2783482

30   Bill Mitchell, "Castilla Mentors Mexican Prospects:
      Former 3B Managing in Winter Ball," *Baseball America,*
      December 16, 2008.

31   Thomas Harding, "Rox Will Be Represented by Castilla In
      HOF Classic: Former Player Set for First Trip to Cooperstown
      for Memorial Day Weekend Event," MLB.com, May 23, 2014.
      mlb.com/news/former-rockies-player-vinny-castilla-to-repre-
      sent-club-in-hall-of-fame-classic/c-76501512.

32   Saunders, "2016 Inductees."

33   "Vinny Castilla's High-Octane Energy."

34   Brandon Rivera, "An Interview With Vinny Castilla," *La Voz,*
      April 29, 2015.

35   "Game Plan for Success," educatorsforhighstandards.org/
      game-plan-for-success/.

AARON COOK

BY JOY HACKENMUELLER AND BILL NOWLIN

SOMETIMES, LET'S SAY MOST OF THE time, knowing exactly what we want out of life is the key to making it happen. Aaron Lane Cook, born February 8, 1979, at Fort Campbell, Kentucky, was asked in the eighth grade to fill out a questionnaire on what he wanted to do when he grew up.

"My teacher didn't understand," Cook recalled. "She said, 'You can't do that, you have to do something serious.' I said, 'I want to be a professional baseball player.'"[1]

Cook grew up in Hamilton, Ohio, where his father worked in the local paper mill. Garry Cook, Aaron's father, offered support to his son by coaching his teams as often as he could. Garry mentioned a pivotal moment when young Aaron was one out away from defeating the New England Mariners at a national AAU tournament in Des Moines, Iowa, "Aaron motioned for me to come out to the mound. Keep in mind he was just 13. I thought he wanted me to take him out. Instead, he said 'I just need a minute here to calm down.' On the way back to the dugout, I thought, 'He's actually got a chance to do something big with baseball."[2] Aaron added, appreciatively, "He was always there for me. He never missed a tournament or anything until I was 16. He helped me chase my dreams."[3]

Aaron's mother, Veronica, left when he was 15, after a divorce. Aaron's best friend growing up was Curtus Moak. As Patrick Saunders wrote, "Cook and Moak competed against each other in Little League before becoming best friends the summer before their sophomore year at Hamilton High. Because Cook's house was far out of town, he often spent the night at Moak's house. 'We'd sleep in these bunk beds and we'd talk for hours,' Moak recalled. 'We became like brothers. My mom became his second mom.'"[4]

The two Hamilton High teammates helped lead the team to two statewide baseball titles. Moak, a left-handed pitcher, later played for the University of Cincinnati and in 2001 was drafted in the 25th round by the Cincinnati Reds. He played four years in the minors, but never rose as high as Double A.

As a young teenager, Cook threw a fastball in the low 80s. By the time he was 18 years old he had harnessed a 90-mph fastball with exceptional control. On June 3, 1997, the high-school senior was drafted by the Colorado Rockies in the second round of the amateur draft. He grew to 6-feet-3 and was listed at 215 pounds.

The Rockies placed Cook in Mesa, pitching Rookie-league ball in the Arizona League; he was 1-3 in 46 innings of work, with a 3.13 earned-run average. He devoted five years to development before rising as high as Double A. In 1998 he was with the Portland Rockies (Northwest League), and in 1999 he pitched ball for the Asheville Tourists in the Class-A South Atlantic League. There he might have felt discouraged, winning only four games against 12 losses and with an ERA of 6.44. Asheville finished in last place in the six-team league. But Cook kept working, trying to hone his craft.

In 2000, his second year with Asheville, he began to turn things around and, though the Tourists still had a losing record at 66-69, Cook improved dramatically in his control, converting his 1.74 strikeouts/walks ratio to 5.13, halving his walks to 23 while striking out 118. His ERA dropped to 2.96 and he was 10-7 in wins and losses. He spent part of the season in high-A ball, pitching for Salem (Virginia) Avalanche in the Carolina League. He was overmatched (1-6, 5.44), but once more he improved with experience, and in 2001 he started 27 games for Salem and worked to a 3.08 ERA. He was 11-11 for the 70-68 Avalanche.

In 2002 Cook climbed the ladder rapidly. First, in Raleigh with the Double-A Southern League's Carolina Mudcats, he was 7-2 (1.42); and then in Triple A with the Pacific Coast League Colorado Springs Sky Sox, he held his own (4-4, 3.78).

Cook got the call to come to the big leagues. On August 10, 2002, at age 23, he made his debut for the Rockies against the Chicago Cubs. After five innings, the Cubs were winning 14-1, and manager Clint Hurdle called on Cook as the third of five Rockies pitchers that day. The first batter he faced was Cubs left fielder Moises Alou, who homered to make it 15-1, but Cook retired the next three batters. He also worked the top of the seventh, giving up a leadoff single but then getting the next three batters. On August 26 he was given his first start, against the visiting San Francisco Giants, and acquitted himself well enough, working six innings while giving up three runs, in a game the Rockies ultimately lost. Cook gave up three runs again, working seven innings in San Diego in his second start, but lost his first decision; the Rockies were shut out, 3-0. Cook then won back-to-back starts, against the Padres in Denver and the Astros in Houston. He finished the season appearing in nine games, five of them starts, with a record of 2-1 and a 4.54 ERA in 35⅔ innings.[5]

In both 2003 and 2004, Cook spent some time on Interstate 25 traveling the hour or so between Colorado Springs and Denver and working for both teams, though the lion's share of his time was with the big-league club in 2003, when he pitched in 43 games, 16 of them starts. Cook's ERA was a disappointing 6.02 and his final record 4-6, but the Rockies kept the faith.

By the 2004 season, Cook had developed full trust in his sinkerball, one he worked diligently to develop with Rockies minor-league pitching coach Bryn Smith.[6] His sinker developed from his straight fastball. Eventually, a conventional grip of two fingers on both seams was tweaked and became one finger across one seam to become his signature sinkerball.

Bob McClure of the Rockies' minor-league pitching staff taught Cook that contact was OK. "One thing I give Bob McClure credit for is teaching me how to pitch to contact and trusting that I can get guys out with groundballs," said Cook. "Swings and misses, for me, are more of a timely thing—certain situations with guys on, less than two outs, less than one out, that's the time I really try to go for the strike-outs. But other than that, I really try to make guys mis-hit the ball, hit pitches that I'm trying to make."[7] Once Cook trusted contact, he went from throwing 110-115 pitches per game to around 80. His sinkerball technique in combination with a pitch flying at upward of 90 mph made his pitches unhittable.

After beating the Diamondbacks with a complete-game 10-2 win on August 1, 2004, Cook was feeling good about himself; he was 25 years old and seeing the fruits of his technique training. Six days later, on August 7, Cook took the mound against the Cincinnati Reds at Coors Field. After three innings, 10 batters and five hits, Cook complained of dizziness and shortness of breath. He left the mound and was taken to Rose Medical Center, where he was diagnosed with pulmonary embolisms, a sudden blockage of the arteries, in both lungs. Doctors, medics, and the Rockies medical team all told Cook later that it was a miracle he was alive. Indeed, he told the *Boston Globe*'s Nick Cafardo several years later, "I had the paramedic and doctor telling me as I was lying on the stretcher that I should be dead," Cook recalled. "At that point, I'm fighting for my life. I wasn't thinking about baseball. I was thinking about my family and my health and whether I was going to make it."[8]

Cook had essentially gone from the peak of his young career to a debilitating condition. "I had experienced trouble breathing for a couple of days before that start," Cook said. "I don't think I could have thrown another pitch in the game."[9] The clots originated near his first rib, constricting flow against his collarbone. He had two surgeries; his top rib was removed to correct the problem that was causing the clots. After rehabilitation lasting the better part of a year, Cook got back to baseball.

It was a bit of a slog to get back in the big leagues after recovery, and in 2005, Cook pitched for four minor-league teams. First he pitched in two games for the Tri-City Dust Devils (Pasco, Washington) of the Northwest League. Then he advanced to the Modesto Nuts (Class-A California League) for one game, then on to the Double-A Tulsa Drillers for one game, then to the Triple-A Sky Sox in Colorado

Springs for three games. In late July he was deemed ready for the Rockies.

Cook was activated from the disabled list in time to start on July 30 at Coors Field against the visiting Phillies. It did not go well; he was hit for seven runs, all earned, in 4⅓ innings. But he had made his way back to big-league baseball and was pitching from a major-league mound. Next time out, on August 5, he yielded only one run in six innings. Then he won six games in a row. He took one more loss, and then added another win. By the end of his half-season, Cook was 7-2 with an ERA of 3.67. It was a remarkable recovery after a near-fatal illness.

Bob Apodaca, the Rockies' pitching coach, commented on Cook's dedication after his surgeries: "I think that changed him. … Any success he is getting now is the result of pure hard work. Before, I think he did rely on pure ability. I think that's why we would scratch our head and wonder, what kind of pitcher he would be? Now we don't have to wonder any more. He's shown us."[10]

In January 2006 Cook was given the Tony Conigliaro Award for his quick comeback and dedication to the game. The day after receiving the award, he signed a two-year, $4.55 million contract with the Rockies.

Cook had 32 starts in 2006, winning nine and losing 15 with a 4.23 ERA. That he had worked 212⅔ innings was a testament to his having regained full health.

In 2007 Cook worked a full load through August 10, when he suffered an oblique injury that kept him out for the rest of the regular season. He was 8-7, 4.12. That was the year the Rockies caught fire and won 14 of their last 15 games, earning them a wild-card slot in the postseason. Cook was not on the postseason roster for either the Division Series, which they swept in three games from the Phillies, or for the NLCS, which they swept in four from the Arizona Diamondbacks. With the back-to-back sweeps, the team had now won 21 of its last 22 games and was headed to the World Series against the Boston Red Sox. Cook was with the team in Phoenix and enjoyed the champagne the Rockies sprayed on one another.

Cook was activated for the World Series, and he started Game Four at Coors Field. The pendulum of sweeps had started to go the other way, with Boston taking the first three games of the World Series and on the brink of a sweep if Cook couldn't stop them. It could hardly have been a more emotional time for a return. Rockies manager Clint Hurdle said, "The opportunity to tell him, 'You're going to get the ball in Game Four' was very special. And it was meaningful, but again, for all the right reasons. If it was about sentiment, he would have pitched in the NLCS, and he understood that." For his part, Cook said, "I feel ready to go. I feel as strong as ever."[11]

Game Four was, as the *New York Times* observed, "a duel of survivors. [Red Sox pitcher Jon] Lester fought his way back after offseason treatment for lymphoma, and Colorado's Aaron Cook once missed almost a year with blood clots in both lungs."[12]

Both pitched good games. Cook gave up a leadoff double to Jacoby Ellsbury, who moved to third base on a grounder by Dustin Pedroia, then scored when David Ortiz singled to right field. In the top of the fifth, the score still 1-0, Mike Lowell doubled to lead off and Jason Varitek singled him in. Lowell homered leading off the seventh, making it 3-0 Red Sox, and Hurdle brought in Jeffrey Affeldt to take over from Cook. Lester had departed after 5⅔ innings. The Rockies came back with a run in the bottom of the seventh. Boston's Bobby Kielty pinch-hit for Mike Timlin in the top of the eighth and homered, so when the Rockies got two more in the bottom of the eighth, they still trailed, 4-3, and that was the final score. Cook bore the loss.

Cook had his winningest season in 2008. He was 11-5 through July 1, and had won six consecutive starts from April 13 to May 9. Cook was named to the National League All-Star team. He pitched three scoreless innings, the 10th, 11th, and 12th. In the 10th he faced a bases-loaded situation with no outs after second baseman Dan Uggla made back-to-back errors, and Carlos Guillen was walked intentionally. Cook worked his way out of the jam, inducing three groundouts, the first two resulting in forces at home. It was said that he could have been named the game's MVP had the National League won,[13] but AL prevailed in 15 innings, 4-3.

Cook finished the 2008 season 16-9 (3.96). In 2009 he was 11-6 in 27 starts with a 4.16 ERA. He had also enjoyed the day on May 29 when he attended the dedication of a "Field of Dreams" baseball complex in Windsor, Colorado, a facility for which he had been a major donor.[14]

In 2009 Cook had another opportunity to play postseason baseball. The Rockies were the wild-card team again after Clint Hurdle (18-28) was replaced as manager by Jim Tracy (74-42). They faced the Phillies in the Division Series, and Cook started and won Game Two, 5-4, giving up three runs in five-plus innings of work. All three runs scored in the top of the sixth, when he allowed two singles and a double without securing an out. The two runners inherited by reliever Jose Contreras both scored, but then the bleeding was stopped and Cook got the win, the only game Colorado won in the NLDS.

In 2010 Cook started 23 games and was 6-8 (5.08), while in 2011 he had another subpar year (3-10, 6.03),

his most disappointing year, after accidentally breaking his index finger in a screen door during spring training. He said, "I couldn't pick up a baseball for four weeks after I broke my finger."[15]

The Rockies granted Cook free agency after the season. With the Rockies he had been 72-68 over the course of 10 seasons, as of 2016 second only to Jorge de la Rosa in wins among Rockies pitchers.

The Red Sox took a chance on Cook, signing him to a minor-league deal in early January 2012. The incoming Red Sox pitching coach was Bob McClure, who had tutored Cook as Cook was ascending through the minors.

After arriving in Boston, he spoke about receiving the Tony Conigliaro Award. "It was an honor to be recognized for what had happened to me and that I was able to overcome what happened to me to resume my career," Cook said. "I grew up in church, and what happened to me renewed my faith in the Lord. He got me through a challenging time in my life, and the whole experience made me stronger as a person. It's allowed me to put everything in perspective. I know what's important. I know better what things I need to worry about and what things I have no control over. But it's made me stronger. No doubt about that."[16]

With the Red Sox Cook was 4-11, 5.65, pitching in only three games before July 4. He was 3-0 in Triple-A Pawtucket, but working in the majors in what proved to be his last season in the big leagues was difficult. In his four wins combined, he allowed a total of only four earned runs, but the rest of the time he was challenged.

A free agent after the season, Cook signed with the Phillies for 2013, but was released in spring training and later signed a minor-league contract with the Rockies. With Colorado Springs he added a cutter to his repertoire, but finished 0-5 with an 8.15 ERA.

In 2014, as a free agent, Cook decided to put a hold on his career, recuperate from repeated instances of severe inflammation in his elbow, and focus on getting himself in front of major-league teams for the 2015 season. He was unable to find a team willing to take a chance.

Longtime friendships and strong faith have supported Cook. A longtime member of the Hamilton Christian Center,[17] he met his wife, Holly there, and counted as one of his best friends Curtus Moak, youth pastor at the church.[18]

Cook and Holly have three children—daughter Alexis and sons Elijah and Colton. When he realized in 2013 that retirement might be in his future, he said, "I'd be a better dad with my summers open."[19]

SOURCES

In addition to the sources mentioned in the Notes, the authors also consulted baseball-almanac.com and baseball-reference.com.

Joy dedicates this article to her father, Gary, born with cerebral palsy in the 1940s, long before he could benefit from the Americans with Disabilities Act; the ADA specifies that students with disabilities must have the same opportunities to participate in sports and activities as anyone else.

NOTES

1   Patrick Saunders, "Aaron Cook: Midwestern Success Story," *Denver Post*, July 12, 2008.

2   Ibid.

3   Ibid.

4   Ibid.

5   Baseball-almanac.com, Aaron Cook 2002 Game-by-Game Pitching Logs.

6   Alex Speier, "Outlier: Why Aaron Cook Is a Pitcher Like Few Others," WEEI.com, May 5, 2012. weei.com/sports/boston/baseball/red-sox/alex-speier/2012/05/05/outlier-why-aaron-cook-pitcher-few-others.

7   Ibid.

8   Nick Cafardo, "Cook's Story Is Stirring," *Boston Globe*, March 1, 2012: C1.

9   Irv Moss, "Colorado Classics: Aaron Cook, Colorado Rockies' Winningest Pitcher," *Denver Post*, May 28, 2013.

10   Saunders.

11   John Powers, "Game 4 Is on Cook's Menu," *Boston Globe*, October 28, 2007: F7.

12   Tyler Kepner. "Red Sox Coronation," *New York Times*, October 29, 2007: D1.

13   "National League All-Stars vs. American League All-Stars," ESPN, July 15, 2008.

14   Colorado Rockies press release, May 27, 2009.

15   Cafardo.

16   Ibid.

17   Associated Press, "Blood Clots Unable to Block Cook's Faith," ESPN, July 29, 2005. espn.com/espn/wire/_/section/mlb/id/2119671

18   Ibid.

19   Moss.

JEFF FRANCIS

BY ALEX MARKS

FOR THOSE OF YOU HAVE NEVER heard of the Magnus Force, as first described in 1852 by the German physicist Heinrich Gustav Magnus, it is a force generated by a spinning object moving through a fluid experience with a sideways deflection in its path. The force is perpendicular to the velocity vector of an object, and the resulting force (the "Magnus Force") is in the downward direction perpendicular to the direction of the air. Like the Magnus Force, pitching is all about physics: a) the most efficient transfer of momentum from body to baseball, b) the maximum effectiveness of the arm as a lever, and c) the rotational dynamics of the baseball leaving the fingertips, all within four-tenths of a second after the ball leaves the pitcher's hand. Based on this, who would have guessed that close to 155 years after the Magnus Force was discovered, a baseball pitcher from Canada who had an affection for three things in life: baseball, Canada, and of course physics, would use these passions to make his life go to the fullest.

Jeffrey William Francis was born on January 8, 1981, in Vancouver, British Columbia. When he was two weeks old, his grandfather William Francis nicknamed him Boomer (actually he was called Boomboom, then shortened to Boomer).[1] Jeffrey attended Burnsview Junior Secondary School and North Delta Senior Secondary School in North Delta, British Columbia. It was there that his good childhood friend, Gary Moraes, noticed that he had a future in physics, and in baseball. "His ball had so much movement and it would banana into me," Moraes said.[2]

After his senior year Francis played on the Canadian Junior National Team, where he went 3-1 with a 1.71 ERA. After playing for the North Delta Blue Jays of the B.C. Premier Baseball League, the highest-caliber junior league in British Columbia, Francis went undrafted and so went to the University of British Columbia. It was there that he brought his knowledge of physics into his world of baseball,

pursuing a major in physics and a minor in astronomy while playing for the UBC Thunderbirds. Jeff would constantly think about physics during his baseball career. "I think all baseball players, whether they're superstars or not, are aware of certain physical aspects of the game by just being around baseball and observing," he once said.[3]

During his sophomore year, 2001, Jeff went an impressive 13-2 with a microscopic 0.92 ERA and was named Canadian Baseball Network Player of the Year and a member of the CBN all-Canadian First Team. In his 15 starts, he had eight complete games, a 46-inning scoreless streak, 118 strikeouts in 98⅓ innings, and only 15 walks. He was also named NAIA Region I Player of the Year. In 2002, during his junior year, Francis went 7-2 with three complete games, a 1.93 ERA, and 101 whiffs in 74⅔ innings. He again earned first-team honors on the Canadian Baseball Network All-Canadian team and again made the NAIA all-region team.

After his junior year, before the June 2002 amateur draft, Francis headed north to Alaska to pitch for the Anchorage Bucs, where he threw a club-record six shutouts, finishing 7-1 with a 1.20 ERA and 83 strikeouts in 76 innings. He was named Alaska Player of the Year and was invited by the league winner, the Anchorage Pilots, to pitch in the National Baseball Congress tournament in Wichita, Kansas. He was named the tournament MVP after hurling 14 shutout innings, becoming a tournament all-star and being tabbed "best pro prospect."[4]

The Colorado Rockies originally wanted to draft outfielder Denard Span with their first-round pick in 2002, but could not reach a preliminary agreement with him before the draft. Instead the Rockies selected Francis in the first round (ninth pick overall).

In his first year of minor-league ball, Francis made three starts for the Tri-City Dust Devils (Pasco, Washington) of the low Class-A Northwest League and four starts for the Asheville Tourists of the Class-A South Atlantic League. Over the seven starts and 30⅔ innings, he had no decisions and a 1.17 ERA. His season was cut short by an injury caused by a foul ball.

In 2003, while pitching for Visalia in the Class-A California League, Francis went 12-9 in 27 starts with an ERA of 3.47 and two shutouts including a no-hitter.

Moved up to Double-A Tulsa in 2004, Francis was 13-1, a record that earned him a promotion to Triple-A Colorado Springs, where he was 3-2. Overall he had an ERA of 2.21 and 196 strikeouts in 154⅔ innings pitched. He had more strikeouts than hits (108) and walks (29) combined. Francis was named Minor League Player of the Year by both Baseball America and USA Today, becoming the first player in Rockies organization to win either of the awards and the fourth player to be honored in the same season by both publications, joining Andruw Jones (1995, '96), Rick Ankiel (1999), and Josh Beckett (2001).

The 6-foot-5, 200-pound left-hander was called up by the Rockies in August and made his major-league debut on August 25, 2004, against the Atlanta Braves, losing an 8-1 decision. He pitched five innings, allowing six runs (on three home runs), walking one and striking out eight. He earned his first major-league victory on September 5 against the San Diego Padres at Petco Park, tossing 5⅓ scoreless innings in a 5-2 game. Francis finished with a 3-2 record and a 5.15 ERA for the Rockies. Francis was unhappy that the Rockies wouldn't let him pitch for Team Canada at the 2004 Summer Olympics in Athens, where he would have been the team's number-1 starter. "Regrettably I didn't get the chance to pitch," he said in 2016. "I made it a goal to pitch for Team Canada again."[5]

Francis would soon get another chance to represent his country, when he played for Canada in the 2006 World Baseball Classic. In his only game, against Mexico, he fared poorly, retiring only four of the 11 batters he faced as Canada lost, 9-1. (Canada lost out in the second round to Mexico and the United States on run differential.)

In 2005, Francis led the also-ran Rockies (67-95, last place in the NL West) with a 14-12 record, the only pitcher with double figures in wins. But his ERA was 5.68 and his WHIP was at 1.62 as he allowed 228 hits in 183⅔ innings.

Francis finished the 2006 season with a record of 13-11 and an ERA of 4.16, more than a run lower than in 2005. On September 23 he defeated Atlanta for his 30th win with the Rockies, passing Brian Bohanon to become the left-handed pitcher with the most career wins for the team.

After the 2006 season Francis signed a four-year deal worth $13.25 million with a club option for a fifth year at $9 million. Under MLB rules, the option year would be his first year of eligibility for free agency. The contract would allow Francis and the Rockies to avoid going to arbitration every year.

For the 2007 season, Francis had a career year while leading the Rockies into the postseason for the first time since 1995. He finished the season with 17 wins while pitching over 200 innings for the first time in his career. On October 3 Francis became the first Canadian starting pitcher to win a postseason game by beating the Philadelphia Phillies, 4-2, in Game One of the National League Division Series. It was his first postseason appearance. He also won the first game of the NLCS, throwing 6⅔ innings against Arizona while allowing just one run.

On October 24 Rockies manager Clint Hurdle gave Francis the start in Game One of the World Series against the Boston Red Sox. He thus became the second Canadian starting pitcher to pitch in the World Series. He struggled, lasting only four innings and allowing six runs.[6] The Rockies lost the game, 13-1, and the Red Sox swept the Series. Although the Series did not have a happy ending for Francis, he did not let the outcome ruin his experience. "It was special to be able to be a champion," Francis said in a 2016 interview with MLB.com. "I know we didn't win it all, but that was a team that came together, even though I don't know what was expected of us. We did special things in dramatic fashion."[7]

Like many of his Rockies teammates, Francis struggled to replicate his 2007 success during the 2008 season. He finished the year with a 4-10 record and a 5.01 ERA in 24 starts, although he reported pitching through shoulder soreness for much of the season. What Francis didn't realize at the time was that because of his passion for physics, when he started to experience shoulder discomfort in mid-April, he was altering his motion and release point to adjust to the soreness. At that point, soreness and discomfort led to pain. His shoulder refused to let his arm get his fingers in the proper position on top of the ball, causing his changeup to cut instead of fade, his sinker to stop sinking, and his control to evaporate. "As much as I [would] think of throwing it the proper way, I think my body does it by itself," Francis said. "[That] summer, my body wouldn't turn the ball over because it knew it was going to hurt."[8]

Francis tried to work through the pain during the offseason and spring training, but when it did not subside, he had it looked at, and turned out he had a torn labrum. He underwent arthroscopic surgery on his left shoulder on February 25 and missed the entire 2009 season. While rehabbing, Francis found himself reverting back to his knowledge of physics. It didn't matter if he was using an upper-body ergometer while doing throwing motions, or in the pool punching forward using vented paddles, he would analyze the motions using Newton's third law.[9] But when Francis took it all out to the field, especially for throwing sessions at Coors Field, physics knowhow was no match for the subconscious pulleys that act on every pitcher.[10] Pitching in 2010 the way he once did would require months more of exercise whose physics he understood. Such is the curse of a physicist.

Francis began the 2010 season on the disabled list, but was able to get back to pitching by late May. In his first game back, he pitched seven innings, allowing two walks and seven hits in a 2-1 win over the Washington Nationals on May 16. Francis pitched in 20 games that season, posting a 4-6 record with a 5.00 ERA.

After the 2010 season the Rockies chose not to exercise Francis's option and he became a free agent. From then on his career resembled that of a typical journeyman pitcher. In January 2011 Francis agreed to a one-year contract with the Kansas City Royals for $2 million plus performance bonuses. He became Kansas City's number-two starter and led the staff in most pitching categories throughout the first half of the year.

Francis was 3-7 at home for the Royals with an ERA of 4.18, and 3-9 on the road with a 5.48 ERA, for a 6-16 record. After the season, he again became a free agent.

In January 2012, Francis agreed to a minor-league contract with the Cincinnati Reds. Assigned to Triple-A Louisville, Francis exercised a June 1 opt-out clause, and on June 8 he agreed to a major-league deal with the Rockies. The next day, he started against the Los Angeles Angels of Anaheim. Francis finished the season in the rotation with a 6-7 record and an ERA of 5.58.

Again a free agent after the season, Francis re-signed with the Rockies. He pitched half the 2013 season out of the bullpen, making only 12 starts in his 23. He finished 3-5 with an ERA of 6.27, his worst in the major leagues.

Once more a free agent, Francis signed a minor-league contract with Cincinnati for 2014 with an invitation to spring training. He started the season with Louisville and was called up on May 15. He was designated for assignment the next day after allowing San Diego three runs in five innings to pick up the loss.

On May 18 Francis was claimed off waivers by the Oakland Athletics. He was designated for assignment on July 3. On July 11 the A's traded him to the New York Yankees, who released him on August 5 after two relief appearances.

In October 2014 Francis signed a minor-league contract with the Toronto Blue Jays that included an invitation to spring training. On the eve of the 2015 season, he was assigned to Triple-A Buffalo. Called up on April 19, he made his Blue Jays debut that day, and in pitching to Russell Martin, formed the first all-Canadian battery in the Blue Jays' history. Francis was outrighted to Buffalo on May 20. On September 1 he was called up again. He made a total of 14 relief appearances for the Blue Jays in 2015.

In the summer of 2015, Francis was selected for the Canadian team in the Pan American Games, held in July in Toronto. Having not been allowed by the Rockies to play for Team Canada in the 2004 Olympic Games for fear being injured, Francis took pride in his selection. He made three appearances, including a start in the Gold Medal Game against the United States. He pitched seven innings and gave up eight hits and four earned runs, striking out seven. Canada won, 7-6 in 10 innings. As a Canadian, Francis was especially proud to have one last shot to go out as a champion. "We know how important Canada's program is, and we try to put back into it what we get out of it," he said. "We know if we can give the program notoriety, it can continue and keep producing prospects. To repeat (Pan Am Gold), and

to do it at home, was special and hopefully Canadian kids were watching."[11]

That was enough for Francis. On December 15, 2015, he announced his retirement. For his 11-year career, he won 72 games and lost 82 with an ERA of 4.97.

In January 2016, Francis was honored by Baseball Canada as the eighth member of the Baseball Canada's Wall of Excellence.

Francis and Allison Padfield were married on December 31, 2005, in London, Ontario. As of 2018 they lived in the Denver area (during the baseball season), and in London, with their daughter, Cameron (born in 2009) and son, son, Miles (2011). While the couple were expecting their first child in 2009, Jeff was still thinking about ways to introduce not only the world of baseball, but also the world of physics. "I hope my interest in physics and science is something I can pass on," he said. "If my kid doesn't like baseball, maybe that's something I can mentor them in. Now that I think about it, I just bought a mobile for the crib."[12] So what is it? Baseballs? Gloves? Bats? ..."Nope […] the solar system."[13]

After retiring as a player, Francis got involved with a number of causes, including a Wiffle Ball tournament benefiting a charity that brings used computers and other technology devices to underprivileged people in Canada.

SOURCES

In addition to the sources mentioned in the footnotes, the author also utilized baseball-reference.com.

NOTES

1   Bob Elliot, "Things to Know About Jeff Francis," *Independent Sports News*, November 12, 2014. independentsportsnews. com/2014/11/12/things-to-know-about-jeff-francis/.

2   Bob Elliot, "Ex-UBC, Blue Jays Pitcher Jeff Francis Honoured by Baseball Canada," *Vancouver Province*, June 17, 2016.

3   American Physical Society, "Jeff Francis and the Physics of Baseball," *Symmetry*, June/July 2016.

4   Bob Elliot, "Things to Know About Jeff Francis."

5   Bob Elliot, "Ex-UBC, Blue Jays Pitcher Jeff Francis Honoured by Baseball Canada."

6   Reggie Cleveland of the Boston Red Sox was the first
Canadian, when he started Game Five of the 1975 World Series
against Cincinnati.

7   "Jeff Francis Calls It a Career," Baseball Canada, December 16,
2015. baseball.ca/jeff-francis-calls-it-a-career.

8   Alan Schwarz, "While Recovering, Rockies' Francis Revels in
Physics of Pitching," *New York Times* June 27, 2009.

9   Ibid. Newton's Third Law states: For every action there is an
equal and opposite reaction.

10   Ibid.

11   Baseball Canada, "Jeff Francis Calls It a Career."

12   Alan Schwarz, "While Recovering, Rockies' Francis Revels in
Physics of Pitching."

13   Ibid.

BRIAN FUENTES

BY RYAN KEELER

WHENEVER A MAJOR-LEAGUE closer comes in for a save opportunity, the lights shine the brightest and the pressure increases immensely. Any closer will tell you that he has one of the most nerve-wracking positions in all of sports. Nobody knows about this feeling more than former pitcher and closer Brian Fuentes.

Fuentes was born in Merced, California, on August 9, 1975, coming from a Mexican-American heritage. Fuentes' father, David, was a Merced police officer and the Fuentes family has always been well admired in the town.[1] Fuentes discovered his talent when he attended Merced High School and noticed that he had a talent for pitching—the year after being cut from the team as a junior, while trying to make it as a first baseman and outfielder. "It was like the end of the world, getting cut from the team," Fuentes said. "I was really embarrassed. I'd never been cut from anything. It was a tough time, but I kind of rode it out. And I'm glad I stuck with it. I was raised not to be a quitter."[2]

After graduating from high school, Fuentes found his next path at Merced Community College, where he played three seasons for the Blue Devils. The 6-foot-4 left-handed pitcher was drafted in the 25th round of the 1995 free-agent draft, number 678 overall, by the Seattle Mariners. From 1996 through 2000, he pitched for four different teams in the Mariners' farm system.

The first team was the short-season Single-A Everett AquaSox, for whom he pitched in 13 games in 1996 with a record of 0-1 and a 4.73 ERA. In 1997 Fuentes was advanced to the Wisconsin Timber Rattlers of the low Class-A Midwest League, where he saw more playing time. Fuentes was the starting pitcher in all 22 of his games with a record of 6-7 and an ERA of 4.39.

In 1998 Fuentes moved up again, to the Lancaster JetHawks of the high-A California League. Still a starter, he was 7-7 with an ERA of 4.17 and 137 strike-

outs. Then he spent two seasons with the New Haven Ravens of the Double-A Eastern League. Over the two seasons, still a starter, he was 3-3 and 7-12, with elevated ERAs of 4.95 in 1999 and 4.51 in 2000. The 2001 season was Fuentes' final stop in the minor leagues; converted to relief duty with the Triple-A Tacoma Rainiers (Pacific Coast League). His ERA, at 2.94 in 35 games pitched (52 innings) was below 3.00 for the first time in his minor-league career. In June Fuentes was called up by the Mariners, and on June 2, 2001, he made his major-league debut, retiring two Tampa Bay Devil Rays in a brief relief appearance. After relieving in 10 games (1-1, 4.63 ERA in 11⅔ innings), Fuentes was sent back to Tacoma.

After the season Fuentes was traded to the Colorado Rockies with Jose Paniagua and Denny Stark for third baseman Jeff Cirillo. In his first four years as a major-league player, Fuentes had a record of 8-8 with a 4.04 ERA with only four saves in 163 games. The Rockies planned to make him a closer. His unusual side-arm pitching style was often confusing to hitters, and his slider was especially effective against left-handers. Between 2002 and 2004, Fuentes was shuttled back and forth between the Rockies and Triple-A Colorado Springs. In mid-May of 2005 he took over the closer role for the Rockies after Chin-hui Tsao was placed on the DL with a shoulder injury. He quickly showed enough to be selected for the National League All-Star squad, the first reliever and third pitcher in Rockies history to be named an All-Star. His 31 saves in 2005 matched Dave Veres for the third-highest single-season total, trailing only Jose Jimenez and Shawn Chacon.

In 2006 Fuentes was chosen to help represent the United States in the inaugural World Baseball Classic. "That's probably the one memory that sticks out most in my mind," he said years later. "Probably the proudest moment of my career was pitching in the World Baseball Classic. I remember that first game against Canada. To be out on that line wearing

USA on your jersey, surrounded by Hall of Famers, while the national anthem played. It was a special feeling."[3]

In 2006 Fuentes totaled 30 saves, and his performance earned him his second All-Star Game appearance. He pitched one inning, the sixth, and retired all three batters.

The 2007 season was one of negatives and positives for Fuentes. His dominance as closer started to fade in late June as he blew four saves in an eight-day period. After the fourth blown game, Fuentes was removed from the Rockies' closing role and replaced by 24-year-old Manuel Corpas. Corpas continued to close for the rest of the 2007 season and into the postseason. Perhaps because Fuentes' struggles came so close to the midsummer classic, he was named an All-Star for the third straight season. (He did not pitch in the game.)

Asked about the change in Fuentes' role, manager Clint Hurdle said, "We are going to keep him in the bullpen, but take him out of the role of closing. We just want to try and get him out of the spotlight a little bit and off the burner. We want him to reacquire his weapons and then get him back involved."[4] Hurdle said Fuentes took his demotion with class. "He took it like a pro, he's a high-character guy. He's already overcome a lot and this is a bump in the road for him. As I've told many of the players, this last week won't define them. Where he goes from here will define him."

As it turned out, Fuentes wasn't the only one being defined that season. The Rockies wound up going on a historic late-season run, winning 13 of their final 14 games of the regular season and defeating the San Diego Padres in a deciding 163rd game to determine the NL wild card. For Fuentes, his appearance in this game was a frustrating one. He struggled with his command in the bottom of the eighth inning, giving up the tying run on two hits. The Rockies eventually won the game in the bottom of the 13th inning, giving the franchise its second playoff berth.

Fuentes' struggles still lingered but for the first time in his career he was playing in the postseason. He started strong in the Division Series against Philadelphia. In a three-game sweep of the Phillies, Fuentes worked in all three games, was the winner in the deciding game. In 2⅓ innings pitched in the series, he gave up one hit and struck out four.

In the National League Championship Series against Arizona, Fuentes also worked in every game of the four-game sweep, throwing one scoreless inning in each of the first three games. After working six consecutive games without allowing a run, he gave up a three-run homer to the Diamondbacks' Chris Snyder in Game Four. After a triple followed the homer, Fuentes was lifted for Corpas, and the Rockies held on to win, 6-4. Fuentes earned holds in Games Two and Three.

In the Boston Red Sox' World Series sweep of the Rockies, Fuentes pitched two scoreless innings in Game Two, helping keep the game close; the Rockies lost, 2-1. The Red Sox held a 6-5 lead in Game Three; Fuentes gave up three runs. In Game Four, the Red Sox held a 3-1 lead after seven innings. Fuentes was called from the bullpen to hold the lead, but surrendered a leadoff homer to Bobby Kielty. Though the Rockies rallied for two in the bottom of the eighth, the Red Sox won. Aaron Cook was the losing pitcher.

The season hadn't ended the way Colorado and Fuentes wanted, but the Rockies were National League champions and had capped off a season of epic proportions.

About a month into the 2008 season, Fuentes regained the closing role. Corpas had been losing velocity and struggling with inconsistency, and the Rockies felt it was time to make Fuentes the closer again. From April 24 to the end of the season, Fuentes racked up 30 saves.

Fuentes, now 33 years old, chose free agency after the 2008 season and took a two-year, $17.5 million deal with the Los Angeles Angels of Anaheim.[5] Fuentes left the Rockies as their career saves leader (115) and leader in strikeouts by a reliever as well. "It was a great experience all the way around," he said of his seven years in Colorado. "I was fortunate to have the opportunity to pitch quite a bit and work my way up. I'm definitely happy to have the opportunity to play for a team that I've watched for a long time."[6]

As for his role with the Angels, general manager Tony Reagins committed to stick with Fuentes as his closer while players Scot Shields and Jose Arredondo would take on the seventh- and eighth-inning roles. Former teammates Darren Oliver and Justin Speier were also on the Angels roster. "It's going to be nice to have a little bit of a comfort zone," said Fuentes.[7]

Fuentes led the American League with 48 saves in 2009. He was picked for the All-Star Game for the fourth time. The Angels were champions of the AL West Division and swept the Red Sox in three games in the Division Series. Fuentes got saves in Games Two and Three, pitching 1⅔ hitless innings. The Angels lost the ALCS to the New York Yankees in six games. Fuentes pitched in three of the games and got a save in Game Five. All told, he gave up one hit and one run in three innings of work.

The following year, 2010, was a different story as Fuentes struggled with his command. Manager Mike Scioscia had to call upon other relievers to help

spell Fuentes late in games. In late August he was traded to the Minnesota Twins for a minor leaguer. Because the Twins already had a reliable closer in Matt Capps, manager Ron Gardenhire made Fuentes the eighth-inning setup man. Gardenhire said, "It's a positive whenever you can acquire a player of his caliber, a closer from another team, to help fill out your bullpen. We knew he was out there, and as all players go through waivers, we put in a claim for him along with everyone else. We got to him first, and he got to us."[8]

As for Fuentes, the trade brought a sense of comfort and relief. Of his Angels experience, he said, "It was funny. I felt like I was pitching on the road quite a bit. I came in to a lot of boos, but the fans here come out in droves. They're here to be entertained. They're entertained one way or another, through my frustrations or through my success. I felt like I've given them a lot more success than failure."[9]

Fuentes pitched in 9⅔ innings for the Twins in September as they wrapped up the AL Central Division title. They were swept by the Yankees in three games in the Division Series. Fuentes pitched in two of the games, giving up one hit in 2⅔ innings.

Once again Fuentes was on the move when he signed as a free agent with the Oakland Athletics for 2012 and was demoted from being a closer. Released in July, he pitched briefly for the St. Louis Cardinals. (He requested time off in August for personal reasons.) He retired after the season. In the major leagues he had 26 wins and 43 losses, with 204 saves and a 3.62 ERA. He was a four-time All-Star.

As of 2017 Fuentes lived in his hometown, Merced, with his wife and four children.

SOURCES

In addition to the sources cited in the Notes, the author consulted Baseball-Reference.com.

NOTES

1   Susan Slusser, "Brian Fuentes: From a Modest Start to Bold Relief," *SF Gate*, March 8, 2011, sfgate.com/athletics/article/Brian-Fuentes-From-a-modest-start-to-bold-relief-2456206.php.

2   Ibid.

3   Sean Lynch, "Merced's Fuentes Announces Retirement from Baseball," *Merced* (California) *Sun-Star*, November 14, 2012. mercedsunstar.com/news/local/article3271946.html#storylink=cpy.

4   Patrick Saunders, "Fuentes Out as Rockies Closer," June 30, 2007. denverpost.com/2007/06/30/fuentes-out-as-rockies-closer/Notes.

5   Associated Press, "Angels Agree to Terms With Brian Fuentes," ESPN.com, December 31, 2008, espn.com/espn/wire/_/section/mlb/id/3802383.

6   Ibid.

7   Ibid.

8   Mark Saxon, "Twins Get Angels LHP Brian Fuentes." ESPN.com, August 28, 2010, espn.com/mlb/news/story?id=5504887.

9   Ibid.

ANDRES GALARRAGA

BY BRIAN WERNER

ANDRES JOSE PADOVANI GALARRAGA was known as the Big Cat, or El Gato Grande, during his 19-year major-league baseball career, a career in which he became the Colorado Rockies' first big star. He looked like a slugger but what made him so popular, and helped secure his nickname, was his quickness around the first-base bag. Along the way he helped establish the Rockies' tradition of great infield defense.

Galarraga was the first of the "Blake Street Bombers" and one of the key reasons the Rockies established a major-league record for attendance during their first year and by year three were in the playoffs.

During his big-league career, he hit 399 home runs, became a five-time All-Star, two-time Gold Glove winner, and two-time Comeback Player of the Year. Most importantly, Galarraga is a two-time cancer survivor.

When his career ended in 2005, after a brief stint with the New York Mets in spring training, he had hit more home runs than any native Venezuelan (since broken by Miguel Cabrera) and was considered a national hero in his native land.[1]

Andres Galarraga was born June 18, 1961, in the capital city of Caracas. His father, Francisco Padovani, was an Italian immigrant who painted houses for a living, while his mother, Juana, helped raise his three brothers and one sister. Orlando, Alfonso, Francisco, and sister Haide were Andres' siblings.[2]

Andres played sandlot ball growing up until the age of 16, when he began playing professional ball in the Venezuelan winter league. He began his career as a third baseman and catcher. It was there in 1979 that Felipe Alou first saw him play and, after getting over his "chubbiness," recommended to Montreal farm director Jim Fanning that the Expos sign him.[3]

The signing is an interesting story. According to an Alou recollection, he was friends with the Caracas manager, Oscar Minaya.[4] He brought a rooster to give him as a present and in return Oscar told him about this player named Andres Galarraga. Alou watched him play and proceeded to call Fanning and recommend signing the young slugger. Fanning balked at the $10,000 figure Alou gave him, and while there is some discrepancy over how much Galarraga actually signed for—either $5,000 (per Alou's memory) or $1,500 according to most other reports—the Expos had him under contract as an amateur free agent.[5]

He was given the moniker "Big Cat" by his manager (and former big leaguer) Bob Bailey while playing Rookie League ball at Calgary in 1979, for his cat-like quickness and agility around the first-base bag.[6] He stood 6-feet-3 and listed at 235 pounds.

Galarraga's first impression of the United States was not all that favorable and he experienced many of the same frustrations other Latino ballplayers do when arriving in the country for the first time. According to Bob Kravitz, Andres didn't speak a lick of English when he arrived in West Palm Beach.[7] In an interview with Kravitz years later, Galarraga remembered he was so homesick when he first arrived that he wanted to call his parents every day but only had the money to do so on a weekly basis. He was also the only Latino on his teams in Calgary and at Jamestown in the Class-A New York-Penn League.

Galarraga's road to English understanding mimicked many other Latin players' efforts in adapting to a new country and a strange language. He watched TV and he read the dictionary and newspapers to understand the language. According to Jill Leiber, Galarraga had the TV on 24 hours a day to learn English.[8] He recalled the frustration with simple day-to-day tasks such as ordering food from a menu in an American restaurant where he and his fellow Latinos had to simply point at the item to order it.

Future big leaguer Randy St. Claire was a teammate of Galarraga's at Jamestown and also helped with his English.[9]

Perhaps because of these cultural adjustments, Galarraga's career did not get off to a rousing start. In fact, he was so bad in his first professional appearance in West Palm Beach that he was demoted to Rookie League Calgary during his first professional season. He stayed in Calgary until he was promoted to the Expos' low Single-A club in Jamestown, New York, for the 1981 season.

He was back in West Palm Beach and high Single-A ball for the 1982-83 seasons before being promoted to Double-A Jacksonville in 1984. There he became the Southern League's Most Valuable Player by hitting .289 with 27 home runs and 87 RBIs. He had now also established himself as a full-time first baseman. He was promoted to Montreal's top farm club at Triple-A Indianapolis in 1985 and was named the International League's Rookie of the Year. He hit .269 with 25 homers and had 85 RBIs before being promoted to Montreal in August.

Galarraga made his major-league debut on August 23, 1985. Getting into 24 games that first year, he hit .187 with 2 home runs and 4 RBIs.

His official rookie year, 1986, was off to a promising start but he injured a knee that required arthroscopic surgery. Later in the season he also pulled a rib-cage muscle. Despite the injuries, he played in 105 games and slugged 10 home runs.

Galarraga's career took off in 1987 when he played a full season, batted.300 for the first time (.305), knocked in 90 runs and finished second in the NL with 40 doubles. The next year he fully blossomed with his first All-Star berth while being named the Expos Player of the Year. He hit .302 with 29 home runs, 92 RBIs, and 99 runs scored while leading the league in hits (184) and doubles (42).

That was to be Galarraga's high point for the Expos as he suffered through injuries and a lack of production while leading the league in strikeouts for three consecutive years (1988-90). After knee surgery again during the 1991 season and the worst batting average of his career (.219) outside of his 1985 season, he was traded in November to the St. Louis Cardinals for pitcher Ken Hill.

The 1992 season started miserably as Galarraga broke his wrist in the second game of the year. When he returned from the injury he hit only .243 with 10 home runs and 39 RBIs. He did, however, meet the man who was to transform his game and his batting approach: St. Louis hitting coach Don Baylor. Baylor liked Galarraga and when he became the Colorado Rockies' first manager for their inaugural 1993 season, he persuaded team ownership to sign the player as a free agent following his release by the Cardinals.

Toward the end of Galarraga's tenure in St. Louis, Baylor got him to alter his batting stance. This transformed Galarraga's career: He hit .301 over his last 45 games. His stance was soon to be recognizable by baseball fans everywhere for its unconventionality. Baylor persuaded Galarraga to stand so that both eyes were facing the pitcher and then stride into the pitch from that stance.[10]

Galarraga signed as the Rockies' first free agent on November 16, 1992, one day prior to the expansion draft that produced the team's first-ever roster. With him coming off two subpar seasons in succession, the Rockies were able to sign Galarraga for a mere $600,000, probably the team's best-ever free-agent signing. Galarraga's 1993 contract included $250,000 in incentives, bringing his total to $850,000.[11]

Galarraga was 31 years old and his career was about to take off as he became an immediate fan favorite in the Rockies' inaugural season. He was the cleanup hitter for the Rockies' first game, against the New York Mets on April 5, 1993. It was the first of five consecutive Opening Day starts for the Big Cat as a member of the Rockies. With his new open stance paying huge dividends, Galarraga flirted with .400 for much of the season. He was hitting .391 at the All-Star break and became the Rockies' first participant in the midsummer classic.

He ended the season with a major-league-leading .370 batting average. He knocked in 98 runs, hit 22 home runs, and finished with a 1.005 OPS, the best of his career, all of this despite missing 42 games with two stints on the disabled list. During his second DL stint, the Rockies lost a team-record 13 consecutive games, a record that still stood as of 2018.[12]

His .370 batting average was the highest by a right-handed hitter since Joe DiMaggio hit .381 in 1939.[13] Galarraga was named the Comeback Player of the Year (the first of two such selections in his career) by *The Sporting News* and finished 10th in MVP voting.

Galarraga underwent yet another knee surgery during the offseason, but also capitalized on his 1993 year by signing a $12 million, four-year contract in December 1993. With incentives and bonuses, Galarraga eventually made $17.2 million over the course of the next four years.[14]

During the Rockies' second season, which was cut short at midseason by the players strike, Galarraga had an April to remember. He drove in 30 runs during the month, a National League record that Barry Bonds was to break two years later. But he broke his hand on July 28 and when the strike began on August 12, his season was over. He did lead the Rockies in home runs with 31, hit .319, and knocked in 85 runs while playing in only 103 games.

The 1995 season was to be one of the most memorable in Rockies history with the opening of Coors Field in a renovated area of downtown Denver known as LODO, for lower downtown. Galarraga played a key role in the Rockies' playoff push culminating in their first appearance in postseason play.

He was also healthy for a full season for the first time in four years and produced again with a .280 average, 31 home runs, and 106 RBIs. Galarraga also led the league in strikeouts (146) for the fourth and last time in his career.

He became part of the Blake Street Bombers that year, a reference to the location of Coors Field at the corner of 20th and Blake. The Bombers consisted of Galarraga, Larry Walker, Vinny Castilla, Dante Bichette, and Ellis Burks. In 1995 Galarraga, Bichette, Walker, and Castilla made major-league history and tied the 1977 Dodgers with four players on a team hitting 30 or more homers in the same season.

Galarraga also made more major-league history that year by hitting home runs in three consecutive innings against San Diego on June 23 to tie a National League record. Two weeks later he went 6-for-6 with two home runs and five RBIs against Houston on July 3.[15] (His six hits in a game for the Rockies were matched by Charlie Blackmon in 2014.)

The Rockies lost to eventual World Series champion Atlanta Braves in the Division Series.

The next year Galarraga led the NL in homers with 47 and RBIs with 150. He stroked 39 doubles and had a slugging percentage of .601 while playing in 159 games, the most of his career.

The 1997 season was Galarraga's last in Colorado. He went out with a flourish, leading the NL again in RBIs with 140, scoring 120 runs (the most of his career) and being named to his third All-Star team.

Galarraga hit the most famous of his many home runs, a grand slam, on May 31, 1997, off the Marlins' Kevin Brown at Pro Player Stadium in Miami. There is no doubt where he hit the ball—it landed 20 rows up in the upper deck on a blue tarp in a closed-off section—and while initial estimates put the distance at 573 feet, it was later recalculated at 529 feet and then recalibrated 14 years later using ESPN's Home Run Tracker at 468 feet.[16] However, a recent exhaustive study of the home run by Jose Lopez and others has seemingly answered the question once and for all. Lopez and his fellow authors used the latest LIDAR technology along with a 3D mathematical model to determine that his mammoth shot probably traveled 524 feet, making it "one of the few hit prior to Statcast proven to have exceed the 500-foot distance in the history of MLB."[17]

With young prospect Todd Helton on the horizon, the Rockies said goodbye to the Big Cat after the 1997 season. He signed with Atlanta in November and earned more than $25 million during the next three years with the Braves.

His initial season with the Braves saw him play in 153 games, hit .305, knock in 121 runs, and hit 44 homers. He made the All-Star team for the fourth time. He became the first major leaguer to hit 40 home runs in two consecutive seasons for different teams.

The 1999 season was a nightmare for the Big Cat. He missed the entire season after being diagnosed with non-Hodgkin's lymphoma in spring training. It had settled into his lower back on the second lumbar vertebra. He went through five months of chemotherapy and radiation. Yet he was determined to play baseball again and went through a rigorous rehabilitation routine at the Powerhouse Gym in West Palm Beach, where he lived in the offseason.[18] It was successful and he was back to playing baseball in the spring of 2000.

In the Braves' first game he hit the game-winning home run in the seventh inning and also provided a game-saving defensive gem in Greg Maddux's 2-0 win. He played in 141 games in his comeback season and received his second Comeback Player of the Year Award by hitting .302 with 28 home runs and 100 RBIs.

After the 2000 season Galarraga asked the Braves for a two-year contract. They offered only a one-year deal and Galarraga switched leagues for the first time in his career by signing with the Texas Rangers.

His did not adapt to the American League well and, with star Rafael Palmeiro a fixture at first base, he mostly DHed and pinch-hit. After 72 games and with a .235 batting average, 10 home runs, and 34 RBIs, the Rangers traded Galarraga back to the NL and the San Francisco Giants on July 24. He finished the season with the Giants playing in 49 games and hitting .288 with 7 more homers and 35 more RBIs.

A free agent again after the season, Galarraga signed with his original team, the Montreal Expos, in the spring of 2002. At 41 years old, he played in 104 games for the Expos and saw a decline in his batting numbers. He hit 9 homers, knocked in 40 runs, and batted .260.

The decline had begun and, although he managed to hang on and play 110 games with San Francisco in 2003, Galarraga was never again the player he was before going to the American League. He hit a respectable .301 with the Giants but his power numbers were fading. He hit 12 home runs with 42 RBIs in his last full season in the majors.

After the season, Galarraga once again faced cancer. After being diagnosed with the same form of non-Hodgkin's lymphoma in November, he spent most of January 2004 at the Robert H. Lurie Comprehensive Cancer Center at Northwestern University. He went through a stem-cell transplant and chemotherapy and radiation again.[19]

Not wanting to give up his baseball career yet, Galarraga battled back from his second bout with cancer and signed a contract with the Anaheim Angels' minor-league club in Salt Lake City. He was called up to the Angels when rosters expanded on September 1. He hit his final major-league home run, the 399th of his career, while getting 10 at-bats. His last major-league appearance came on October 3, 2004, 19 years after his first major-league game.

The next season Galarraga, at 43 years old, was invited to the New York Mets' spring training. Realizing it was the end of a long and productive career, he retired officially on March 29, 2005.[20]

Galarraga's final career numbers are impressive. He finished with a .288 career average, 399 home runs, and 1,425 RBIs. He had 444 doubles, 32 triples, and 128 stolen bases—not bad for someone once considered too chubby to play professional baseball.

Galarraga and his wife, Eneyda, whom he married on Valentine's Day 1984, took up residence in West Palm Beach after his retirement. They have three children. Katherine, Andria and Andrianna.

SOURCES

In addition to the sources cited in the Notes, the author also consulted Baseball-Reference.com and the following:

Beaton, Rod. "Galarraga Says Support Makes Me Feel So Strong," *USA Today*, March 18, 1999.

Heyman, Jon. "Big Cat's Doggedness Provides Inspiration," Newsday.com, January 14, 2005.

MacDonald, Ian. "Cooperstown Bound?" *The Sporting News*, July 4, 1988.

Price, S.L. "Cat and Mouth Game," *Sports Illustrated*, March 13, 2000.

Saunders, Patrick. "Andres 'Big Cat' Galarraga Still a Big Hit in Denver," *Denver Post*, June 5, 2013.

Tucker, Tim. "Even Schuerholz, Kasten Are Moved by Galarraga," *Atlanta Journal Constitution*, April 4, 2000.

Vecsey, George. "Sports of the Times; Galarraga Brought Angels to the Gym," *New York Times*, June 28, 2000.

York, Marty. "Expos' Unknown Superstar," *Globe and Mail* (Toronto), June 10, 1988.

NOTES

1   Carlos Frias, "Beloved Big Cat," *Atlanta Constitution*, February 6, 2000.

2   Bob Kravitz, "Rocky Mountain High: Colorado Fans are Seeing Galarraga at His Peak," *Houston Chronicle*, June 27, 1993.

3   Felipe Alou, "Fat Cat Is Big Hit at Third in Venezuela," *Rocky Mountain News* (Denver), September 25, 2003.

4   Michael Farber, "Cat Quick," *Sports Illustrated*, June 2, 1997.

5   Jill Leiber, "The Big Cat," *USA Today*, August 27, 1998.

6   Farber.

7   Kravitz.

8   Leiber.

9   Kravitz.

10 Farber.

11 Doug Pappas, Baseball Reference website/SABR; John Mossman, "Galarraga Re-Signs with Rockies," *Deseret News* (Salt Lake City), December 7, 1993.

12 Mossman.

13 Morris Eckhouse, "The Ballplayers: Andres Galarraga," Baseball Library.com.

14 Mossman, and Pappas.

15 Owen Perkins, "Rox Reflect Fondly on Blake Street Bombers," special to MLB.com, October 19, 2007.

16 Patrick Saunders, "Rockies Legend Andres Galarraga Talks About His Famous Homer vs. Marlins," *Denver Post*, June 13, 2015.

17 Jose L. Lopez, Oscar A. Lopez, Elizabeth Raven and Adrian Lopez, "Analysis of Andres Galarraga's Home Run of May 31, 1997," *Baseball Research Journal*, 46 (2), (2017): 83-90.

18 Tracy Ringolsby, "Galarraga Diagnosed With Cancerous Tumor," *Rocky Mountain News* (Denver), February 19, 1999; Frias.

19 George Vecsey, "The Princely Smile Says Galarraga, the Big Cat, Is Back," *New York Times*, February 16, 2004.

20 Pat Borzi, "Galarraga Decides to Retire to Spare the Mets Some Angst," *New York Times*, March 30, 2005.

BOB GEBHARD

BY PAUL PARKER

BOB GEBHARD, THE MAN WHO became the first general manager in the history of the Colorado Rockies, emerged from modest working-class roots in rural Minnesota.[1]

Born on January 3, 1943, Gebhard grew up in Lamberton, population 1,100, about 150 miles southwest of Minneapolis. He is of German and Scandinavian heritage, and his family has called Minnesota home for several generations.

Bob's father, Leo, was the local barber in Lamberton, and his mother, Viola (Albertson), served as head cook at Lamberton High School. His sister, Leola, was four years older.

Gebhard grew into a very talented athlete at Lamberton High, earning 16 varsity letters in football, basketball, track and field, and baseball. By the time he graduated in 1961, Bob had filled out into a strapping young man at 6-feet-2 and 210 pounds. He decided to accept an athletic scholarship to the University of Iowa.

At Iowa, Gebhard was a two-sport athlete, playing three seasons of basketball for the Hawkeyes and four seasons of baseball, serving as captain of the baseball team his senior year. Bob completed his undergraduate studies in January of 1966, receiving a bachelor of science degree in recreation. He studied for a time at Mankato State, now Minnesota State, and earned another bachelor's degree in physical education and math.

The previous summer, in June of 1965, the first-ever draft of amateur players was conducted by major-league baseball. Rick Monday, an outfielder at Arizona State, was selected first overall by the Kansas City Athletics. Back in the 44th round, Bob Gebhard, a right-handed pitcher out of the University of Iowa, was picked by the Minnesota Twins at number 732 overall.

During college, Bob had a student deferment as the Vietnam War heated up. He later completed his military obligation by serving in the Minnesota National Guard.

Gebhard began his professional baseball career with the short-season St. Cloud Rox of the Northern League. Over the next six years he made his way up the ladder in the Twins' minor-league system. For players, this is not ordinarily a straight climb, and Bob was no exception.

As he hurled for a variety of teams in the Southern, Carolina, and Pacific Coast Leagues, and the American Association, Gebhard's high-water marks included an 11-2/1.91 ERA in 1965 for Class-A St. Cloud, 13-3/1.23 for Double-A Charlotte in 1969, and an 8-3 record with a 4.02 ERA for Triple-A Portland in 1971. His PCL performance for Portland earned Gebhard a promotion to the big leagues, and on August 2, 1971, Gebhard made his major-league debut for the Minnesota Twins. At the age of 28, Gebhard pitched two scoreless innings against the Chicago White Sox.

He stuck with the Twins the rest of the season and throughout the entire 1972 season, but 1973 found him back in Triple A, hurling for Tacoma. In the offseason, he was released by Minnesota. On January 14, 1974, he signed as a free agent with the Montreal Expos.

Gebhard was briefly with the parent Expos team in 1974, but spent the bulk of the year toiling as a player-coach for the Memphis Blues, their Triple-A affiliate, posting a 10-6 record with a sterling 1.69 ERA. One more go-round as a player for Gebhard in 1975, going 4-3/2.67 for Memphis, and at 32 Bob Gebhard decided it was time to make the transition in his baseball life from player to coach and administrator.

Montreal judged in 1976 that Gebhard, now a retired pitcher of 33, showed significant potential as an administrator and offered him a position as minor-league field director and roving pitching coach. Gebhard served the Expos in that capacity for five years through 1980, honing his instructing proficiencies as well as his interpersonal skills.

Paying his dues in the minors finally paid off for Gebhard in 1981 when the Expos, undergoing a midyear shakeup under general manager John McHale, elevated him to pitching coach with the major-league team. He continued in that position through the 1982 season and then was named director of minor league clubs, a position he held for the following four years, 1983-1986.

Returning to the team he made his major-league debut with, Gebhard, then 44, rejoined the Minnesota Twins as director of major league personnel in 1987, adding the title of vice president a year later. Twice during his tenure with Minnesota (1987, 1991), the Twins captured World Series championships.

The Colorado Rockies were born on July 5, 1991, being named one of two National League expansion franchises, the other being the Florida Marlins. With major-league action slated to begin for the expansionists in the 1993 season, the new Rockies organization wasted little time in selecting a general manager. In September 1991, Colorado named Bob Gebhard senior vice president/general manager.

The Rockies had less than two years between the awarding of the franchise and the beginning of major-league play. The first order of business was building a minor-league system and creating an administrative staff.

Gebhard first built a scouting staff, picking Pat Daugherty as the Rockies' first director of scouting. Together, along with a rapidly growing scouting department, Gebhard and Daugherty became known as "the road warriors," scouting all 26 existing major-league teams during the 1992 season in preparation for the expansion draft, which was to take place on November 17, 1992.[2]

At the conclusion of the baseball season and before the draft, it was time to name a field manager. Gebhard chose longtime player and coach Don Baylor to lead the Rockies in their inaugural year. Baylor and Gebhard had crossed paths briefly during their championship season in Minnesota in 1987, but Baylor left a lasting impression on his future boss. "I

used to watch him in the clubhouse," Gebhard later recalled. "He was only with us for six weeks, but our players would go up to him for advice. I never forgot what I saw."

Don Baylor had spent the 1992 season as hitting coach for the St. Louis Cardinals. During that season the Cardinals had journeyman first baseman Andres Galarraga on the roster. Galarraga had enjoyed several productive years in Montreal, but by 1992 he seemed to be on the downside of his career and was holding on to stay in the majors. Hitting coach Baylor went to work on "The Big Cat," completely rebuilding Galarraga's swing to an almost exaggeratedly open stance.

Galarraga's numbers for 1992 were unimpressive, and after the season he became a free agent. But Baylor knew what talent was there after working diligently with Andres, and shared this with his new boss in Colorado, Bob Gebhard. So the stage was set for the Rockies to grab Galarraga, and on the day before the expansion draft, November 16, 1992, Gebhard signed Galarraga.

The Inaugural Year Rockies had their first baseman locked up, and all Galarraga did to reward his new team was play stellar defense and win the National League batting title, swinging at a .370 clip.

For three weeks before the expansion draft the Rockies brain trust was sequestered at the team's offices on Broadway in Denver. The principal decision makers were Gebhard, Pat Daugherty, John McHale Jr., Randy Smith, Paul Egins, Herb Hippauf, Don

Baylor, and Dick Balderson. They analyzed every player on every existing major-league roster and ranked them in order of desirability for each position, using age, talent, contract status, sign-ability, and trade-ability as criteria. But it was not until November 7, 10 days before the draft, that Major League Baseball made available to Florida and Colorado the list of protected players from all the other clubs.

Each existing franchise could protect 15 players during the first round of the draft. In each subsequent round, they could then pull back additional players from the selection process for protection. Both before and after the protected list was made available to the Rockies, there was much guesstimating involved. As soon as the process began, picked players came off the board and altered the selection strategy. Gebhard and the Rockies would need to adapt their thinking on the fly. Colorado won a coin toss and selected first.

With the first pick the Rockies went with David Nied from the Atlanta Braves. The tall right-handed pitcher from the Dallas-Fort Worth area had been a late-season callup to the Braves at the end of the 1992 season, and went 3-0. But with the likes of Greg Maddux, John Smoltz, Tom Glavine, and Steve Avery already on the roster, Nied was left unprotected for the expansion draft, and Colorado snapped him up.

Gebhard and his team selected journeyman third baseman Charlie Hayes from the New York Yankees with their second pick, Milwaukee reliever Darren Holmes with their third, and Jerald Clark of the San Diego Padres with their fourth.

Before the draft Gebhard had decided he needed a power-hitting right-handed-hitting outfielder, and had coveted the Brewers' Dante Bichette. The trouble was that Bichette was on the Brewers' protected list, so Gebhard turned to an old friend, Sal Bando, who was the Milwaukee general manager at the time. Gebhard asked Bando what he was in the market for, and Sal didn't hesitate. If the Rockies could secure a left-handed-hitting designated hitter, the Brewers would be willing to part with Bichette. With their fifth pick Colorado selected Kevin Reimer from

Texas, and then swapped him to Milwaukee for Bichette. The deal was consummated on Draft Day.

Other notable Rockies picks from the first round of the draft included Eric Young Sr., an infielder from the Los Angeles Dodgers who would secure his place in Rockies history during the 1993 home opener, and future New York Yankees manager Joe Girardi, a catcher selected from the Chicago Cubs.

The second round provided 1993 starting shortstop Freddie Benavides from Cincinnati and starting third baseman Vinny Castilla from Atlanta. The Rockies also picked Detroit's Kevin Ritz in the second round. Ritz would go on to become a 17-game winner for the Rockies in 1996.

With their participation in the amateur draft in June 1992 and their harvest during the expansion draft, the Rockies had the personnel to fill the first spring-training roster. After considerable research, Tucson, Arizona, was selected as the site for spring drills. The Rockies took over Hi Corbett Field in Tucson, where the Cleveland Indians had trained since 1947. The Tribe pulled up stakes in Arizona and set up their spring camp in Winter Haven, Florida, in 1993.

With an expansion team just starting out, everything and everybody was new. Gebhard arrived in Tucson to find the practice fields badly in need of work, and the day before the first workout found Gebhard doing manual labor with his new coaching staff. Don Zimmer, Larry Bearnarth, Ron Hassey, and Amos Otis, along with Gebhard and Don Baylor, all grabbed shovels and were working on pitching mounds 24 hours before the first Rockies team trotted out into the Arizona sun.

When the new Rockies did arrive they were a mixture of veterans and rookies, but few knew one another. To help break the ice and bring some levity to camp "Hello, my name is ————." name tags were distributed to all. It seemed to help mold the group into a real ballclub over the next six weeks.

On April 5, 1993, Bob Gebhard was ready to present his first major-league team to baseball. Although their debut was inauspicious, with Colorado getting shut out, 3-0 at the hands of the Mets' Dwight

Gooden at Shea Stadium in New York, they were underway: the Rocky Mountain region was now part of the major-league baseball fraternity, and Bob Gebhard was the principal architect.

The Rockies came home to Denver for the inaugural home opener on April 9, 1993. It was a spectacular day in many ways. The Rocky Mountain region, starved for major-league baseball for so many years, turned out in record fashion. The first game in Denver drew 80,227 to Mile High Stadium, still a major-league record for a home opener.

In the bottom of the first, in the first at-bat of a Rockie on Colorado soil, Eric Young electrified an already energetic crowd with a solo home run. The home team went on to notch an 11-4 win over the visiting Montreal Expos.

The Rockies went on to draw 4,483,350 in their first year, also an attendance record that as of 2018 still stood.

The parent club was now supported by the minor-league system Gebhard had developed, with the Triple-A affiliate Sky Sox down the road from Denver in Colorado Springs, in the Pacific Coast League, the New Haven Ravens the Double-A team in the Eastern League (starting in 1994), and Single-A squads in Visalia, California, and Asheville, North Carolina.

That first big-league season in 1993 was typical of expansion franchises. After enduring a 13-game losing streak in midsummer, the Rockies' main goal was avoiding 100 losses. They accomplished it, posting a 67-95 mark.

Bob Gebhard did much that was right in his eight years as general manager of the Colorado Rockies. But by his own admission, his worst move came during that first major-league season of 1993. He, along with others in the front office, had been impressed with San Diego Padres right-hander Greg Harris. A midseason trade made Harris a Rockie. But Harris struggled once he reached the Mile High City, and never did get on track; his 4-20 record while with the club remains one of the low points in franchise history.

The 1994 season started with considerable optimism, as most baseball seasons do. The Rockies were on pace to break their own record for single-season attendance. But the storm clouds of a strike in baseball soon began to gather. The season came to a screeching halt after the games of August 11, and for the first time in 90 years the World Series was canceled.

Like everyone else in the game, Bob Gebhard was very upset. On top of the aborted season, the Rockies were scheduled to move into their new home, Coors Field, for the 1995 season. Uncertainty abounded as the strike dragged on through the winter. Eventually, the owners decided to proceed with replacement players, pleasing almost no one. Mercifully, a settlement in the dispute was reached in time for an abbreviated spring training for the "real" players, but it dictated that the regular season be only 144 games in 1995.

That year Colorado became the first National League team to win the wild card in the new playoff format. In just their third season the Rockies became the fastest expansion team to reach the postseason, up until that point, a fact that provided Gebhard with much pride. He had created a competitive team from scratch and was duly rewarded for his efforts.

One of Bob Gebhard's more notable achievements while general manager in Colorado came away from major-league action. One day he was waiting in his car near some ballfields for a meeting to begin. He noticed seven or eight kids playing catch and hitting fly balls to one another. After a short time a group of older kids came by and simply chased the younger kids from the field and took over. Gebhard thought to himself: "Hey, why aren't there enough fields in the Denver area to accommodate all the kids that want to use them?"

This experience gave rise to Gebhard's idea of building new fields or refurbishing existing ones and financing the project through discretionary community money written right into the contracts of Rockies players. The Field of Dreams Program was started in 1995 and as of 2018 consisted of 55 fields spread around the Denver area, the Colorado Front

Range, the Western Slope, and Wyoming. It proved to be so successful and impactful that within a few years the Los Angeles Dodgers, St. Louis Cardinals, and San Diego Padres had started fields programs of their own, using the Rockies program as a model.

After the eventful season of 1995, when the Rockies moved into their new Coors Field home and reached the postseason, 1996, 1997, and 1998 turned out to be less than satisfying years for the team. Gebhard always believed the Rockies had the makings of a good team during that stretch, but underperformed.

After the disappointment of the 1998 season, Gebhard was faced with making what he termed "the most difficult decision of my life." After taking a chance on a previously inexperienced manager to launch the franchise, it was time to let Don Baylor go. Gebhard was also aware that Jim Leyland, a longtime baseball man he admired, was available, and so Gebhard made the change.

But despite the managerial switch, 1999 was another down year for Colorado, and this time it was Gebhard's turn to part ways with the Rockies. The ax fell on August 20. Gebhard was replaced as general manager in September by longtime Orioles and Indians executive Dan O'Dowd.

Gebhard was very well connected and respected throughout the game, and within a few days of his Colorado dismissal he had been contacted with offers on the table by Chicago Cubs President Andy McPhail, St. Louis Cardinals general manager Walt Jocketty, and Minnesota Twins GM Terry Ryan. On September 1, 1999, he became special assistant to Jocketty, a man who had earlier worked for Gebhard in Denver. It was a position he was to hold for the next five years, through 2004.

Late in the 2004 season Arizona general manager Joe Garagiola Jr. called Jocketty in St. Louis to ask permission to talk to Gebhard about a position with the Diamondbacks that Garagiola considered an upgrade. In October 2004, Gebhard became vice president and special assistant to Garagiola in Arizona. When a vacancy occurred with the Diamondbacks GM position in July of 2005, Gebhard was installed as interim GM until Josh Byrnes was hired as permanent GM in October of that year. Gebhard then returned to his previous job.

Gebhard was to stay in Phoenix with the Diamondbacks until October 2016, when he made his return to the Cardinals in a similar capacity. In the small universe of major-league baseball, Bob Gebhard was lured out of Arizona by John Mozeliak, who years earlier had been a clubhouse employee under Gebhard with the Rockies. Gebhard related that Mozeliak had a standing offer to him: "When you get tired of the desert, call me."[3] Bob Gebhard finally took him up on his offer.

Entering the 2018 season, Bob Gebhard was senior special assistant to the general manager of the St. Louis Cardinals, a title he shared with Mike Jorgensen and Hall of Famer Red Schoendienst.

SOURCES

In addition to the sources cited in the Notes, the author also consulted Baseball-Reference.com. All other information was obtained from the Gebhard interviews and from the author's personal knowledge as Colorado Rockies club historian.

NOTES

1   All personal biographical information was obtained through a series of one-on-one author interviews with Bob Gebhard in late 2017. Unless otherwise indicated, all direct quotations come from these interviews.

2   *Colorado Rockies Media Guide* of 1993 and 1994.

3   Author interview with Bob Gebhard.

BRAD HAWPE

BY JOHN PAUL

WHAT DO YOU, A YOUNG BALLPLAY-
er, do when your college of choice doesn't offer you
a scholarship to play baseball? If you're Brad Hawpe,
you pick up the phone, dial the campus, and invite
them to see you play. In Hawpe's case, that led
to a nine-year big-league career, mostly with the
Colorado Rockies.

Bradley Bonte Hawpe was born on June 22, 1979,
in Fort Worth, Texas, to Richard Hawpe, owner of
an auto dealership, and his wife, Paula, an elementa-
ry-school teacher. Four years later a brother, Todd,
came along.

Brad was a three-year baseball letterman at
Boswell High School in Fort Worth. He began as a
pitcher, but after he hurt his arm in his junior year,
he switched to first base. A "wow" hitting moment
occurred in a 1996 game against Springtown High
School. With the bases loaded, Brad hit a Roy Hobbs-
type shot that cleared the right-field fence, struck a
light standard, and set off a "Natural" moment with
electrical sparks and broken bulbs dropping onto the
field. (He and his teammates collected the ball and
pieces of glass, and he kept them as a souvenir.)[1] In
his senior year he pitched and played first base as his
team won the Texas 4A state championship.[2]

Hawpe also starred for the Dallas Mustangs
American Legion team, and began to attract the
attention of scouts.[3] Unfortunately from Hawpe's
viewpoint, they were interested in him as a pitcher,
and he wanted to move up as a first baseman. In the
June 1997 amateur draft he was selected in the 46th
round by the Toronto Blue Jays as a pitcher, but he
did not sign. He wanted to go to college and pursue
his dream of becoming an outstanding hitter. Many
colleges made scholarship offers, but not his desired
Louisiana State University or University of Texas
at Austin. While attending Navarro Junior College,
south of Dallas, Hawpe continued to focus on his
passion to play for LSU, so much so that he picked up
the phone, called the LSU athletic staff and invited

them to come see him play. LSU took him up on his
offer, watched him in a game and immediately after
the game offered Hawpe a full scholarship.[4]

In the 2000 season Hawpe led all NCAA Division
I players with 36 doubles in 69 games.[5] He topped
that by hitting two three-run homers in a 10-4 victory over the University of Southern California in
the College World Series.[6] LSU won the national
championship and Hawpe was named to the All-
Tournament Team.[7]

In the 2000 free-agent draft, the Rockies selected
Hawpe in the 11th round—as a pitcher.[8] Since he
had made up his mind to play as a first basemen or
outfielder he almost decided to return to LSU for his
senior year rather than turn pro. His signing scout,
Damon Iannelli, explained to Hawpe that it was an
internet mistake and that the Rockies wanted to sign
him as a first baseman or outfielder, so he agreed to
sign with the Rockies. [9]

The Rockies sent Hawpe to the Portland Rockies
of the short-season Class-A Northwest League.
Splitting his playing time between first base and right
field, he finished third in the league with a .900 OPS
(on-base average plus slugging percentage).

The next season, Hawpe was advanced to the low
Class-A Asheville Tourists (South Atlantic League).
Again splitting time between first base and right field,
he hit 22 homers and 22 doubles with an .870 OPS.
Hawpe had a breakout season in 2002 with Salem
of the high Class-A Carolina League. Leading the
league in batting average (.347), slugging percentage
(.587), and OPS (1.033), he was named the circuit's
Most Valuable Player. (He placed second in the
league with a .447 on-base percentage, 87 runs scored,
and 97 RBIs, and third with 38 doubles and 22 home
runs.) Hawpe played all but two of his 122 games at
first base. But a position switch had to be considered;
Todd Helton, the Rockies' first baseman with the
Rockies, was well entrenched as a team leader and a
major-league star.[10]

Hawpe knew he had to try to become a better outfielder especially since he had minimal experience at the position. He had to improve his positioning, reading baseballs hit his way, and improving his arm slot while throwing for improved accuracy. His learning began with his assignment in 2003 to Double-A Tulsa, where he played mostly right field. On July 14 he injured his right shoulder diving for a ball and missed the final six weeks of the season.

Nevertheless, the Rockies promoted Hawpe to the 40-man roster in 2004 and assigned him to the Triple-A Colorado Springs Sky Sox. Though he was still listed as an infielder,[11] he played 86 of his 92 games with the Pacific Coast League club in the outfield. He batted a strong .322 with 31 home runs and 86 RBIs.

Hawpe's early-season performance earned him a summons to the big leagues on May 1. With the Rockies playing a doubleheader at Coors Field, he pinch-hit for pitcher Tim Harikkala in the seventh inning of the first game and hit a ground-ball single

to center field, his first major-league hit. Starting the second game batting seventh and playing right field, he went 3-for-4 with a two-run homer, a triple, and a line-drive single to center field.

Hawpe was sent back to Colorado Springs on May 30 and lit up the PCL with a hot .352 batting average for his second go-round. He hit 14 of his season's 31 home runs in August, when he averaged one homer every 7.7 at-bats. His efforts earned another call-up to the Rockies for the final 20 games of the season.[12] In 2005 spring training Hawpe knew that his prowess at the plate was a strength, but that he needed to improve as an outfielder. He found help from future Hall of Famer Goose Gossage, who attended spring training with the Rockies and provided Hawpe with instructions for making strong and accurate throws from the outfield. Rockies first-base coach Dave Collins helped with tips on positioning and throwing.[13] Collins later commented that "when runners try and test him, they will pay the price," and teammate Aaron Cook noted his reputation for throwing runners out, especially at home plate.[14]

Opening the 2005 season with the Rockies, Hawpe placed well among the NL's rookies, and his hard work with Gossage and Collins as mentors began to show as well; he led the team with 10 outfield assists. But his season was cut short on July 9, when he injured his left hamstring trying to break up a double play. He was on the disabled list from July 10 until September 2.[15]

In 2006, Hawpe, healthy again, batted .293 with 22 home runs, 84 RBIs, and 16 outfield assists, the second highest in the majors that season. "One of my favorite parts of the game now is throwing somebody out at the plate," he said.[16]

During the Rockies magical "Rocktober" run to the postseason in 2007, Hawpe contributed strongly. In the Rockies' last 14 games, Hawpe had six doubles, a triple, and four home runs. Two of his homers were game-winners. His 116 RBIs and 29 home runs for the season were career highs. Working in the team's front office at the time, Walt Weiss said, "Hawpe has the ability to carry a club, he is that dangerous at the plate."[17]

In the wild-card tiebreaker on October 1, Hawpe was hitless in the Rockies' 9-8 victory. In the third game of the National League Division Series, against the Philadelphia Phillies, Hawpe hit a key single in the Rockies' winning rally, advancing Garrett Atkins from first base to third, after which he scored on a single by Jeff Baker. Hawpe also had several key at-bats in the Rockies' sweep of the Arizona Diamondbacks in the Championship Series.

The Rockies took on the Boston Red Sox in Colorado's first World Series appearance. The Rockies were swept, but Hawpe had a slugging percentage of .563, delivering a single in the second game, a triple in the third game, and a homer in the bottom of the seventh inning of the fourth game.

In 2008 Hawpe had a team-high 25 home runs, his third straight season with more than 20. He suffered a strained hamstring on May 21 and was on the disabled list until June 6. His injuries may have slowed him down after his return.[18]

Hawpe was slowed down by several injuries during first half of the 2009 season: a left hamstring injury on April 13, a neck contusion that kept him out from April 27 until May 1, and a groin strain from May 26-29. Still, he had his fourth consecutive year with more than 20 home runs (he hit 23) and he led the team with a career-high 42 doubles. He became a first-time National League All-Star in 2009. The 2009 Rockies won 92 games and took on the Phillies in the National League Division Series, but lost the series in four games.[19] Hawpe was one of the team's best offensive players during the season, but struggled at times against left-handed pitchers.[20] Against the Phillies, he played in only two games and was hitless.

Hawpe's 2010 season was hampered by a strained left quadriceps injury in April, which got him a stay on the disabled list.[21] He suffered a rib injury on June 25 running into a low right-field wall in Anaheim while chasing a pop fly, and was listed as day-to-day for several games. Playing hurt probably affected his performance with a downward spiral in his batting and landed him on the bench as a reserve.[22] On August 26, Brad Hawpe, 31 years old, cleared waivers and was released.[23]

Between his release and August of 2013, Hawpe played in five major-league organizations, the Tampa Bay Rays, San Diego Padres, Texas Rangers, Pittsburgh Pirates, and Los Angeles Angels of Anaheim. During his time with the Padres he went on the disabled list on June 21, 2011, and underwent Tommy John surgery five days later. With the Angels he played with the Salt Lake Bees and was called up to Los Angeles in June of 2013 but managed a batting average of just .185 after 17 games and was released on August 4, after which he retired as a player.

As of 2018 Hawpe, his wife, Kim, their daughter, Avery, and their son, Drake, lived in the Dallas-Fort Worth area. He spent some of his time coaching his daughter's softball team and his son's baseball team. He was a co-founder of The FUEL Nutrition, which prepares and markets health-food supplements. An avid outdoorsman, mainly hunting, he was the co-owner of Triple C ranch and deer farm with Matt Belisle and Todd Helton. He is one of the founders and a part-owner of the Cooperstown Cobras baseball program, serving the Dallas-Fort Worth area. Though he no longer had formal ties to any professional baseball team, he remained close to the game as a fan.

NOTES

1   *2010 Colorado Rockies Information Guide*, 115.

2   *Rockies Magazine*, May 2007: 24.

3   Ibid.

4   *Rockies Magazine*, May 2007: 26.

5   NCAA Baseball Division I Baseball Records, fs.ncaa.org/Docs/stats/baseball_RB/2012/D1.pdf.

6   "Baseball—College World Series; LSU Snaps USC's Streak," June 13, 2000, nytimes.com/2000/06/13/sports/plus-baseball-college-world-series-lsu-snaps-usc-s-streak.html. See also W.C. Madden and Patrick J. Stewart, *The College World Series a Baseball History 1947-2003* (Jefferson, North Carolina: McFarland, 2004), 216.

7   *2010 Colorado Rockies Information Guide*: 116.

8   My Draft, mydraw.com/1997 and /2000.

9   *Rockies Magazine*, May 2007: 26.

10   Ibid.

11   *Tucson Citizen*, Colorado Rockies Preview, tucsoncitizen.com/morgue2/2004/03/02/17581-colorado-rockies-preview/.

12   MiLB.com, milb.com/gen/articles/printer_friendly/clubs/t551/
      y2007/m08/d14/c289354.jsp.

13   *2010 Colorado Rockies Information Guide:* 115.

14   *Rockies Magazine,* May 2007: 28.

15   *2010 Colorado Rockies Information Guide:* 115.

16   *Rockies Magazine,* May 2007: 29.

17   *Rockies Magazine,* May 2007: 31; KUSA, 9news.com/sports/
      mlb/colorado-rockies/rocktober-relived-september-21-2007-
      one-hawpe-closer/477470748.

18   *2009 Colorado Rockies Information Guide:* 123.

19   *2010 Colorado Rockies Information Guide:* 114.

20   Fangraphs Hawpe Batting Splits, fangraphs.com/statsplits.
      aspx?playerid=1885&position=OF&season=2009.

21   ESPN: Colorado Rockies Transactions—2010, espn.com/mlb/
      team/transactions/_/name/col/year/2010.

22   "Hawpe Day-to-Day With Bruised Ribs," *Rockies News,* June
      25, 2010, m.rockies.mlb.com/news/article/11591482//.

23   Troy E. Renck, "Rockies' Hawpe Talks About His Exit,
      Thanks Fans," *Denver Post,* August 19, 2010, blogs.denverpost.
      com/rockies/2010/08/19/rockies-hawpe-talks-about-his-exit-
      thanks-fans/4585/

TODD HELTON

"THE FACE OF THE COLORADO FRANCHISE"

BY ALAN COHEN

You come to Colorado, the first guy you talk about is Todd Helton. We try to stay down in the zone and not give him anything to hit."

—Cubs pitcher Kerry Wood[1]

IN THE SO-NEAR-YET-SO-FAR-AWAY category, Todd Helton has a place of honor. In 2003, the batting race in the National League came down to the last day of the season. The Colorado Rockies were playing the San Diego Padres in an otherwise meaningless game. Helton, who had won the title with a .372 batting average in 2000, was going for his second title. He had hit safely in 19 of his most recent 20 games, and the Rockies' first baseman brought a .358 average into the game in San Diego. Meanwhile, in Phoenix, the St. Louis Cardinals were facing off against the Diamondbacks. The Cardinals' Albert Pujols came into the game in a virtual tie for the batting lead with Helton. Both teams had been eliminated from Wild Card contention and the only issue at hand was the batting race.

Pujols went 2-for-5 with a double to raise his average to .35871 (212-for-591). After the Cardinals easily defeated the D-backs, 9-5, he could only be a spectator to events in San Diego. The game in San Diego, with nothing on the line between two teams with losing records, wound up being an exciting affair for the 60,988 spectators at the final game ever held at Qualcomm Stadium (formerly known as Jack Murphy Stadium). In the top of the eighth inning, the Rockies had scored two runs and extended their lead to 10-7. There was a runner on second with two outs.

Helton stepped to the plate. He was already 2-for-4, and needed a hit to secure the batting title. His average stood at .35849 (209-for-583). Padres manager Bruce Bochy, looking to avoid further scoring and set up a force play, had his pitcher, Rod Beck, issue an intentional walk to Helton. It wound up being Helton's last plate appearance of the season. The next batter, Jay Payton, flied out, and the Rockies were retired in order in the ninth inning. The Padres cut into the lead with a Mark Loretta eighth-inning homer, but it would not be a happy ending for the Padres fans as they lost, 10-8. Helton lost the batting title by .00022.

Four years later, there was a sweet redemption. The date was September 18, 2007. The Rockies entered the doubleheader at Coors Field on that date with a 77-72 record. They were fourth in the NL West, six games out of first place. They were five games out in the wild-card race. Only 13 games remained in the season. They defeated the Dodgers in the first game of the doubleheader, but Los Angeles was on the verge of gaining a split as the second game entered the bottom of the ninth inning, leading 8-7. Reliever Takashi Saito retired the first two Rockies before yielding a single to Matt Holliday. Up stepped Helton. Behind in the count 1-and-2, the 11-year veteran homered over the right-center-field wall. Helton circled the bases in a fit of emotion, pumping his fist high in the air before being mobbed at home plate. The Rockies had a modest three-game winning streak. They kept on winning, losing only one game the rest of the way. Todd Helton would play in the postseason for the first time.

Todd Lynn Helton was on born August 20, 1973, in Knoxville, Tennessee. His father, Jerry, had played in the Minnesota Twins organization as a catcher in 1968 and 1969. (He died at the age of 65 on March 7, 2015.) In 2005, Todd remembered that Jerry "taught me how to hit in our garage, batting off a tee he made from a washing-machine hose. I was 5."[2] Jerry and wife Lynda Courville Helton had three children. In addition to Todd, there were brother Rodney and sister Melissa (Missy). Todd's passion for baseball is matched by his love of hunting, and in his youth, he often went duck hunting with his maternal grandfather, Don Courville.[3]

Helton attended Central High School in Knoxville, where Rodney had starred on the gridiron before going on to play at Alabama. Todd was a letterman in football and baseball. In the fall of his sophomore year, playing for his uncle, coach Joel Helton, the quarterback was named the Knoxville Football League's Sophomore of the Year.[4] He was first mentioned in *USA Today* for his baseball exploits on May 28, 1990, when his team was rated 24th in the country, thanks in no small part to his .500 batting average, 7 homers, and 30 RBIs. A week later, the team had surged to 16th as Helton went 5-for-10 and undefeated Central won the Tennessee state championship tournament. By season's end, his batting average stood at .495 and as a pitcher he went 9-0 with an ERA of 0.25.

When not on the playing field, Helton excelled in other areas. His India-ink drawing titled "Shadows" was chosen the best print at the Tennessee Valley Fair Student Art Exhibit.[5]

When fall arrived in 1990, Helton, by then a junior, excelled on the football field for his nationally ranked squad. A win over Sevierville, in which he threw for three touchdowns, resulted in the squad being ranked 20th in the country by *USA Today*. As his team raced through the playoffs, he also excelled at defensive safety, making 11 tackles and picking off a pass in a win over Morristown West. After a 44-19 win over Dayton High School, Knoxville Central was 13th in the country, but its victory march was halted in the state semifinals. For the season, Helton had thrown for 1,617 yards and 20 touchdowns, while rushing for 606 yards.[6]

In his junior year, Todd continued to excel on the ballfield, hurling a no-hitter with 17 strikeouts in the first game of the District 3 Class AAA tournament. He batted .482 with 10 homers and 41 RBIs. On the mound, he was 7-1 with a 2.36 ERA and his achieve-

ments resulted in his being named the Knoxville Interscholastic League's Player of the Year.

Helton's senior year was phenomenal in both football and baseball. In football, he posted 2,666 total yards. He passed for 1,904 yards (22 touchdowns), ran for 551 yards (eight touchdowns), and added 211 yards picking off seven passes in the defensive secondary (three touchdowns). By the time the season ended, the highly recruited Helton could basically go wherever he chose for college. It would come down to a choice between Tennessee and North Carolina, and on January 31, 1992, he announced that he would be going to Tennessee.[7] In baseball as a senior, Helton posted a .655 batting average and 12 home runs and was named the Regional Player of the Year. Todd was drafted in the second round (55th overall) by San Diego in the 1992 draft. He did not sign and honored his commitment to attend the University of Tennessee.

Eight years later, Helton reflected on the decision. "It was a very hard decision for me not to leave (Tennessee) when I was drafted out of high school. I always really wanted to be a baseball player. I had some pressure from my family to stay around and play football, and I don't regret the decision that I made. I'm glad I got an opportunity to do what I did at Tennessee."[8]

While his football talents got him his scholarship to play at Tennessee, Helton was no slouch on the diamond. As a freshman, during walk-on tryouts for the baseball team, Todd grabbed a bat and it took little time to convince coach Rod Delmonico that his talents were not confined to the gridiron. With the Vols, he played first base and was the team's mound closer. Said Delmonico, "He's the best pitcher I ever coached."[9]

Helton's football career, however, hit a snag. He was sandwiched between two great quarterbacks. In his first two years, he backed up Heath Shuler. After Shuler graduated, Jerry Colquitt took over as the starter. An injury to Colquitt in the season's first game gave Helton an opportunity to start. His time as first-string quarterback was brief. In the team's fourth game of the season, against Mississippi State,

Helton injured his knee. He had played his last football game. In his time at Tennessee, Helton had appeared in 12 games. He completed 41 of 75 passes for 484 yards and threw for four touchdowns. Peyton Manning replaced Helton at quarterback and went on to a great NFL career. When Manning joined the Denver Broncos at the end of his career, his longtime friend Todd Helton was there to greet him.[10]

After his junior year at Tennessee (1995), in which he batted .407 with 20 homers and 92 RBIs, and had a Tennessee-record 11 saves (with a 0.89 ERA) as a pitcher, Helton was awarded the Dick Howser Award as National Collegiate Baseball Player of the Year. On October 13, 2017, he was inducted into the University of Tennessee Athletics Hall of Fame.

Helton was drafted in the first round of the June 1995 draft by the Rockies, and signed for a bonus of $892,000. His time in the minor leagues was brief. After signing on July 1, he was assigned to Asheville of the Class-A South Atlantic League, where he batted .254 in 54 games. Part of the reason for the low average was Helton's trying to pull the ball, aiming for the short right-field wall at his home ballpark. That wasn't his style. His style, as practiced in the family garage, was to hit line drives and not pull the ball. He reverted to form in 1996. He began the season with the New Haven Ravens in the Double-A Eastern League, batting .332 in 93 games, and went on to Colorado Springs (.352 in 21 games) in the Triple-A Pacific Coast League. In the autumn of 1996, Helton participated in the Arizona Fall League and was ultimately inducted into the AFL Hall of Fame in 2003. In 1997, he was once again batting .352 (through 99 games) at Colorado Springs when the call came to report to the big leagues, two years and one month after he signed his first contract with the Rockies.

On August 2, 1997, the day after he was promoted to the Rockies, Helton made his major-league debut in a 6-5 road loss at Pittsburgh, going 2-for-4 with a walk. Helton started in left field, batted fifth, and flied out to short left field in his first at-bat. He singled in his second at-bat off Francisco Cordova. After walking in the sixth inning, he hit his first home run, a solo shot in the eighth off Marc Wilkins. The homer was part of a four-run uprising that brought Colorado to within one run of tying the game, but they could get no closer. In his first season, Helton had 26 hits in 93 at-bats and kept his rookie status.

In 1998, his first full season, Helton hit .315 with 25 home runs and 97 RBIs in 152 games. He led all major-league rookies in batting average, homers, RBIs, multi-hit games (49), total bases (281), slugging percentage (.530), and extra-base hits (63). He also led all National League rookies in runs (78), hits (167) and on-base percentage (.380). He finished second in the Rookie of the Year balloting to Chicago pitcher Kerry Wood.

Before the 1999 season, Helton was awarded a four-year, $12 million contract by the Rockies. In 1999, he batted .320. He hit 35 home runs and had 113 RBIs, while drawing 68 walks. On June 19, in a 10-2 Rockies home win over the Florida Marlins, Helton went 4-for-4, hitting for the cycle. But the Rockies were a disappointment as a team, finishing last in the five-team National League Western Division with a 72-90 record. The losing had an impact on Helton, and in August, he was doing as poorly as his comrades. The Rockies were finishing a road trip in Milwaukee. They had lost five straight games and seven of eight.

T. Helton

The record had dropped to 48-65 and Helton's batting average, after he went 1-for-18 in those five losses, had dropped to .288. On the morning of August 11, Helton and hitting coach Clint Hurdle had a heart-to-heart talk. Hurdle was later quoted as telling Helton, "Every time the pitcher looks on deck (when Helton was in the on-deck circle), you should be looking at him. You don't let him breathe."[11] Helton finished the season batting .320.

Before the 2000 season, Helton married Christy Bollman, whom he had met in his freshman year at Tennessee, and the couple honeymooned at the Rockies Fantasy Camp. They have two children, daughters Tierney Faith and Gentry Grace.

In 2000, Helton had a spectacular season, leading the major leagues in batting average (.372), RBIs (147), doubles (59), total bases (405), extra-base hits (103), and slugging percentage (.698). He led the National League in hits (216) and on-base percentage (.463). Helton's MLB-leading 103 extra-base hits tied for the fourth most in major-league history and the second most in NL history. His 59 doubles were the most in the National League since 1936, when Joe Medwick set the league record with 64. Helton was chosen for the All-Star team for the first time, and entered the game in the fourth inning as a pinch-runner for first baseman and former Rockies teammate Andres Galarraga. He stayed in the game and went 0-for-2 as the NL lost, 6-3.

On May 1, Helton had the first three-homer game of his career, victimizing the Montreal Expos at Denver. The 4-for-5 game brought his average to .362, and it would keep on rising. He spent most of May above .400, ending the month at .421. As late as mid-August, he was still flirting with a .400 batting average. That was after a 36-for-65 run during the first 18 games of August took his average from .371 to .399. He would tail off in September, but his season would have a fairly-tale ending.

The Rockies showed improvement, but were nowhere close to making it to the postseason. They took an 81-80 record into the season's last game, on October 1 against the Braves at Atlanta. Going into the ninth inning, the Rockies trailed 5-3. Braves closer John

Rocker entered the game in search of the save. Five batters later, the score was 5-4. There were runners on first and second with two outs, both strikeouts. Up stepped Helton. The right-handed Rocker got ahead, 0-and-2, and went for the game-ending strikeout with a thigh-high fastball on the middle-inside portion of the plate. The left-handed-hitting Helton, who was a difficult player to strike out (61 in 581 plate appearances in 2000), took a level swing and deposited the pitch over the right-field wall to give the Rockies an 8-5 lead. They won the game 10-5. But they still finished in fourth place, 15 games behind the division champion Giants.

There were abundant accolades at the end of the season. Helton received the second annual Hank Aaron Award as the league's best hitter. He was named Player of the Year by *Baseball Digest*, *The Sporting News*, and the Associated Press. He received a Silver Slugger Award, but the MVP award did not come his way. Each of the four players who finished ahead of him in the balloting played in the postseason.

After the season the Rockies gave Helton a contract extension worth $141.5 million and tied him to the team through 2011. In terms of overall money, he was in the company of Alex Rodriguez, Derek Jeter, and Manny Ramirez.

In 2001, Helton once again had a big year at the plate. He hit a career-high 49 home runs, tying him with teammate Larry Walker for the most home runs in a season by a Rockies player. Helton's .336 batting average was second only to Walker's .350 in 2001. He had 105 extra-base hits, making him the first major leaguer to total at least 100 extra-base hits in back-to-back seasons. Once again he was on the All-Star team, this time as a starter. He went 0-for-2 as the NL lost 4-1. At season's end, not only was Helton's hitting recognized with another Silver Slugger Award, but his fielding earned him his first Gold Glove.

During the season, Helton reached a milestone with his 500th RBI. It came against Montreal on September 21 before 10,510 fans at Montreal's Olympic Stadium. The game between two teams that were long since out of contention went into extra innings tied at 9-9. In the top of the 11th, Helton came up with the bases loaded and singled in the winning run. The 11-9 win was a bright spot in another futile season for the franchise as the Rockies dropped to last place with a 73-89 record.

During the offseason, Keli McGregor took over as team president and there were changes in playing personnel as well. But the team's key player was still Helton. McGregor said, "He embodies everything you want every person in our organization to embody."[12]

They were still playing the annual Hall of Fame Game in Cooperstown in 2002, and that season the Rockies faced the White Sox in the exhibition. Before the game, Helton was included in a round-table discussion with recently inducted Ozzie Smith of the Cardinals and Frank Thomas of the White Sox, who would be inducted into the Hall of Fame in 2014. (Helton's name was due to go on the ballot for the first time in 2018.)

The respite in July was little consolation in a season that went bad for both Helton and the Rockies. For the first time in his career, he played in pain. The team continued to experience difficulties. After the Rockies lost 16 of their first 22 games, there was a change in managers with Clint Hurdle replacing Buddy Bell. Helton's pains did not have a major impact on his numbers. He batted .329 with 30 homers and 109 RBIs. For most players, these numbers would represent success, but for Helton, the figures were a disappointment. Speaking before the 2003 season, he said, "I did so many things bad that I have tons of room for improvement."[13]

Helton's determination to improve in 2003 was unfortunately not contagious as once again the team struggled despite another set of big numbers from Helton. He brought his batting average back up to .358 with 33 homers and 117 RBIs. It was his fifth consecutive season with more than 100 RBIs. His 49 doubles gave him over 35 two-baggers for the seventh consecutive season. He once again started the All-Star Game, and his two-run homer off Shigetoshi Hasegsawa in the top of the fifth inning gave the National League a 2-1 lead. The American League came from behind with three eighth-inning runs to win, 7-6.

The Rockies hovered around the .500 mark for most of the season and were 61-61 on August 12. However, they slumped and finished in fourth place with a 74-88 record. Helton's season was highlighted by a game on May 29 when he went 4-for-5 with three homers in a 12-5 win at Denver over the Dodgers. The win concluded a three-game sweep, the first ever at home against the Dodgers. It was the second time in his career that Helton had homered three times in a game. His six RBIs were the best of his career to that point. For the fourth straight season, he won the Silver Slugger Award.

"I would like to scoreboard watch at least one day."[14]

In his years with the Rockies the team had failed to reach the postseason. They weren't even close. Speaking with Troy Renck of the *Denver Post*, he said, "It's like a dog who has never had table scraps. I really don't know what it tastes like. I would love to get a taste of the playoffs. I hope I will get to, and I hope it's this year. I am not on the three-year or four-year plan to get there. I am on a one-year plan."[15]

The Rockies once again failed to make the postseason in 2004, despite another great season from Helton at first base, where he won his third Gold Glove Award, and was named to his fifth consecutive All-Star team, this time as a reserve. He appeared as a pinch-hitter in the ninth inning and fouled out. His .347 batting average in 2004 placed him second in the National League to Barry Bonds. His 96 RBIs ended his streak of consecutive years over 100, and he would never reach the 100 plateau again. His 32 homers gave him at least 30 home runs in six consecutive seasons. These numbers enabled Helton to become the first major leaguer to hit at least .315 with 25 home runs and 95 RBIs in each of his first seven full seasons.

Despite another team failure to make it to the postseason (the Rockies went 68-94 and finished in fourth place), Helton remained optimistic about the future, and did not seek a trade outside the organization.

And then came a disturbing report. St. Louis Cardinals broadcaster Wayne Hagin implied that Helton had used steroids in 1998. Don Baylor, Helton's manager in 1998, in an interview with Hagin, had said that he had advised Helton "to get off the juice," because Helton was a good-enough hitter and didn't need any supplements. The juice to which he was referring was creatine, a legal over-the-counter bodybuilding supplement. His use of the term juice did not refer to steroids, but the damage had been done. By 2005, the term juice had become synonymous with steroids. Certain print media sources quoted Hagin as saying, "Baylor told me that he suspected Todd Helton of experimenting with steroids early in his career." An apology was tendered by Hagin, but Helton could not bring himself to forgive the former Rockies broadcaster. Baylor supported Helton, as did the Rockies. The players, in a display of clubhouse humor, covered Helton's locker with police tape and a sign saying, "This area closed pending a search for evidence."[16]

Helton's 2005 season was truly disappointing in terms of power production. Although he batted .320 with 20 homers and 79 RBIs, it took a tremendous finish to get him there. He got off to his worst start ever and, as the season passed the one-third mark (his first 66 games, to be precise), he was batting only .250 with 6 homers and 26 RBIs. Speaking with *USA Today*'s Gary Graves in late June, he said, "I've changed my stance 42 times in 42 games. I haven't allowed myself time to see the baseball. That's what I see (as the problem) and that's what I'm trying to correct. I feel pretty comfortable right now, and that's what I'm going to stick with."[17]

In July, although he was not selected for the All-Star Game, Helton turned things around, batting .400 (with 5 homers and 12 RBIs) and raising his average to .294, before spending two weeks on the disabled list (for the first time in his career) with a strained left calf muscle. On July 7, he had passed Larry Walker to become the Rockies' all-time home run leader. After his return from the DL, Helton kept on hitting, with 9 homers and 36 RBIs in his last 48

games, but the Rockies could not turn their season around, finishing in the cellar with a 67-95 record.

Fifteen games into the 2006 season, Helton was batting .347 when he awoke in pain on April 20. At the hospital he was diagnosed with acute terminal ileitis, a painful inflammation of the lower intestine. He was released from the hospital after three days, rehabbed at Colorado Springs and returned to the lineup on May 5, missing 14 games.[18] Although his numbers for the season were down from prior seasons (.302/15/81), and the Rockies finished at 76-86, there were better times ahead.

After 10 years of frustration, Helton would find himself in postseason play. Prior to the 2007 season, there was discussion of his being sent to the Boston Red Sox, but the Rockies wanted too much in exchange and the deal fell through.

"The face of the franchise is hitting .396 in September. He's Beltin' Helton again."[19]

Helton's walk-off homer against the Dodgers on September 18 was his third of the month and the 301st homer of his career. His 300th had come on September 16 against Mauro Zarate in a 13-0 romp over the Marlins. His five homers in September gave him 17 for the season to go with 91 RBIs, His .320 batting average made it 10 consecutive seasons over .300 for Todd. His 42 doubles made it 10 years in a row with more than 35 in that department. Nobody in the major leagues had ever done that before.

By winning 13 of their last 14 regular-season games, the Rockies tied San Diego and faced the Padres in a one-game playoff for the wild-card berth in the National League. On October 1, Helton homered in the fourth inning as the Rockies defeated the Padres, 9-8 in 13 innings, and advanced to the Division Series. Helton tripled off Cole Hamels in his first at-bat in the Division Series against the Phillies, and scored on a double by Garrett Atkins. The Rockies won, 4-2, and went on to sweep Philadelphia in the best-of-five series. Colorado advanced to the League Championship Series, and once again Helton hit safely in his first at-bat of the Series. This time he singled off Brandon Webb of Arizona in the second inning and came around to score his team's first run. Colorado went on to win the game, 5-1, and swept the Diamondbacks in the best-of-seven series. It was then on to the World Series for the first time in franchise history. The Cinderella season came to an end when the Rockies were swept by Boston. Helton batted .333 (5-for-15) with a pair of doubles in his only World Series appearance.

In 2008, Helton played in only 83 games. He went on the disabled list in early July, and played in only two late-season games thereafter. In August, he was diagnosed with a degenerative back condition, and he had surgery in September. For the season, he batted only .264 with 7 homers and 29 RBIs.

As Jerry Crasnick of ESPN noted in August 2009, Helton, after his surgery, "found a way to stick around and remain productive into his late 30s. Helton is living proof that second acts — and second winds — are as much fun as they're cracked up to be."[20]

Helton found that second wind when 2009 dawned, and was back to playing every day. He had a great comeback season that was highlighted by two milestones. The first was his 2,000th hit, at Atlanta off Jair Jurrjens on May 19. The Rockies had little to celebrate that evening after their season's record went to 15-23, but after Helton's third-inning single in an 8-1 loss, his teammates presented him with a full range of gifts including a hunting rifle from the players and champagne from manager Clint Hurdle.[21]

Hurdle's days as manager were numbered, and he was replaced by Jim Tracy on May 28, when the team was 18-28. With Tracy at the helm, the Rockies turned their season around and on July 22, against Jon Garland of the Diamondbacks, Helton stroked his 500th double, a third-inning RBI two-bagger. Helton's eighth-inning homer gave the Rockies a 4-3 victory that put their record at 52-43. They were in second place in the NL West, but they were on the way to their second wild-card berth in three years. They secured that wild-card berth as Helton batted .325 with 15 home runs and 86 RBIs. He finished 13th in the MVP balloting, the first time he had

finished in the top 20 since 2004. The Rockies faced Philadelphia in the best of-five Division Series, and were eliminated in four games.

Before the 2010 season, the Rockies extended Helton's contract through the 2013 season, meaning that he would finish his career in Denver. But 2010 turned out to be a year of frustration for the face of the franchise. Playing in only 118 games, Helton, now 36 years old, batted .256 with 8 homers and 37 RBIs. The team stayed in the wild-card hunt, but Helton's once powerful bat could not take them to the postseason this time. His back problems returned. He missed games sporadically during the first three months and was finally forced to the disabled list for an extended stay from July 5 through August 2, missing 23 games. The Rockies finished in third place with an 83-79 record.

As Helton faced a new round of challenges, manager Jim Tracy offered this assessment:

"The mentality, the character, the work ethic of this team, it's easy to have all that when the best player in the history of the franchise is the hardest worker on the team. It's absolutely tearing him to pieces not to be involved with us, to not be the player we've known him to be."[22]

Proud and determined, the 37-year-old Helton returned for the 2011 season, and the career .324 hitter batted .302 in his 15th season. He had 14 homers and 69 RBIs in 124 games. Another milestone was reached when he played in his 2,000th major-league game on June 30. But the team tumbled to a 73-89 record, finishing fourth in the NL West.

Pain returned in 2012, and the season had few highlights for Helton. This time he went on the disabled list in July and had season-ending surgery on August 10 to repair a torn labrum in his right hip. He played in only 69 games and his numbers were eroding. He batted .238 with 7 homers and 37 RBIs. The next season would be Helton's swan song, and trainer Keith Dugger was of a mind that the surgery would enable him to come back strong and go out on top. "He was having good days and bad days. But we weren't going to give him anti-inflammatories or shots to get through this," Dugger said. "This (surgery) gives him a chance to get it right. This is going to give him a chance to focus on one thing—rehabbing and getting this right for spring."[23]

After the surgery, Helton, speaking as the season drew to an end, was looking forward to 2013. He said, "I know there are going to be days when I am not going to be out there and perform, but the days I do feel good and feel like I can go out there and hit there all over the ballpark, I want to be out there."[24]

But before Helton headed off to spring training, there was an embarrassing incident when he was pulled over for driving under the influence on February 6 in a Denver suburb. He was sentenced to one year's probation and 24 hours of community service. He apologized to his family, teammates, and fans, saying, "Part of making a mistake, making a monumental mistake like I made, is recognizing the mistake and making sure it doesn't happen again."[25]

"He's one of those guys who wakes up on Christmas morning when he's 52, and he can go hit a ball in the gap."[26]—Walt Weiss, February 17, 2013

When Helton woke up on Sunday, September 1, 2013, he was not quite 52 years old yet, but the was ready to go out to the ballpark, find a pitch, hit the ball, and send it to a gap. The Rockies were at home playing the Cincinnati Reds in the finale of a three-game series. The 40-year-old first baseman came to the plate in the seventh inning. The Rockies had just extended their lead in the game to 7-4 on Michael Cuddyer's home run. Helton stepped in to face Reds reliever Curtis Partch. Using that all-to-familiar left-handed grip and swing that his dad had taught him in the garage more than 30 years earlier, Helton slammed a 3-and-2 pitch to the opposite field. The ball zipped past third base near the foul line, and Todd slid into second base with a double, the 584th two-bagger and 2,500th hit of his career. The crowd of 30,594 stood and cheered and Helton reciprocated by removing his helmet and waiving it high.[27]

On September 14, after the Rockies had lost to the Diamondbacks, 9-2, in Phoenix, Helton announced what had been anticipated all season—that he would soon be retiring. The Denver fans would get to see him in one last nine-game homestand. In making his announcement, he said, "I'm going to miss walking out of the tunnel at night, trying to figure out how I'm going to get a hit the next day or how we're going to win a game the next day. To me, that's going to be the hardest (part)."[28]

During that last homestand, Helton had the last two of his 369 homers. On September 25, before his last game in Denver, a sellout crowd of 48,775, including friend and former college teammate Peyton Manning, showered him with admiration as the team presented him with a 6-year-old horse named NXS A Tru Bustamove. (As of 2017 the horse was a four-time American Paint Horse Association world champion.) In the pregame festivities, Todd's daughter Tierney threw out the first pitch.[29] In his first at-bat, against the Red Sox, he homered off Jake Peavy, but it was in a losing cause as Boston won, 15-5. In subsequent at-bats in his home finale, Helton drove in runs with a third-inning sacrifice fly and a fifth-inning double, sliding in head-first for the last of his 592 career two-baggers. His three RBIs brought his career total to 1,406. After the game, he took a final lap around the ballpark to say goodbye to the fans.[30] The last of Helton's 2,519 major-league hits came in the first at-bat of his final game, against the Dodgers in Los Angeles on September 29. His final season batting average was .249, and he left baseball with a career average of .316.

Helton wore number 17 for 17 seasons with the Colorado Rockies and they honored him by retiring the number on August 17, 2014. He became the first Rockies player to have his number retired by the team. The number has become special to Helton. His ranch outside of Denver is known as the 17 Ranch. Daughter Tierney, then 11, spoke as her 4-year-old sister, Gentry, stood by her side. She said, "My daddy has been a Colorado Rockie my entire life. This stadium has been my second home. Thank you for that. Now that my daddy has been home with us this season—a lot—I want to ask you one question. Do you want him back?" The game's 42,310 spectators, on cue, screamed, "Yes!"[31]

SOURCES

In addition to Baseball-Reference.com, the Todd Helton player file at the National Baseball Hall of Fame and Museum, and the sources shown in the Notes, the author used:

Kuenster, John. "Rockies' Todd Helton *Baseball Digest*'s 2000 Player of the Year," *Baseball Digest*, January 2000: 19.

Verducci, Tom. "Historic Quest," *Sports Illustrated,* September 4, 2000: 45-48.

NOTES

1 Jeff Mahony, ed., *Baseball Superstars: Who Are These People, Anyway?* (Middletown, Connecticut: Checkerbee Publishing, 2001), 54.

2 Todd Helton, as told to Michael Bamberger, "SI Players on and Off the Field," *Sports Illustrated*, May 9, 2005: 23, 25.

3 Patrick Saunders, "Former Rockies Great Todd Helton Content in First Year Away From Game," *Denver Post*, August 17, 2014.

4 Bill Luther, "Super Soph Fulton's Cotner Caught on Quickly," *Knoxville News Sentinel*, November 21, 1990: D1.

5 Eleni Chamis, "Young Artists Display Prize-Winning Work in Variety of Media at Candy Factory," *Knoxville News-Sentinel*, September 26, 1990.

6 Sammy Batten, "Recruiting Wars Begin," *Fayetteville* (North Carolina) *Observer*, September 14, 1991.

7 "Helton Fulfills a Dream, Commits to Being a Vol," *Knoxville News-Sentinel*, January 31, 1992: C1.

8 Todd Helton, as told to Seth Livingstone, "Dugout Direct: Comfy at Coors, With No Apologies," *USA Today Baseball Weekly*, May 24-30, 2000: 19.

9 Austin Murphy, "Baseball," *Sports Illustrated*, June 5, 2000: 46.

10 Mark Kizla, "Peyton Manning and Todd Helton—Best Buddy System Ever," *Denver Post*, March 27, 2012.

11 Murphy, "Baseball."

12 Tracy Ringolsby, "Helton's Leadership Qualities Set Him Apart," *Rocky Mountain News* (Denver), February 22, 2002.

13 Troy E. Renck, "Back to Business: A Painful Season Behind Him, Rockies Star Todd Helton Wants a Big Year," *Denver Post*, February 4, 2003.

14 Troy E. Renck, "Helton Out to Complete Picture in Playoffs," *Denver Post*, February 11, 2004.

15 Ibid.

16 Jack Etkin, "Helton Receives Support," *Rocky Mountain News*, March 22, 2005.

17 Gary Graves, "Helton Tries to Swing Back Into Groove," *USA Today*, June 20, 2005: 3C.

18 Associated Press, "Colorado's Helton Is Up Off His Back and Back on the Field," *New York Times*, May 7, 2006.

19 Mark Kiszla, "Big Brother Helton Watching With Glee," *Denver Post*, September 27, 2007.

20 Jerry Crasnick, "Helton Stresses Team-First Mentality," ESPN. com, August 11, 2009.

21 Thomas Harding, "Rox Throw Clubhouse Party for Helton," MLB.com, May 20, 2009.

22 Jim Armstrong, "Helton Facing Uncertain Future With Rockies," *Denver Post*, August 1, 2010.

23 Troy E. Renck, "Injured Todd Helton Deserves to Go Out on His Terms," *Denver Post*, August 8, 2012.

24 Tracy Ringolsby, "Helton Wants One More Kick at the Can in 2013," MLB.com, September 26, 2012.

25 Associated Press, *Boston Herald*, February 17, 2013.

26 Ibid.

27 Patrick Saunders, "Hurray for Rockies Star Todd Helton, Who Joins the 2,500 Hit Club," *Denver Post*, September 4, 2013.

28 Associated Press, "Rockies Pay Tribute to Todd Helton," ESPN.com, September 17, 2003.

29 Mark Townsend., "Todd Helton Homers in Final Home Game, Receives Horse From Rockies as Retirement Gift," Yahoo, September 26, 2013.

30 Troy E. Renck, "Todd Helton Will Be in Cooperstown ... or at Least His Bat Will Be," *Denver Post*, September 26, 2013.

31 Patrick Saunders, "Longtime Star Todd Helton Is Honored by Rockies, Who Retire His No. 17," *Denver Post*, August 18, 2017.

CLINT HURDLE

BY BRIAN C. ENGELHARDT

THE COVER OF THE MARCH 20, 1978, annual baseball preview issue of *Sports Illustrated* featured a picture of Kansas City Royals rookie Clint Hurdle looking ready for action, with the caption "This Year's Phenom" in bold yellow letters right next to his smiling face. Keeping with the "phenom" theme, the article described the 20-year-old Hurdle as "tall, dark, handsome and brash and able to hit a baseball nine miles."[1] Batting instructor Charlie Lau described Hurdle as "the best hitting prospect I've ever seen in our organization." Manager Whitey Herzog rated Hurdle "the best player in the minors last year."[2] General manager Joe Burke called him "one of the top prospects I've seen in the 17 years I've been in the major leagues."[3]

Hurdle's playing career—politely described as "utterly modest"[4]—fell far short of the hype. Appearing in 515 games over 10 seasons for the Royals, New York Mets, Cincinnati Reds, and St. Louis Cardinals, Hurdle batted .259 with 32 home runs and 193 RBIs. In only three of those seasons did he make more than 200 plate appearances in major-league games.

Hurdle made more of a mark in baseball as a successful manager, for both the Colorado Rockies and the Pittsburgh Pirates. Both teams were in the midst of prolonged periods of losing at the time Hurdle took over. He led each to a level of success including postseason play—once with the Rockies in 2007, when they went to the World Series, and three times with Pirates in 2013 through 2015.

Hurdle's life off the diamond has been a journey in which he has experienced difficult circumstances, but has been very public in sharing his experiences when he believes he can help others. During Hurdle's playing career, he enjoyed the nightlife and the fast lane. As a recovering alcoholic, he continued as this writing to remain involved with Alcoholics Anonymous and became a prominent advocate of therapy and the benefits of treatment programs.[5]

Clinton Merrick Hurdle was born on July 30, 1957, in Big Rapids, Michigan, to Louise Hurdle and Clint Hurdle Sr. When he was 3 years old the family moved to Merritt Island, Florida, site of NASA's Apollo space program at the Kennedy Space Center, when his father joined Grumman Aircraft, which had a contract with NASA.

The senior Hurdle worked for 37 years in Grumman's computer data systems lab, supervising more than 300 employees. His management style was to try to meet each month with as many of his subordinates as possible so that "they felt they were part of the program," adding that in the process, "people learn to trust you, you gain credibility."[6] Clint described his father as a "connector of people," who "put people in the right spots."[7]

During Hurdle's childhood it was not unusual for his family to watch NASA launches from their front porch or the nearby schoolyard.[8] (On January 28, 1986, Hurdle and his father watched as the space shuttle *Challenger* broke apart and its crew of seven was killed.[9])

Baseball was a family tradition. His paternal grandfather had been offered a contract by the Cincinnati Reds at age 15, a day before his own father died, but turned it down so he could work to help support his family. Clint Sr. played college baseball at Ferris State University but had to forgo a baseball career after being drafted into the military.[10] A Hurdle family ritual occurred regularly on the baseball field behind the family home, with Clint Sr. pitching batting practice to his son, with Hurdle's mother, his two sisters, and the family dog playing outfield.

Hurdle starred in baseball and football at Merritt Island High School. He was named an all-state quarterback in his senior year after leading the team to a state championship. He received more than a dozen scholarship offers. The University of Miami wanted him to play both baseball and football, and an offer came from Harvard.[11] Hurdle chose instead to make himself available for the 1975 first-year player draft.

Kansas City Royals scout Bill Fisher, who lived near the Hurdles, spent three years watching games, tossing batting practice, and filing reports during Hurdle's high-school years. Before the 1975 draft, Fisher pitched to Hurdle in front of a group of Royals front-office executives whom the scout had persuaded to come and watch. After Hurdle finished hitting, providing the group with what Fisher termed "the greatest exhibition you ever saw," Fisher asked the executives if they'd like to see him run and throw.[12] The response was unanimous: if he could hit like that, no one cared whether or not he could run or throw.[13]

The Royals selected Hurdle with the ninth over-all pick in first round, ahead of future major-league stars Lee Smith, Carney Lansford, Andre Dawson, and Lou Whitaker. Anxious that Hurdle begin his professional career right away, he and his parents met with Fisher at a nearby restaurant, where a paper napkin with proposed numbers was passed back and forth until a $50,000 signing bonus was agreed to and Hurdle signed a contract.[14]

Hurdle's ascent through the Royals' minor-league system was rapid. The 6-foot-3, 195-pounder played in the outfield at each level, batting left-handed and throwing right-handed. With the Royals rookie league team at Sarasota in 1975, he was named to the Gulf Coast League All-Star team, batting .274 and leading the league with 31 RBIs. The next season, playing for the Waterloo Royals in the Class-A Midwest League, he was named "Prospect of the Year," clubbing 19 home runs, tying him for second in the league, with 89 RBIs in 127 games.

Hurdle was invited to the fall Florida Instructional League and Royals spring training in 1977. Although he started out at 1-for-19 in the Instructional League, Royals hitting instructor Dennis Paepke told him to relax, and "go out and have some fun."[15] Hurdle then smacked 11 hits in 27 at-bats, including seven extra-base hits. Paepke said, "When Clint hits the ball, it just explodes. He hits the ball as hard as the big-league hitters do right now."[16]

When the Royals headed north for the 1977 season, they promoted Hurdle to Triple-A Omaha, where he batted .328 with 16 home runs and was named American Association Rookie of the Year. A September call-up, he made his major-league debut on September 18, 1977, starting in right field and batting fifth in a home game against the Seattle Mariners. After grounding out to third base in his first at-bat, Hurdle hit a two-run homer off the Mariners' Glenn Abbott. Hurdle was 20 years old, and the youngest player in Royals history. He was also the first Royal to hit a home run in his first start.[17] Playing in nine games over the remainder of the season, Hurdle hit .308 with two homers and seven runs batted in.

Hurdle managed to focus on producing on the field during spring training in 1978 despite any distraction created by the *Sports Illustrated* cover, performing well enough that the Royals moved veteran first baseman John Mayberry to Toronto. Although this made room in the lineup for Hurdle, it had him playing a position at which he had no experience except for about 14 games in winter ball.[18] Nonetheless, beginning Opening Day and until July 2, Hurdle was the Royals' everyday first baseman.

By July 1 Hurdle was hitting only .251 with not much power, so Herzog moved him to the outfield. His problem adjusting to first base was believed to be one of the reasons for his problems at the plate.[19] That batting coach Lau pushed a technique for him to hit line drives, while Herzog encouraged development of a home-run stroke added to Hurdle's problems at the plate.[20]

Hurdle relaxed at the plate in the second half of the season and finished the year with a batting average of .264. Among his offensive highlights that season, he drove in six runs, going 3-for-3 with a three-run homer off Dennis Eckersley in a 9-0 Royals home victory over the Boston Red Sox on July 21. In the 1978 American League Championship Series, which the Royals lost to the New York Yankees, Hurdle started two games and pinch-hit in two games, getting two singles, a triple, and two walks in 10 plate appearances. At season's end Herzog said, "Clint had a good year. If it wouldn't have been for all the ballyhoo, we would be saying it was a hell of a year."[21]

Batting .240 two months into the 1979 season, Hurdle was demoted to Triple-A Omaha. Bitter about the demotion, Hurdle said afterward, "When they sent me back to Omaha … it was a shock, but it really shouldn't have been. I was beaten out of my job by Willie Wilson and they explained to me that I'd be doing the team and myself no good by sitting on the bench."[22]

Working with his father at the batting cage, he changed from a negative frame of mind to a positive one, relaxing and finding a more comfortable stance at the plate.[23] Recalled to the Royals in mid-August, he hit an identical .240 over the rest of the season.

Under Jim Frey, who replaced Herzog, the 1980 Royals not only won a division crown but swept the Yankees in the 1980 ALCS. Moving on to the World Series, they lost in six games to the Philadelphia Phillies. The 1980 season was the most productive of Hurdle's playing career, with a .294 batting average and career highs of 10 home runs, 31 doubles, and 60 RBIs.[24]

Although Hurdle was the regular right fielder for most of the season, over the last few weeks Frey platooned him with veteran outfielders Jose Cardenal and Rusty Torres. The platooning continued during the ALCS, in which Hurdle was platooned in right field with John Wathan. In the World Series Hurdle started all four games in right field and batted .417 with two walks in 14 plate appearances.

Hurdle began the 1981 season as the Royals' starting right fielder, going 7-for-15 with two home runs in the first five games. On April 14 he injured his back sliding into third base and spent two stretches on the disabled list for a total of 72 days.[25] Another major disruption was the players strike from June 12 to August 10. During the strike Hurdle tended bar, saying that he was doing it just to keep busy.[26] After the strike Hurdle was the Royals' regular right fielder for the last two weeks of the regular season, batting .310. Limited to 89 plate appearances, Hurdle batted .329 with a .553 slugging percentage. The Royals were swept by Oakland in three games in the AL Division Series. Hurdle had three hits and a walk in 12 plate appearances.

In December Hurdle was traded to the Cincinnati Reds for Scott Brown, a relief pitcher with 10 games of big-league experience. Hurdle's value had perhaps diminished in the eyes of team brass due to the back injury.[27]

As a member of the Reds, Hurdle was united with Bill Fisher, the scout responsible for his signing with the Royals, who was the Reds' pitching coach.

Penciled in by manager John McNamara as the team's starting left fielder at the outset of the 1982 season, Hurdle batted only .182 with four hits and one RBI in his first eight starts and was reduced to a reserve role before being optioned to the Reds' Triple-A affiliate, the Indianapolis Indians, on May 15.[28] In 88 games with Indianapolis, Hurdle batted .245 with 12 home runs. He was not recalled.

Released by Cincinnati at the end of the season, Hurdle signed as a free agent with the Seattle Mariners, who were desperately in need of left-handed hitters.[29] Although Hurdle hit .317 in spring training, and manager Rene Lachemann and his coaches were unanimous in recommending that the team keep him, Mariners President Dan O'Brien decided to release him. Disappointed, Hurdle said O'Brien "had told me that if I had a good spring, I'd make the club. Obviously, I didn't have a good enough spring."[30] A spokesman for the Mariners said Hurdle's run production "was not where everyone thought it would be."[31]

Hurdle then signed with the New York Mets and was assigned to the Triple-A Tidewater Tides (Portsmouth, Virginia). To broaden his appeal to the Mets, Hurdle undertook to learn to play third base.[32] His .910 fielding average with 20 errors in 115 games was evidence that it didn't come easy, but Hurdle described how "my footwork got better and I picked up my range a little bit."[33]

After batting .285 with 22 home runs and leading Tidewater in doubles, hits, runs scored, RBIs, and walks, Hurdle got a September call-up. Mets manager Frank Howard moved Hubie Brooks to second base to give Hurdle an opportunity at third base. In nine games Hurdle made four errors in 20 chances and batted .182 with only two extra-base hits and two RBIs in 34 at-bats. After the season he was sent outright to Tidewater, where he spent the full 1984 season.

While Hurdle played mostly first base in 1984, he also played in 21 games as a catcher—the continuation of an experiment initiated by the Mets in spring training.[34] His progress was impaired when he injured his thumb in mid-May and missed three weeks.[35] In the 21 games behind the plate, Hurdle was charged with seven passed balls, but only one error. He joked that his goal was to drive in more runs than he let in.[36]

Although his batting average dropped to .243, Hurdle led the Tides in home runs (21) and walks (79). Because of his versatility in the field, the Mets brought him to 1985 spring training as a nonroster invitee. Hurdle spent the entire 1985 season with the Mets but played in only 43 games, among them 17 games behind the plate and 10 in the outfield. In 97 plate appearances, he batted .195 with 3 home runs and 7 RBIs, and was 0-for-16 as a pinch-hitter.

Dropped from the Mets' major-league roster, Hurdle was selected by the St. Louis Cardinals in the 1985 Rule 5 draft. Making the Cardinals roster as a utility player, he played in 78 games, at third base, first base, two outfield positions, and even catching in five games. Hurdle's versatility made him particularly desirable that year, during which major-league rosters were trimmed from 25 players to 24.

At that year's All-Star Game, Hurdle received the annual Danny Thompson Award, presented by Baseball Chapel to a player "for exemplary Christian spirit in baseball."[37] On the field, he batted .195 with 3 home runs and 5 doubles in 184 plate appearances. After the season the Cardinals declined to offer him arbitration and he became a free agent.

Hurdle signed a minor-league contract with the Mets in 1987 and was invited to spring training.[38] Calling Hurdle a "leader," Mets manager Davey Johnson described him as a "great guy to have in the clubhouse" and an "insurance policy" due to his versatility.[39] After playing in one game, Hurdle was sent to Tidewater in late April. Recalled for a brief time in mid-June, he made his final appearance as a major-league player in a 5-2 loss to the Phillies on June 26, pinch-hitting for Sid Fernandez. Kevin Gross struck him out looking.

On December 1, 1987, in Port St. Lucie, Florida, Hurdle announced his retirement as a player and accepting appointment as manager of the Port St. Lucie Mets of the Class-A Florida State League. He was candid with sportswriters about his mixed feelings over retiring at age 30: He said that while he still thought he could play in the major leagues, he had come to terms with himself—that he was not going to be a Hall of Famer as a player. "Maybe I can do it this way," he said.[40] By the time he retired Hurdle had already managed the Mets team in the Florida Instructional League that fall, getting a head start on his next career.[41] It was the first of five consecutive seasons that the Mets would name him as Instructional League manager—a testimonial to the Mets organization's opinion of his ability in teaching the game.

In Hurdle's first season as a manager, St. Lucie won the second half of the Florida State League's split season and the league playoffs. Hurdle managed St. Lucie again in 1989, with the team winning both halves of the season.

Hurdle's coaching technique impressed Mets first baseman Keith Hernandez, who after a four-day rehab stint in St. Lucie described him as a "teacher as well as a manager."[42] That offseason Hurdle returned briefly to the diamond as a player, splitting the catching duties for the St. Lucie Legends of the Senior Professional Baseball Association with another Mets veteran, Jerry Grote.[43]

Moved up to the 1990 Jackson Mets of the Double-A Texas League, Hurdle again won praise for his techniques and approach. Mets director of minor league operations Gerry Hunsicker described him as a "great teacher" with "great rapport with his players and the ability to communicate with them," adding, "There is no question he will not only manage in the big leagues, but he has a chance to be one of the top managers of the future."[44]

Hurdle was named Texas League manager of the year.[45] Notably, despite the team's success in being first in its division, no Jackson position players made the league all-star team, further evidence of Hurdle's skill in managing.[46]

Hurdle remained at the Double-A level in 1991, managing the Williamsport Bills of the Eastern League, in a makeshift move when an intended transfer from Jackson to Binghamton, New York, could not be completed on time.[47]

Promoted to manage the Mets' Triple-A affiliate Tidewater Tides (International League) in 1992, Hurdle faced a challenging season: The team finished a league-worst 56-86.[48] Hurdle described the challenge of keeping players at Triple A happy: "You do have a little different athlete here. You've got a third of the guys who think that they should be in the big leagues and never have been. You've got another third who have been and don't think they should be here. And you've got the other third who are just happy to be where they are at."[49]

For 1993, the Mets retained Hurdle to manage the renamed Norfolk Tides, who improved to 70-71 and were in the race for a playoff spot until late in the season.[50]

Immediately after the season ended the Tides announced that Hurdle was being released "to seek other opportunities in baseball."[51] A major factor in Hurdle's release was that Mets minor-league director Steve Phillips didn't like Hurdle's open and highly communicative approach to managing, favoring instead a stricter, more traditional approach.[52]

In October 1993 Hurdle joined the Colorado Rockies as their minor-league hitting instructor. At the end of the 1996 season Rockies manager Don Baylor named him the team's hitting coach and first-base coach. Hurdle was the Rockies' fifth hitting coach in five seasons. Baylor had been a hitting coach for several teams and had his own ideas on the right way go about it, leading to occasional conflicts with whoever was the incumbent Rockies hitting coach.[53]

To start, Hurdle asked Baylor for his own evaluation of each player so that Hurdle would know what to look for. Baylor praised Hurdle's approach, calling him "always positive with (the players), but … truthful too."[54] Hurdle obtained outstanding results. The Rockies as a team batted .294 in 2000 and .292 in 2001, the National League's top averages in 70 years; they also set a major-league record with 2,748 total bases in 2001. Rockies All-Stars Larry Walker and Todd Helton won four batting titles between them in Hurdle's five seasons on the coaching staff.[55] When Jim Leyland replaced Baylor as manager for the 1999 season, he kept Hurdle, explaining, "When I talked with some of the players, Clint got great reviews. Sometimes, when you look around for great coaches, they're already there."[56]

Every season from 1996 to 2001, the Rockies finished last or next to last in the NL West. When they started 2002 with a record of 6-16, manager Buddy Bell was fired and Hurdle succeeded him. Under Hurdle, the Rockies won the next six games and posted a record of 19-8 over the next month, putting the team over the .500 mark on May 25. Hurdle didn't take credit for the turnaround and felt bad that it didn't take place under Bell. "We were due to play better. We played so poorly we got a good man fired," he said.[57]

In June Hurdle said he and his coaches were just trying to "simplify the game—slow it down, play it inning by inning, win and inning, play today's game, don't worry about tomorrow's game. ... We're capable of playing in the present. We've proven that over the last month."[58] Hurdle said the team had been winning with "pitching and defense" and praised the pitchers, who over the past month had a 3.47 ERA, in contrast to the 5.48 ERA of the team's initial 22 games.[59]

In June and July the Rockies' pitching woes returned; the team ERA over that time was 5.99. The Rockies finished the season in fourth place. Two high-priced free-agent pitchers, Mike Hampton (7-15, 6.15 ERA) and Denny Neagle (8-11, 5.26, ERA), could not compensate for Jason Jennings's record of 16–8 with a 4.52 ERA; Jennings became the first Rockies player to win the National League Rookie of the Year Award.

For 2003, Hurdle assembled his own coaching staff. Most remained with him during his time with the Rockies until after the 2008 season.

Despite Hurdle's enthusiasm and open communication with his players, the 2003 Rockies again finished in fourth place. They ranked second in the league in home runs and doubles and third in batting average and runs scored. After the season the Rockies extended the club options on Hurdle's contract to include 2005 and 2006. They also extended general manager Dan O'Dowd's contract through 2006. Rockies managing general partner Charlie Monfort said Hurdle and O'Dowd were not "just good baseball men. ... They are key leaders who will help us continue to build a strong organization and bright future for the club and fans."[60]

The Rockies again finished in fourth place in 2004, and finished last in the division in 2005 with a record of 67-95, matching the record of the inaugural 1993 club as the worst in their history. Top performers from the previous year, Jeromy Burnitz and Vinny Castilla, had gone elsewhere as free agents, and first

baseman Todd Helton missed a number of games with injuries, posting the lowest home-run total of his career up to that point (20). In August Hurdle experimented with using a four-man rotation with a controlled pitch count because the performance of whoever was used as a fifth start was so poor. The experiment didn't work and was scrapped by the end of the season.[61]

The 2006 Rockies finished tied for fourth place (or last place, if you see the glass as half-empty) with a slightly improved 76-86 record. It was noted that Hurdle is "the only manager in major league history to start a career with five losing seasons and not get fired."[62] His longevity was attributed to his being an "organizational advocate ... never afraid to take blame for the organization, ... (shepherding) the youth movement, and ... (charming) the community with his big heart."[63]

Going into 2007, Hurdle declared that he needed to "prepare (the team) more effectively." He admitted that he overmanaged during the second half of 2006, and promised a slightly different approach. "I am going to do things differently, because it's time," he said.[64] In February his contract was extended through the end of the 2007 season.[65]

After 149 games of the 2007 season, the Rockies were four games out of the NL wild-card spot. At that time what became known as "Rocktober" materialized; the Rockies won 13 of their last 14 regular-season games and tied the San Diego Padres for the wild-card berth. The Rockies then won an unforgettable tiebreaker with the Padres, 9-8, overcoming a two-run deficit by scoring three runs in the bottom of the 13th inning off future Hall of Fame pitcher Trevor Hoffman.

After sweeping the Philadelphia Phillies in three games in the Division Series, the Rockies swept the Arizona Diamondbacks in four games in the National League Championship Series. When it was over the Rockies had won an incredible 21 of 22 games to reach the 2007 World Series. There, a four-game sweep at the hands of the Boston Red Sox was a disappointment. But after Game Four, Hurdle said that although the Rockies were outplayed by

Boston, he was proud of what they had achieved, and that he had told the team "they've brought me more joy this year than I've had in 35 years of professional baseball."[66]

After a 74-88 record in 2008, followed by an 18-28 start in 2009, Hurdle was fired and replaced by Jim Tracy. Dan O'Dowd said later that letting Hurdle go was his biggest regret during his tenure as GM.[67]

Offered an unspecified role in the Rockies organization, Hurdle chose instead to join the nascent MLB Network, working as a studio analyst for the remainder of the 2009 season. During his brief time there he worked with younger analysts and assistants, in the process becoming acquainted with new-age baseball thought and the world of sabermetrics.

In November 2009 Hurdle was hired as the hitting coach of the Texas Rangers. Among a group of talented young players on the Rangers was outfielder Josh Hamilton who, like Hurdle, had been labeled a "can't-miss" prospect and who had a history of substance-abuse issues, including alcoholism. The Rangers hoped Hurdle could help Hamilton in view of his own history as a recovering alcoholic.

Hurdle met daily with Hamilton in sessions which were more about life in general than baseball. He related his own experiences—from his days as a phenom, to the drinking and divorces, and also to the process by which Hurdle eventually found himself.[68] That season the Rangers won their first pennant since the franchise moved to Texas from Washington; Josh Hamilton was the American League batting champion and its Most Valuable Player, batting .359 with 32 home runs, the best year of his career.[69]

At the end of the season Hurdle was contacted by both the Mets and Pittsburgh Pirates about their managerial vacancies. In November 2010 he signed a three-year contract to manage the Pirates.[70] Although he considered the Mets offer, people close to Hurdle said he was wary about the Mets organization's perceived micromanaging, and felt he would be just another manager in New York, no matter what happened. Hurdle embraced the challenge presented in Pittsburgh, where if he was successful, he "would be king forever."[71]

In addition, the location of the Children's Institute in Pittsburgh, facilitating any needs his daughter Madison would have, was another factor. Madison had Prader-Willi syndrome and the institute is considered to be one of the top providers of care for that genetic disorder. He moved his family to Pittsburgh, declaring that he should live where he manages. "If you're going to tell people you are all in, you need to be all in," he said.[72]

The Pirates had not been to the postseason since 1992, had finished last or next to last in their division for seven straight seasons, and had not had a winning season for 18 years, a period of futility that continued for the first two seasons under Hurdle and resulted in a major-league record of 20 losing seasons in a row.[73]

Neal Huntington, the Pirates general manager, who hired Hurdle, was adapting the Pirates organization to the use of sabermetric techniques of player evaluation. Although Hurdle's baseball background was clearly "old school," the time he spent with his colleagues at the MLB Network had opened his eyes to many of the concepts underlying sabermetrics.[74] Hurdle and Huntington worked together exploring and considering various sabermetric concepts, including defensive shifts. While initially Hurdle was not totally on board with shifts, he embraced them fully within two years. The Pirates went from shifting 87 times in 2011 to 105 times in 2012 and 494 times in 2013.[75]

The 2011 season started off with a bang. One game after the All-Star break the Pirates were tied for first place in the National League Central Division. It was the first time the team had been above .500 at the All-Star break since 1992. On July 26, hanging onto first place by percentage points, they lost a 19-inning heartbreaker to the Braves. After that the Pirates went 19-42 and finished in fourth place. Despite the second-half slump, Hurdle came away with a positive read, declaring, "We want to win. That being said, we haven't won enough. We have a core group in place. Obviously we have some areas that we need to improve upon."[76]

The 2012 season followed a similar pattern. On August 6 the Pirates (62-46) were 3½ games out of first place in the Central Division and in the running for one of the two wild-card spots. After that date, the team collapsed, losing 37 of its final 54 games and finishing with a 79-83 record. It was the team's 20th consecutive losing season. In a meeting with Huntington after the season, Hurdle stated that he wanted to fully embrace analytics.[77]

Over the last two months of the 2013 season, the Pirates were in a dogfight with the St. Louis Cardinals for first place in the division, separated by two games or less for most of that time. The Cardinals won out, finishing in first, three games ahead of the Pirates, but the Pirates qualified for the wild-card game as the home team, and defeated the Cincinnati Reds, 6-2.

Facing the Cardinals in the Division Series, the Pirates lost, three games to two. Before the deciding game, Hurdle's message to his team was: "Find a way to play your heart. Play the size of your heart, not the size of the audience. Go get in the backyard and get after it. Play to win."[78] *The Sporting News* named Hurdle the National League Manager of the Year. He also was named the Sportsman of the Year by Dapper Dan Charities in Pittsburgh.[79]

The Pirates also reached the postseason in 2014 and 2015, but lost the wild-card game each time, to the San Francisco Giants, then to the Chicago Cubs. The team failed to make the playoffs in 2016 and 2017. At the end of the 2017 season, Hurdle signed a four-year contract extension, through 2021.[80]

In his family life, Hurdle went through the emotional trauma of two divorces prior to his marriage in 1999 to his third wife, Karla, whom he credited with being the major factor in his straightening his life out. While managing in Williamsport, Hurdle met Karla Yearick, an accountant, while having his taxes prepared.[81] After six years of dating, Hurdle asked Karla to marry him. She turned him down, telling him that he had to clean up his drinking binges and declaring, "Until you find a way to make yourself happy, you will never make me happy."[82] Hurdle went sober for good in 1998, and "put his demons to rest," including those that haunted him from the *Sports Illustrated* cover.

When he asked her again, satisfied that Hurdle had accomplished what she asked, Karla said yes.

Hurdle and Karla have two children, a daughter, Madison, born in 2002, and a son, Christian, born in 2004. Hurdle also has a daughter from his second marriage, Ashley, born in 1985. Madison was born prematurely with a genetic disorder that was later diagnosed as Prader-Willi syndrome, characterized by low metabolism and unrelenting hunger. Despite the considerable demands on his time as manager of the Rockies, Hurdle became a spokesman for the Prader-Willi Syndrome Association, taping public-service announcements, participating in charity events to raise money to fight the disease, and offering encouragement to parents whose children suffer from the disorder.[83]

Clint and Karla lead the annual "Wins for Kids" campaign, in conjunction with ROOT Sports and Pirates Charities to raise funds for the Children's Institute of Pittsburgh's Center for Prader-Willi Syndrome. The campaign raised more than $360,000 in its first six years.[84] For his work in this area, Hurdle in 2014 received the Brooks Robinson Community Service Award, presented by the Major League Baseball Players Alumni Association.[85]

Hurdle sends daily email or text messages to his players, colleagues, associates, and others. They embody a wide range of themes, from inspiration to humor. With each such message the closing is always the same: *"Make a difference today. Love, Clint."*[86]

Hurdle's managerial style works well with the modern ballplayer. He respects his players. He acknowledges the temptations that come with being young and a major leaguer. He often tells players, "Anything you've done wrong, I've done worse, and I've done it twice!"[87]

Asked once about good judgment, he said that it came with experience. "How do you get experience?" he was asked. His response: "Through bad judgment."[88]

SOURCES

In addition to the sources cited in the Notes, the author also consulted Retrosheet.org, Baseball-Reference.com, and Clint Hurdle's player file at the National Baseball Hall of Fame. Thanks to Phil

Davis, on whose initial rendition of a Hurdle biography this article was built.

NOTES

1   Larry Keith, "The Eternal Hopefuls of Spring," *Sports Illustrated*, March 20, 1978: 20. si.com/vault/issue/70772/21/1?-cover_view=0

2   Ibid.

3   Ibid.

4   Tom Singer, "Phenom to Manager, Hurdle's Brain Matches Brawn," MLB.com, September 13, 2012.

5   Tom Friend, "Love, Clint," ESPN.com, September 30, 2013. espn.com/mlb/playoffs/2013/story/_/id/9726637/pirates-manager-clint-hurdle-inspiring-others-daily.

6   Travis Sawchik, *Big Data Baseball* (New York: Flatiron Books, 2015), 18.

7   Ibid.

8   Stephen J. Nesbitt, "Note to Self," Pirate Baseball Issue (supplement), *Pittsburgh Post-Gazette*, April 3, 2016, newsinteractive.post-gazette.com/pirates/2016/clints-climb/.

9   Ibid.

10 Clay Latimer, "Life's Lessons Had Sting for Hurdle," *Rocky Mountain News* (Denver), October 8, 2007.

11 In addition to his athletic prowess, Hurdle was an excellent student, graduating from high school with all A's except for an offending "B" in driver's education. Sawchick, 20.

12 Sawchick, 20.

13 Ibid.

14 Ibid.

15 John Brockman, "Clint Hurdle Takes Major Strides," *The Sporting News*, October 30, 1976: 40.

16 Ibid.

17 Del Black, "Kansas City Cookie Quits Without Crumbling," *The Sporting News*, October 8, 1977: 11.

18 Sid Boardman, "Royals Crowing Over Bat Feats of LaCock," *The Sporting News*, August 26, 1978: 17.

19 Del Black, "Clint Faces New Hurdle as Royals Right Fielder," *The Sporting News*, January 12, 1980: 42.

20 Mike DeArmond, "Popeye Saves Hurdle From Kaycee Taunts," *The Sporting News*, July 19, 1980: 29.

21 Edwin Pope, "Life Just Starting, Hums Hurdle," *The Sporting News*, March 31, 1979: 40.

22 Bill Madden, "Hurdle Changes Attitude," *New York Daily News*, August 22, 1979.

23 Ibid.

24 All 10 of his home runs were off right-handers.

25 "Hurdle Traded to Cincinnati," *Florida Today* (Cocoa, Florida), December 12, 1981: 1C.

26 Associated Press, "Serving the Hard Stuff," July 1, 1981 (Hall of Fame Archives).

27 "Reds Hinting a Foster Deal," *The Sporting News*, December 26, 1981: 42.

28 Playing in the Reds loss to the Pirates on the date he was optioned, Hurdle entered the game in the second inning as a pinch-hitter, then remained in the game, hitting two singles and raising his average from .161. to .206 which kept his final average for the season above the Mendoza Line (.200).

29 Tracy Ringolsby, "Hurdle Looking for a Second Chance," *The Sporting News*, February 21, 1983: 40.

30 "Hurdle Annoyed by M's Decision," *The Sporting News*, April 18, 1983: 28.

31 "Mariners Release Hurdle Despite Impressive Spring," *Florida Today*, April 5, 1983: 1C.

32 Barry Jacobs, "Hurdle Trying to Clear Path Back to Majors," *USA Today*, June 15, 1983: 5C. The Mets had been unhappy with third baseman Hubie Brooks' offensive output.

33 James Tuite, "Mets Give Hurdle Third Base Tryout," *New York Times*, September 14, 1983: 89.

34 Jack Lang, "Keystone Combo Is Mets Top Concern," *The Sporting News*, March 5, 1984: 19.

35 Joe Gergen, "Hurdle's Enthusiasm Is Definitely Catching," *Newsday*, May 12, 1985.

36 Ibid.

37 Rick Hummel, "Daley May Go on Disabled List," *St. Louis Post-Dispatch*, July 16, 1986: 36.

38 "NL East—Mets," *The Sporting News*, February 16, 1987: 34.

39 Joseph Durso, "Hurdle Is Heading for Mets Again," *New York Times*, February 10, 1987: D31.

40 Barbara Caywood, "Playing Days End for Hurdle," *Florida Today*, December 1, 1987: 23.

41 "NL East - Mets," *The Sporting News*, December 14, 1987: 54.

42 Peter Kerasotis, "Skills Pass From Father to Son," *Florida Today*, July 16, 1989: 14.

43 "NL East - Mets," *The Sporting News*, November 6, 1989: 71. The team folded after one season, finishing in last place.

44 Rob Rains, "Hurdle Charts New Course," *The Sporting News*, July 2, 1990: 32.

45 Jackson finished with the league's best record, 73-62, winning the second half of the league's split season but losing in the league playoffs.

46 Joe Powell, "Hurdle, Young Are Top TL Manager, Pitcher," *Clarion-Ledger* (Jackson, Mississippi), August 31, 1990: 23.

47 John W. Fox, "Eastern League Says Farewell to an Old Friend," *Press and Sun Bulletin* (Binghamton, New York), September 4, 1991: 21. The Bills finished in seventh place. One of the few bright spots was the performance of the Mets' top pick in the 1990 draft, Jeromy Burnitz, who led the league with 31 home runs and tied for the league lead with 85 RBIs.

48 A rash of injuries on the parent club required that a number of players be moved up to the Mets; over the course of the season, 46 players appeared with the Tides.

49 David Jones, "Mets' Hurdle Continues Climb Up Minors," *Florida Today*, August 25, 1992: 21.

50 Mike Holtzclaw, "Going, Going …Gone," *Daily Press* (Newport News, Virginia), August 15, 1993.

51 Mets vice president Gerry Hunsicker issued a statement the next day that "[W]ith the hiring of Dallas Green, it became apparent that the advancement of Clint's manager career in New York would not be able to happen in the future." "Hurdle Felt Path to Mets Blocked by Green's Hiring," *Daily Press*, September 7, 1993.

52 Bob Klapisch, "Hurdle's Dismissal No Minor Matter," *New York Daily News*, September 12, 1993.

53 "NL," *The Sporting News*, March 10, 1997: 33.

54 Cheryl Rosenberg, "Hurdle an Expert on Unfair Expectations," *Palm Beach Post*, May 3, 1998: 720.

55 Troy E. Renck, "Rockies Turn to Tracy as Manager," *Denver Post*, June 2, 2009.

56 Ibid.

57 Murray Chass, "Hurdle Works Magic With Pitching Staff," *New York Times*, June 2, 2002: G3.

58 Ibid

59 Ibid.

60 Tracy Ringolsby, "Retention of Hurdle, O'Dowd Shows Faith in Direction of Team," *Rocky Mountain News*, November 13, 2003.

61 Sawchick, 122.

62 Troy Renck, "Hurdle Couldn't Have It Both Ways," *Denver Post*, May 30, 2009.

63 Ibid.

64 Troy E. Renck, "Hurdle on Hot Seat in '07 Season," *Denverpost.com*, January 19, 2007.

65 "Crisp Agrees to Boston Deal," *Albany Times Union*, February 7, 2006.

66 Jeremy Sandler, "Curse Obliterated as Sox Sweep," *Nanaimo* (British Columbia) *Daily News*, October 29, 2007: 15.

67 Nesbitt.

68 Nesbitt.

69 Friend.

70 Ron Cook, "Hurdle Is a Terrific Hire," *Pittsburgh Post-Gazette*, November 16, 2010.

71 Ibid.

72 Bill Brink, "Clint Hurdle's 'Yinzer' Life Suits Him Fine," *Pittsburgh Post-Gazette*, October 19, 2011.

73 DJ Gallo, "Sports Biggest Losers," ESPN.com, September 5, 2013, espn.com/sportsnation/story/_/id/9636396/with-pirates-streak-dj-gallo-takes-look-sports-current-big-losers.

74 Sawchick, 13.

75 Sawchick, 105.

76 Bill Brink, "A Glimpse of What Could Be," *Pittsburgh Post-Gazette*, October 2, 2011: 43.

77 Kevin Creagh, "How Clint Hurdle Stayed the Course After 2012's Implosion," *The Point of Pittsburgh*, Nov 25, 2015. thepointofpittsburgh.com/how-clint-hurdle-stayed-the-course-after-2012s-implosion/.

78 Michael Sanserino, "Hurdle Keeps Message Simple," *Pittsburgh Post-Gazette*, October 10, 2013: 26.

79 *Pittsburgh Post-Gazette*, December 22, 2013: 33.

80 Bill Brink, "Clint Hurdle Agrees to Four-Year Contract Extension With Pirates," *Pittsburgh Post-Gazette*, September 4, 2017. post-gazette.com/sports/pirates/2017/09/04/Clint-Hurdle-agrees-to-four-year-contract-extension-with-Pirates/stories/201709040104.

81 Sawchick, 24.

82 Phil Rogers, "Hurdle Has Had Big Dreams Since First Day on the Job," MLB.com, October 2, 2013.

83 For a more detailed discussion on Prader-Willi Syndrome, see Vicki Michaelis, "Clint Hurdle Balances Family Concerns With Baseball," *USA Today*, September 12, 2005, usatoday30.usatoday.com/sports/baseball/nl/rockies/2005-09-12-hurdle-family-cover_x.htm; see also Barry Syrluga, "Hurdle Manages to Find Ways Through Difficulties," *Washington Post*, October 23, 2007. washingtonpost.com/wp-dyn/content/article/2007/10/22/AR2007102202430.htm.

84 "Clint Hurdle's 2017 Win for Kids Charity Campaign in Full Swing," Pirates Breakdown.com piratesbreakdown.com/2017/05/19/clint-hurdle-pirates-wins-for-kids-charity/.

85 Staff Report, "MLBPAA Announces Clint Hurdle as Brooks Robinson Community Service Award Winner for 2014," *Cision*, May 15, 2014, a report found in Hurdle's player file at the National Baseball Hall of Fame.

86 Friend.

87 Perkins.

88 Bob Cohn, "Pirates Manager Hurdle Is Guided by History," *Pittsburgh Tribune-Review*, August 14, 2011.

JASON JENNINGS

BY MICHAEL T. ROBERTS

JASON JENNINGS HAD WHAT MIGHT be the greatest debut in baseball history. His first game at the major-league level was so impressive that no less an authority on greatness than the National Baseball Hall of Fame contacted the Colorado Rockies to inquire about displaying memorabilia from the game.

The Rockies promoted pitcher Jennings from Triple-A Colorado Springs on August 23, 2001, to replace reliever Jose Jimenez, who had been placed on the disabled list. Jennings was immediately summoned to start the game that evening at Shea Stadium in New York against the Mets. All he did was pitch a five-hit complete-game shutout, striking out eight and walking four. He also added three hits, including a home run. He is the only pitcher in baseball's modern era to pitch a shutout and hit a home run in his major-league debut.

Jason Ryan Jennings was born on July 17, 1978, in Dallas, the oldest child and only son of Jim and Connie (Cummings) Jennings. As of 2017 his father worked in the sporting-goods business in the Dallas area, and his mother was an administrative assistant in the athletic office of the Mesquite Independent School District. Sisters Krystal and Jamie joined the family in 1981 and 1984. Jason was influenced by his father, a former football player at the University of Texas, Uncle Bobby Cummings, a former TCU linebacker, and his grandfather. His father and uncle coached him growing up, and taught him to be "super competitive and humble."[1] His grandfather was a Dallas area broadcaster, with the result that young Jason spent time around many successful people.

A standout in both football and baseball at Poteet High School in Mesquite, Texas, Jennings was drafted by the Arizona Diamondbacks in the 54th round of the 1996 first-year player draft. Rather than sign with Arizona, he hoped to attend the University of Texas. But it was Baylor University that offered a baseball scholarship, and thus Jason became a Baylor Bear.

Texas's loss was Baylor's gain, as Jennings became one of the greatest players in Baylor history. He was a standout two-way player, excelling both as a hitter and on the mound. On offense, in 172 career games he had a .344 batting average on 207 hits that included 41 doubles and 39 home runs. His career as a pitcher includes 69 appearances with 34 starts, a 27-11 won-lost record, 3.56 ERA, 15 complete games including three shutouts, 13 saves, 377 strikeouts, and 125 walks in 313⅓ innings.

Jennings was a three-time All-American, and earned Division I Player of the Year honors in his senior season of 1999. He was elected to the Baylor University Hall of Fame in 2009, and the university retired his number 17 in 2014. He also pitched for the USA National team in 1997 and 1998.

The Rockies made the brawny Jennings (6-feet-2, 235 pounds) their first pick in the 1999 first-year player draft, the 16th player chosen. Drafted as a pitcher, Jennings was assigned to the low-A Portland Rockies of the Northwest League to start the 1999 season. He pitched in two games and dominated the nine innings he worked, striking out 11, walking two, and giving up five hits. This earned him a quick promotion to the low Class-A Asheville Tourists of the South Atlantic League, where he went 2-2 in 12 starts with a 3.70 earned-run average. He struck out 69 batters and walked only eight in 58⅓ innings. His teammates included future Rockies standouts Matt Holliday, Juan Uribe, Juan Pierre, and Aaron Cook.

Promoted along with Uribe and Holliday to Salem of the high Class-A Carolina League for the 2000 season, Jennings made 22 starts, pitched 150⅓ innings, struck out 133, and walked 42. This earned him a late promotion to Carolina of the Double-A Southern League, where he went 1-3 in six starts, but continued to have an impressive K/BB ratio, striking out 33 and walking only 11.

Jennings started the 2001 season with Carolina, but was promoted to Triple-A Colorado Springs after four starts. In 22 starts for the Sky Sox, he went 7-8 with a 4.72 ERA. Those numbers do not stand out on their own; however the 2001 Pacific Coast League featured mostly hitter-friendly ballparks averaging five runs per team per game, and had an aggregate batting average of .275. In addition, Jennings was 22 years old, which was over five years younger than the average PCL player.

Brought up to the Rockies in August after the Jimenez injury, Jennings followed the memorable first start with six more starts down the stretch. He won again in his second start, going six innings against the Los Angeles Dodgers allowing eight hits and two runs. He won again in his third start, giving up only three hits in seven innings against the Giants in San Francisco. (One of those hits was Barry Bonds' 58th home run of the season, on his way to a record 73.)

Five days later, again facing the Giants but at Coors Field, Jennings suffered the first loss of his big-league career. He gave up four runs on nine hits and three walks in 5⅔ innings in a game the Giants won, 7-3. It was his only major-league loss of the season.

In his final start of the season, on October 5 at San Diego, Jennings threw six shutout innings to earn the win in a 4-0 Rockies victory. His record with the major-league Rockies was 4-1, with a 4.58 ERA and 26 strikeouts in 39⅓ innings pitched.

Despite his impressive work late in the 2001 season, Jason was not a lock to be in the Rockies' 2002 rotation. Veteran left-handers Mike Hampton and Denny Neagle, both big-name free agents the Rockies had signed before the 2001 season, were assured of two spots. The Rockies were hopeful two other veterans with past success, Scott Elarton and Pete Harnisch, the latter signed in February, would secure starting spots. This left Jennings in a battle with a couple of recent farm-system graduates, John Thomson and Shawn Chacon, as candidates for the fifth rotation spot. Jennings was a long-shot entering spring training, as both Thomson and Chacon had big-league experience.

Although he struggled early in spring training, Jason's stock grew as injuries hampered both Elarton and Harnisch. By late March, the *Denver Post's* spring-training notes declared that Jennings had all but earned a spot. The *Post* opined, "Jason Jennings didn't want to offend the chamber of commerce, but he made it clear he has no interest in leasing a place in Colorado Springs. After his start today, he may not have to worry about it. Jennings, barring injury or Pete Harnisch's remarkable recovery, should secure the fifth spot in the rotation."[2]

Jennings did earn that last spot. Using primarily an effective sinker, he went six innings in three of his first four starts. He closed the month of April with his strongest effort in start number five, pitching seven shutout innings against the Phillies in Coors Field, surrendering only four hits to get the 4-2 win. This squared Jennings's record at 2-2, with his ERA at 3.67. From that point on, he did not lose a game until June 18. He also reeled off a stretch of victories in five straight starts in August. He was especially effective at home, which was noteworthy as Coors Field was notoriously tough on pitchers.

In a *USA Today Baseball Weekly* feature, columnist Bob Nightengale commented that "Jason Jennings might be the best arm to hit Colorado since John Elway. . . ."[3] Jennings was developing a reputation for toughness on the mound, not letting any particular ballpark, especially Coors Field, or any recent struggles affect his current work.

By September, Jennings was being talked about in terms of the likely 2002 Rookie of the Year. After his 16th win, the *Denver Post* exclaimed, "Despite their barren offense and shaky bullpen, the Rockies are nearly unbeatable every fifth day when Jason Jennings takes the mound. Further cementing his rookie of the year status, the burly right-hander devoured the Padres for seven innings as Colorado posted a 5-2 win Monday night before 31,837 at Qualcomm Stadium."[4] Jennings dropped two of his final four starts, the other two being no-decisions. He finished 2002 with a 16-8 record and a 4.52 ERA, a respectable number for a guy pitching half of his games in Denver. (The Rockies' team ERA for 2002 was 5.20, worst in the National League.) Jennings's victories were the most for a National League rookie pitcher since 1985. He was also a tough out at the plate, hitting .306 and driving in 11 runs. His batting mark was the best for a National League rookie pitcher since 1947.[5]

Jennings indeed won the National League Rookie of the Year Award, winning 27 of the 32 first-place votes. It was the first significant award won by a Rockies pitcher.

A strong 2003 spring training cemented Jennings's spot as the Rockies' number-one starter. His heroics were especially welcome to a franchise historically known only for its hitters. With hopes high, the 2003 regular season started with a thud. Playing the Astros in Houston to start the season, Jennings was rocked for eight earned runs on nine hits, surrendering three home runs in four innings of work. It was the most earned runs Jennings had allowed in a game up to that time. Relying more on a slider than the vaunted sinker, Jennings continued to struggle in the early going. He finished April with a 2-3 record and 6.97 ERA, which was primarily due to poor command as evidenced by 12 walks in 31 innings pitched. Despite Jennings's struggles, the Rockies as a team looked to be much improved over the team that finished 73-89 in 2002. With a 15-12 record in the first month,

fans were optimistic that once Jennings found his stride the Rockies could be serious contenders for the National League West title.

It was June before Jennings looked like the 2002 version. He went 4-1 during the month, winning his first four starts, and lowering his ERA from 5.40 to 4.70. Perhaps his best outing of the season occurred on June 10 in Minnesota, where he threw 7⅔ innings of three-hit shutout ball, striking out seven.

The second half of the season saw both Colorado and Jennings unable to find consistency. The Rockies finished only one game better than the previous season. Jennings fell victim to the time-honored sophomore jinx, with a 12-13 record and a 5.11 ERA. He walked hitters at a rate of 4.4 per nine innings, up a full walk per game from the prior year. He was especially vulnerable to multiple-run innings. "I don't know what causes it, but it has been a problem," he commented after his final start, a game in which Randy Johnson threw a one-hitter against the Rockies. "Last year, it seemed I could make that big pitch to get out of that inning. I could get the double play."[6]

The 2004 season was more of the same, with similar numbers as the previous year. Jennings again struggled with his control, walking batters at a rate of 4.5 per nine innings. And as in 2003, he started the season slow. After his first six starts his ERA was a whopping 10.57. There were even rumors that he was headed back to Triple A. Jennings did regain some consistency with his sinker, and won eight of 11 decisions from late May through July. But he failed to win a game after August 17. The Rockies' weak bullpen was a big reason; Jennings had no-decisions in six of his final eight starts. He finished 11-12 with an ERA of 5.51. The Rockies regressed as a team, finishing at 68-94. Only their initial season as an expansion team in 1993 was worse.

The Rockies had some decisions to make after the poor showing in 2004. The top priorities were to improve the bullpen and to sign Jennings and fellow starter Joe Kennedy. Both were eligible for arbitration and thus had some leverage in negotiating an agreement. Despite his struggles the previous two years, Jennings was durable, starting a combined 65 games and throwing over 382 innings.

In January 2005, the Rockies and Jennings came to an agreement on a two-year, $6.9 million contract. It was only the third multiyear deal given to a pitcher by the Rockies, and a significant increase over his 2004 salary of $340,000. Jennings had become the franchise's most successful home-grown pitcher, with 43 wins under his belt in just over three full seasons. What made him particularly valuable was a stellar 23-13 record in Coors Field, normally a death sentence for a pitcher's statistics. In addition, ESPN named Jennings the best hitting pitcher in baseball. His career batting average of .257 was the best among active pitchers heading in to the 2005 season.

As spring training got underway, a *Rocky Mountain News* article claimed Jennings was to the pitching staff what slugger Todd Helton was to the lineup, "a cornerstone for the long-term building plan."[7] He had a strong spring, his best since joining the Rockies, however he was not chosen to be the Opening Day pitcher. That assignment went to left-hander Joe Kennedy. Never one to get off to a good start, Jennings hoped things would be different in 2005. "I think I'm more ahead of schedule coming out of spring (training) than I have been in the past," he said.[8] Pitching coach Bob Apodaca worked with him during the spring to refine his mechanics and be more consistent in his delivery.

Starting the second game of the season, things were no better for Jennings than past April starts. After facing three batters, he was already down 3-0. He lasted just four innings, giving up seven hits and six runs, four earned. He did fare better later in the month, throwing a complete game in a 9-1 win against the Dodgers on April 22. But that was Jennings's only win until May 26, when he yielded a single run in seven innings at Wrigley Field. At that point in the season his record stood at 2-6, with a 6.37 ERA.

By July, Jennings had returned to the consistency that kept him atop the rotation. In his first three starts of the month, he pitched 20 innings, yielding only four earned runs and lowering his ERA from 5.75 to 5.08. He went seven scoreless innings and got the win on July 9, in the first-ever 1-0 game at Coors Field. With the July 31 trade deadline approaching, both the San Francisco Giants and Boston Red Sox showed interest in acquiring the big right-hander, but the Rockies were not willing to part with their ace. He looked to be headed toward a strong finish.

Then came July 20, and a start in Washington against the Nationals. Jennings had gone five strong innings, continuing a stretch of effective starts over the last two months. In the top of the sixth, with the Rockies up 3-2 and no one on base, he singled. Cory Sullivan bunted. Nats first baseman Brad Wilkerson fielded it and threw to second attempting to get the force out. Jennings slid into second and awkwardly caught his right hand on the base. As a result, his middle finger was fractured, ending his season. After seasons of 32, 32, and 33 starts, the injury held him to 20 starts in '05. His final record stood at 6-9, with a 5.02 ERA.

Jennings's goal heading in to 2006 was to put the injury behind him and earn the Opening Day starting assignment. He hoped to change his early-season misfortunes by adjusting his offseason workout, concentrating on routines to strengthen his back, shoulders and abs. "What I am doing has changed my body composition. I feel more solid," Jennings said in a *Denver Post* interview. "I am happy with the way the workouts are going and hope it makes a difference in (the way the season starts)."[9] In addition, pitching coach Apodaca changed the pitchers' spring-training work schedule, having starters throw more than in prior springs.

On February 24, manager Clint Hurdle announced that Jennings would indeed start on Opening day, becoming the fourth pitcher in Rockies history to make two Opening Day starts. By this time Jennings was the senior member of the Rockies staff, despite having only four full seasons in the big leagues. He was also the Rockies' second-longest-tenured player, behind only Todd Helton.

Despite battling a flu bug, Jennings was impressive in the 2006 opener, a 3-2 win in 11 innings over the Arizona Diamondbacks. He threw seven innings of one-run ball. In postgame comments, Jennings said, "Hopefully, this is a sign of things to come. Usually as I get more tired (and) as the season wears on, I get better. Most sinkerball guys are like that. Hopefully, I can just come out this year and change the trend I've had since I've been here."[10]

Things did go a little better early on. Jennings earned his first win in start number two, going six innings at San Diego, giving up five hits and three runs. His final two April starts were rough, though; he allowed seven earned runs in San Francisco on April 21, and again in Philadelphia on April 26. But those were Jennings's two worst starts of the season, as he settled in after that and pitched the best ball of his career. By July his earned-run average had dipped below 4.00. From June 15 through mid-August, he had an NL-best 2.03 ERA.[11] He was threatening to break Joe Kennedy's mark (3.66) for the lowest season ERA for a Rockies starter, checking in at 3.34 as of August 16.

Jennings pitched well, but his won-lost record did not benefit much due to some tough luck and the Rockies' unusually weak offense in 2006. As of August 23, he had 19 quality starts (defined as at least six innings with three or fewer earned runs) second most in the National League, yet was only 6-6 in those games. He had the third lowest run support in the league.

As the innings piled up over the second half of the season, Jennings was less effective. By season's end he was gassed. "I think it is fatigue as much as anything," manager Hurdle said after his final start of the season. "He had five walks and zero punchouts. He did not have a crisp fastball. The workload has piled up on him a little bit."[12] His ERA had climbed to 3.78. There was some thought about giving him the start in the final game of the season, October 1. He would break the Rockies' season ERA mark with seven shutout innings in that game, but due to the fatigue of the long season he decided to forgo the start and shut it down for the year.

In 2006 Jennings pitched a career-high 212 innings, the fourth highest total in Rockies history up to then. He had a career-low 3.78 ERA. His 9-13 record did not reflect his true value, and would have much better with more run support.

Because Jennings would be eligible for free agency after the 2007 season, rumors circulated that the Rockies were shopping him in the offseason to plug gaps in other areas, most notably center field. Despite his success at home, Jennings was open to the notion of pitching away from Coors Field. Negotiations grew tense between the club and Jennings in early December, when the Rockies made what amounted to a "discounted" offer to their star right-hander. The proposal was less than pitchers of his caliber had signed, and Jennings would not respond to the offer. Rockies owner Charlie Monfort felt Jennings was being unfair in not responding. General manager Dan O'Dowd felt he had no choice but to trade Jennings, given the likelihood that he would not sign the contract extension and could potentially leave the team as a free agent once the 2007 season concluded.

Jennings's career with the Rockies came to an end on December 12, 2006. The Rockies traded him to Houston. While the trade was viewed as a good one for the Rockies, who received two promising young pitchers and speedy center fielder Willy Taveras, it involved arguably the best pitcher in Rockies history. Jennings held the club records for wins (58); innings pitched (941); games started (156); and shutouts (3). As the 2002 Rookie of the Year, he was also the only Rockies pitcher to earn an award.

But Jennings's major-league career went downhill after he left Colorado. In 2007, his lone season with Houston, he struggled to a 2-9 record with an ERA of 6.45. Elbow problems, which he disclosed in August as having dealt with "for well over a year now," kept him on the disabled list most of April and May.[13] His season ended in August when it was determined surgery was required.

Houston did not bring Jennings back for 2008. A free agent, he signed a one-year agreement with the Texas Rangers at a guaranteed $4 million, with incentives based on pitching appearances and milestones. Everything looked bright: Jennings would be pitching for his hometown team, and felt healthy for the first time since early 2006.

Despite the optimism, it was more of the same in 2008. Jennings struggled, with what was becoming a chronic sore elbow. After just six starts, he was placed on the disabled list. He missed the rest of the season.

Jennings re-signed with the Rangers for the 2009 season, and was moved to the bullpen. It turned out to be his last season in the major leagues. He pitched well over the first half of the season, but was hit hard from late July on, and was released in August. He closed out his career with 44 appearances in the season and a 4.13 ERA. He signed a minor-league deal with the Oakland Athletics for 2010, but did not make their major-league roster.

Jennings continued to play minor-league ball through 2011. He was 10-2 for the independent American Association champion Grand Prairie AirHogs before retiring from professional baseball in 2012.

Through the 2017 season, Jennings was in the Rockies' top 10 in nearly all major pitching categories. He was fourth in wins (58), innings pitched (941), and games started (156). He was tied with Ubaldo

Jimenez for the club lead in shutouts (3), and was fifth in strikeouts (622).

As of 2018 Jennings lived in Frisco, Texas, with his wife, Kelly; sons, Keathan and Braden; and daughter, Bailee. He founded and operates Pastime Training Center in Frisco, dedicated to training youngsters in baseball and softball skills, and life lessons.

SOURCES

In addition to the sources cited in the Notes, the author consulted thebaseballcube.com, Baseball-Reference.com, and Retrosheet.org.

NOTES

1   Email correspondence with Jason Jennings, September 2017.

2   Troy E. Renck, "Colorado Rockies Spring Training," *Denver Post*, March 24, 2002: C-4.

3   Bob Nightengale, "Jennings Proves Coors Can Be Tamed," *USA Today Baseball Weekly*, August 28-September 3, 2002: 5.

4   Troy E. Renck, "Jennings Lights Up Dim Scene, Rookie Making Case for Award," *Denver Post*, September 3, 2002: D-06.

5   Troy E. Renck, "Jennings Top NL Rookie/Pitcher Says Changeup Will Keep Him in Groove," *Denver Post*, November 5, 2002: D-01.

6   Ibid.

7   Tracy Ringolsby, "Jennings Armed For '05 — Rockies Pitcher, With 2-Year Deal, Ready for Business," *Rocky Mountain News*, February 19, 2005: 1B.

8   Jack Etkin, "Jennings Eyes Quicker Start — Right-Hander Confident He Will Bring an End to His April Woes This Year," *Rocky Mountain News*, April 6, 2005: 6C.

9   Troy E. Renck, "Rockies — Getting to Core of the Matter — Jennings Uses New Winter Workout," *Denver Post*, January 2, 2006: C-02.

10   John Henderson, "Sinkerball Lifts Jennings' Recovery — Flu Bug Squashed — The Opening-Day Starter Reverses a Trend of Getting Off on the Wrong Foot With Seven Strong Innings," *Denver Post*, April 4, 2006: D-09.

11   Troy E. Renck, "Untimely Generosity Puts L.A. Back in First/ Dodgers 4, Rockies 3," *Denver Post*, August 11, 2006: D-01.

12   Tracy Ringolsby, "Dodgers Get in Way of Jennings' Pursuit — Pitcher Loses Game, Ground in Quest for Rockies ERA Record," *Rocky Mountain News*, September 27, 2006: 4C.

13   Jose de Jesus Ortiz, "Astros' Jennings Faces Season-Ending Surgery," *Houston Chronicle*, August 22, 2007.

KELI MCGREGOR

BY ALEX MARKS

"NO MATTER WHAT YOUR ROLE OR title, model greatness and invite others on the journey." That is the quote that is stapled into a sign outside the baseball park at the Salt River Fields baseball complex on the Pima-Maricopa Indian Community in Scottsdale, Arizona. It greets you as you arrive at the entrance of the Keli McGregor Reflection Trail, which is a small walking trail that circles the west side of the baseball complex. It was a dedication from the Pima-Maricopa tribe because they were so touched by the interest McGregor had in their tribe and community as a whole. The Reflection Trail also allows those who walk it to reflect on Keli McGregor as a person; someone who always cherished people over projects, friendships over fare, above all else, relationships over records.

Keli Scott McGregor was born on January 23, 1963, in Primghar, Iowa. Shortly after he was born, his parents, Brian and Margaret McGregor, left Margaret's family farm and moved to the Denver area. Brian joined the coaching staff at Lakewood Junior High School. "I wanted to be a teacher and a coach," he said.[1] He moved to Arvada West the following year as assistant football coach and head track and field coach. He soon became the head football coach, and his 1972 Arvada West team won the state championship. Keli's father was very passionate about football, and baseball was something to just fill the summer months. "Baseball never was a big thing for me," said Brian.[2]

Keli McGregor was a multisport athlete at Lakewood (Colorado) High School from 1977 through 1980. For college, McGregor decided to stay close to his childhood home and was accepted by Colorado State University. (Of course, he had other motivation: He wanted to marry his high-school sweetheart, Lori.) He took his skills as an all-state running back to play for the university's football team as a walk-on. Considered to be an undersized halfback when he arrived on campus, McGregor went

from freshman walk-on to second-team all-American tight end in 1984. He grew to 6-feet-8 and was listed at 250 pounds, and went on to become an all-Western Athletic Conference tight end from 1982 to 1984. He set a single-season school record with 69 catches in 1983, a mark that stood for 10 years. In his four years at CSU, he had 153 receptions, 1,604 yards, and 8 touchdowns.[3] He was voted to Colorado State's all-century team in 1992 and was named to the CSU Hall of Fame in 1996.

McGregor was selected by Denver in the fourth round of the 1985 NFL draft and played for the Denver Broncos and the Indianapolis Colts during the 1985 NFL season for a total of eight games. In 1986 he tried to catch on with the Seattle Seahawks, but never made it out of training camp. When he could not catch on with any other professional football team, he decided to hang up his playing career. He never accumulated any offensive stats.

McGregor then embarked on a career in sports administration. He worked as an associate athletic director at the University of Arkansas for four years, and then as assistant football coach for two years at the University of Florida (1988-89), where he earned a master's degree in education with an emphasis on athletic administration.

Although he had been very passionate about football through his early adult life, he was finding it was not such a fulfilling career. Little did he know that because of a close friendship, he would truly make his mark in professional baseball.

During his time at Colorado State University, Keli had become friends with Mike McMorris, whose father, Jerry McMorris, had become the initial principal owner of the Colorado Rockies, in 1993. Jerry McMorris was looking for some new and fresh ideas from outside the baseball world.

McMorris hired Keli in October 1993 as director of stadium operations. "The way that Keli came in and handled everything so smoothly, and the way he worked with others in baseball, I just knew it would be a matter of time before he would be the man sitting in the big chair with the ultimate authority," said McMorris.[4] McGregor held that position until 1995; he was promoted to senior vice president in 1996 and then executive vice president in 1998. His meteoric rise in the Rockies organization reached its apex when he took over from the very man who had believed in him, believed that he could change the organization. Jerry McMorris decided to step down as the team's president and McGregor replaced him in 2001.

Despite coming from a football background, McGregor quickly learned the inner workings of major-league baseball and was highly respected by players, administrators, and owners throughout the sport. The health-conscious McGregor often worked out at Coors Field with Rockies players. He knew that the future of the Rockies not only had to come from within, by bringing in and developing young baseball talent, but by also establishing great relationships with communities, those who followed baseball and even those who did not.

He worked to fortify the team's farm system, declaring that the franchise would emphasize character while building the team with home-grown players. He also strongly emphasized community involvement from players and others within the organization. He cofounded and served as president of the Reaching Out to Youth (ROY) Foundation in the battle against cystic fibrosis, which had claimed the life of his dear friend Mike McMorris. He served on numerous boards, including the Denver Metro Chamber of Commerce and the Colorado Commission on Higher Education. The Rockies helped build more than 100 youth baseball fields during his 18 years with the franchise. McGregor believed in building strong and trusting relationships throughout the Rockies organization and the state of Colorado in general.

"I talked to (Commissioner) Bud Selig, who is a good friend of mine, the day after Keli died," Jerry McMorris said. "He told me Keli was on the short list of people being considered to be the next com-

missioner of baseball. That's how highly regarded he was. It makes me sad when I think about how much more he could have accomplished."[5]

McGregor's passion and vision for the Rockies paid off in seven short years. In the fall of 2007, the Rockies made an impressive late-season charge that carried them into their first World Series. Even though they were swept in four games by the Boston Red Sox, reaching the World Series was the ultimate affirmation that McGregor's emphasis on player development and character were the keys to the franchise's future success. McGregor had built the relationships he wanted, and now the whole Rockies franchise was celebrating his impact.

Once McGregor had steered the Rockies franchise in a better baseball direction, he wanted to bring them closer to their respective communities as well, starting with their spring-training operations in Arizona. The team had been at Hi Corbett Field in Tucson since its beginning, but the Rockies and the only other team training in Tucson, the Arizona Diamondbacks, wanted to move to a better facility, one closer to all spring training teams in the Phoenix area. So in July 2009, McGregor led the negotiations and agreement to build a new spring training-facility in Scottsdale, Arizona, within the Salt River Pima-Maricopa Indian Community on land that is called Talking Stick. "The complex will provide for our fans and organization the best pure spring experience in major-league baseball," McGregor said in a statement once the deal was finalized. "We're excited to partner with the Salt River Pima-Maricopa Indian Community and the Arizona Diamondbacks."[6]

It was McGregor's desire to bring the communities of the Colorado Rockies (along with the Diamondbacks) and the Salt River Pima-Maricopa Tribe together to help one another, for that was what he believed in: the power of relationships. Sadly, McGregor would not live long enough to see his true vision come to pass.

On April 20, 2010, he was found dead at the age of 47 in a Salt Lake City hotel room while on a business trip. He was in his 17th season with the Rockies, his ninth as club president. Initial indications were that he died of natural causes. Major figures in McGregor's life paid tribute to him, including members of the Rockies and Diamondbacks, Commissioner Selig, and representatives of Major League Baseball, Colorado State University, the Denver Broncos, and his family and friends.[7] The power of these relationships was on full display to show the world it had lost such a wonderful person.

On August 30, 2010, it was announced that McGregor had died of a rare virus that infected his heart muscle. The infection caused lymphocytic myocarditis, an inflammatory disease of the heart muscle, killing an otherwise healthy McGregor. His family (he was survived by his wife, Lori, three daughters, and a son) issued a statement about the diagnosis and how they could remember him:

"Keli McGregor had the heart of a lion. He did not die of a heart attack or of any other preventable heart condition. Instead, his healthy heart was attacked by a rare virus which unfortunately infected the heart muscle, causing the lymphocytic myocarditis that led to Keli's death. In an unusual manifestation of a viral illness, this organism infiltrated his heart muscle and disrupted the electrical pathways that signal the heart to beat properly. The heart muscle may have recovered from the viral attack had these electrical pathways not been destroyed, but the muscle may have been permanently weakened and destined for eventual heart failure. This infectious process most likely occurred during the last week of Keli's life, causing nothing more than flu-like symptoms. Just as a healthy brain can be infected with viral meningitis, a healthy heart can be infected with viral myocarditis. Fortunately, the vast majority of viral illnesses do not damage the heart or the brain. Keli McGregor was a champion of the physical and spiritual health of the heart. He acted as a strong advocate for the early detection and prevention of cardiovascular disease, both with the Rockies and throughout Denver and Colorado. Keli lived an active life and had his cardiovascular status evaluated regularly. Unfortunately, even a heart as strong as Keli's can, in rare cases, fall victim to these microscopic viral invaders. Like you, we miss Keli every minute of every day."[8]

During one of the final home games of the 2010 season, the Rockies honored McGregor by placing his initials "KSM" among the retired numbers at Coors Field.

Before his death, McGregor had spent much of the year putting the finishing touches on the Rockies' new spring-training facility near Scottsdale. Before the facility's official opening for 2011 spring training, on February 11, a blessing was given at sunrise on a spot that is dedicated to McGregor.

McGregor had a huge impact on the Salt River Fields project before his passing. The Salt River Pima-Maricopa Indian Community president, Diane Enos; its vice president, Martin Harvier; community manager Bryan Meyers; and Derrick Hall and Dick Monfort, the Rockies' owner/chairman and CEO, took turns sharing their memories about McGregor during a private dedication outside the Salt River Fields main stadium. Lori McGregor, Keli's widow, also shared memories of her late husband, including how he would come home to Colorado after visiting the Community and would talk about the coming spring training facility. She thanked everyone and the Community for their support, and shortly after she spoke she was presented a miniature sculpture of three water birds identical to the sculptures featured in the facility's Reflections Trail, which is dedicated to the memory of McGregor. The Maricopa singing group Bird Singers and Dancers by the River sang as the guests walked along the trail to see the sculptures being revealed. At the beginning of the trail, the Maricopa group showed to Lori the plaque that had Keli's famous quote, as they felt it embodied what Keli McGregor was all about, and that was the power of relationships.

NOTES

1   Irv Moss, "Death of Former Rockies Keli McGregor Still Stings Father," *Denver Post,* December 23, 2015.

2   Ibid.

3   sports-reference.com/cfb/players/keli-mcgregor-1.html.

4   Todd Phifer, "Keli McGregor," *Colorado Sports Hall of Fame — Who's in the Hall* coloradosports.org/index.php/who-s-in-the-hall/inductees/item/161-keli-mcgregor.

5   Ibid.

6   Kevin Reichard, "D-Backs, Rockies Break Ground on New Spring Complex," *ballparkdigest.com,* November 17, 2009. ballparkdigest.com/200911172324/major-league-baseball/news/d-backs-rockies-break-ground-on-new-spring-complex,

7   Remembering Keli McGregor — a tribute, Coloradorockies.com. colorado.rockies.mlb.com/mlb/news/tributes/obit_keli_mcgregor.jsp?c_id=col.

8   Michael Roberts, "Keli McGregor, Late Rockies President, Died of Rare Virus That Attacked His Heart, Family Says," *Westword,* August 31, 2010. westword.com/news/keli-mcgregor-late-rockies-president-died-of-rare-virus-that-attacked-his-heart-family-says-5869497.

JERRY MCMORRIS

BY BOB LEMOINE

"I'll never forget the experience of going to spring training for the first time. Then, there was our first opening day against the Mets in New York. We came back to Denver for our first home game and Eric Young hit the home run leading off the bottom of the first inning. The home run and the great crowd were huge. Then fast forward to the opening game in Coors Field, making the playoffs in 1995 and our All-Star Game in 1998. All of those things were great for Denver."
—Jerry McMorris.[1]

JERRY MCMORRIS KNEW WHAT A championship baseball team looked like because he had been on one. In Little League. "I played first base," the future millionaire entrepreneur and baseball team owner said, referring back to when he was 12. "I was tall and not especially quick of foot, so that's where they put me."[2] He certainly wasn't going to make money playing baseball. Instead, he started his own trucking company and three decades later was a successful businessman with enough money to buy a "major-league baseball team everybody in Colorado can be proud of,"[3] he promised. He discovered building a championship team wasn't anything like Little League, and running a baseball team wasn't like running a trucking company. But both Colorado and baseball itself needed Jerry and his business know-how when it seemed the team wouldn't even get off the ground, and the 1994 players strike threatened to dig baseball's grave. McMorris, always exuding confidence, guided the Colorado Rockies through their first decade of existence and put the Mile High City on the baseball map.

Jerry McMorris was a baseball fan at heart and loved the American West, with its culture and traditions. He was a small part of the original ownership group of the Colorado Rockies, who were awarded an expansion franchise in 1991. When the major partners of the group were involved in legal and financial trouble and it looked as if Denver would lose its new franchise before it even started, McMorris stepped up at the eleventh hour to take control. McMorris can be called the savior of the Colorado Rockies; it might not have existed if not for him. He helped create not only an expansion franchise but also a team that was the talk of baseball in the 1990s. The Rockies led all of baseball in attendance from 1993 to 1999, made the postseason in just their third year of existence, and were often seen on baseball highlights slamming home runs consistently through the mountain air. But as fans and sportswriters regularly do with club owners, McMorris was criticized for what he did or didn't do to get the club to the next level. Quality pitching was hard to find and McMorris's record-breaking contracts to top pitchers couldn't stop their ERAs from soaring like mountain peaks. But it wasn't for lack of trying, and the Rockies in their infancy were led by a pioneer who was "a man more inclined to set a trend than follow a crowd."[4]

"Jerry quickly established himself as a leader within our industry," Commissioner Bud Selig said, "playing a key role on a number of our committees and serving not only the Rockies franchise but all of Major League Baseball very well."[5]

Jerry Dean McMorris was born on October 9, 1940, in Rock Island, Illinois, to Donn and Evelyn McMorris. Both parents were from Illinois. Later siblings included a brother, Jeffrey, and a sister, Caryljo. At the 1940 census, Evelyn worked for a rubber boot manufacturer. Donn was a truck driver and would spend his career in the trucking industry. He drove for the Denver-Chicago (D-C) Trucking Company and worked his way up to vice president of the company. His upward mobility created a transient life for the family, and young Jerry lived in Iowa, Denver, Nebraska, Minnesota, Ohio, and Denver again by the time he reached his junior year at Denver's Cathedral High School. Always being the new kid in class probably made him the success he was in the business world. "I wonder if that didn't have a long-term effect on my life," McMorris pondered. "I found it easier to go in and meet people than most men do."[6] "He was a very smart person," his future wife, Mary, remembered. "He was a total 'A' personality. He just had a certain charisma when he walked into the room." Mary remembered being "swept off my feet" at a young age as even then Jerry "was so positive and knew exactly what he was going to do with his life."[7]

He loved the New York Yankees, and despite the distance from New York, McMorris felt a connection through the Denver Bears, a Yankees minor-league affiliate. He played baseball for Cathedral and fondly remembered his coach, Cobe Jones. "I remember he hollered a lot, and I got my share," McMorris recalled. "He was a taskmaster, but he was a healthy influence on my life, because he made us aware that he expected me to do my best."[8]

When he was 19, Jerry attended the University of Colorado and worked for D-C Trucking in the summer. He brought some ideas on how to improve the company to his father. "If you're so smart, you should go into business for yourself," his father told him. So Jerry did. He borrowed money, bought three trucks and established Westway Motor Freight trucking company. He began a relationship with the Adolph Coors Company and transported beer from the Coors Brewing Company in Golden, Colorado, to Denver. The energetic Jerry would haul beer, answer the phones, and change flat tires from sunup to sundown, believing no time in the day should be wasted. He later bought out Northeast Trucking and the combined companies were then called Northwest Transport.[9] Jerry and Mary married in 1962.[10]

In 1965, he and his father merged, forming NationsWay Transport.[11]

In 1979 the McMorris family moved from Denver to a farm in Timnath, Colorado, an hour north of the city. Jerry and Mary had three children. The farm

grew to 1,300 acres[12] and in 1982 he went into the cattle business. By the mid 1990s his Belvoir and Red Mountain ranches encompassed 53,000 acres from Colorado to Wyoming.[13] There was no doubt McMorris was a man who loved the West. "Nothing strikes a chord in him like the sight of father and son riding side-by-side on a tractor," wrote Jerry Crasnick in *Baseball America*. "Or a little boy, dressed in cowboy boots, jeans, workshirt and cap, chewing on a toothpick like dad. He figures it's the closest life can come to a Norman Rockwell painting."[14]

In August of 1990, Colorado Governor Roy Romer turned to McMorris when early attempts to land professional baseball in the Mile High City were stalled. John Dikeou, owner of the Denver Zephyrs minor-league team, had been influential in persuading major-league owners to consider the city for an expansion team and encouraging voters to approve a ballot measure to fund a new stadium.[15] But Dikeou had to remove himself from the position while major-league baseball was still entertaining pleas for an expansion team from Miami, St. Petersburg, Buffalo, and Washington. McMorris had previously considered investing in a sports team. "We had talked about joining the Denver Broncos ownership many years ago, and we had talked about the Denver Nuggets," McMorris said. "But the opportunity to help bring baseball to the area meant more to me, and I know it means more to the community than buying an existing franchise."[16]

On July 5, 1991, team owners approved a National League expansion franchise for Denver and the Michael Monus/John Antonucci/Steve Ehrhart ownership group. Monus and Antonucci were Youngstown, Ohio, businessmen. Monus was the president of the discount drugstore chain Phar-Mor Inc. Antonucci was an Ohio beverage distributor. Ehrhart, a Denver-area businessman, became chief operating officer. These new general partners also had secured financing for the future home of the Rockies, Coors Field. But the future of the franchise was in doubt a year later when Monus was forced out as president of Phar-Mor amid charges of embezzlement. Monus was forced to resign his position with the Rockies, was later indicted on charges of fraud and embezzlement of $1 billion, and spent time in prison.[17] All of this hit the fan on July 29, 1992, a mere nine months before Opening Day. Monus and Antonucci's $20 million investment was mainly through loans and not cash. An unsung hero in this story is Denver attorney Paul Jacobs, who on the very day Monus confessed his wrongdoings, had the Monus family transfer $10 million of stock in the team to himself and team accountant Stephen Kurtz. The Antonucci $10 million investment was also "bad money" since it was linked with Monus. So Jacobs arrived at the National League's New York office to meet with NL President Bill White and Commissioner Fay Vincent, saying he now owned the team but didn't have the $20 million needed.[18]

Enter McMorris, who was one of eight limited partners in the ownership group, having paid $7 million of the necessary $95 million expansion fee. McMorris was the limited partner to step up into a leadership role to keep the franchise afloat. He not only had to try to figure out a way to make up the shortfall, but also organize a new ownership team. Yet his optimism was apparent from the beginning. "The Colorado partners, once we get all the facts, will do what it takes to solve the problem," he said. "There's no reason for people here to be concerned, the commissioner to be concerned, or the league to be concerned. The Monus thing will not be a significant hurdle. I've talked to another partner, and knowing the character of the other families and businesses, I have no concerns. What I don't want to see happen is for us to lose sight of the excellent management team they've put together."[19]

"I remember I was in my backyard when Jerry came walking up," Charlie Monfort remembered. Monfort and his brother Dick Monfort were part of a family that owned a meatpacking and distribution company in Greeley, Colorado. The company was later purchased by ConAgra Foods. "(Jerry) said: 'We've got a problem. We've got to step up or we're going to lose this franchise. What can you do?'

Jerry McMorris and Don Baylor

I said, 'I'm in.' But he's the one who led the charge."[20] McMorris pledged half of the $20 million himself, and secured the rest through Monfort and Oren Benton, a Denver-area entrepreneur with holdings in uranium trading.[21]

"I believe it is fair to say without the efforts of Jerry, there may have never been major league baseball in Denver," Dick Monfort said in 2012.[22] "We have three new major partners—myself, Oren Benton, and Charles Monfort," McMorris announced. "The major partners essentially have equal ownership positions, but I have been appointed chairman and chief executive officer of the general partnership and will represent our interest in the operation of the ownership group and related entities."[23] Coors Brewing Company was the fourth partner in the new ownership. Antonucci remained with the organization for a few more months, and Ehrhart became president of the Rockies Stadium Development Corporation, which was involved in the creation of Coors Field.

Other fine-tuning with just months to go before the 1993 season included the hiring of Bob Gebhard as general manager and Don Baylor as manager, as well as the expansion draft in November. "We've waited a long time for this," McMorris said as he and Gebhard watched the first player workout at the first spring training in Tucson, Arizona. "This is a special day. Everybody here today is in on a little bit of history. It all starts right here, right now."[24] In less than two months, McMorris was in Shea Stadium in New York as the Rockies played on the first Opening Day in their history. They lost 3-0 and finished 0-2 on their brief season-opening series. Now they came home for their first home opener at Mile High Stadium. The legendary stadium had been home to Denver's minor-league team since 1948, but because it shared space with the Denver Broncos of the National Football League, the left-field wall was adjusted to only 335 feet, a hitter's paradise.[25]

McMorris addressed the team before it took the field in front of a crowd of 80,227, the largest ever in the National League. "Guys, the sky's the limit. The dreams are out there for you guys to chase. Here's your opportunity." "That was big for us,"

Dante Bichette recalled. "I don't think major-league baseball would have happened in Denver if not for him."[26] The energized team won that home opener over Montreal, 11-4, with leadoff batter Eric Young, the first Rockie to bat at home, homered in a four-run first inning. The team had plenty of offense. The 1993 Rockies finished third in the National League in batting average, fourth in runs per game, tied for fourth in runs scored, and third in slugging percentage. The thin mountain air contributed to their power and huge discrepancies were evident in their home/away averages. The Rockies had a higher batting average (.306/.240), scored more runs (489/269), produced more RBIs (449/255), and had more total bases (1,328/1,001) at home by wide margins than they did on the road. But the opposite was also true. Colorado pitchers had a collective ERA nearly a run higher at home than on the road (5.87/4.99), far more runs allowed (551/416), and more home runs allowed (107/74).

McMorris was determined to show the multitude of fans (the brand-new Rockies drew a major-league record of 4,483,350 or 55,350 per game) he was determined to improve the troubled pitching staff. In July, the Rockies acquired veteran starting pitchers Bruce Hurst and Greg Harris in a trade with the San Diego Padres. "Our fans deserve to have a winner," McMorris said. "If we aren't willing to take some financial gambles in our position, then shame on us."[27] But the salaries were high and the players were a gamble. The 35-year-old Hurst never won a game for the Rockies; Harris suffered a horrendous 1-8 with a 6.50 ERA. "Regrets? None," McMorris said. "I don't even have any second thoughts."[28] The Rockies' inaugural season saw them finish 67-95, in sixth place in the National League West.

McMorris was named the 1993 Business Leader of the Year by the Colorado Association of Commerce and Industry.[29] The 1994 season, in which both leagues divided into three divisions with a wild-card playoff team, saw the Rockies improve to third place despite the worst ERA in the league (5.15). When player David Nied's son was born prematurely in New York City and needed to be transported to Denver by Air

Ambulance, McMorris paid the $13,000 bill. "They were in a tough, tough deal, and I was in a position where we could at least cushion that a little. So that's what we decided to do," he said.[30]

McMorris would have a major role in baseball beyond the Rockies franchise. The 1994 season has forever been a black mark on the game. With the collective-bargaining contract up for renegotiation, the owners, who had colluded to limit the signing of free agents in previous years, sought to control soaring salaries via a salary cap, a revenue-sharing plan, and limits on the power of free agents. With little progress toward settlement, the players union struck on August 12. Many expected the situation to be resolved shortly, but the remainder of the season and postseason were canceled. As a late December deadline for the owners to impose a salary cap approached, the owners negotiating committee called on McMorris to make their last good-faith effort before imposing the cap.[31] Acting Commissioner Bud Selig remarked, "Jerry is the best person to come."[32]

"Both parties are probing and trying to find a way," McMorris said after a three-hour meeting that ended in the wee hours of the morning. "My sense is if we're deadlocked again on Thursday, there won't be any flexibility. If we can break the deadlock and get the thing moving, we shouldn't need to go beyond Thursday [December 22]." McMorris had experience negotiating with the Teamsters Union and players had respect for his demeanor and manner. "He's a nice guy who's sometimes shrewd," said Don Baylor, the Rockies manager. "He's confident he can get it done by negotiating. That's how Jerry looks at himself. He's not trying to intimidate; he's trying to negotiate. His attitude is, 'We can work it out.'" "He's approachable," said David Cone, a player representative. "We admire him as a second-year owner who has the guts to speak his mind."[33] This was the Jerry his wife, Mary, knew so well: "He could see a path to negotiating when no one else could."[34]

McMorris said his previous success in negotiating "has had something to do with treating people with dignity and respect, which is always how I conduct myself. I think that's important. A proper relation-ship with everybody is important. And certainly your relationship with your employees and your associates in any business is. This sport is no different."[35]

In 1994, NW Transport changed its name to NationsWay Transport to better reflect a national company that recently opened 28 new freight terminals, mostly in the Northeast and Southeast. This expansion was possible when St. Johnsbury Truck Lines, a New England-based service McMorris had as a marketing partner, went out of business and McMorris took over the routes.[36] By 1995 NationsWay saw profits around $400 million, had 6,500 employees and 13,000 pieces of equipment, and had expanded into Texas, Louisiana, Arkansas, Tennessee, Mississippi, Alabama, Georgia, and Florida.[37] But McMorris was still known as an everyday, caring individual who contributed to his church: St. Benedict's Church in Florence, Colorado, and let employees just call him Jerry. "I could get along without the attention," McMorris said in 1995. "It's something I can handle, but I don't thrive on it."[38]

In January 1995 *Baseball America* listed McMorris as number three among the 25 most influential people in baseball. "No one has risen as far, as fast as McMorris," the publication wrote. "He is already an important member of the owners' negotiation committee, and many think he'll be the key to straightening out the mess in baseball. McMorris looks at the big picture better than other owners and is a calming force in a sea of hotheads."[39] His net worth, including his trucking business, farm, and ranch as well as the Rockies, was estimated at $100 million.[40]

The 1995 season was a landmark season for the franchise. The team unveiled Coors Field as the new home of the Rockies, and also made the playoffs for the first time. Coors Field was the first baseball-only park built in the National League since Dodger Stadium in 1962. A downtown-friendly stadium would easily become the most hitter-friendly stadium in baseball and the biggest nightmare for pitchers. The design placed outfield fences farther back, in light of the history of home runs flying out of Mile High Stadium. But this only meant more doubles and triples. Left field was 347 feet, left-center 390 feet, and the deepest part of right-center 424 feet. Because of the enormous crowds at Mile High, the original 43,800 seats planned for Coors Field were increased to 50,200.[41]

The first game at Coors Field was a spring-training contest against the New York Yankees on March 31, 1995, even as the strike still lingered and replacement players were brought in. The absence of star players didn't dampen the enthusiasm, however; the shiny new stadium was the star of the show. "This is a special day for the whole region," McMorris said. "After waiting more than 30 years, we now have the most unique urban ballpark in the majors."[42] Baseball lifer Don Zimmer, now a Rockies coach, said, "Were this game not in a brand-new park, it'd be just another spring-training game. But when nearly 50,000 people come out, that's special."[43] In the crowd was Buck O'Neil, the legendary Negro League player. "I've played in some great parks—even in old Yankee Stadium," he said. "But nothing like this."[44]

Fans were obviously eager for the regular players to return and the gloomy strike to end. That announcement came the very next day. Having been rebuffed by the courts, the owners couldn't garner enough votes to continue a lockout, and agreed to the union's offer to return to work. The season would be limited to 144 games instead of 162, but replacement players never set foot on the diamond for an actual regular-season game. Baseball was finally back. "I hope we'll be very aggressive and get to the table very quickly," McMorris said. "We've both proven how strong we are, and I think we've severely damaged our game."[45] Nevertheless, McMorris invested money to improve the team, giving $35.1 million for free-agent pitcher Bill Swift and free-agent outfielder Larry Walker. "There's only one reason we can do this," McMorris said. "The fan support in Denver. Who would have ever known that they would have stepped up like they did? And we're trying to give them back a financial commitment. We think we've made more advancement in a shorter period of time than any other expansion franchise."[46]

The first Opening Day at Coors Field, on April 26, harkened back to the beginnings of the franchise two years earlier. Eric Young had homered in the first Rockies at-bat in 1993 and now it was a walk-off home run by Dante Bichette in the 14th inning to christen Coors Field as the Rockies prevailed in the cold opener, 11-9. "This was exciting," McMorris said. "The weather was cold and it was gratifying to see the fans still there at the end."[47] They would also have a walk-off win the next day, 8-7. Their two initial games set a tone: The pitching was again bad at home, but the bats were ferocious. The Rockies led the NL in home runs (200), RBIs (749), slugging percentage (.471), and batting average (.282). At home they batted .316 (134 home runs), on the road, .247 (66 homers). The Rockies' pitching was again last in the NL in ERA at 4.97 (6.17 at home, 3.71 on the road). But it was enough to get them into the playoffs. Walker hit 36 home runs with 101 RBIs and was joined by teammates with similar numbers: Andres Galarraga (31-106), Vinny Castilla (32-90), and Bichette (40-128). "Tears of joy," McMorris said as the club clinched a postseason berth. "It was a very emotional time for me. This is why we wanted to have baseball here in the first place."[48] Fittingly, the Rockies clinched by winning the season finale 10-9 after trailing 8-2. "The 30-year wait to get major-league baseball here gave a lot of people the opportunity to be part of this."[49] It was their only playoff appearance during the McMorris ownership era.

Jerry and Mary had a son, Michael Dean McMorris, who was born in 1964. At 14 months Michael was diagnosed with cystic fibrosis and was not expected to live past the age of 2. He survived and thrived, however, becoming a high-school athlete who loved to scuba-dive, hike, and ski. He graduated from Colorado State University in 1988 and while a student assisted the CSU football program in videotape, budgeting, and recruitment. After college Michael worked with his father in the trucking business, and then joined the Rockies as director of operating services. Despite his constant need for medical and physical care, Michael lived to age 32, succumbing to the disease in 1996. The Rockies wore the initials MDM on their sleeves during the season.[50] "Mike was loved by everybody who took care of him.

He was a role model for people who have to face adversity," said his physician, Dr. Lawrence Kline.[51] The research for a cure for the disease goes forward in his name at the Mike McMorris Cystic Fibrosis Research and Care Center at Children's Hospital Colorado, in Aurora, Colorado. The center is "the largest CF clinical care center in the United States," according to its website.[52] "We hope that funding this center in celebration of Mike's life will help conquer the disease once and for all," McMorris said at the center's grand opening in 1998. Mary echoed his sentiments and applauded the medical advances on the disease. "We're quite encouraged by the progress," she said, "but at the same time, we're disappointed that we're not really solving the problems of children who have it now."[53]

Another son, Scott McMorris, attended Colorado University.

The Rockies had back-to-back third-place finishes of 83-79 records in 1996-1997, experiencing the same problems with pitchers. The Rockies didn't even have a starting pitcher with 10 wins in 1997. After two off-seasons of no blockbuster pitcher signings, McMorris dug into his pockets again and acquired free-agent pitcher Darryl Kile.

Coors Field hosted the All-Star Game on July 7, 1998. Hometown hero Walker started in center field, batting seventh. Appropriately, it was the highest-scoring All-Star Game in history, with the American League winning 13-8 before a crowd of 51,267. McMorris summarized the occasion succinctly enough: "I think we put on a good show."[54] A 77-85 season by the Rockies, however, soured the rest of the season and it cost Baylor the managerial job he had held since day one of the franchise. "I personally will accept a large part of the responsibility for our disappointments," McMorris said, deflecting the blame from Baylor. "This issue wasn't to point fingers. In the end, the players are the ones who have to play. We know that. We felt that the quickest way to get to the level we want was a change in chemistry."[55]

Before the 1999 season, Commissioner Selig appointed McMorris to a panel to discuss the issue of revenue-sharing and a player salary cap. Also on the committee were author George Will, representatives of the MLBPA, and Yale academics. That offseason, the Los Angeles Dodgers had signed free agent Kevin Brown to a $105 million, seven-year contract. McMorris was firm in the belief that baseball needed to overhaul how it divided TV revenue "so that each city has some chance of winning." "We're not owned by a [Rupert] Murdoch, Disney, or Ted Turner, and baseball can't afford the kind of imbalance where the Dodgers' Kevin Brown alone makes twice the Montreal Expos' entire payroll." Citing the salary-cap system of the National Football League, where small-market teams could compete against the larger markets, McMorris said baseball should adopt a system "to put a brake on those who simply want to spend their way to the moon."[56]

Jim Leyland, considered the best manager available and the skipper who had led Florida to a world title in 1997, became the Rockies' manager in 1999. "He was a winner," McMorris said. "And we had a sense that he liked Coors Field, and he liked it in Colorado. Jim has a different approach in the way he manages. And his approach is enhanced by the World Series ring he's won as a manager."[57] Mike Klis of the Denver Post reported that the Rockies' payroll jumped 14.7 percent to $59.7 million, a 707 percent increase over the $8.8 million payroll on McMorris's first Opening Day, in 1993. "And I'm the cheapskate," McMorris said, referring to criticisms that he was unwilling to spend money.[58] At the top of the payroll was Kile, the expected ace of the staff, who at over $8 million a year led the league in losses (17) with a 5.20 ERA in 1998. Yet the biggest expense would come just days later. Walker signed a six-year extension for $75 million, or $12.5 million per season. Recognizing that he had to spend to compete, McMorris said, "What it really came down to is we are constantly being pressured on what players are being paid in New York and Los Angeles. But not everybody wants to play in New York and Los Angeles."[59]

Depressingly, the 1999 season was another poor one for McMorris (72-90, fifth place), and though the Rockies led baseball in attendance for the seventh straight year, it was down by 300,000 from the year before. Leyland could not figure out what to do with the pitching staff. The Rockies' team ERA was 6.01 and they surrendered the most home runs in the league (237). Yet once again their hitters led the league in batting average (.288) and home runs (223). Bob Gebhard, who had built the team from scratch, resigned as GM. "Bob Gebhard was the heart and soul of this franchise," McMorris said. "He's a stand-up guy. But I could tell today that he was totally drained and beat. It wore on him. It was showing. He was in a tough spot. He couldn't effectively handle his job, especially from the All-Star Game on. But he worked day and night for this organization."[60] Leyland also departed after the season, and Buddy Bell became the new manager.

The year was also a difficult one financially for McMorris. NationsWay had been struggling and needed to be restructured in 1997, slashing routes and returning to a regional service. The $450 million in revenue in 1996 represented an 11 percent decline.[61] The restructuring plan McMorris enacted was only temporary, however, and NationsWay filed for Chapter 11 bankruptcy in May of 1999. "A bankruptcy judge in Phoenix is now the CEO of NationsWay," McMorris said.[62] "This was a challenge bigger than I could find a solution for," he said, referring to the $19 million debt the company accrued, much of it through the failure to make payments to the employee pension fund. McMorris blamed deregulation in the industry, which allowed smaller trucking companies to eat into NationsWay profits over the previous five years. "The fundamental problem is a tough, competitive industry that has had inadequate profits," McMorris said. "The reality was simple — we were not producing a profit."[63] More than 3,000 employees lost their jobs. By contrast, WestWay Express, a smaller trucking company McMorris owned, was thriving.[64]

The reality in the business world is that companies do "go under" and people do lose their livelihoods. But when you are one of those hard-working employees who has a family to support, and your boss, who filed bankruptcy for the company, is the same person who gave a $12-million-a-year contract to

Larry Walker, it is understandable that hard feelings persisted. Such was the image problem McMorris suffered. On the one hand, NationsWay was in a hole, but the Rockies, his other, unrelated business, were prospering. Members of the Teamsters began picketing outside Coors Field. "When the owner of your company pays the Rockies millions and millions of dollars and they can't pay us, it makes you a little hot under the collar," said Valerie Whiddon, a NationsWay employee.[65] "I'm sure that my owning the Rockies is a lightning rod for criticism from people who don't understand that the Rockies are a completely separate legal entity with completely different partners," McMorris said. "What we decided we wanted to pay to keep Larry Walker doesn't have a darned thing to do with wages being competitive in the trucking industry. The [trucking] business has struggled for five years, and it hasn't changed the Rockies' foundation or the other things this organization stands for. I hope everyone can get on with their lives with a minimal amount of disturbance. But it is what it is. It's very distasteful for everyone. We feel very sorry for everyone involved."[66] Most business owners don't have such a high profile as that of a baseball-team owner, or have such a source of revenue, something his truckers took notice of in terms of income disparity. "I've had drivers ask me over the years how I can pay these type of wages when not one of these ballplayers can drive a truck over Loveland Pass, let alone do it with chains on. Well, nobody's ever paid me to watch those guys chain up and go over Loveland Pass."[67]

In response to the financial hit, McMorris sold all but $8.5 million of his investment to the Monfort brothers, increasing their ownership stake to 46.3 percent of the club.[68]

The 2000 season saw the Rockies finish over .500 (82-80) with an improved fourth-place finish, and the team ERA (5.26) actually wasn't the worst in baseball. Their .294 batting average still topped the NL. To build on the success, McMorris and new GM Dan O'Dowd gave a $121 million contract to free-agent pitcher Mike Hampton for eight years, the largest contract in baseball history to that point. Just days earlier, they had also opened their wallet for free-agent pitcher Denny Neagle for $51.5 million for five years. Beaming at the press conference over the $172.5 million paid for two pitchers, McMorris took congratulatory handshakes, but then uttered an off-hand remark, "If it doesn't work out …"[69]

It didn't. Hampton's ERA soared to 5.41 in 2001 and in 2002 he finished 7-15 with a 6.15 ERA. The Rockies (73-89) finished in the basement in 2001. Neagle was 9-8 with a 5.38 ERA. "We really thought that we would be contenders," McMorris stated.[70] "The heralded free-agent signings were a flop and a failure and a fiasco of epic proportions," wrote Woody Paige in the *Denver Post* two years later.[71]

After the 2001 season, McMorris stepped aside as team president while remaining CEO. Keli McGregor became team president and handled day-to-day operations. McMorris was content with the move. "It means I won't have to be at the office at 7 every morning," McMorris said. "But I'll still be around. In today's economic climate, with the salaries the way they are, ownership has to be involved in the major decisions made by the baseball people. The difference now is we'll become involved only after Keli and Dan and Buddy sort through them first."[72] In 2002, he relinquished his title of CEO and chairman to Charlie Monfort, and remained as vice chairman.

The Rockies again went 73-89 in 2002, a fourth-place finish that was gasoline on the fire for fans and sportswriters clamoring for a change in the front office. "Everything that's wrong with the Rockies starts at the top," wrote Mark Kiszla of the *Denver Post*. "The primary aim is to find a way to dump the salaries of pitchers Denny Neagle and Hampton. They were $175 million mistakes that proved McMorris and the Monfort brothers lack the deep pockets to cover the inevitable errors of free agency. Compounding their lousy investments, the Rockies futilely try to cover their blunders with nickels and dimes. Hampton, Neagle, Walker and first baseman Todd Helton devour a staggering 65 percent of the team's budget for players."[73] McMorris was an architect who helped build the club and see it rise to the playoffs in a short time. Now he had watched the team have

four losing seasons over the last seven, never finishing higher than third. "Once upon a time," Kiszla wrote, "a Colorado trucking magnate rode to the rescue of a National League expansion franchise in need of a jump-start. McMorris, however, has driven baseball in Colorado as far as a man of his resources can go. He and the Rockies would be best served by unloading the team to new ownership, and hauling his well-earned profits into the sunset."[74]

The Rockies finished two more poor seasons in 2003-2004 (74-88, 68-94), and attendance was now far from the top in the National League. In November of 2004, McMorris was removed as vice chairman by the Monfort brothers. McMorris retained his 12.4 percent financial stake in the ownership group but no longer had voting rights. "I didn't decide it," he said. "I've put 12 years in helping to bring major-league baseball to Colorado, building the franchise and working with what was in the best interest of major-league baseball. I've given it my best effort. I don't understand any of this."[75]

In December of 2005, the Monfort brothers bought out McMorris's 42.5 percent share of the general partnership. McMorris received between $17 million and $20 million for his remaining $8.5 million investment. Satisfied with the deal, he took time to reflect on his time running the ballclub. "Getting Coors Field built was a big accomplishment for our franchise. And I enjoyed all of the relationships with the fans and players," McMorris said. "I am just sorry we weren't able to put the pitching together to maintain a consistent run (at the playoffs). It wasn't because of a lack of effort or a lack of money. Those first few years were as special a time as anyone has seen in all of sports."[76] By this time, McMorris acknowledged that his time in baseball ownership had drawn to a close. "I didn't get into baseball thinking it would be the rest of my life," he said. "The plan all along was for Charlie (Monfort) to assume the leadership role."[77]

McMorris, his days as a trucking magnate and baseball executive over, returned to where his heart always was: a ranch in the west. He had been involved with the Western Stock Show Association, serving as chairman for six years and on the executive committee for 18 years. "It was an honor to learn from Jerry and witness his passion for the Western way of life and the values we at the Stock Show represent," said Paul Andrews, president and CEO of the show.[78] McMorris continued to serve the Denver community as vice chairman of the Denver Police Foundation and a member of the board of directors of the Poudre Valley Fire Authority.[79] He never settled into a retirement role, which Mary said didn't fit his energetic style. "His entertainment was taking on a new business deal," she said. "He was a businessman, and he thrived."[80]

While McMorris was ranching, the Rockies put together a memorable 2007 season. The club was largely based on home-grown talent like Matt Holiday, who paid tribute to McMorris for not giving up on him when he was struggling in the minor leagues. "He was always vocal about his support of me and thinking I would be a good player," Holliday said. "He was a big reason why I stayed with baseball."[81] McMorris turned out to Coors Field to watch the Rockies advance to the National League Championship Series. "I am extremely pleased for everybody involved with the franchise," he said. "I feel great about what is going on. This is how it is supposed to be."[82] The Rockies won the National League pennant, but lost to the Boston Red Sox in the World Series.

McMorris was inducted into the Colorado Sports Hall of Fame in 2009. In his induction speech, McMorris's interests in baseball and the American West appropriately came together in a story he told of Gene Autry, the American icon and owner of the California Angels. Meeting Autry at an owners' meeting, Autry told him how he voted for Denver to be a franchise because "Colorado always treated him No.1."[83]

Jerry McMorris died on May 8, 2012, at the Colorado Anschutz Medical Campus in Aurora, Colorado, after a lengthy battle with pancreatic cancer. He was survived by his wife, Mary, his two children, and two grandchildren. He is buried at Mount Olivet Cemetery in Wheat Ridge, Colorado.

Players lined up at Coors Field before the game on May 16, and a video tribute was aired on the JumboTron. Another video tribute aired during the game, and the crowd gave a standing ovation.[84] Mary, who as of 2017 was still attending one Rockies game per month, noted how pleased she was to have been a part of the Rockies franchise and the friendships she made.

"I believe it is fair to say without the efforts of Jerry, there may have never been major-league baseball in Denver. He will be greatly missed by us all," Dick Monfort said.[85] Charlie Monfort summarized the McMorris legacy well: "Jerry McMorris will always have a special place in the history of the Colorado Rockies."

SOURCES

In addition to the sources listed in the Notes, the author benefited from the following sources:

Baseball-reference.com.

Jerry McMorris file from the Giamatti Research Center at the Baseball Hall of Fame, Cooperstown, New York.

Retrosheet.org.

NOTES

1   Irv Moss, "Catching up with Jerry McMorris—Running His Own Farm Club—Rockies Owner Exited Baseball Stage After 12 Years," *Denver Post*, September 25, 2006: C-02.

2   Mark Kiszla, "McMorris May Be Man to Fuel Trust in Rockies," *Denver Post*, August 8, 1992: 1D.

3   Ibid.

4   Jerry Crasnick, "A Driven Man," *Baseball America*, May 29-June 11, 1995: 11.

5   "What Others Are Saying," *Denver Post*, May 9, 2012: 3B.

6   Crasnick, "A Driven Man."

7   Mary McMorris, phone interview with the author, November 10, 2017.

8   Irv Moss, "McMorris at Home as Owner—Rockies' Principal Taps Local Roots," *Denver Post*, October 27, 1992: 1D.

9   Irv Moss, "McMorris at Home as Owner."

10   Mary McMorris interview.

11   Crasnick, "A Driven Man."

12   Ibid.

13   Ibid.

14   Ibid.

15   Irv Moss, "John Dikeou Played Role in Bringing Major-League Baseball to Denver," *Denver Post*, March 31, 2015.

16   Irv Moss, "McMorris at Home as Owner."

17   Gene Wojciechowski, "Rockies Born of Monus' work, but He Never Saw His Baby Grow Up," ESPN.com, October 23, 2007. Retrieved March 18, 2017. espn.com/espn/columns/story?id=3074665&columnist=wojciechowski_gene&sportCat=mlb.

18   Mike Klis, "25 Years Ago: How Denver Attorney Paul Jacobs Helped Bring Major League Baseball to Denver," KUSA News. Retrieved April 1, 2017. 9news.com/news/25-years-ago-how-denver-attorney-paul-jacobs-helped-bring-major-league-baseball-to-denver/262421119.

19   Jim Armstrong, "Rockies Partners Pull Out—Phar-Mor's Monuses Resign Amid FBI Investigation," *Denver Post*, August 4, 1992: 1A.

20   Patrick Saunders, "Jerry McMorris, 1940-2012," *Denver Post*, May 9, 2012: 1B.

21   "Oren Lee Benton," *Sioux City Journal*, May 21, 2006. Retrieved March 19, 2017. siouxcityjournal.com/news/local/obituaries/oren-lee-benton/article_36ed878d-d068-5e42-92b8-129a717082a1.html

22   denverpost.com/2012/05/08/mcmorris-one-of-rockies-original-owners-dies/.

23   Irv Moss, "McMorris Running the Show," *Denver Post*, September 3, 1992: 5D.

24   Jim Armstrong, "Rockies Spring to Life in First Workout—Special Day Quenches Major Thirst," *Denver Post*, February 20, 1993: 1D.

25   Philip J. Lowry, *Green Cathedrals: The Ultimate Celebration of Major League and Negro League Ballparks* (New York: Walker & Co, 2006), 80.

26   Patrick Saunders, "Jerry McMorris, 1940-2012."

27   Mark Kiszla, "Investment Pays Fans for Loyalty," *Denver Post*, July 27, 1993: 1D.

28   Mark Kiszla, "Harris Hopes to Become Fixture in Future," *Denver Post*, September 15, 1993: 3D.

29   "Spotlight on McMorris, CACI Winners," *Denver Post*, July 19, 1993: 6C.

30   Jim Armstrong, "Rockies' McMorris Is a Shy Samaritan," *Denver Post*, September 18, 1994: B-4.

31   Cliff Corcoran, "Who Was Right, Who Was Wrong, and How it Helped Baseball," *Sports Illustrated*, August 12, 2014. Retrieved March 17, 2017. si.com/mlb/2014/08/12/1994-strike-bud-selig-orel-hershiser ;

Associated Press, "McMorris, One of Rockies' Original Owners, Dies," *Denver Post*, May 8, 2012. Retrieved March 18, 2017.

32   Claire Smith, "It's Down to the Wire; McMorris Is at Plate," *New York Times*, December 22, 1994.

33   Ibid.

34   Mary McMorris interview.

35   Claire Smith, "It's Down to the Wire."

36   Jeffrey Lieb, "NW Rolls Out National Name—McMorris Trucking Firm on the Road to Growth," *Denver Post*, December 29, 1993: 1C.

37   Crasnick, "A Driven Man"; Smith, "It's Down to the Wire."

38   Crasnick, "A Driven Man."

39   Quoted in Norm Clarke, "National Acclaim Rains on McMorris," *Rocky Mountain News* (Denver), January 10, 1995: 2B.

40   Crasnick, "A Driven Man."

41   *Green Cathedrals*, 81.

42   J. Sebastian Sinisi, "Coors Field Intoxicates Sports Fans," *Denver Post*, April 1, 1995: AA-4.

43   Ibid.

44   Ibid.

45   Jerry Crasnick, "Ball Strike Over. Owners Approve April 26 Opener; Issues Unresolved," *Denver Post*, April 3, 1995: A-1.

46   Woody Paige, "Rockies Lay Hefty Bet to Win Big-Ticket Talent," *Denver Post*, April 9, 1995: B-1.

47   Irv Moss, "Ice Cold Coors. Coors Opener Packs Pizzazz at Finish," *Denver Post*, April 27, 1995: D-12.

48   Hal Bodley, "Rockies' Wild-Card Berth a Credit to McMorris, Fans," article of unknown origin in McMorris's Hall of Fame file.

49   Bodley, "Rockies' Wild-Card Berth."

50   Todd Phipers, "Rockies Mourn Loss of Mike McMorris," *Denver Post*, March 31, 1996: CC-04.

51   "Michael Dean McMorris, 32, of California," *Denver Post*, March 30, 1996.

52   childrenscolorado.org/doctors-and-departments/departments/breathing-institute/programs/cystic-fibrosis/, retrieved March 17, 2017.

53   Ann Schrader, "Cystic-Fibrosis Center Dedicated at Children's," *Denver Post*, October 21, 1998: B-01.

54   Woody Paige, "Baseball, the Rockies and Denver Can Be Proud," *Denver Post*, July 8, 1998: AA-02.

55   Irv Moss, "No Ring, So Bell Tolls for Baylor," *Denver Post*, September 29, 1998: D-06.

56   J. Sebastian Sinisi, "McMorris Favors Level Playing Field," *Denver Post*, January 20, 1999: D-07.

57   Mike Klis, "It's a Deal! Leyland Agrees to 3-year Pact," *Denver Post*, October 6, 1998: D-01.

58 Mike Klis, "Rockies' 1999 Payroll: Money Talks $59.736 Million Going to Players," *Denver Post*, March 2, 1999: D-08.

59 Mike Klis, "Walker Strikes a Deal: $75 Million for Six Years," *Denver Post*, March 5, 1999: D-01.

60 Irv Moss, "End of an Era For the Colorado Rockies; Given a Choice, Gebhart Resigns; Sources Say GM Was Gone Either Way," *Denver Post*, August 21, 1999: C-01.

61 Henry Dubroff, "McMorris gets NW Transport Moving Again," *Denver Business Journal*, October 5, 1997. Retrieved March 17, 2017, bizjournals.com/denver/stories/1997/10/06/newscolumn1.html.

62 Gregory S. Johnson, "NationsWay Transport Goes Out of Business," *Journal of Commerce*, May 23, 1999. Retrieved March 17, 2017, joc.com/nationsway-transport-goes-out-business_19990523.html.

63 Donald Blount and Jeffrey Leib, "McMorris Lost Race Against Time," *Denver Post*, May 22, 1999. Retrieved March 18, 2017, extras.denverpost.com/business/biz0522.htm.

64 Jeffrey Lieb, "The Way to Go: Westway Thrives While Sister Firm in Bankruptcy," *Denver Post*, June 27, 1999: J-01.

65 Bill King, "Rockies Owner Draws Fire," *Street & Smith's Sports Business Journal*, June 7-13, 1999: 13.

66 Ibid.

67 King; Located on the Continental Divide, Loveland Pass (US Route 6) is considered to be the highest mountain pass in the world (nearly 12,000 feet above sea level) to stay open even during the winter months. Weather conditions often force the road to be closed, and its hairpin turns and steep grades can make driving treacherous, especially for truck drivers. dangerousroads.org/north-america/usa/62-loveland-pass-usa.html.

68 Mike Klis, "Rockies Fire McMorris as Their Vice Chairman. The Former No. 1 Boss Retains His Stake With the Franchise, but His Voting Rights Have Been Lifted," *Denver Post*, November 10, 2004: D-01.

69 Woody Paige, "Rockies Run Off M Factor," *Denver Post*, November 14, 2004: BB-01.

70 Tony E. Renck, "Rockies' Motto: Team Comes First," *Denver Post*, February 10, 2002: D-02.

71 Paige, "Rockies Run Off M Factor."

72 Mike Klis, "McMorris Hands Off Daily Duties," *Denver Post*, October 19, 2001: D-01.

73 Mark Kiszla, "M&M Boys Should Contemplate Selling," *Denver Post*, September 22, 2002: C-01.

74 Ibid.

75 Klis, "Rockies Fire McMorris as Their Vice Chairman."

76 Troy E. Renck, "Monforts Buy out McMorris — The Team's Former CEO Was Instrumental in Bringing Major-League Baseball to Denver," *Denver Post*, December 16, 2005: D-02.

77 Tracy Ringolsby, "Former Rockies' Owner's Heart Still in It," *Rocky Mountain News*, October 12, 2007.

78 "McMorris, One of Rockies' Original Owners, Dies."

79 Moss, "Catching Up with Jerry McMorris."

80 Mary McMorris interview.

81 Irv Moss, "Farm Teams Yield Top Crop — Homegrown Talent Forms the Foundation of the Team That Is Excited About the Future," *Denver Post*, October 3, 2007: R-08.

82 Ringolsby, "Former Rockies' Owner's Heart."

83 Irv Moss, "Regier Gives Inspiring Speech — Disabled Athlete Among Honorees at Hall of Fame Induction Banquet," *Denver Post*, April 15, 2009: C-08.

84 Troy E. Renck, "Moyer Inspires With Effort, Not Age — That's All People Want," *Denver Post*, May 17, 2012: 1B.

85 "What Others Are Saying."

DICK AND CHARLIE MONFORT

BY ROGER L. KINNEY

DICK AND CHARLIE MONFORT brought a new breed of ownership to the Colorado Rockies with a long-term commitment for financial stability, a caring entrepreneurship, and a steadfast desire to build a winning franchise.

The two brothers became the primary owners of the Colorado Rockies in a most peculiar way. Shortly after Commissioner Peter Ueberroth announced plans for expansion of the National League in 1989, the Colorado Baseball Commission had two major problems: They lacked the initiation fee of $95 million, and they did not have an ownership group that would be acceptable to the MLB expansion committee.

At the request of the Colorado Baseball Commission, Dick Anderson, a Denver businessman, approached Governor Roy Romer to explain the unfortunate state of affairs. Romer agreed to form a finance committee that involved business leaders Dick Robinson, Tryg Myhren, and Jim Baldwin. The group contacted Jerry McMorris, who agreed to make an initial investment as a limited partner. McMorris offered to contact Ken Monfort, a legendary beef-industry pioneer in northern Colorado who was known for his business acumen and good humor, as well as his generosity for any worthy cause in his beloved state of Colorado.

After a lengthy presentation, Ken Monfort agreed that the long-term benefits of having a major-league baseball team in the state could be significant, but in his opinion the proposal was somewhat crazy—the ownership structure was out of balance with the general partners providing only about 22 percent of the capital investment and the limited partners providing about 78 percent. In addition, he questioned the accuracy of the estimated financial projections, in fact he agreed with some skeptics who thought the potential population for buying tickets for the games included many of the jackrabbits and antelopes in northern Colorado. Monfort's response was that he personally was too old to consider such an investment. However,

if any of his children were interested, then he and the family would support them. In addition, he told his sons that he did not like to invest in such a project as a limited partner. Based on his experience, he preferred to retain personal control of his investments.

It didn't take long for Charlie Monfort to agree to support the project. He became a limited partner and one of the club's original founders with his initial investment in 1991. His initial investment was intended, first to support their friends Jerry McMorris, Pete Coors, and the other investors, and second, to support the organized effort to provide a long-term financial benefit for the state of Colorado. Another important investment came from Peter Coors, representing Coors Brewery, who agreed to invest $25 million, of which $15 million would go for the naming rights for the ballpark.[1] The ownership group eventually reached its goal and the franchise was awarded to the Colorado Rockies on July 5, 1991.[2]

Shortly thereafter, in July 1992, the franchise faced an unexpected crisis when Michael "Mickey" Monus, one of the out-of-state owners, was accused of embezzlement and faced with multiple lawsuits. He and his father, Nathan Monus, resigned when it became apparent that Mickey Monus would be unacceptable to Major League Baseball. Paul Jacobs, legal counsel, and widely recognized as the driving force for the ownership group, quickly arranged for the sale of Monus's stock to Steven Kurtz and himself. John Antonucci, the Rockies CEO, and his father also sold their stock to Kurtz and Jacobs and left the franchise. Within several months, Jacobs and Kurtz sold their stock in a buyout agreement to Charlie Monfort, Jerry McMorris, and Oren Benton, giving the local owners control of the franchise.

Jerry McMorris became the chairman and CEO and Charlie Monfort became a managing general partner, and was named vice chairman of the Rockies in 1993. Thus, Charlie fulfilled his father's advice by becoming a general partner on September 2, 1992.[3]

In April 2003 Charlie traded positions with Jerry McMorris and became the chairman and CEO while McMorris became a vice chairman.[4] Dick Monfort, who was involved in other business activities, became involved in an ownership role by becoming a vice chairman on December 8, 1997.[5]

Another ownership crisis developed when Oren Benton filed for bankruptcy protection on February 23, 1995. Benton had been a pioneer in the uranium business and had originally committed $20 million for the Rockies. The disposition of the stock would be tied up in the courts for several years. But in time, Charlie and Dick Monfort stepped to the plate again and purchased additional stock from the bankruptcy, giving them the ownership control of the team. As Dick became more involved in the management of the team, Charlie said, "It is something we've been talking about for quite a while and I'm happy he's in. He is a really good businessman and is really going to be helpful."[6]

As the baseball seasons progressed, there were ongoing financial constraints throughout major-league baseball involving revenue sharing, player contracts, a fair and equitable draft system, free agency, and the threat of a players' strike. On the national scene, the entire country was shocked and horrified by the 9/11 attack in 2001, the global financial crisis, and the 2008 business recession. These conditions had a staggering impact on the banks and their lending policies for many businesses, including the Colorado Rockies. The Rockies, eager to attract fans with high-profile, veteran players, signed some free agents, only to suffer the consequences of large, guaranteed contracts that brought minimal results on the field. The borrowing policy for covering some deficits became an increasing problem. On the field, the team's record was subject to ongoing criticism by the media and some disgruntled fans.

Dick Monfort, who was recognized for his analytical expertise with numbers, financial forecasting, and business common sense began to formulate a long-term plan with Keli McGregor, who was the club's president and quickly becoming the organizational leader of the franchise.

Charlie Monfort was once asked if he was interested in selling the team. He responded, "All the rumors about people wanting to buy the team, it's flattering because it tells you people see the potential of this market. But to sell the club now doesn't make sense. I would compare it to a woman who has been in labor for nine months then hands off the baby. We have gone through the labor pains. We want the reward."[7]

Contrary to the rumors circulating in 2005 that the Monforts might be contemplating selling their interests in the Rockies, just the opposite was true. They were negotiating to purchase an additional 12.5 percent interest from Jerry McMorris. McMorris had served the Rockies admirably during the first 10 years of the franchise, but his trucking company was in bankruptcy and the club's history of borrowing to meet financial requirements needed to be addressed. The Monforts responded by purchasing McMorris's stock, paying about twice the original value, which was considered more than fair under the circumstances. Consequently, it was at that time, that the Monforts gained full ownership control of the Rockies. Dick Monfort became the owner/chairman and chief executive officer and Charlie became owner/general partner.

Over the years, Charlie and Dick Monfort answered the call every time an ownership crisis developed. They experienced their share of "growing pains" on and off the field, but they were steadfast in supporting and growing the franchise. As of 2017 they represented the only surviving founders and owners, chairman, and chief executive officer of the Rockies.

The Monfort Families

Dick Monfort was born on April 27, 1954, and Charlie Monfort was born on October 30, 1959. They have two sisters, Kyle (born in 1952) and Kaye (born in 1958). Dick has three children—a daughter, Lyndsey, and two sons, Walker and Sterling, who both work for the Rockies. Charlie has four children—two daughters, Clara and Danica, and two sons, Kenny and Lucas. Danica and Lucas are twins.

The original patriarch of the Monfort family was Dick and Charlie's grandfather, Warren Monfort, who was eulogized by his son Kenny as "not only a good father but the finest man I have ever known."[8] The strong family legacy passed from Warren to his son Kenny, who became a legend in his own right. Kenny was an innovator, leading his packing company and revolutionizing the beef industry. In 2011 it was reported that the company "was slaughtering 350,000 cattle and 60,000 lambs each year with revenue exceeding $150 million."[9] Kenny was known for his personal charm, fabulous sense of humor, strong family values and enormous generosity. As stated by his friend Senator Hank Brown," Kenny epitomized the best of the Colorado spirit—a pioneer who truly cared for his neighbors.[10]

Kenny's sons, Dick and Charlie grew up in a rural community with strong, traditional values associated with the Western agricultural culture. They received their elementary education in a small schoolhouse with 13 students and three teachers for all grades, 1 through 6. They moved to Eaton, Colorado, for junior high school and then to Greeley, where they attended Greeley West High School. The family attended the local church. In 1937-38 the noted author and historian James A. Michener was the Sunday school teacher for Kenny's brother, Richard. The boys became avid readers of Michener's writing, including his historical novel *Centennial*. Consequently, as a result of their father's influence, Charlie and Dick Monfort were well schooled in the history of Colorado's agriculture, especially that in the northern part of the state.

As a young baseball player and fan, Dick rooted for the Los Angeles Dodgers. His first major-league experience came when the family traveled to Los Angeles to see the Dodgers play.

Dick graduated from the University of Northern Colorado in 1976 with a degree in business management. He joined the family business and spent 25 years in the cattle business. He was the president of

Dick and Charlie Monfort

Monfort of Colorado, Inc., a subsidiary of ConAgra, and of ConAgra Red Meats. Colorado, Inc. was highly successful and was listed as a Fortune 500 company. In March 1989, the company had 2,780 employees. Dick retired from ConAgra in 1995 to pursue other business opportunities, including the Rockies.

Charlie graduated from the University of Utah in 1982 with a degree in marketing and business management. Joining the family business, he served in several areas and became the president of Monfort International Sales Corporation in 1988. The company became one of the largest beef exporters in the world, with offices in Japan, Hong Kong, Taiwan, and Moscow. In 1996, he became president of ConAgra Refrigerated Foods, Inc. In 1998, he resigned to pursue the Rockies and other business interests.

Philanthropy

Dick and Charlie continued the family tradition of widespread community participation and philanthropy throughout Colorado. They have contributed more than $100 million to charities, universities, and hospitals.[11] The Monfort family gave $10 million to Children's Hospital, where the oncology floor is named in memory of Rick Wilson, a cousin of the family. Other recipients of the Monforts' generosity include Colorado State University, Craig Hospital, the Colorado University Cancer Center, the University of Northern Colorado, the United Way, the Denver Art Museum, the Special Olympics, Habitat for Humanity, the Rocky Mountain Chapter of SABR, and the Boys and Girls Clubs of Denver and Weld County.[12]

The Monfort College of Business at the University of Northern Colorado is named in honor of Kenny Monfort. Dick Monfort was awarded an honorary doctorate by Colorado State University in recognition of his contributions to Colorado industry and higher education. Dick was inducted into the Colorado Tourism Hall of Fame in 2013.

Charlie Monfort has been a member of the board of trustees at Colorado Mesa University. He has served on other boards including the Kempe Foundation, the Special Olympics, and the Monfort Foundation. He was the president of his Kappa Sigma fraternity at the University of Utah.

Dick Monfort has been chairman of the board of trustees at the University of Northern Colorado and of the University of Colorado Health. He is the chairman of Major League Baseball's Labor Relations Committee. He serves on other boards including the Colorado Economic Development Council and CoBiz Financial.

Rocktober

In 2007 the Colorado Rockies accomplished one of the greatest comebacks in history when they won 14 of their last 15 games to tie the San Diego Padres for the National League wild-card spot. The Rockies, led by manager Clint Hurdle, defeated the Padres in a classic playoff game, going 13 innings to win, 9-8. Matt Holliday scored the winning run when he came home and bowled over catcher Michael Barrett. Barrett argued that Holliday did not touch home plate, but the umpire called him safe and the victory celebration began.

The Rockies went on to sweep the Philadelphia Phillies in three games and the Arizona Diamondbacks in four games to win their first National League pennant. Their amazing record was 21-1 when they reached the World Series to face the Boston Red Sox. Their winning streak came to an end when the Red Sox won the World Series in four games. After the final game, Charlie Monfort spoke directly to the team, acknowledging their accomplishments throughout the season and encouraging them to come back to win the World Series next year.

The Rockies were recognized by *Baseball America* as the "Organization of the Year" for 2007. It had been an exciting season for the entire organization as well as the Rockies' fans. The future looked promising as Dick and Charlie Monfort worked closely with their management team to build upon the success of the 2007 season.

In 2008 the team finished with a disappointing record of 74-88, finishing third in the West Division. Jim Tracy became the new manager in May 2009, guiding the team to a successful season and a return to the playoffs. That September, the team won 10 of their first 11 games en route to their second wild card in three years. In the playoffs, they lost to the Philadelphia Phillies, three games to one. In retrospect, the team had competed well over the past three years and there was optimism for the future.

In April 2010, the Rockies were stunned by the death of their president, Keli McGregor. He was young, very popular, and the picture of good health. Doctors identified the cause of death to be a rare case of viral myocarditis. The impact of his loss would be felt throughout the Rockies organization and the Denver sports community.

McGregor was instrumental in building a strong organizational base for the franchise, including putting together a highly competent and professional staff. With his untimely death, Dick and Charlie Monfort were faced with a major decision regarding the future path of the franchise. Ultimately, rather than bring new personnel into the organization, they decided to keep the business staff and managerial team in place. Dick Monfort assumed the presidency and worked with general manager Dan O'Dowd and manager Jim Tracy as the baseball season moved on.

Past experiences in dealing with family tragedies and unforeseen business circumstances helped Dick and Charlie Monfort confront the Rockies' continuity and move forward in a positive way. Their family was shaped with a similar loss when Richard Lee Monfort, Charlie and Dick's uncle, was killed in World War II on a bombing mission in Germany. Richard Lee had been groomed to assume the leadership of the Monfort cattle operations. Kenny, Richard's younger brother, had plans to be a writer, but he adjusted his plans for the future and assumed the stewardship of the family business.

During the period 1975 to 1987, the cattle business faced many challenges including fluctuating beef prices, labor unrest, alterations in government regulations, changes in monetary policies including banking and lending restrictions, and, as always, the possibility of extreme weather conditions. In addition, Monfort management was increasingly concerned about consolidation in the meat-packing industry.[13]

In 1979, Ken Monfort purchased a meat-packing plant in Grand Island, Nebraska, and Dick Monfort, then in his 20s, was sent to help run the operation. On June 3, 1980, a massive tornado hit Grand Island. The damage was so severe that the plant was forced to close. Dick faced the disaster head-on. He organized the employees, asking them not to quit. He gathered volunteers and, as quickly as possible, they made the necessary repairs. It took eight days of working around the clock to get the plant back into operation. Dick provided the leadership while working side by side with the workers. The experience proved to be a valuable lesson for him. With a determined spirit, Dick, the employees, and the volunteers worked very hard, succeeding in rebuilding the plant and reviving a vibrant community. The plant was saved, the employees kept their jobs, and the economy in the greater Grand Island area was saved with the positive economic impact from the plant's operation.

The business experiences in the meat packing industry proved to be a good education for Dick and Charlie Monfort. They learned to deal with the emotional highs and lows of managing a successful business, to develop strong personnel skills including the ability to delegate authority and build teamwork, and to analyze financial data and plan for future contingencies. As young business entrepreneurs, they were confronted with a multitude of managerial problems. To solve those problems, they developed business skills and a philosophy that would prepare them well for owning and managing a major-league baseball team.

Major-league players have described the baseball season as a marathon requiring long-term physical and mental strength. It's fun and exciting when the team is playing well and the fans are packing the stadium. But there are difficult times as well. An extended slump by a team can be depressing for the fans, but the owners of a team must also endure the financial burden and sometimes, the wrath of the media and fans. With their business experience and background, the Monforts were well trained to confront adversity. Dick and Charlie developed a working philosophy within the Rockies organization of keeping moving, counting your blessings, uniting the troops, providing "open door" communications, and building on your strengths.

Loyalty and devotion to the common goals of the team became hallmarks for the future of the Monforts' organization. Shortly after the Monfort brothers took controlling interest of the Rockies before the 2005 season, "they immediately shifted the focus to a more sustainable business model, focusing on drafting and developing players.[14]

Draft and Develop

One of the lessons taken from the success of the 2007 Rockoctober team was how the development of a very good group of young players could lead to long-term success. Actually it began in 2004 with a successful draft of talented players. Affectionately termed "Todd (Helton) and the Toddlers," the team featured Jeff Francis, Matt Holliday, Brad Hawpe, Garrett Atkins, Jason Jennings, and Aaron Cook, all outstanding players who came together primarily through the Rockies farm system to form perhaps the best team in Rockies history. It took patience and three years for the team members to reach their championship level together. But the policy of drafting high-quality players and developing them in the Rockies farm system became the Monforts' model for the future. It is a model that continues as they work with the entire organization to give full support for the plan. They made related improvements to the business operations, including the creation of a department for communications and marketing, promoting capable and talented staff members from within the organization.

To support the player development program, Dick and Charlie Monfort made a commitment to improving the scouting program and the training facilities in Latin America. They created an active scouting program in Venezuela and they have built a new baseball facility in the Dominican Republic.

In 2009, the Monforts joined forces with the Arizona Diamondbacks to open a new spring training facility at the Salt River complex in Phoenix, Arizona. The complex is used as a year-round fa-cility, including spring training, rehabilitation, and offseason conditioning for all players in the Rockies organization.

Coors Field

Charlie Monfort has often said, "We are always striving to improve the fans' experience at Coors Field." One of the Rockies' most innovative im-provements came in 2013 with the building of the rooftop party area beyond right field. When Dick Monfort looked at the vacant space above the out-field seats, he visualized a robust viewing area, ideal for young millennials and happy-go-lucky baseball fans. The area features an early-bird cocktail hour before every game. It also has a fabulous view of the playing field and the Denver skyline, as well as the Rocky Mountains to the west.

The playing field is recognized as one of the best maintained diamonds in major-league baseball. Mark Razum, the head groundskeeper, has been at Coors Field since its opening in 1994. In addition to main-taining Coors Field, Razum and his crew have given valuable advice for many of the youth baseball fields in the metropolitan area.

In recent years, the Coors Clubhouse, the press box, the Mountain Ranch Club, and the club level seating areas have all been upgraded to improve the fans' experience. The Sandlot, which is located on the first-base side, has a microbrewery on the premises. The popular Blue Moon beer was originally created at the Sandlot brewery. Plans were in the works for a new scoreboard, an increased lighting system, and an improved sound system. The 2017 team was greatly improved and returned to the National League play-offs for the first time in several years.

In 2017, Dick Monfort and the Colorado Baseball Stadium Authority signed an extension of the lease for Coors Field. The lease runs for 30 years, ensuring that the Rockies will remain there through 2047.[15] By then, Coors Field will be 53 years old and likely the oldest ballpark in the National League. (As of 2018 it was the third oldest.) The new agreement with the Stadium Authority includes a 99-year lease on a one-block property on Wazee Street, just south of Coors

Field. In 2018 plans were underway as to what would be developed in that location.

Since the inception of the Rockies, Dick and Charlie Monfort have consistently shown their optimism for the team and its future in and for Colorado. Whenever difficulties have arisen, they have confronted the problems and offered solid solutions. They have looked for opportunities to improve the team, the business operations, and the fans' experience at Coors Field. They are persistent and dedicated to the long-term success of the team. As a result, they have created and now represent one of the leading sports franchises in America.

One must believe the best is yet to come.

SOURCES

In addition to the sources cited in the Notes, the author also consulted:

Cady, Lew. *They've Got Rockies In Their Heads* (Aurora, Colorado: Mile High Press, 1993).

Clark, Norm. *High Hard Ones* (New Haven, Connecticut: J Phoenix Press, 1981).

DeMarco, Tony. *Tales From the Colorado Rockies* (New York: Sports Publishing LLC, 2008).

Michener, James Albert. *Centennial* (New York: Random House, 1974).

Monfort, Kenny. *Random Thoughts, Town & Country News, Greeley Tribune*, 1980-1990.

Ringolsby, Tracy. "Inside Corner, Rockies Commentaries," *Colorado Rockies Magazine* (Denver: American Web, a Publication of Printers Co., 2017).

NOTES

1   Mary Kay Connor, *Dick Connor Remembered* (Golden, Colorado: Fulcrum Publishing, 1995), 119.

2   Irv Moss and Mark Foster, *Home Run in the Rockies, The History f Baseball in Colorado* (Denver: Publication Design, Inc., 1995; now available from Hirschfeld Press), 62.

3   *Colorado Rockies Media Guide*, 2017, 5.

4   Ross Maak, "New Role Suits Owner Monfort," *Greeley Tribune*, April 5, 2003: C2.

5   *Colorado Rockies Media Guide*, 2017, 5.

6   Bill Jackson, *History of Monfort, Inc.*, fundinguniverse.com, January 23, 1994, 2.

7   Toggle Navigation, *Top 10 Quotes by Charlie Monfort*, quoter.net/ 1.

8   Walt Barnhart, *Kenny's Shoes, A Walk Through the Storied Life of the Remarkable Kenneth W. Monfort* (West Conshohocken, Pennsylvania: Infinity Publishing, 2010), 11.

9   "John Maday, Bovine Veterinarian," *Cattle Network*, carnivore.com, November 17, 2011, 3.

10 Barnhart, iii.

11 Woody Paige, *Rockies' Monforts May Come Around to Being Appreciated*, gazette.com/woody paige, April 11, 2017: 3.

12 *Colorado Rockies Media Guide*, 2017, 6.

13 Monfort, Inc. History, International Directory, Vol. 13, St. James Press, Steamwood, Illinois, fundinguniverse.com/company-histories/monfort-inc-history, 2.

14 Troy Renck, "Rockies Owner Dick Monfort Provides Look at Team's Budget," denverpost.com, November 13, 2013: 3.

15 Nick Groke, "Dick Monfort Reflects on Team's New 30-Year Lease," denverpost.com, March 31, 2017: 2.

DAN O'DOWD

BY CHRISTOPHER WILLIAMSON

DAN O'DOWD WAS A BASEBALL MAN from the beginning. Born in Morristown, New Jersey, on September 6, 1959, Dan grew up working on his parents' (Marty and Anna Mae) dairy farm and in O'Dowd's Milk Bar on Route 46 in Pine Brook. As it is for most, his love of baseball was cultivated from playing the game throughout childhood and young adulthood. As a high-school freshman, he was the starter at third base on the 1974 Morris County, New Jersey Tournament championship team. During senior year, his high-school coach, John Gallucci, had the "what do you want to do with your life" conversation with Dan. "He said he wanted to be in sports management," Gallucci recalled. "He knew right from the very beginning. You don't see that very often."[1]

O'Dowd went on to play college ball at Rollins College in Florida but recognized early on that he was an average ballplayer without a professional future. A nose-shattering line drive during his sophomore year virtually ended his playing days and by his senior year he had transitioned into a coaching position assisting Rollins coach Boyd Coffie and soaking up every ounce of baseball knowledge and nuance available.[2]

After graduation, O'Dowd was accepted into the executive development program with Major League Baseball and from there secured employment in the Baltimore Orioles' front office in 1983 and more importantly with his baseball mentor, Orioles general manager Hank Peters.[3] He instantly got to savor the sweet taste of victory as the Orioles won the 1983 World Series. Over the next few years he was rotated through several positions within the organization and became versed in both the baseball and business sides of the game.

By October of 1987, the relationship between Orioles owner Edward Bennett Williams and Hank Peters had soured to the point that Williams decided to clean house in his front office. Both Peters and

O'Dowd were out of a job—but not for long. The Jacobs brothers had bought the Cleveland Indians in 1986 and had been interested in bringing in Hank Peters as their general manager and president of baseball operations to lead a turnaround effort for the decades-long American League doormat team. Peters, who was known as a very loyal man, brought on many of his former associates who that had been casualties during the purge in Baltimore, including the now 28-year-old Dan O'Dowd as his farm director.

The Cleveland media viewed the hiring of Dowd skeptically in view of his relative inexperience. Peters acknowledged O'Dowd's greenness and commented, "We are going to train him. I was trained. He has some interesting qualifications. And I think with time and guidance, he will grow into a very competent baseball executive."[4]

A few of the noteworthy changes Peters instituted were a return to the policy of developing from within, rebuilding through the farm system to create a sustainable fount of continuous talent for the Indians. He also drastically improved the organization's relationship with its current players by offering some multiyear contracts prior to free agency and agreeing to generous one-year deals to avoid arbitration with star players such as Joe Carter. Rebuilding the farm system and making the team's current players happy were sound and logical first steps toward getting the organization on a path to relevance.

The first six years of the rebuild were slow and O'Dowd's farm did not bear much fruit initially. The philosophy put into place by O'Dowd, Peters, and Tom Giordano (special assistant to Peters) heavily favored drafting high-school over college players. In spring training of 1990, O'Dowd noted, "It's not that there aren't some good college coaches, but with most college players, you have to spend time trying to overcome all the bad habits they've learned."[5] That same spring, the Indians' hottest young prospect was 20-year-old shortstop Mark Lewis of Hamilton,

and his 25 errors tied for the most in the American League. Lewis was traded to the Cincinnati Reds in 1994 and bounced around the National League until 2001 as a low-impact, glove-first utility infielder who had some nice seasons defensively.

Near the end of the 1991 season, John Hart was promoted from director of baseball operations to general manager and executive vice president, replacing Peters. O'Dowd became Hart's right-hand man as the assistant GM. This helped set the stage for Indians to become a powerhouse during the mid/late-'90s. The organization endured two more losing seasons in 1992 and 1993 but the farm system began to strengthen under the dual management of O'Dowd and Hart. Manny Ramirez was drafted in the first round in 1991 and quickly blossomed into a superstar.

For the Indians' minor-league system, 1993 was a banner year. From the rookie leagues up through Triple A, all six of the organization's affiliates made the playoffs. O'Dowd said, "I know wins and losses don't always indicate the success of your system, but we've never even had five teams in the playoffs, and this year we could have six. I really believe this is an indication that our scouts are doing the job of bringing the right kids in our system."[7] Several future major leaguers were in the system in 1993, including Brian Giles, Kelly Stinnett, David Bell, Mitch Meluskey, Chad Ogea, Albie Lopez, and Paul Shuey.

By 1994, the Indians were ready to move out of decrepit Municipal Stadium and into beautiful new Jacobs Field. The major-league clubs put together by Hart and O'Dowd over the next five years were formidable and won the division every year until O'Dowd's departure after the 1998 season (not including strike-shortened 1994).

Ohio, whom they drafted in the first round and second overall in the June 1988 draft. (Charles Nagy was drafted 17th overall with their second first-round pick in 1988.) O'Dowd said of Lewis, "Defensively, he's a major league shortstop. ... I won't tell you he's now a major-league hitter, or possibly even a Triple-A hitter. ... Right now, he's a fastball hitter. What he's got to work on is hitting the breaking ball and the changeup."[6]

O'Dowd's lack of hyperbole was prescient. Lewis debuted with the Indians in 1991 and started 78 games at shortstop and second base but made virtually no impact at the plate. His 1992 season was very similar: He played in 122 games with an OPS under .700,

The 1994-1998 Opening Day lineups:

Batting Order	1994	1995	1996	1997	1998
1)	Kenny Lofton, CF	Kenny Lofton, CF	Kenny Lofton, CF	Marquis Grissom, CF	Kenny Lofton, CF
2)	Omar Vizquel, SS	Omar Vizquel, SS	Julio Franco, 1B	Omar Vizquel, SS	Omar Vizquel, SS
3)	Carlos Baerga, 2B	Carlos Baerga, 2B	Carlos Baerga, 2B	Jim Thome, 1B	Shawon Dunston, DH
4)	Albert Belle, LF	Albert Belle, LF	Albert Belle, LF	Matt Williams, 3B	Manny Ramirez, RF
5)	Eddie Murray, 1B	Eddie Murray, 1B	Eddie Murray, DH	David Justice, LF	Geronimo Berroa, LF
6)	Candy Maldonado, DH	Jim Thome, 3B	Jim Thome, 3B	Manny Ramirez, RF	Travis Fryman, 3B
7)	Sandy Alomar Jr, C	Manny Ramirez, RF	Manny Ramirez, RF	Julio Franco, 2B	Sandy Alomar Jr, C
8)	Manny Ramirez, RF	Paul Sorrento, 1B	Sandy Alomar Jr, C	Kevin Mitchell, DH	Jeff Manto, 1B
9)	Mark Lewis, 3B	Tony Pena, C	Omar Vizquel, SS	Sandy Alomar Jr, C	Enrique Wilson, 2B
	Dennis Martinez, P	Dennis Martinez, P	Dennis Martinez, P	Charles Nagy, P	Charles Nagy, P

After decades of futility, the Indians won four straight division titles (1995-1998) and made World Series appearances in 1995 and 1997. The star power on the field during those years was clearly evident. However, the star power off the field was almost equally impressive. During or immediately after the 1998 season the Indians' front office was loaded:

- John Hart, general manager
- Dan O'Dowd, assistant GM
- Mark Shapiro, player development director
- Josh Byrnes, scouting director
- Paul DePodesta, advance scout
- Ben Cherington, advance scout
- Neal Huntington, assistant director of minor-league operations
- Chris Antonetti, baseball operations assistant

Every one of those eight went on to become a general manager. Three became club presidents, and one became an NFL chief strategic officer. O'Dowd and Shapiro were the visionaries who originally came up with the idea to sign young players to contract extensions before arbitration. This created a sustainable model for small-market clubs to achieve long-term cost certainty and gave young players financial security early in their careers and before reaching free agency. The Indians were the first clubs to create

personalized player-development plans and not fall victim to the one-size-fits-all mentality; early on they embraced advanced statistics like OPS (On Base + Slugging Percentage) and data analytics. "I don't know what it was like to work at Apple or any of the tech firms in their heyday," said O'Dowd, "but I'd imagine it was a lot like that. It was a creative think tank, and it was invigorating."[8]

After the 1998 season, O'Dowd was a hot commodity on the open market to fill general-manager vacancies. He had created quite a name for himself as the assistant general manager of the American League's model organization and both Hart and Dick Jacobs were getting calls for permission to interview the 39-year-old hot shot. With Pat Gillick retiring, the Orioles were in the market and were given permission to speak to O'Dowd with the stipulation that if he was hired, no other members of the Cleveland front office would follow him. But the GM position never materialized for O'Dowd and he decided to take the 1999 season off to fully pursue other GM positions around baseball.

After a year of pursuit, O'Dowd was hired in September 1999 as general manager of the Colorado Rockies. "Dealin' Dan" didn't waste any time overhauling the roster in preparation for the franchise's eighth season. Sixteen new players were added to the club's 25-man roster and only Todd Helton, Mike Lansing, and Neifi Perez were in both the 1999 and 2000 Opening Day lineups. O'Dowd's goals were for the team to become younger and more athletic with the intent of improving defensively and on the basepaths. He made six trades, and a bevy of other roster moves before the 2000 season. Notable departures were Vinny Castilla, Dante Bichette, Darryl Kile, and Dave Veres. Notable arrivals included Jeff Cirillo, Tom Goodwin, and Julian Tavarez. The Denver media and the fan base were taken aback by the sheer quantity of roster turnover and the departures of fan favorites like Castilla and Bichette. O'Dowd's response: "I don't know what the downside is. We lost 90 games last year. Any time you trade away marquee players for guys who may not be as well known, it's tough for the fans to swallow. But we definitely have a plan here. I think it's going to take some time when you make this many changes. But maybe change can create a better environment. I trust that Buddy (Bell) and his staff can create that."[9]

After a surprise 82-win season in 2000, Dealin' Dan was at it again in the offseason and made the two most scrutinized free-agent signings of his career. O'Dowd inked two big-name left-handed free-agent pitchers to long-term contracts. Denny Neagle was signed to a $51 million, five-year contract and Mike Hampton was signed for $121 million spread over eight years. To say these deals were a disaster is an understatement. Hampton pitched to a 6.15 ERA in 2002 and was shipped out of town after two years (with the Rockies eating most of the remaining $90 million on his deal), and Neagle was equally ineffective; injuries ended his career in 2003. Needless to say, these two contracts were very detrimental to the Rockies' payroll flexibility and made it very difficult for the organization to make free-agent signings over the next few years.

The Rockies were cellar dwellers in the NL West with seven straight fourth- and fifth-place finishes from 2000 through 2006 until a shocking 90-win, wild-card postseason berth and World Series appearance in 2007. The key contributors to the 2007 team included superstar Todd Helton, Matt Holiday, Brad Hawpe (11th round, 2000 draft), Garrett Atkins (fifth round, 2000 draft), Troy Tulowitzki (first round, 2005 draft), Ryan Spilborghs (seventh round, 2002 draft), Willy Taveras (international free-agent signing), Kaz Matsui (international free-agent signing), Jeff Francis (first round, 2002 draft), and the entire bullpen that was either drafted or acquired by O'Dowd and his front office. The 2007 campaign was an absolute dream season for the organization and its fans. Despite being swept by the Red Sox in the World Series, fans and Denver got to witness a Cinderella story: reaching the playoffs for the second time in franchise history; making an incredible run with an offensive juggernaut, a questionable-at-best starting rotation, and an overachieving bullpen that was masterfully built by O'Dowd's front office. One could infer that O'Dowd learned his lesson after the failures of Hampton and Neagle. Those contracts hamstrung the organization for years and forced the front office to focus on player evaluation and development combined with shrewd short-term free-agent deals. This lower risk/ lower reward strategy bore fruit in 2007.

The 2008 season ended in disappointment as the club mustered only a 74-win season. Matt Holiday was sent to Oakland for Huston Street, Greg Smith, and Carlos Gonzalez, and several changes were made to the coaching staff as the front office attempted to retool for the 2009 season. Without taking big risks in free agency, the 2008 squad didn't have enough to repeat their 2007 successes.

The 2009 Rockies season featured an exciting run in the second half that coincided with Jim Tracy being brought on as manager to replace Clint Hurdle. The 2009 Rockies set a team record with 92 wins, but lost to the Philadelphia Phillies in the NLDS three games to one. The next five years until O'Dowd resigned on October 8, 2014, are considered an all-around disappointment. However, O'Dowd and his staff did set up the Rockies for future success by drafting virtually all of the Rockies' near-term major contributors including Nolan Arenado, Charlie Blackmon, Kyle Freeland, Ryan Castellani, Ryan McMahon, Pat Valaika, Jon Gray, Mike Tauchman, David Dahl, Tom Murphy, Scott Oberg, Tyler Anderson, Trevor

Story, Chad Bettis, and Dustin Garneau. That is a stunning run of draft success over a seven-year period and the organization was left in tremendous standing for incoming GM Jeff Bridich.

Dan O'Dowd's foundation was built in Baltimore, where he learned the business and sales functions of a major-league organization before moving into the baseball operations/player development side of the house. Moving to the Cleveland Indians with his mentor Hank Peters, his career blossomed; he gained acclaim as one of the top baseball operations minds as part of the historic Indians teams of the '90s. Success in Cleveland allowed O'Dowd to leverage his substantial reputation into a 15-year stint as the general manager of the Colorado Rockies. The overall body of work can be scrutinized by detractors but the 2007 World Series appearance and 2009's incredible second-half run can be noted as key highlights. In the end, Dan O'Dowd's analytical mind and opinionated persona found a great fit at the MLB Network as he became a top analyst who speaks his mind and draws upon his life as a baseball man to provide wonderfully insightful commentary.

SOURCES

In addition to the sources cited in the Notes, the author also consulted Baseball-Reference.com and MLB.com.

NOTES

1   Mark Kitchin, "Rockies," *Morristown* (New Jersey) *Daily Record,* October 25, 2017: A6.

2   Ibid.

3   Ibid.

4   "Hank Peters Running the Whole Show in Cleveland, and Couldn't Be Happier," *Baltimore Sun*, April 10, 1988: 24B.

5   Hal Lebovitz, "Bonus for Fans Who Attend Tribe Opener," *Mansfield* (Ohio) *News-Journal*, April 1, 1990: 3C.

6   Ibid.

7   Sheldon Ocker, "Adair, of Course! He Had to Be at Fault All Along," *Akron Beacon Journal*, September 5, 1993: E9.

8   Anthony Castrovince, "Cleveland's 'Dream Team' Front Office," January 7, 2016. sportsonearth.com/article/161217636/1998-indians-front-office-executives-tree.

9   John Mossman, "Dealin' Dan O'Dowd Overhauls the Rockies," *Hazelton* (Pennsylvania) *Standard-Speaker*, January 23, 2000: B16.

KEVIN RITZ

BY CHAD MOODY

FOLLOWING A PROMISING ROOKIE
year in 1989, pitcher Kevin Ritz found his career on
shaky ground after struggling with extreme control
problems for the Detroit Tigers over his next couple
of seasons. This was exacerbated by a serious elbow
injury suffered at the end of his tenure in Detroit
that sidelined him for a full season. Undeterred
despite the setbacks, however, Ritz resurrected his
flagging career and set a prominent club record that
held for 14 seasons with the Colorado Rockies — despite pitching in the notoriously hitter-friendly
Mile High City.

Kevin D. Ritz was born on June 8, 1965, in
Eatontown, New Jersey, where his father had been
serving in the US Army. Like his father, Ritz was only
given a singular letter for his middle name. Within
six months of his birth, his family relocated to the
rural Midwestern town of Bloomfield, Iowa, where
he grew up.[1] There, his father, Carl, was a bus driver,
and his mother, Darlene, worked at a plastics factory.
Living in a "modest" home on a gravel road, Ritz was
the second youngest of five children, with siblings
Dana, Renetta, Rose, and Stacey rounding out the
family.[2] Although his parents did not instill in him a
love for the game — they were not particularly ardent
baseball fans — the dream of playing in the major
leagues became a passion early on for Ritz due to
the innate skills he displayed on the diamond.[3] "My
interest started like most boys. I went through Little
League, Babe Ruth, and then on to the high-school
team," he reflected. And the game came naturally to
Ritz: "I really didn't have to work at it and I didn't
have to practice very hard."[4]

As a teenager, when not working as a dishwasher
at a local restaurant, Ritz excelled on the mound at
Davis County High School. Coach Pat Perry knew
the big right-hander threw hard, so he used the local
police department's radar gun to measure his exact
pitch speed. Ritz was throwing in the mid-80s.[5]
He utilized this talent to toss a no-hitter for Davis

County in 1983, and earned an all-state selection.[6]
Further illustrating his athleticism, Ritz was also recognized as an all-state basketball player during his
time with the Mustangs.

After high school, Ritz enrolled at William Penn
University in nearby Oskaloosa, Iowa. His freshman
season with the Statesmen, 1984, did not go as he had
hoped. "I wasn't too thrilled with William Penn," Ritz
said. "The coaching staff wasn't what I expected and I
found myself playing on the junior varsity. It was just
a long year."[7] Still, Ritz's potential was noticed by the
San Francisco Giants, who drafted him in the fourth
round of the January 1985 amateur draft. Not having
been offered a signing bonus, however, he decided to
stay in school.[8]

For his sophomore year, Ritz decided to play baseball at Indian Hills Community College, a junior
college in Centerville, Iowa, even closer to home, on
whose home field he had played many times during
high school. "We had a great rivalry with Centerville
when I was at Davis County," he said. "It was just
nice to be close to home so the family could come
and watch, but we also played on that field against
Centerville a lot. That area has always been a big part
of my life."[9] Ritz immediately felt much more comfortable playing for the Falcons. "There were a lot of
older guys on the team, guys like Mitch Knox who
I think was ancient. He was like 40," Ritz quipped.
"There was good leadership there, different guys from
different cities. It was a great atmosphere right from
the get-go."[10] This change of scenery translated into
success for the young hurler. Ritz finished the season
at Indian Hills with a 7-3 record, and struck out 78
batters in 57 innings while allowing only 42 hits. His
efforts — which included winning two postseason
games — helped lead the Falcons to a Junior College
World Series appearance in 1985.[11] Although the 1985
campaign ultimately was his only season with the
Falcons, Ritz's contributions were recognized by the

school with his induction into the school's Athletics Hall of Fame in 2013.[12]

Ritz's strong performance at IHCC again attracted the attention of a major-league club, this time the Detroit Tigers. Scouted by George Bradley, he was selected by Detroit in the fourth round of the June 1985 amateur draft. Ritz struggled with the decision whether to sign or remain in college—albeit at a different school. "The coaching [at IHCC] wasn't very good, so I felt a change was needed," he explained.[13] Several larger universities including Georgia, Missouri, Nevada-Las Vegas, Oklahoma, and Southern Mississippi had given him offers to transfer to their baseball programs.[14] While taking time to decide, Ritz continued to work at his craft by playing in the summer for the Alaska Goldpanners of Fairbanks in the amateur collegiate Alaska Baseball League. Pitching primarily in relief, he led the team with four saves.[15] Finally, after initially announcing that he had decided to attend Nevada-Las Vegas because he felt he needed more seasoning, Ritz reconsidered when Detroit sweetened its contract offer with a bonus of $12,000.[16] On September 3, 1985, he signed with the Tigers.

For the 1986 season, Detroit assigned the 6-foot-4, 195-pound hurler to the Class-A level. Splitting time with the Gastonia Tigers of the South Atlantic League and the Lakeland Tigers of the Florida State League, Ritz struggled in his first stint in the minor leagues. Between the two clubs, he finished the year with a 4-11 record in 25 games (22 starts), and posted a 5.16 ERA and 1.71 WHIP. Despite the disappointing results, Tigers farm director Frank Franchi was still "delighted" with Ritz, considering his lack of experience, and touted him as one of the team's top prospects to watch.[17]

Showing confidence in the 21-year-old, Detroit promoted Ritz to the Glens Falls Tigers of the Double-A Eastern League for the 1987 season, where he was used strictly in a starting role. Although facing more formidable competition, Ritz showed improvement in nearly all statistical categories, and led the club in wins and innings pitched. In 25 starts, he finished the season with an 8-8 record, 4.89 ERA,

and 1.59 WHIP. Although he expected to advance to Triple A, at the beginning of the 1988 season, Ritz found himself back with Glens Falls. "[In 1988] I was expecting to make the Triple-A roster and on the next-to-last day they sent me to Double A. Sometimes it's kind of disappointing when you see younger guys getting a chance," Ritz said.[18] Although his confidence was shaken, Ritz again showed marked improvement, posting an 8-10 record, 3.82 ERA, and 1.35 WHIP in his 26 starts. He limited opposing batters to a .229 batting average (fifth lowest in the league), and picked up a victory in a playoff start which according to Ritz was "probably the highlight of the season."[19]

Added to Detroit's 40-man roster for the 1989 season, the promising Ritz attended the Tigers' spring training in Lakeland, Florida. He did not make the Tigers' regular season roster, but performed well with the Toledo Mud Hens of the Triple-A International League, posting a 3.16 ERA after 16 starts into midseason, with wins in his last four decisions. Meanwhile the parent Tigers were languishing as one of the worst teams in baseball. And with both injuries and lackluster performance plaguing their aging starting rotation, the Tigers called up the promising 24-year-old to replace struggling fill-in starter David Palmer in the rotation.[20]

With the team's season all but lost, the move was an indication that the Tigers were planning for the future. Asked whether Ritz would have been called up had Detroit been in contention, manager Sparky Anderson responded, "No way."[21] On July 15, Ritz made his first major-league appearance, getting the start against the Seattle Mariners at Tiger Stadium. With a contingent of 15 family members and friends who made the 12-hour trek from Iowa to Detroit to support him, Ritz pitched reasonably well through four innings, allowing five hits and two runs.[22] His night ended, however, after he allowed four consecutive baserunners and two runs to begin the fifth inning, and he left the game down 4-3. The Tigers were unable to mount a comeback, and Ritz was tagged with the loss.

Ritz bounced back in his next start with a strong performance against the California Angels in a no-decision, and followed that with his first major-league victory in a start against the Minnesota Twins on July 28. Twins manager Tom Kelly said of the rookie, "Ritz has a very good arm. He has a nice, easy windup, can throw hard, has a good curve, and a little bit of a changeup."[23] While celebrating his first big-league win by enjoying a ham sandwich after the game, the low-key Ritz kept things in perspective, confessing, "I'm glad to have this out of the way. It's just a win in another league. I didn't expect to get hyper, because it's just another game."[24] After he won his next two starts, the Tigers maintained him in their starting rotation for the balance of the season. Ritz got positive reviews within the organization based on his solid overall performance. "A couple years from now, hitters won't want to get out of bed on the day he pitches," manager Anderson quipped.[25] Ritz finished the season with a 4-6 record and 4.38

ERA in 12 starts, and was named Tigers Rookie of the Year.

Ritz's success was a much-needed "Cinderella story" inspiration to residents in his Iowa hometown, many of whom made the 3½-hour drive to attend his start in Kansas City in August. "It's been a tough decade for Bloomfield. We've had our hard knocks," said Bloomfield merchant Susan Howard. "So because this is a small town there's a special feeling about what's happened to Kevin. A community is full of independent people, but we become one under both good and bad circumstances. That's why I'm so happy at seeing this decade finishing on this nice high note."[26] In another indication of the pride Ritz instilled in his community, after the season he was guest of honor at a civic luncheon at the Bloomfield United Methodist Church.

Deciding against re-signing 39-year-old Doyle Alexander for the 1990 campaign, Detroit instead targeted the more youthful Ritz to fill the starting-rotation void. Instead of building on the promise of his rookie year, however, Ritz got off to a disastrous start. Struggling to find the strike zone and hit hard when he did, after his first three starts he had allowed 13 hits and 10 walks in 7⅓ innings. Things hit rock bottom for Ritz in his fourth start, when he was removed from the game against Minnesota without recording an out after allowing four walks and one hit to the first five batters he faced. Although Ritz complained about battling a "dead arm" during his struggles, teammate Frank Tanana diagnosed Ritz's problems as stemming from a lack of confidence. "After the confidence goes the fastball, then the location. That's the usual course of events," said Tanana. "In Kevin's case, it looks like he's trying to overthrow to compensate for his control problems. It's something every young pitcher goes through. Once he starts having a little success, he'll be fine. All he needs is that first victory."[27] Ritz did not get a chance to get that first victory, however, as Detroit had little choice but to send him to the minor leagues after he compiled a 0-4 record with an 11.05 ERA and 3.82 WHIP in his four starts. Spending the rest of the season back at Toledo, Ritz continued to battle wildness. He finished the disappointing year there with a 3-6 record, 5.22 ERA, and 1.70 WHIP in 20 games (18 starts). Ritz walked 59 batters in 89⅔ innings.

Because of his sophomore slump, Ritz was not in the Tigers' plans at the beginning of the 1991 campaign, and again found himself in Toledo to start the year. Featuring a newly developed slider, Ritz rebounded. His 4-0 record with a 1.77 ERA for the month of May, coupled with an unreliable Detroit starting rotation, afforded Ritz another chance with the parent club. Mud Hens pitching coach Ralph Treuel noted of Ritz's prevailing successes, "A lot of hard work and more self-confidence have been the keys. With his mound presence and poise, he looks like a pitcher. He just decided to take the bull by the horn. This is not the same Kevin Ritz from the past."[28] On his return to the Tigers, however, it did indeed look very much like the Kevin Ritz from the past. After five starts with Detroit between late May and late June, he posted a 0-3 record with an abysmal 18.00 ERA. And the wildness had returned, with Ritz walking 18 batters in nine innings. Unsurprisingly, he was sent back to Toledo. Although Ritz was again recalled to the Tigers late in the season, he accomplished nothing particularly noteworthy there in his six appearances out of the bullpen.

"Some type of mental block" was pointed to by members of the Detroit and Toledo coaching staffs as the cause of Ritz's inability to throw strikes. "Who knows what's going through the guy's mind? I like Kevin an awful lot. He's got a great arm. There's no explanation," said Detroit pitching coach Billy Muffett. Manager Anderson also shared his thoughts: "I told him, 'You gotta overcome that block.' That's all it is. It's easy to say, but hard to cure. I don't think there's anything harder to cure than that." At the time, Ritz revealed that he might consider consulting a psychiatrist if the problem persisted. "In my mind there's a subconscious block," he confessed.[29]

Despite his incredible struggles at the major-league level over the prior two years, Ritz still figured in the Tigers' plans for the 1992 season; he had "too good an arm to give up on."[30] Beginning the campaign pitching in relief for Detroit—although still featuring a high walk rate—Ritz seemed to have finally overcome his mental block. He pitched reasonably well out of the bullpen, carrying a 4.03 ERA into late May after 10 appearances. And with Detroit starter Eric King struggling on the mound and dealing with a sore shoulder, Ritz rejoined the starting rotation.[31] Although lacking consistency, he pitched well enough to become a mainstay in the rotation for the next two months. In his July 29 start against the Chicago White Sox, however, Ritz suffered another setback, in the form of an elbow injury that caused him to exit the game early. "I felt it a couple of pitches before I came out. Hopefully, it's nothing too serious," Ritz said after the game.[32] But it was serious—enough to keep him sidelined for the rest of the year. Ritz had posted a 2-5 record with a 5.60 ERA in 23 games (11 starts) when his season—and tenure as a Detroit Tiger—came to an unceremonious end.

Injury situation notwithstanding, on November 17, 1992, Ritz was drafted by the Colorado Rockies as the 46th pick in the major-league expansion draft. He was not bitter about having been left unprotected by Detroit, saying, "I most definitely was given every opportunity. I just didn't take advantage."[33] While he sought a fresh start with the expansion Rockies for the 1993 campaign, the elbow problems resurfaced, however, requiring him to battle through pain during spring training and negatively affecting his performance. Although the Rockies attempted to send him to the minor leagues to open the season, Ritz refused the assignment, instead opting to test the free-agent market, knowing the Cleveland Indians had strong interest. Upon undergoing a physical examination by Cleveland, Ritz was diagnosed with a torn elbow tendon requiring surgery. This voided the deal with the Indians, and left Ritz sidelined for the 1993 season while dealing with a potentially career-threatening injury. "I was close to giving up and looking for another job," Ritz said.[34] Encouraged by his wife to not give up, he underwent surgery in April and spent months rehabbing, unable to throw a ball until August.[35] Released by the Rockies in October, he found himself without a team. Less than two months later, however, the Rockies re-signed Ritz, offering him a glimmer of hope of getting back in the game as the 1994 season approached.

With his surgically repaired elbow feeling "fine" and having been given a clean bill of health from his doctors, Ritz went to spring training in 1994 with the Triple-A Colorado Springs Sky Sox. "It feels good to just be out playing baseball again. Things are looking pretty good for me," he said of his comeback.[36] His first preseason appearance also looked pretty good, with Ritz tossing three hitless innings against the California Angels' top farm club on March 22. He carried that strong performance into the Sky Sox' regular season, posting a 5-0 record with an outstanding 1.29 ERA into late May, and only six walks in 35 innings—particularly impressive considering his history of high walk rates. With Colorado starter Armando Reynoso lost for the season with an elbow injury, Ritz's efforts were rewarded with a summons to the Rockies. He made his first start on May 25 against the Cincinnati Reds. After throwing 34 pitches and allowing two runs in a rough first inning, he settled down, not allowing another run in his next four innings. Although he got a no-decision, Rockies pitching coach Larry Bearnarth said of Ritz's performance, "That was a Herculean effort. Going against [Jose] Rijo, coming off surgery, not pitching in the big leagues in nearly two years, and overthrowing like crazy in the first inning. ... He settled down, and that was the pitcher we scouted."[37] Ritz remained a fixture in Colorado's starting rotation until the players strike cut the season short, and finished with a 5-6 record and a 5.62 ERA. Rockies manager Don Baylor put things into perspective when he said, "What he has done as far as coming back from an injury that has ended the career of some players is simply remarkable."[38]

In spring training in 1995, Ritz was named the Rockies' fifth starter to begin the team's first season in what became a noted hitters' park, Coors Field. With the other members of Colorado's starting rotation struggling in the early going, however, he soon became the ace of the staff, tying a team record with nine strikeouts on June 8 against the Chicago Cubs.

Heading into the All-Star break, Ritz had a 7-3 record with a solid 3.50 ERA, and was touted as the team's "savior" by manager Baylor.[39] Despite his success, the low-key Ritz was not comfortable with the associated media attention. "I just want to do my job. Maybe it's because I just come from Iowa, I never had that kind of attention, and don't want it," he said.[40] Although he suffered through a dreadful August (0-5, 6.12), Ritz still finished the season with an 11-11 record and 4.21 ERA (tops among Rockies starters), and led the club in wins, innings pitched (173⅓), and strikeouts (120). Helping the Rockies advance to the playoffs in only their third season, Ritz saw action in two National League Division Series games against the Atlanta Braves. He started the series opener against Greg Maddux and pitched relatively well, receiving a no-decision in a 5-4 loss. Ritz also appeared in relief in the series finale, a 10-4 loss. Unsurprisingly, he was named the Rockies Pitcher of the Year.

Coming off his breakthrough year—and with veteran aces Bill Swift and Bret Saberhagen on the disabled list—Ritz was named the starter for the Rockies' 1996 season opener. "I'm looking at it as just another start. It's just day one of a long season," was his restrained comment.[41] Ritz responded to the honor by firmly establishing himself as the number-one starter on the staff, giving up just one hit (but seven walks) in 5⅓ innings as the Rockies defeated the Phillies, 5-3. On May 5, in defeating the Florida Marlins 5-4, he became the first Rockies pitcher to toss a complete game at Coors Field. And by the end of June, Ritz was tied for second in the NL with nine wins, leading to media speculation that he might be named to the All-Star team. Although it did not happen, he said years later, "I couldn't be too disappointed about the All-Star Game, especially where I had come from in my career. At least I was mentioned."[42] By season's end, Ritz had smashed several franchise records en route to his second consecutive selection as the Rockies Pitcher of the Year. Compiling a 17-11 record, he became the team's leader in career victories with 33, and also set single-season records for most innings pitched (213), games started (35), and victories.

Ritz's record 17 victories held for 14 years before being supplanted, and remains as of 2018 tied for second. Among NL season leaders for 1996, he finished tied for second in games started, tied for third in wins, and 10th in won-lost percentage. Despite these successes, Ritz's statistics featured some counterintuitive peculiarities. His 125 earned runs were the most in the league, his 236 hits and 105 walks were both second, and his 10 wild pitches were eighth highest. This all translated into a rather lofty 5.28 ERA and 1.60 WHIP. Nonetheless, that winter Colorado signed Ritz to his first major contract—a two-year deal with a third year at Ritz's option for a reported $3 million per year. "With the dearth of pitching in the major leagues the fact, as we have found out, that bringing a new pitcher in here is no guarantee he will be successful, and with Kevin having pitched here for three years, we had a higher level of comfort that he can continue to be a major factor for us," Rockies general manager Bob Gebhard explained regarding the signing.[43]

Asked in 1997 spring training whether he would perform differently now that he was the recipient of a lucrative contract, Ritz responded, "It's hard to say because I've never made that kind of money. But the few days that I've been here, I've been relaxed and had a good time. I'm throwing well." He was again named the Rockies' Opening Day starter, and expectations were high. "I think Kevin Ritz is at a point in his career where he can be categorized in that elite group they call 20-game winners," proclaimed Rockies pitching coach Frank Funk. "He should be able to get real close to that 20-win mark on a consistent basis."[44] But Ritz was battered around in taking the Opening Day loss to the Reds, and continued to struggle into midseason as he dealt with an ailing shoulder throughout June.[45] A medical examination in July revealed a torn labrum in his throwing shoulder that required surgery; thus, Ritz's season came to a premature end.[46] His final statistics for the disappointing season featured a 6-8 record and a 5.87 ERA.

With his repaired shoulder not quite ready for Opening Day in 1998, Ritz started the year on the disabled list, and did not fare well in some early-season rehabilitation outings with the minor-league Sky Sox. Still, the 32-year-old was activated in May by the big-league club, declaring himself "ready."[47] After two starts with the Rockies, however, Ritz had allowed 17 hits and 11 earned runs in nine innings, and was placed back on the disabled list. According to manager Baylor, his lack of success appeared to be due to reduced velocity on his fastball, which at 88 mph was down 4 mph from his pre-injury form.[48] Ritz pitched reasonably well in three rehabilitation starts for the New Haven Ravens of the Double-A Eastern League, but struggled when given a start with the Triple-A Sky Sox in June. Shortly thereafter, he underwent season-ending surgery to repair tears in both his labrum and rotator cuff.[49] Although hoping for yet another comeback in the 1999 season, Ritz was realistic about his chances considering his age and injury history. "They did five surgeries on my arm and hopefully it will heal properly. It feels good right now, but who knows what the future will hold," he said. For Ritz, the future did not hold any further professional baseball.

The effects of Ritz's arm injuries from his playing days lingered into his post-baseball life, causing him to undergo additional surgeries after settling down with his family in Cambridge, Ohio, his wife's hometown.[50] He and his wife, Sally, whom he met in the late 1980s through a former minor-league teammate, have four children: Molly, Kyle, Eli, and Lilly.[51] Although Ritz involved himself in business pursuits including batting cages, golf and hunting simulators, and a sporting-goods store, he primarily spent his time as a "professional father," following the activities of his children—some of whom have played collegiate athletics. "I'm really just a family man," Ritz said in 2008. "My family is more important to me than any baseball accomplishments I've had."[52] He and Sally spent a significant amount of time doing volunteer work, and started the Kevin Ritz Family Foundation, which has helped support youth baseball and football leagues in addition to other activities benefiting children. As spare-time hobbies, Ritz took up hunting, fishing, camping, and golf.[53]

Ritz continued to support the Rockies, cheering them on at Fenway Park with his two sons when they reached the World Series in 2007.[54] He did not mince words when reflecting on how he approached pitching in Denver. "I've never been scared of Coors Field," Ritz said. "There's a lot of guys who come in there and mentally can't pitch there because of the bad things that they've heard. If you give up a cheap, three-run homer, you just say the hell with it."[55] Despite the challenges he faced pitching before a humidor was installed to help normalize ball flight in the high-altitude environment, he still enjoyed his time with the Rockies. "I had a great time in Denver," Ritz said. "That season [1995] kind of put me on the map."[56]

Acknowledgments

The author wishes to thank Kevin Ritz, Sally Ritz, and Kevin Pink for their time and research assistance.

SOURCES

In addition to the sources noted in this biography, the author accessed Ritz's file from the library of the National Baseball Hall of Fame and Museum in Cooperstown, New York; Ancestry.com; Baseball-Reference.com; Facebook.com; GenealogyBank.com; NewspaperArchive.com; Newspapers.com; and Retrosheet.org.

NOTES

1 Kevin Ritz, phone interview with author, April 10, 2017. Ritz said he was uncertain of his heritage, but believed it to be predominantly German.

2 Gene Raffensperger, "Detroit Tiger Kevin Ritz Is a Hit in His Hometown," *Des Moines Register*, October 8, 1989: 2B.

3 Ritz phone interview, April 10, 2017.

4 Brenda Macy, "Ritz Ready for Spring Test," *Ottumwa* (Iowa) *Courier*, February 26, 1986: 12.

5 Raffensperger, "Detroit Tiger Kevin Ritz."

6 "Ritz Fires 8-Inning No-Hitter for Davis County," *Des Moines Register*, June 21, 1983: 2S.

7 Scott Jackson, "Kevin Ritz Returns to His IHCC Roots," *Ottumwa Courier*, February 19, 2013: B3.

8 Jeff Rivers, "Ritz Passes on Dip Into the Big League," *Ottumwa Courier*, June 13, 1985: 13.

9 Jackson, "Kevin Ritz Returns to His IHCC Roots."

10 Ibid.

11 Rivers, "Ritz Passes on Dip Into the Big League"; Kevin Pink (sports information director at Indian Hills Community College), email correspondence with author, August 29, 2017.

12 IHCC Athletic Dept., "IHCC Announces 2013 Athletic Hall of Fame Class: Ex-Pros Kevin Ritz, Tony Galbreath Among Five Athletes Honored," *Ottumwa Courier*, January 16, 2013: B1.

13 Macy, "Ritz Ready for Spring Test."

14 Rivers, "Ritz Passes on Dip into the Big League."

15 Lew Freedman, *Diamonds in the Rough: Baseball Stories from Alaska* (Kenmore, Washington: Epicenter Press, 2000), 244; Alaska Goldpanners of Fairbanks, "1985 Alaska Goldpanners Pitching Statistics," pannervault.com/Seasons/1985/statistics.html, accessed March 6, 2017.

16 Rivers, "Ritz Passes on Dip into the Big League;" Macy, "Ritz Ready for Spring Test."

17 Mark Kram, "Unkindest Cut of All: Released Players Feel Anger, Shock, Relief," *Detroit Free Press*, July 9, 1986: 6D; "Farm Crisis Could Mean Famine for Tigers," *Detroit Free Press*, July 6, 1986: 4D.

18 John McPoland, "Bloomfield Native Hurling Toward Tiger Town," *Ottumwa Courier*, March 21, 1989: 9.

19 Larry Paladino, ed., *Detroit Tigers Yearbook 1989* (Detroit: Detroit Baseball Club, 1989), 60; McPoland, "Bloomfield Native Hurling Toward Tiger Town."

20 Gene Guidi, "6 Moves: Guillermo on DL; Palmer Cut," *Detroit Free Press*, July 14, 1989: 4D.

21 John Lowe, "M's Rock Ritz; Tigers' Skid Hits 10," *Detroit Free Press*, July 16, 1989: 11E.

22 John Lowe, "Henneman Experiences Game's Ups and Downs," *Detroit Free Press*, July 17, 1989: 8D.

23 John Lowe, "Tigers Win for Ritz, Then Do the Splits," *Detroit Free Press*, July 29, 1989: 7C.

24 Ibid.

25 Tom Gage, "Tigers Rookie Pitcher Is Putting on the Ritz," *The Sporting News*, August 28, 1989: 21.

26 John Lowe, "Whole Town Turns Out to See Kevin Ritz Pitch," *Detroit Free Press*, August 31, 1989: 6D; Raffensperger, "Detroit Tiger Kevin Ritz Is a Hit in His Hometown."

27 John Lowe, "Dead Arm Might Have Been Burying Ritz," *Detroit Free Press*, April 24, 1990: 4D; Randy Peterson, "Iowan Finds Patriarchal Advice About Losing From Those Who Know," *Des Moines Register*, April 26, 1990: 2S.

28 John Lowe, "Unreliable Rotation Speeds Need for Ritz," *Detroit Free Press*, May 30, 1991: 4E.

29 Victor Chi, "Out of Control: Mental Block Keeps Ritz From Major Success," *Detroit Free Press*, July 20, 1991: 5B.

30 John Lowe, "Gibson Deal Helps Push Young Arms," *Detroit Free Press*, February 24, 1992: 3D.

31 John Lowe, "King's Ailing Shoulder, ERA Out of Rotation," *Detroit Free Press*, May 26, 1992: 4C.

32 Gene Guidi, "Tigers' Skid 6—8-6," *Detroit Free Press*, July 30, 1992: 1C.

33 Gene Guidi, "Tigers Will Face Competition to Keep Lou," *Detroit Free Press*, November 23, 1992: 2C.

34 John Lowe, "Ritz's Tenacity, New Confidence Rewarded," *Detroit Free Press*, January 15, 1997: 1D.

35 Ibid; Dereck Lewis, "Iowan Ritz Seeks Return to Old Form on Mound," *Des Moines Register*, March 29, 1994: 3S.

36 Ibid.

37 Tracy Ringolsby, "Colorado Rockies," *The Sporting News*, June 6, 1994: 26.

38 Randy Peterson, "Elbowing His Way Back Into the Majors," *Des Moines Register*, July 5, 1994: 1S.

39 John Lowe, "Bosox Take Huge Lead Despite Injuries, and Help's on the Way," *Detroit Free Press*, June 9, 1995: 4G.

40 Mike Klis, "Ritz, Castilla Pace Rockies in Chicago," *Colorado Springs Gazette Telegraph*, June 9, 1995: C3.

41 Randy Peterson, "Ritz-y Opener," *Des Moines Register*, March 29, 1996: 4S.

42 Irv Moss, "Ritz Won Sweet 17 With 1996 Rockies," *Denver Post*, denverpost.com/2010/06/07/ritz-won-sweet-17-with-1996-rockies/, June 7, 2010, accessed April 25, 2017.

43 "Colorado Signs Ritz for $3 Million a Year," *Des Moines Register*, January 4, 1997: 4S.

44 Mike Klis, "Ritz's Maturity Makes Him a Winner at Coors," *Colorado Springs Gazette Telegraph*, February 18, 1997: C3.

45 Associated Press, "Rockies Pitcher Ritz Sidelined by Injury," *Des Moines Register*, July 13, 1997: 3D.

46 Mike Burrows, "Torn Shoulder Shelves Ritz for Season; Bailey Next Off DL," *The Gazette* (Colorado Springs), July 13, 1997: SP7.

47 Ray McNulty, "Thompson's Torn Muscle Idles Hurler Two Months," *The Gazette* (Colorado Springs), May 8, 1998: SP5.

48 Mike Burrows, "Once Again, Ritz Shows He's Still Far From Being First Class," *The Gazette* (Colorado Springs), May 17, 1998: SP7.

49 Ray McNulty, "Ritz's Season Is Over," *The Gazette* (Colorado Springs), June 25, 1998: SP5.

50 Jeff Birnbaum, "Where Are They Now? Kevin Ritz," MLB. com, m.mlb.com/news/article/3370097, August 27, 2008, accessed March 6, 2017.

51 Jeff Harrison, "We've Got Our Own Rockie Right Here—Kevin Ritz," *Daily Jeffersonian* (Cambridge, Ohio), daily-jeff.com/local%20sports/2007/10/21/we-ve-got-our-own-rockie-right-here-kevin-ritz, October 20, 2007, accessed April 25, 2017.

52 Birnbaum, "Where Are They Now? Kevin Ritz."

53 Ibid; Moss, "Ritz Won Sweet 17 With 1996 Rockies."

54 Birnbaum, "Where Are They Now? Kevin Ritz."

55 Klis, "Ritz's Maturity Makes Him a Winner at Coors," C1.

56 Moss, "Ritz Won Sweet 17 With 1996 Rockies."

LARRY WALKER

BY ALAN COHEN

"WHAT IF?" IT IS A PERENNIAL QUES- tion and in baseball, the "what if?" usually pertains to injury. What would have a team accomplished had not half of its players been on the DL at one point or another during a season? What if a pitcher's promising career had not been torpedoed by a line drive off the bat of the opposing team's infielder? Would have Larry Walker's statistics been deemed worthy of the Hall of Fame had he not lost the equivalent of three full seasons to various injuries in his 17-year major league career? The folks from Western Canada may never have the opportunity to wave their flags on the green lawns of Cooperstown, but their pride and joy's accomplishments on diamonds stretching from Montreal to Denver to St. Louis can never be diminished and will never be forgotten.

Larry Kenneth Robert Walker was born December 1, 1966, in Maple Ridge, British Columbia. He was the fourth son born to Larry and Mary Walker. Brothers Barry, Carey, and Gary preceded him into an athletic family, and the five men in the family often played together in a fast-pitch softball league. Larry never played baseball at Maple Ridge Senior Secondary School, as they didn't field a team. He played volleyball and hockey in high school. He learned his baseball in a Canadian amateur league in Vancouver, roughly the equivalent of the Senior Babe Ruth Leagues in the United States.[1]

After graduation in 1984, he elected not to go to college. Hockey was his main sport growing up. His brother Carey, a goalie, had been drafted by the Montreal Canadiens, but did not play in the NHL. Larry, also a goalie, advanced through the youth hockey ranks, along with his friends Rick Herbert and Cam Neely. The latter would go on to a career with the Boston Bruins. Herbert and Walker tried out for the Regina Pats of the Junior A Western Hockey League, but Larry was disappointed when the best offers he got involved playing for Tier II

teams. One was to play in Swift Current, 1,000 miles from his home. One trip to Swift Current convinced him that his future would not be in hockey. "It wasn't the greatest place. It was a tough place, kind of dirty. I said to myself, 'What am I doing here?' Then we went to the rink, and when we got there I told myself, 'No.' I didn't want to do it. It just wasn't what I wanted. We hopped back in the car and drove home."[2]

At 17, Walker began to concentrate more on baseball. During the summer of 1984, he played with the Coquitlam Reds in Vancouver, British Columbia. He made Canada's national team and played in the 1984 World Youth Championships in Kindersley, Saskatchewan. After finishing high school, he was disenchanted about his future. "I warned Larry back then that he would have to be prepared to spend the next 50 years as a laborer," his dad, Larry Sr., the manager of a building supply company, recalled. "He said he understood that." Not long after deciding not to continue his schooling, Walker got a call from Bob Rogers, an Expo scout who realized he could sign Walker to a minor-league contract. No other teams showed interest,[3] and he was signed by the Montreal Expos as a free agent on November 14, 1984, for a $1,500 signing bonus. He spent 1985 through most of 1989 in the minors in the Expos organization, batting .274 with 73 homers and 258 RBIs in 437 games.

He was raw when he first joined the organization and hit only .223 with 2 home runs in 62 games on loan to the unaffiliated Utica Blue Sox of the New York-Penn League in 1985. "I'd never seen a forkball, never seen a slider. I didn't know they existed. I had never really seen a good curveball. In Canada, as a kid, we'd play 10 baseball games a year. Fifteen, tops. Some pitchers had a thing they'd call a spinner, but nothing like this. Baseball just wasn't big. The weather was against it. Nobody ever played baseball thinking about making the major leagues. It was just a game, just something to do."[4] He was not even aware of all of the rules. Years later he remembered the instance where, on a hit and run play, he raced from first to third. On the play, however, the batter hit a fly ball that was caught by one of the opposing team's outfielders. Walker raced back to first base, taking the direct route. Although he beat the throw back to first base, he was called out for failing to touch second base. He couldn't understand that he had to retouch the bag. He exclaimed, "Why? I was already there."[5] But Utica manager Ken Brett kept him in the lineup because "he was just so tough."[6]

Another person in the Expos' organization who had faith in Walker was hitting coach Ralph Rowe. After the 1985 season and for several seasons thereafter, Walker was in West Palm Beach, Florida honing his skills in the Florida Instructional League. It didn't take long for him to show improvement.

He blossomed in 1986 with the Burlington (Iowa) Expos of the Midwest League, hitting .289 with 29 home runs with 73 RBIs, before, in late July being transferred to Montreal's other Class-A team, West Palm Beach in the Florida State League. The move was made necessary when West Palm Beach's Mike Day, batting .316 at the time, was sidelined for the season with a broken arm.[7] Walker hit four more dingers (and 16 extra base hits) in 38 games with West Palm Beach.

Although he was but a 19-year-old, the folks in Canada couldn't wait for Larry's arrival on the big-league stage. A legion of Canadian reporters followed his every move. "Mentally, I`ve improved so much," he said, explaining his progress. "I really want to play every day, go out and do my best. I know now I can hit the ball. I have a lot of confidence even though I still strike out a lot. I swing at too many bad pitches." Manager Felipe Alou said, "If he keeps improving the way he has the last 12 months, there`s no telling what he could do. You have a kid with his kind of potential, they don`t last long in the minor leagues."[8] With Walker's firepower, West Palm Beach won the FSL's Southern Division.

Walker spent the following season with the Class-AA Jacksonville Expos in the Southern League. After slugging 25 doubles, 7 triples, and 26 homers for Jacksonville, and being named to the Southern

League All-Star team, he missed all of 1988 due to an injury, the first of several that would cut into his playing time over the years. He tore up his knee while playing winter ball in Hermosillo, Mexico. Scoring from first base on a single, he slipped on home plate and his knee locked up causing him to flip over. He needed surgery and a long rehab program. "I was told my career might end, but I never thought about the negative part of it. I was thinking positive all the time and how good I was going to be when I came back."[9] Over the course of his major league career, Walker was to miss the equivalent of more than three full seasons, spending 536 games on the disabled list. His nine trips stints on the DL allowed Walker to play in more than 140 games a season only four times during his career.

The following spring, a groin injury slowed his progress even further. He was sent to the club's minor league training facility and opened the season with Indianapolis in the Triple-A American Association. In 104 games with Indianapolis, he batted .270 with 12 homers and 57 RBIs. He also stole 36 bases. The Expos considered him ready for the big leagues, and he made his major league debut at the age of 22 on August 16, 1989, against the Giants at Montreal. The superstitious Walker favored the number "3," and he wore uniform number 33 throughout his career.

Remembering his long road from hockey goalie in Canada to the big leagues, Walker said, "People have to stick with you, but the most important person is you. You have to go to these minor-league cities, and take the bus rides, and play in little parks lit by candlelight, and not get much sleep, and eat the worst food in the world. It comes with the territory. You might not make it. But sometimes it pays off."[10]

After walking in his first two plate appearances, he singled to right field off Mike LaCoss for his first major league hit. He came around to score the Expos' first run of the game, as they went on to win 4-2. His call-up had come 10 days after Expos lost their hold on first place in the NL East after having held it since June 26. They had slipped to third place, four games behind the division leaders. They hoped that two young but talented outfielders, Walker and

Marquis Grissom, would provide the spark to push them back to the top of the standings, but it wasn't to be. The Expos lost 27 of their last 43 games and dropped to fourth place. The most memorable game during Walker's time with the Expos in 1989 was a 22-inning game at Montreal against the Dodgers—the longest in team history—on August 23. In the 16th inning of a scoreless game, Walker was called out on an appeal play for leaving third base early after scoring the apparent winning run on a sacrifice fly. But in the 18th, he made a spectacular catch of a line drive off the bat of Eddie Murray against the wall in right field, and the teams played on. The Expos lost eventually 1-0 when Dodger catcher Rick Dempsey homered to lead off the 22nd inning. Walker went 1-for-7 in the contest, and his average plummeted from .333 to .280. He ended the season in a prolonged slump during which he went 1-for-22 and saw his average drop to .170 with no home runs.

In spite of the inauspicious start, Walker was not sent back to the minors. Instead he became the regular right fielder for the 1990 Expos, because Hubie Brooks became a free agent at the end of the 1989 season and signed with the Dodgers, clearing a spot in the line-up for Walker. In 1990, the Expos fielded three players with little major league experience that year: Walker, Delino DeShields, and Marquis Grissom. Walker batted .241 with 19 home runs, tying Andre Dawson's rookie record for the Expos. His first homer came on April 20 at Shea Stadium in New York off Ron Darling as the Expos defeated the Mets 2-1. At season's end Topps named him to its All-Star Rookie team.

He didn't hit well during spring training in 1991, and there was even talk about platooning him. After an 0-for-3 performance on May 4, his average stood at .169. And then he warmed up, going 16-for-46 with four homers over a 12-game stretch to increase his average by 79 points. But the streak was temporary. Not only wasn't he hitting, but he sustained a pulled hamstring and wound up on the DL at the end of June. He came off the DL on July 14 and, in August, he finally found his stroke. He began the month with a 10-game hitting streak, his best of the season, during which he batted .439. From the time he came off the DL in mid-July through the end of the season, he had 10 homers, 41 RBIs, and a .338 batting average. For the season, he batted .290 in 137 games as the Expos (71-90) finished last in the NL East.

In 1992, Walker hit .301, reaching .300 for the first time, and his 23 home runs were the most of his young career. He became the first and only Canadian to win the Expos Player of the Year award. He also won the Silver Slugger award, and his 16 assists propelled him to the Gold Glove award. One of those assists came on July 4, when he fielded a ground ball in right field and threw out Padres shortstop Tony Fernandez at first base! He was named to his first All-Star team, getting a pinch-hit single in his only at-bat. And he finished fifth in the MVP voting as the Expos finished in second place, their best performance since 1981. Bringing on Felipe Alou as manager 37 games into the season was one of their keys to success.

Walker was just starting to show his stuff and over the balance of his career, he would go on to win seven Gold Gloves and be named to five All-Star teams. Before the 1993 season, hitting coach Tommy Harper predicted that if "everything goes right for him, he can hit 40 home runs and drive in 100-something runs. He has that kind of potential. The thing about Larry is, he works so hard. I saw him in the weight room in the minors, so I know. But he's also very tough on himself. It's like he's always trying to have a perfect game. I've told him, `You've worked to reach this point. Give yourself a little credit.'"[11]

In 1993, Walker had an off-season at the plate as his average dropped to .265. However, his power numbers were consistent with those in the prior season, 22 homers and 86 RBIs. He also won his second consecutive Gold Glove Award. On a revolving door Expo team that saw 48 different players on the roster during the course of the season, he also had four fellow Canadians, Joe Siddall, Matt Stairs, Denis Boucher, and Mike Gardiner, as teammates for parts of the season. Alou, in his first full year at the helm took the team to a 94-68 record and a second-place finish. The best was yet to come.

Walker's 1994 season got off to an unusual start. Through his team's first 18 games, he was batting .284 with three homers and 14 RBIs—nothing unusual there. Then on Sunday, April 24, Walker made his way on to the all-time blooper reel at Los Angeles. In the third inning, with one out and the Dodgers leading 2-0, Mike Piazza lifted a fly ball towards foul territory and Walker made the catch. Thinking it was the third out of the inning, Walker handed the ball to six-year-old Sebastian Napier who was sitting with his mom along the right field foul line. The next thing Walker saw was Jose Offerman, who had been on first base, tagging up and flying around the bases. Walker was able to retrieve the ball from the youth and keep Offerman from going beyond third base. And the issue became somewhat moot when Tim Wallach slammed Pedro Martinez's next pitch over the left field wall for a two-run homer. The embarrassed Walker "told the little kid that maybe next time I'll give him a ball when there are three outs

instead of two. Everybody around him was laughing." True to his word, when the Expos took the field for the bottom of the fourth inning, Walker gave little Sebastian another ball, and received a standing ovation. Catcher Mike Piazza, who himself had had an embarrassing moment, told Walker, "You know, it's kind of hard to count to three, sometimes."[12]

As the 1994 season wore on, the Expos were sailing along in first place, six games ahead, with Larry Walker tied for the National League lead with 44 doubles (the first of four times when he would have 40 or more doubles in a season) when the players went on strike in August. In late June that season, he had suffered a shoulder injury, tearing his rotator cuff. Although he only missed four games, the injury affected his throwing, and upon his return to the lineup he was moved to first base. The move didn't hurt Walker's hitting: he batted .364 in 35 games at first base. At the time of the work stoppage, he was hitting a career high .322. The Expos seemed poised to be a contender for years to come with a healthy Walker at first, and Marquis Grissom and Moises Alou patrolling the outfield.

It did not happen. Despite their success, the Expos suffered attendance woes. They were 11th in the league in attendance (1,276,250) and lost their top players to free agency, including Walker, who signed with the Colorado Rockies. After the financial wreckage of the 1994 strike, Expos general manager Kevin Malone was instructed to cut payroll no matter what, so the team declined even to offer Walker arbitration, meaning that they received absolutely no compensation when he signed with the Rockies.

In 2002, manager Felipe Alou spoke of his team's missed opportunity. "It's not the sweetest thing to talk about. It took away an opportunity. I only managed that one club. That took away my only opportunity to be in the playoffs. It's frustrating, it's emptiness. That was it."[13] Alou, who managed in Montreal from 1992 through the first 53 games of the 2001 season, would return to managing in 2003 and get to the postseason with the Giants. Larry Walker would not have to wait that long.

Although a good hitter in Montreal, in Denver's thin air he significantly improved his statistics. He had his first 100-RBI season in 1995, and took part in postseason play for the first time as the Rockies became the first wild card team in NL history. A quartet of players collectively known as The Blake Street Bombers — Walker, Andres Galarraga, Dante Bichette, and Vinny Castilla each of whom hit more than 30 homers—anchored the team. In postseason baseball, the dictum is "good pitching beats good hitting," and the Rockies were eliminated by the Atlanta Braves in the Division Series, three games to one. Walker went 3-for-14 with a three-run home run off Tom Glavine in the sixth inning of Game Two, won by the Braves 7-4.

Walker's 1996 season was interrupted in June when he broke his collarbone running into the outfield wall in a game against the Braves in Denver. Through his first 53 games, he was batting .283 with 14 homers and 41 RBIs and performing efficiently on the base paths, with 12 stolen bases in 13 attempts. He returned to the lineup on August 15 after missing 60 games. Less than two weeks later, however, against Cincinnati, he strained his shoulder in a collision at second base with Barry Larkin. The new injury hampered in his hitting, and over the balance of the season he only went 1-for-14. For the season, he batted .276 with only 18 home runs and 58 RBIs.

The following spring, he said, "I've got a lot to prove this year. Not only to myself, because I'll never make myself happy, no matter how good I do. I've got a lot to prove to the city of Denver and the fans. I want to win, and I want to do well. I know it's there. It's just a matter of doing it."[14]

And did he do it! As June turned into July, he was in a magnificent groove. As late as July 17, he was batting .402. He told a reporter, "The thing is I just step in the box, see the ball, and hit it. Or try to hit it. That's how I learned to do it. Ralph Rowe, who was my hitting coach in the Expos' chain when I was in Utica and Burlington, told me, 'Kid, just see the ball and hit the ball. That's all there is to it. Just see it and hit it.' I said, 'OK,' He said it was real simple. So I took it real simple."[15]

Also hitting for a lofty average that season was perennial All-Star Tony Gwynn of the San Diego Padres. Although both players fell off from the July highs, they finished 1-2 in the batting race. Gwynn won the title batting .372, and Walker finished in second place at .366. Walker won the MVP Award, leading the NL with a career-high 49 homers, more than anyone in the league had hit since Andre Dawson had hit 49 for the Cubs in 1987. He also led the league in total bases with 409. His 130 RBIs were third best, as were his 46 doubles. He joined the 30-30 home run/stolen base club with his 33 stolen bases, and for the only time in his injury riddled career, had more than 200 hits, finishing with 208, second most in the league. His 108th hit of the season on June 20 against Andy Ashby of San Diego was also the 1,000th of his career.

Walker had a home run spurt in mid-September, hitting dingers in four consecutive games (five homers in all) including the 200th of his career. Both it and the 199th came in a game at San Diego on September 17 and accounted for all the Colorado scoring in a loss to the Padres, 5-4. Don Baylor's Rockies, however, were unable to fully capitalize on Walker's contributions finishing in third place that season with an 83-79 record.

One remarkable aspect of Walker's 1997 season was his performance away from his home ballpark in Denver. Twenty-nine of his 49 homers were on the road, and his average away from home was .346. "I'm really happy about that. Last year, I got ripped because I was really [so bad] away from Coors Field. This year I think I've proven that I can hit outside of Denver."[16]

He never forgot his Canadian roots. After winning the MVP, he said, "I've done something good for me personally, and I've done something good for my country. Maybe kids will look up to me and it will push them to reach for their goals."[17]

And Canada would never forget Walker's achievements. He became the all-time leader in games, at bats, hits, doubles, home runs, runs batted in, runs, stolen bases, and walks by a Canadian-born player. He is the only Canadian to reach the milestones of

2,000 hits, 300 home runs, and 1,000 RBIs, and he has paved the way for other Canadian players, such as 2004 National League Rookie-of-the-Year Jason Bay, 2006 American League MVP Justin Morneau, and 2010 National League MVP Joey Votto to slug their way to awards and recognition. During his best ever season in 1997, he played in a career-high 153 ballgames, but the injury bug struck again late in the season. He injured his right elbow swinging at a pitch just before hitting his 49th homer of the season, in his team's 160th game, and missed the last two games of the schedule.

Although he rested the elbow during the off-season, the pain persisted, and he aggravated the injury while playing golf in January. Although he tried to play through the injury when the 1998 season began, he missed several games and was on the disabled list for the last two weeks of June. Despite his injury, he was batting .331 in July and was chosen as an All-Star game starter. "I don't deserve to start the game," Walker humbly proclaimed. "I probably don't even deserve to be on the team. But the fans get their say, and I'm fortunate enough to be one of the three (National League) All-Star outfielders. I accept it as a great honor."[18] Although injuries forced him to the sidelines during the second half of the 1998 season, when in the lineup, Walker was a force to be reckoned with. He raised his average to .363 and won his first National League batting title.

He had surgery during the off-season. He started the 1999 season on the DL with a strained rib cage and missed the first week of the season. When he returned to the lineup, he got off to a slow start, going 7-for-31. After some advice from hitting coach Clint Hurdle on April 28, he had three homers and eight RBIs in St. Louis as the Rockies defeated the Cardinals 9-7. His batting average jumped that day from .235 to .308, and he was on his way to another strong year at the plate, winning his second of four batting titles with a .379 batting average. He was named to his third All-Star team in as many seasons and also corralled his third consecutive Gold Glove.

Walker could boast of an historic achievement. Hitting for an average of greater than .360 in three consecutive seasons had not been done in more than 60 years. The last time had been when Al Simmons of the Philadelphia Athletics batted .365, .381, and .390 from 1929-31.[19]

In 2000, severe pain in his elbow put Walker on the DL twice, the first trip coming on May 11. Batting .347 at the time, he missed 23 games, and after his return, was so weak that he hit only .286 in his remaining 57 games. Finally succumbing to the pain, he was placed on the disabled list again on August 20. In his 86 games that season, he ended up with a .309 batting average. He went under the knife on September 8. His pain was such that his wife conveyed this story. "I remember his tossing our daughter Canaan in the air—she was five, six months old—and crumpling in agony when he caught her."[20]

In 2001, after spending the off-season undergoing a fitness regimen with a personal trainer, Walker returned to form, led the league for a third time in batting (.350), and hit 38 home runs, the second-best total of his career. Included in this barrage was his 300th career homer off David Williams of the Pirates on August 5 in Denver. Before the season, an optimistic Walker said, "This is the best I've felt going into camp. I know what I have to do and what I'm capable of doing. It's just a matter of staying healthy and doing it. I want to go out there and look good and do good."[21] Although he did not meet his goal of 150 games, he did play in 142, and his 601 plate appearances were the most since 1997. From April 17–May 23, he put together a streak of reaching base safely in 31 consecutive games. Again named to the All-Star team, he picked up another Gold Glove Award as well. On Opening Day, he displayed his healthy arm, gunning down the Cardinals' Fernando Viña at home plate as the Rockies cruised to an 8-0 win. Unfortunately, the Rockies did not have enough good days. They slipped below .500 on June 22 and finished the season in fifth place in the NL West with a 73-89 record

In 2002, the Rockies got off to their franchise-worst ever start, 6-16, and manager Buddy Bell was released on April 16. Clint Hurdle replaced him, and although the team showed some immediate improvement, winning the first six games under Hurdle's stewardship, they stumbled after June 1, notwithstanding another good year from Walker. Walker's season peaked in June and July as he raised his average from .310 to a season's high of .368. However, the team fared far worse, going 19-33 during this stretch en route to a 73-89 fourth-place finish, 25 games behind the division winners. Walker batted .338 with 26 home runs, and a team-leading 40 doubles. The frustration of having been to the post-season only once in his career nagged at Walker. "It'd be nice to get back," he said at one point in the season. "It'd be nice to see that plastic in here again [covering lockers in the Rockies' clubhouse] and champagne flying all over the place and take another crack at it."[22] He would at least do it with improved eyesight. Shortly after the season, Walker, who had been wearing contact lenses, opted for Lasik surgery. Trade rumors swirled during the off-season; a deal with the Diamondbacks for Matt Williams fell through because Williams did not wish to be apart from his family and Walker balked at deferring part of his salary. The celebration, for Larry Walker, was still on hold.

For the first time since 1996, Walker hit below .300 (.284) in 2003. He played through knee and shoulder injuries, getting into 143 games with 16 homers and 79 RBIs. The knee injury resulted from a collision with Rockies center fielder Preston Wilson during a 1-0 loss at Pittsburgh on August 2. Manager Hurdle noted, "Even with the injuries and the lack of numbers from what they used to be in the past, Larry is still pitched to very carefully and fearfully throughout the league. He's played beaten up and bruised. He's done what he could do."[23] The Rockies continued to drift low in the standings, pretty much duplicating the 2002 season, finishing fourth with a 74-88 record. Walker never missed more than three consecutive games during the course of this season. But besides his regular knee and shoulder ailments, he was bedeviled off and on by hamstring, groin, and hip problems.

He had surgery for both his left shoulder (labrum) and right knee (torn meniscus) in the off-season. And although the surgeries were successful, Walker began the 2004 season on the DL with a strained groin and missed Colorado's first 68 games. Once back in the lineup, he played in 38 of this team's next 40 games and was batting .324 when he was traded to the St. Louis Cardinals on August 7. In the fifth year of a contract that paid him more than $12 million per season, the 37-year-old Walker did not fit into the Rockies' future plans. As a 10-year veteran, Walker had veto power over the trade, but after being in the big leagues for 15 seasons without going to the World Series, he sensed that this was his opportunity. "This is it, this is why you say yes to the trade. I spent almost a decade in Colorado and had a great time, made friends. Loved the place. It was a move that had to be made, and I guess I'm glad I made it."[24]

Before he came to the Cardinals, he had been on the disabled list a total of eight times during his career, but a healthy Larry Walker could help secure a post-season berth for St. Louis. In 44 games with the Cardinals, he batted .280 with 11 homers. The Cardinals won 105 games that season to win the National League's Central Division. Walker excelled in post-season play. In the Divisional Series, he batted .333 with two home runs in four games as the Cardinals eliminated the Dodgers, three games to one. He smacked two more homers in the NLCS as the Cardinals defeated Houston in seven games. It was then on to the World Series for the first, and only, time in Walker's career. Although the Cards were swept by the Red Sox, Walker had a good series, batting .357 with two homers, the only home runs St. Louis hit in the four games.

He returned to the Cardinals in 2005 and showed that he could still hit at the age of 38, batting .289 and adding the last 15 of his 383 career home run total. However, he could not elude the injury bug and was bothered by a neck injury that put him on the DL one last time. He retired after the 2005 season.

Walker finished his 17-year career with a .313 batting average, 2,160 hits, and 1,355 runs scored. His .565 slugging percentage stands 12th on the all-time list as of the end of the 2017 season. He benefited from the mile-high atmosphere of Coors Field, batting

.384/.464/.715 there compared with .280/.385/.514 on the road in the same seasons.

More honors followed: Walker was inducted into the Canadian Baseball Hall of Fame and Museum in 2009. He is a record nine-time winner of that Hall of Fame's Tip O'Neill Award presented to the top Canadian baseball player of the year. Larry was also inducted into Canada's Sports Hall of Fame in 2007 and the British Columbia Sports Hall of Fame in 2009.

Walker coached for Canada in the 2006 and 2009 World Baseball Classics, 2009 Baseball World Cup, 2010 Pan American Games Qualifying Tournament, 2013 World Baseball Classic Qualifiers and Classic, as well as the 2015 Pan American Games

Walker has been married twice. He married Christa Vandenbrink on November 3, 1990, and they had a daughter, Brittany Marie, born on July 15, 1993. The day after the 1998 All-Star game Walker married Angela Brekken. They have two daughters, Canaan and Shayna, and live in West Palm Beach, Florida.

SOURCES

In addition to the sources cited in the notes and Baseball-Reference. com, the author also relied on:

DeMarco, Tony, Larry Walker, *Canadian Rocky*, (Sports Publishing, Inc., 1999).

Gallagher, Danny, "Walker the best position player ever from Canada" in *Remembering the Montreal Expos*, (Toronto, ON, Scoop Press, 2005): 209-212.

McDonald, Ian "Expos Decide Their 'Future' is Now," *The Sporting News*, May 7, 1990.

Mossman, John, "Life is Good for Rockies' Slugger," *Times-Daily* (Florence, AL), July 16, 1997.

Walker's file at the Baseball Hall of Fame Library.

NOTES

1   Bob Hill, "Le Naturel Larry Walker is No Ordinary Class-A Prospect. He's Aiming to be the First Canadian Born Player to Make It Big in Montreal," *Sun-Sentinel* (Fort Lauderdale, FL), August 10, 1986, 5C.

2   Tony DeMarco, *Larry Walker*, (Philadelphia, Chelsea House Publishers, 1999), 19.

3   Marty York, "Expos' Walker Could be Superstar," *Denver Post*, April 11, 1993, 3B.

4   Leigh Montville, "The Accidental Ballplayer: Larry Walker Always Dreamed of Playing in Montreal—For a Hockey Team," *Sports Illustrated*, April 5, 1993.

5   Tony DeMarco, *Larry Walker*, (Philadelphia, Chelsea House Publishers, 1999), 27.

6   Montville, *Sports illustrated*, April 5, 1993.

7   Hill, *Sun-Sentinel*, July 27, 1986, 6C.

8   Hill, *Sun-Sentinel*), August 10, 1986, 5C

9   Jim Shearon, *Over the Fends is Out: The Larry Walker Story and More of Canada's Baseball Legends*, (Kanata, Ontario, Malin Head Press, 2009), 6

10   Jerry Krasnick, "This Time, Stadium will be Full for Walker," *Denver Post*, April 9, 1993, 6AA

11   Ibid.

12   "Larry Walker Discovers that Counting to Three Can be Difficult," *Gettysburg* (PA) *Times*, April 26, 1994, 2B

13   Jack Curry, "Lost Games, Lost Dreams," *New York Times*, August 26, 2002, D1

14   Jack Etkin, "Three for the Show," *The Sporting News*, March 24, 1997, 20

15   Michael Knisley, "Preheat to .400," *The Sporting News*, July 14, 1997, 14

16   Jerry Krasnick, "Who Should and Shouldn't Win Awards," *The Sporting News*, October 6, 1997, 43

17   "Walker wins MVP Award," *New York Post*, November 14, 1997, 112

18   Tony DeMarco, *Larry Walker*, (Philadelphia, Chelsea House Publishers, 1999), 52

19   Bill James, *The New Bill James Historical Baseball Abstract* (New York, Free Press, 2001), 825.

20   Richard Hoffer, "Handy Man: The Rockies Larry Walker has all the Major League Tools, and He Wields Them Like a Master Craftsman," *Sports Illustrated*, June 11, 2001

21   Tracy Ringolsby, "Healthy Walker Determined to Stay that Way This Season," *Rocky Mountain News*, February 18, 2001, 23C

22   Etkin, "In the Midst of Brilliant Season, Walker Looks Stoically at Future," *Rocky Mountain News*, July 5, 2002, 8C

23   Troy E. Renck, "Walker to undergo Surgery on Shoulder," *Denver Post*, September 29, 2003, C-06,

24   Tom Timmerman, "Walker's Childhood Dream Melts into Another Form," *St. Louis-Post Dispatch*, October 24, 2004.

WALT WEISS

BY KEN REED

WALTER WILLIAM WEISS WAS A
tough player—physically and mentally.

"The look in his eye always said, 'Don't even think
about taking me out of the lineup unless the bone's
sticking out and maybe not even then,'" said Weiss's
coach at the University of North Carolina, Mike
Roberts.[1]

His first big-league manager, Tony La Russa,
concurred. "He has always had the physical and
mental toughness you look for in a champion," said
La Russa.[2] While not an outstanding hitter—either
for average or power—he regularly came through in
the clutch—at the plate and in the field. "Nothing
unsettled him," La Russa said.[3]

Walt Weiss's toughness and grit was cultivated in
his youth. Born in Tuxedo, New York, on November
28, 1963, he was raised in nearby Suffern, a village
35 miles north of Manhattan. His parents owned a
video store in Mahwah, New Jersey, and his father
had a second job running a newsstand kiosk in Grand
Central Terminal.[4]

Growing up, Weiss enjoyed playing a lot of sports.
On the baseball diamond, he was considered a field
rat and a grinder. Weiss never wanted to leave the
field. He begged his dad, Bill, to hit him groundball
after groundball.[5] In short, Weiss was a kid who loved
to play, consistently put the team above himself, and
didn't mind diving all over the field for balls.

Once, as a child, Weiss attended a New York
Yankees game and had the chance to stroll on the
warning track. He scooped up some dirt and saved it
in a Ziploc bag. He displayed an unusual confidence
and belief in himself by telling his dad that one day
he would play at Yankee Stadium.

"Yeah, I put that dirt in my scrapbook," said Weiss
with a smile. "It's all I ever wanted, to be in the big
leagues. I was a little scrawny kid and my ignorance
was probably bliss."[6]

Scrawny indeed. Weiss packed 105 pounds on his
5-foot-3 frame as a freshman at Suffern High School.

Despite his lack of size at the time, his sports
idol was a football player, the Miami Dolphins'
Mercury Morris. Weiss's first youth football team
was named the Dolphins. Morris wore number 22
on his Dolphins jersey and Weiss would adopt that
jersey number throughout his career.[7]

As a teenager, Weiss's work ethic matched his
mental and physical toughness. His high-school
baseball coach at Suffern, Jerry Magurno, said he
didn't remember having any player more dedicated
than Weiss.[8]

That dedication served Weiss well in other sports
as well. He was Suffern's quarterback his senior
season and he also excelled on the track, where he was
part of the Mounties' county-championship 4X400
relay team.

But it was on the Suffern High School baseball
field (named Walt Weiss Field in 1999) that Weiss
was at his best.[9] He was the Rockland County (New
York) player of the year in 1982. After his high-school
career, the Baltimore Orioles drafted him in the 10th
round of the 1982 amateur draft.[10]

However, instead of turning pro and joining the
Orioles organization, Weiss chose to attend the
University of North Carolina, the first on either side
of his family to go to college.

Weiss had other interests besides sports as a young
man, one of which was music. He had become a huge
Bruce Springsteen fan. His favorite Springsteen
album was *Darkness on the Edge of Town* and his
favorite song from that album was "Prove It All
Night."[11]

"He had a huge impact on me as a young adult,"
said Weiss. "That's the power of Springsteen.
Everyone thinks the songs were written for them."[12]

After three all-conference seasons at North
Carolina, the Oakland A's drafted Weiss in the first
round with the 11th overall pick in the 1985 draft.[13]
Weiss hit a combined .261 in 1985, splitting time
between Modesto of the California League and

Pocatello of the Pioneer League. In 1986, after hitting .301 through 84 games at Madison in the Class-A Midwest League, Weiss jumped to Double-A Huntsville in the Southern League, where he hit .250.

In 1987 he had successful stints with Huntsville and Tacoma of the Triple-A Pacific Coast League before making his major-league debut on July 12, 1987, at age 23. His first big-league action was as a pinch-runner for Mark McGwire. He was promptly picked off and tagged out at second base.[14]

Nevertheless, Weiss impressed the A's brass enough in that first stint in the big leagues that the team traded incumbent shortstop Alfredo Griffin in December of 1987, opening up the starting shortstop job for Weiss.

The next season, 1988, he was a key player on the Oakland A's team that won 104 regular-season games. Weiss had only a decent season at the plate, hitting .250 with an OBP of .312. However, he was rock-solid in the field with a .979 fielding percentage in 700 chances. He was named American League Rookie of the Year after that campaign, the third A's player in a row to win the honor (following Jose Canseco in 1986 and McGwire in 1987).[15]

The 1988 season ended in disappointing fashion, as the A's lost in the World Series to the Los Angeles Dodgers and Weiss made a critical error in a Game Four loss. Weiss also struggled at the plate in the World Series, hitting .063 after hitting .333 in the ALCS against the Boston Red Sox.

However, 1989 had a happier ending, as the A's became world champions in what was called the "Earthquake Series," due to a major earthquake that hit the San Francisco Bay Area before the start of Game Three. Weiss hit a home run during that World Series.[16] Overall, his postseason hitting woes continued as he hit only .133 in the World Series and .111 in the ALCS against Toronto. Weiss hit .233 during an injury-marred regular season.

In 1990 Weiss had one of his most productive seasons at the plate, hitting .265 with a .337 OBP. However, once again, he struggled hitting in the postseason. He was hitless in seven at-bats in the A's ALCS matchup with Boston. He was injured

during that series and missed the A's World Series loss—four games to none—to the Cincinnati Reds.

Weiss suffered a horrendous injury on June 6, 1991, in a game against Milwaukee. He rolled his left ankle lunging for first base. His left fibula came through the bottom of his leg and was only held on by skin. He was bleeding profusely and needed a transfusion. The doctor told Weiss that if the injury had occurred 15 years earlier he likely would've faced amputation because medical procedures for his injury were less advanced at that time.[17] Weiss hit an anemic .226 during another injury-marred campaign in 1991.

After Weiss hit only .212 for the 1992 A's, he was traded to the Florida Marlins, becoming an inaugural member of that expansion franchise in the process. Early in that 1993 campaign, Weiss drove in the first run in Marlins history.[18] He enjoyed a healthy season and hit .266 while continuing to be a dependable fielder.

In 1994 Weiss moved to the Colorado Rockies via free agency. Thus, he became the first player to play for both of the 1993 expansion teams, Florida and Colorado.[19] He was relatively healthy for the Rockies and hit .251 with 12 stolen bases, a major-league season high at that point.

In 1995 Weiss was the shortstop for the first Rockies team to make the postseason. He was solid, and occasionally spectacular, in the field and hit .260 that season with a .403 OBP. Weiss hit .300 the last month of the season to help the Rockies secure a wild-card playoff berth. His OBP was .375 in the NLDS against the Atlanta Braves but the Rockies fell, three games to one.

During the 1996 campaign with the Rockies, Weiss had the best offensive season of his career, hitting .282 with 8 home runs and 48 runs batted in. There would be no postseason action, however, as the Rockies finished third in the NL West.

Weiss completed his four years with the Rockies by hitting .270 and fielding at a .983 clip in 1997. After the season, he became a free agent. The Rockies were interested in re-signing him but there was internal talk about moving him to second base. Weiss wanted to keep playing shortstop and started to look elsewhere for employment.

Weiss eventually signed with the Atlanta Braves and made the 1998 National League All-Star Team as a starter at shortstop. He had two hits and an RBI in the game. It was the only All-Star Game appearance of his playing career.

The 1998 All-Star Game held special meaning for Weiss because his 3-year-old son, Brody, was in attendance. A week before the game, Brody was in a coma in an Atlanta hospital, a victim of the E. coli bacteria. His recovery was in doubt for several days, so to be able to wave to Brody in the stands at the All-Star Game was the highlight of the night for Weiss.[20]

Weiss ended up hitting .280 for the 1998 season and the Braves won 106 regular-season games but would fall to the San Diego Padres in the NLCS.

Following his outstanding 1998 campaign, age and injuries began to affect Weiss. In 1999 his batting average dropped 54 points to .226. The Braves, however, had a stellar season as a team, ultimately getting to the World Series, where they lost to the

New York Yankees. Weiss was productive at times during the Braves' postseason run, including hitting .286 with two doubles and two stolen bases in the NLCS against the New York Mets.

The standout moment for Weiss during the 1999 playoffs was a game-saving play against the Houston Astros in the NLDS. In the bottom of the 10th inning of Game Three, the Astros loaded the bases in a tie game. Weiss made an outstanding diving play on a groundball and threw home for the force out to preserve the tie. The Braves would go on to win the game.[21]

The 2000 season was Weiss's last as a player. He hit .260 in only 192 at-bats, as injuries and the emergence of Rafael Furcal limited Weiss's time at shortstop. In the NLDS, he hit .667 in limited action. The Braves were swept in three games by the St. Louis Cardinals in the series. Furcal wound up winning NL Rookie of the Year in 2000.

For his career, Weiss made the playoffs in eight of his 14 seasons and played on four World Series teams, including the 1989 world champion A's. He was a middling hitter, even for a shortstop (career marks of .258, 25 home runs, and 386 RBIs). But he had a strong career on-base percentage of .351. His career WAR was 16.5 and his lifetime fielding percentage was .970.[22] An interesting piece of trivia is that Weiss ended his career with 658 walks and 658 strikeouts in 1,495 games.

Throughout his career, Weiss was known as a dependable player. He typically was at his best when the pressure was the greatest.

"There wasn't any deer in the headlights for Walt," said his manager with the Oakland A's, Tony La Russa. "One of the ways to judge a shortstop is how he handles a groundball with the winning run on third base in the eighth or ninth inning. He would field it calmly and coolly."[23]

Somewhat ironically, given his reputation as a very good defensive shortstop — and because he always seemed to make the clutch play in the field — he holds the Rockies franchise record for most errors by a shortstop in a season with 30 in 1996.[24]

Besides being a coach's dream due to his outstanding work ethic and poise on the diamond, Weiss was also known as a great teammate. Seattle Mariners general manager Jerry DiPoto, a former teammate of Weiss's, said Weiss was the best teammate he ever had.[25]

Weiss stayed in shape after his playing career ended by becoming a black belt in taekwondo.

"I knew he was tough, I didn't know he was nuts," said La Russa of Weiss's martial arts adventures.[26]

Weiss also remained close to the game after his playing days ended. He served as an instructor and special assistant to the general manager for the Rockies from 2002 to 2008, filling a variety of roles during that period.

He then took a sabbatical from the professional game to coach his sons. Weiss and his wife, Terri, have four sons, Blake, Brody, Bo and Brock. His property, just outside of Denver, included not only his family's house but also a regulation baseball field and indoor batting cage.[27] It was a dream scenario for baseball-loving kids.

"What makes it neat is they're old enough to really take in some of the finer points of the game and you're involved with them at a time in their lives where they really have most of their goals in front of them," said Weiss at the time.[28]

Weiss would eventually become an assistant football and baseball coach at Regis Jesuit High School in Aurora, Colorado, a suburb of Denver. He eventually took over the head job for the Regis baseball program, leading his team to the state 5A semifinals in his first year at the helm.

All of Walt's sons followed him into baseball. Blake, his oldest, was a center fielder before switching to track. As of 2017, Brody was an infielder at Westmont College. He began his college career at UC Santa Barbara. Bo was a pitcher at North Carolina, his dad's alma mater. Youngest son Brock was a shortstop and right-handed pitcher for Regis Jesuit High School.

After his stint as a high-school coach, Weiss's life and career took a surprising turn. Rockies executives began talking to him about his thoughts regarding potential new managers to replace the departed Jim Tracy. Tracy had left the Rockies after the 2012 season, which produced a franchise-worst record of 64-98. As those discussions progressed, it quickly became clear to Weiss that he had transitioned from team consultant to candidate for the Colorado Rockies managerial opening.

He outlined his managerial philosophy for Rockies general manager Dan O'Dowd and shortly thereafter became the surprise choice to be named the sixth manager of the Colorado Rockies on November 7, 2012.[29]

Fans and members of the media expressed shock at the hire simply because Weiss's only managerial experience to that point had come at the high-school level.

However, after a closer look, it was clear that Weiss had a ton of baseball experience. He was an American League Rookie of the Year, National League All-Star, and world champion as a player. He'd also served as an on-field instructor—and often coached on the bench during Rockies' home games—and assistant to the general manager in his post-playing days. During his 14-year major-league baseball career, Weiss played for, and learned from, some of the game's best managers (Tony La Russa, Bobby Cox, Rene Lachemann, and Don Baylor).

"I hear people saying he's a high-school coach," said former Rockies teammate Dante Bichette, who would become a coach on Weiss's first staff. "I'm like, 'Yeah, he's a high-school coach with a World Series ring, umpteen years (in the majors) and an All-Star Game. There's a little difference.'"[30]

On the home front, the move from the Regis Jesuit High School dugout to the Colorado Rockies dugout was a big change for Weiss's wife and children.

Bo, a pitcher at Regis Jesuit when his father was managing the Rockies, said the shift from having Walt as a full-time dad and high-school baseball coach to Rockies manager took some adjusting.

"We get an inside scoop on a lot of things, which is really cool, and most people would give the world for that," said Bo. "But it also comes with cons: We don't get to see my dad as much and he doesn't get to watch our seasons in the spring. But ultimately I wouldn't have it any other way. Baseball is really all I've known."[31]

Despite the surprise factor, the Weiss hire resulted in a lot of fan excitement in Colorado. Weiss was seen as a popular former player who was coming back to manage the team, and, hopefully, lead the franchise out of its recent doldrums.

Shortly after Weiss was hired, the Denver Beer Company developed a new beer called the "Walt Weiss." It was a wheat beer with banana and clove flavors.[32]

In Weiss's first game as a big-league manager, April 1, 2013, the Rockies lost 5-4 to the Milwaukee Brewers in 10 innings. However, the Rockies soon went on an eight-game winning streak, which put their record at 13-4. That mark represented the franchise's most games over .500 during Weiss's tenure.[33]

Overall, Weiss's first year as manager of the Rockies was a rough one, as the team finished 74-88 in 2013. Nevertheless, that was a 10-game improvement over Jim Tracy's final season in Denver.

The 2014 campaign saw Weiss and the Rockies take a step back. The Rockies finished 66-96. On September 15, the Rockies lost to the Los Angeles Dodgers, 11-3. The loss put the team at 32 games under .500, at 59-91, the low-water mark for Weiss's time as Rockies manager.[34]

The struggles on the field continued in 2015, as the Rockies managed to improve by only two games over the disastrous 2014 season, finishing 68-94.

During the 2015 season, Weiss had to undergo an appendectomy on May 13. He had been struggling with stomach pain for a couple of days and went to the hospital before the game that night against the Angels at Angel Stadium. The Rockies had lost 10 straight games at the time. Bench coach Tom Runnells managed the team against the Angels on May 13 and the Rockies lost their 11th straight, 2-1.[35]

The 2016 season was one of promise for Weiss and the Rockies as the season moved into August. On August 3, the Rockies were only three games back of the second National League wild-card spot after beating the Dodgers to move their record to 54-53.

The team faltered after that, finishing well out of the playoffs.[36] Nevertheless, the 2016 season turned out to be Weiss's best at the helm, as the team finished 75-87.

But it wasn't good enough to keep his job, as Weiss and the Rockies parted ways at the end of the season.

Ultimately, Weiss managed the Rockies to a 283-365 record during his four-year tenure. Despite the mediocre won-lost record, it was commonly felt that Weiss had left the team in a better place than where he found it. For one thing, he was widely credited with creating a positive culture in a clubhouse that had grown complacent with losing.

"Unbelievable grasp of players," said Rockies catcher Nick Hundley in September 2016, shortly before Weiss and the Colorado franchise parted ways. "To a man, everybody respects him. When he talks, everybody listens, and those are great qualities to have."[37]

Officially, Weiss resigned after the 2016 season, but it was widely expected that Rockies general manager Jeff Bridich was about to let him go anyway. Weiss's contract had expired and the Rockies hadn't shown much interest in re-signing him. Multiple reports suggested that Weiss and Bridich simply didn't see eye-to-eye. According to some sources, Weiss was left out of major decisions during his last season as manager.[38]

"I only want to be where I'm wanted," said Weiss at the time. "If I'm not wanted, I just leave. It's one of my rules in life. I don't stay anywhere where I'm not wanted. I just go, I just disappear. … I want to make sure that people want me, from top to bottom. If not, I don't want to be here."[39]

After Weiss's departure, All-Star third baseman Nolan Arenado said that he was a manager whom "every player respects, everyone around the game respects. You don't find those people too often."[40]

Weiss was praised for helping to develop a nice core of young players during his four-year stint as Rockies manager.[41] Those young players would go on to play a big role in the Rockies run to a wild-card playoff spot in 2017, under new manager Bud Black.

In terms of the baseball side of the franchise, Weiss served the Colorado Rockies in more roles than any other person in team history. He had three stints with the Rockies: 1994-97 as a player; 2002-08 as an instructor and special assistant to the general manager; and 2013-16 as manager.

After he sat out the 2017 baseball season, Weiss's career in major-league baseball resumed on November 10, 2017, when he was hired by the Atlanta Braves to be their new bench coach.[42]

NOTES

1   Kevin Armstrong, "Colorado Manager, Walt Weiss, Raised in Suffern, Living the Mile High Life With the Rockies," *New York Daily News*, May 11, 2013.

2   Troy Renck, "Walt Weiss Was Born to Run the Colorado Rockies," *Denver Post*, April 30, 2016.

3   Armstrong.

4   Ibid.

5   Ibid.

6   Renck.

7   Ibid.

8   Ibid.

9   Leland Gordon, "High School Baseball Fields Named After MLB Stars, Managers," MaxPreps.com, June 24, 2014.

10 baseball-almanac.com/draft/baseball-draft.php?yr=1982.

11 Armstrong.

12 Renck.

13 espn.com/mlb/draft/history/_/team/oak.

14 Armstrong.

15 whitecleatbeat.com/2016/03/24/thursday-throwback-oak-land-athletics-trifecta-rookies-1986-1987-1988/.

16 Mike Penner, "The World Series: Oakland Athletics vs. San Francisco Giants," *Los Angeles Times*, October 15, 1989.

17 Neil Devlin, "Managing the Boys," *Mile High Sports*, April 17, 2017.

18 miami.marlins.mlb.com/mia/history/club_firsts.jsp.

19 baseball-almanac.com/players/player.php?p=weisswa01.

20 Ross Newhan, "Stricken Son Tested All-Star Weiss' Faith," *Los Angeles Times*, July 8, 1998.

21 bleacherreport.com/articles/696319-the-best-game-saving-plays-in-sports-history.

22 baseball-reference.com/players/w/weisswa01.shtml.

23 Renck.

24 baseball-almanac.com.

25 Renck.

26 Armstrong.

27 Ibid.

28 Brian Howell, "Former Major Leaguer Walt Weiss Enjoying First Year as Regis Jesuit Baseball Coach," MaxPreps.com, May 4, 2012.

29 "Walt Weiss Named Sixth Manager in Rockies History," MLB.com, November 7, 2102.

30 Armstrong.

31 Morgan Dzakowic, "Bo Weiss, Son of Walt Weiss, Knows the Wins, Outs of the Family Business," *Denver Post*, August 2, 2016.

32 Armstrong.

33 Nick Kosmider, "Walt Weiss Timeline of Four Years as Rockies Manager," *Denver Post*, October 3, 2016.

34 Kosmider.

35 si.com/mlb/2015/05/14/colorado-rockies-walt-weiss-appendectomy.

36 Kosmider.

37 Robert Murray, "Walt Weiss Could Join Braves Coaching Staff," *FANRAG*, October 17, 2017.

38 Patrick Saunders, "Walt Weiss. Run With Rockies Likely Over as Distance From GM Jeff Bridich Grows," *Denver Post*, October 2, 2016.

39 Ibid.

40 Associated Press, "Walt Weiss Out as Rockies Manager After Four Seasons," *Denver Post*, October 4, 2016.

41 Ben Macaluso, "The 100 Greatest Colorado Rockies: 50 Walt Weiss," roxpile.com, March 23, 2017.

42 Mark Bowman, "Former Rox Manager Weiss Joins Braves' Staff," MLB.com, November 10, 2017.

ERIC YOUNG SR.

BY MIKE COONEY

"AND THE 3-2 PITCH. FLY BALL TO deep left field—it's a mile high and it's out of here!"[1]

Not the "shot heard round the world."

But a shot that reverberated among the 80,000 plus fans that rose as one as Colorado Rockies TV play-by-play announcer Charlie Jones called the first Mile High Stadium home run for the first-year expansion Rockies.

A shot called by Rockies' radio announcer Jeff Kingery with his signature home-run call: "The ball's goin and it aint coming back."[2]

A shot that launched the launching pad known as Mile High Stadium.

Despite an 0-2 start in New York against the Mets, Colorado fans anxiously awaited the Rockies' April 9, 1993, Mile High debut against the Montreal Expos. After a scoreless top of the first inning, the bottom of the first started with Rockies second baseman Eric Young walking to the plate.

Young, Colorado's sixth selection in the 1992 expansion draft, stepped to the plate to face Expos pitcher Kent Bottenfield. While many of the 80,000 fans were getting settled in, Young hit the historic first Colorado Rockies Mile High home run.

*Eric Orlando Young was born in New Brunswick, New Jersey, on May 18, 1967. His father, Otis, was a crane operator and his mother, Lucille, was an assistant to a school principal and a worker with special-needs children. Young credited his athletic abilities to his mother, whom he said was a great basketball player.[3]

Young was a multisport standout for New Brunswick High School. His memory of the first time he played baseball: "Playing stickball, 2 of 2, and spray-painting a box against the brick building. That was the first game. Must have been 5 or 6."[4]

After high school, Young stayed in New Brunswick, enrolling at Rutgers, the State University of New Jersey, with a football scholarship.[5]

Young became Eric Young Sr. on May 25, 1985, when his son, Eric Young Jr., was born to his high-school sweetheart. (They were never married.)[6] Even after the birth of Eric Jr., Eric Sr. continued to be identified simply as Eric Young for most of his career. He later had another son, Dallas.

Young started his Rutgers athletic career in his freshman year (1985) as a wide receiver for the Scarlet Knights football team.[7] While Rutgers shows him as a four-year wide receiver, a 2007 article in the *Modesto Bee* said, "Eric Young Sr. was a star defensive back and kick returner at Rutgers."[8]

Young didn't join the Scarlet Knights baseball team until the end of his sophomore year (1987). A two-time Atlantic 10 All-Conference selection as a center fielder, Young batted over .300 in each of his three seasons, with a career high of .337 in his senior year. When he graduated, EY, as he affectionately became known, was the team's career leader in runs, triples, and stolen bases.[9]

Perhaps the hardest decision Young had to face while at Rutgers came during the summer of 1988. Playing for the New Jersey Pilots of the Atlantic Collegiate Baseball League, he was selected to the league all-star team. The all-stars were scheduled to play the United States Olympic team in late August.[10] Scouts from every major-league team would be in attendance.

Playing the Olympic team would give Young a chance to show the major-league scouts what he could do. But it didn't happen. The game was played in Quakertown, Pennsylvania, as scheduled. (The Olympic team gave the All-Stars a 19-1 drubbing.) But Young "was on the Rutgers campus fielding questions, not fly balls, and having his picture taken with a football helmet, not a baseball cap."[11]

With the baseball opportunity of his life conflicting with the Rutgers football team's first practice, Young had a decision to make—play baseball against the Olympians or continue to play football for Rutgers. Young had been allowed to play baseball in the spring and miss spring football practice. But with a new season looming and the first day of practice coinciding with the baseball game, Rutgers football coach Dick Anderson decided that if Young was going to play football for the Scarlet Knights, he would be at practice.[12] Young didn't have to make the decision. Coach Anderson made it for him.

The 21-year-old Young said, "If it was up to me, I would have gone and played baseball. ... I could go to everything during the day at camp and then miss the meetings at night. But I don't have any grudges. My first obligation is football."[13]

As a senior, Young considered both professional football and baseball as the next step in his athletic career. He said, "I wonder where I will be two years down the road, but it doesn't worry me. ... I have to work hard now to put myself in position to make things happen. You only have so many years to play sports, that is why you should play whatever you can."[14]

In the spring of 1989 Young graduated from Rutgers with a degree in business management.[15] He also received the Coursen Award, presented annually to the senior class's outstanding male athlete.[16]

(Further honors included his election to the Rutgers Athletics Hall of Fame in 1999,[17] and induction into the New Jersey Sports Writers' Hall of Fame in 2012.[18])

While Young was deciding whether to pursue a football or a baseball career, he was drafted by the Los Angeles Dodgers in the 43rd round of the June 1989 amateur draft. Ten days later he signed with the Dodgers.[19]

Young quickly moved through the Dodgers' minor-league system. Starting with the Dodgers' team in the rookie Gulf Coast League in 1989, he moved to Class-A Vero Beach in 1990 and to Double-A San Antonio in 1991. At San Antonio he set a Dodgers Double-A record with 70 stolen bases.[20] In 1992, after 94 games at Triple-A Albuquerque, Young was promoted to the major leagues.[21]

Young's apprenticeship lasted 414 games over parts of four years. During that time he hit .303 with a .391 on-base percentage. He hit 10 home runs.[22]

But power wasn't the reason the 5-foot-9, 180-pound Young was promoted to the big leagues. With the bulk of his minor-league playing time (333 games) at second base, he provided potential speed (217 stolen bases) combined with a strong on-base percentage and, in spite of his 20 errors in 1992, a developing second-base defense.

In his major-league debut, on July 30, 1992, against the San Diego Padres at Dodger Stadium, Young helped Los Angeles to a 6-5 victory. His RBI single off Padres pitcher Mike Maddux in the seventh inning tied the game at 5-5. In the 10th, he moved Brett Butler from first to third with another single (he was 2-for-4 in the game), and Butler scored the winning run on a fly ball by Todd Benzinger.

For the 1992 Dodgers, Young played in 43 games, starting 35, and finished with a .258/.300/.288 line in 132 at-bats, one home run and six stolen bases.

After the season, the Dodgers chose not to protect Young in the expansion draft designed to help the brand-new Florida Marlins and Colorado Rockies fill their rosters. The Rockies chose him with their sixth pick, 11th overall.

During spring training in 1993, Young impressed Rockies manager Don Baylor as a defensive second baseman. His first at-bat, and the first in Rockies history, came in New York, against the Mets. At 2:17 P.M. on Monday, April 5, 1993, Young stepped to the plate to face Mets pitcher Dwight Gooden. With a 2-and-1 count, he bunted down the third-base line. Mets catcher Todd Hundley grabbed the ball and threw Young out at first base.[23]

After the game, Young explained: "(The bunt) was my idea. It was a 2-and-1 count and I thought he was going to lay a fastball in there. HoJo (Howard Johnson) took a couple of steps back so I knew if I got it down on the grass I would beat it out."[24] He didn't.

Andres Galarraga got the Rockies' first hit with a second-inning single. With two outs in the third inning, Young got the second, a single to center field.

He quickly set another Rockies first by stealing second base.

Four days later, on April 9, 1993, the Rockies returned to Denver and to their Mile High Stadium home. As the *Central New Jersey Home News* described it: "The halls of the state capitol were empty and the streets were empty as baseball fans decked out in their best purple, black, and silver team colors came to watch the new team play ball."[25]

Young did not disappoint the fans. First, there was his 380-foot leadoff home run to left-center field, and then three more hits to finish 4-for-4—the first four-hit game for the Rockies. He also had two RBIs in the Rockies' 11-4 victory.

After hitting the Rockies' first home run at Mile High Stadium, Young did not hit another home run—home or away—until the final home game of the 1993 season, on September 26 against the Cincinnati Reds, when he hit two in a Rockies victory. In effect he bookended the Mile High season. Young's final 1993 stats included a .269/.355/.353 line with the three home runs, 42 RBIs and 42 stolen bases. Young struggled in the field, making a team-

high 15 errors at second base and 3 more when he was moved to the outfield.

Young's 1994 season started with a bang. With three home runs in the first month, he was on the way to his best season. However, with continued fielding woes and a collapsing batting average, dipping all the way to .196 on May 20, he was benched for much of the early part of the season.[26] But with other Rockies also struggling at the plate, Young played in 90 games in the strike-shortened season, mostly in left field. He finished with a .272/.378/.430 line with 7 home runs, 30 RBIs, and 18 stolen bases. Young continued to be one of the hardest players to strike out, finishing with 38 walks and only 17 strikeouts. On the defensive side, there was great improvement; Young reduced his errors to two for the season.

During the first half of the 1995 season, Young was relegated to pinch-hitting and pinch-running. Then, on June 23, when he was hitting an anemic .189, starting second baseman Jason Bates was injured. Despite his earlier fielding problems at second base, Young was reinserted into the starting lineup.[27] He responded with a .317/.404/.473 line with 35 stolen bases, 6 home runs, and a league-high 9 triples.

After that stalwart 1995 season, Young had an even better 1996. His batting average fell below .300 only once—for two days—during the entire season. He was selected for his only All-Star Game and won the National League Silver Slugger award for second basemen. Perhaps the highlight of the season came on June 30 against the Dodgers when, in the third inning, he walked and stole second, third, and home. For the entire game, he stole six bases.

Young finished the season with a National League-high 53 stolen bases and a .324/.393/.421 line with 8 home runs and 74 RBIs.

The 1997 season brought another change to Young's career. Between seasons he had pushed for a rich three-year contract. Instead, he wound up with a one-year contract, albeit with a $2 million raise, to $3.2 million. While disappointed that he did not get a three-year deal, he generated a 118-game slash line of .282/.363/.408 along with 32 stolen bases and 45 RBIs before he was traded to the Los Angeles Dodgers on

August 19 for pitcher Pedro Astacio. Rockies manager Don Baylor suggested that upcoming contract negotiations might have influenced the trade, saying, "I didn't have a checkbook, so I couldn't pay him."[28]

For his part, Young commented, "I was a little surprised at first, considering the history and everything with me being a Rockie. ... I thought I would be over there for a long time. ... It just shows that you never know, but I'm happy to be coming back to the Dodgers."[29]

Young's 180 stolen bases for the Rockies were still, as of 2018, a Rockies franchise record.[30]

In his first game back with the Dodgers, Young went 3-for-4 with an RBI and a stolen base. For the remainder of the season, he drove in another 16 runs with 13 stolen bases in 37 games.

Young's reunion with the Dodgers, was dampened by an 0-for-20 hitless streak that coincided with the death of his best friend, 30-year-old Dwight Giles. Young would not use Giles' death as an excuse for his batting slump. Instead, in talking about his friend and his batting slump, Young said: "He was like a brother. ... That's not an excuse. Those are things you have to deal with as a professional."[31]

On September 25, the Dodgers went to Denver to take on the Rockies for the first time since the trade. On what was already an emotional day for Young, when he stepped to the plate for the first time, the Colorado Rockies fans gave him a standing ovation. Young raised his batting helmet to the crowd, stepped back up to the plate, and hit a single.[32]

After the season Young became a free agent for the first time, and was rewarded by the Dodgers with a four-year agreement that paid him $4.5 million per year.

Two months into his 1998 season, *Los Angeles Times* sports columnist Jim Murray recognized Young's value to the Dodgers: "What every dynasty team in history needed was that pest in the No. 1 spot, the leadoff hitter, the guy who opened the game for you. ... His job was to be a nuisance, a tough out, a bat manipulator, a schemer, as annoying as a mosquito in a dark room. ... He harassed the pitcher more than he harassed him. Every at bat was a poker game."[33]

Murray went on to say: "The Dodgers have this all-important beat-you ballplayer in their leadoff spot — Eric Young. ... Eric Young can run. He can hit, but he's no Tony Gwynn. He can field, but he's no Bill Mazeroski. But he can beat you."[34]

Young told Murray he would like his initials — EY — to mean "Every Year a Headache" for opposing pitchers.[35]

For the next two years, Young did his best to be that headache. In 1,047 plate appearances, he had 257 hits, 108 walks, and was hit by a pitch 10 times, while striking out only 58 times. Each time he reached base he became a threat to run. His threat to run often gave subsequent batters better pitches to hit.

Still, Young was again on the trading block. On December 12, 1999, in a cost-cutting move by the Dodgers, he was traded along with pitcher Ismael Valdez to the Chicago Cubs for pitcher Terry Adams and two minor leaguers.

The trade to the Cubs reunited Young with manager Don Baylor. Each expressed pleasure with the trade. Baylor commented: "EY will bat leadoff for us. He was a very exciting player for me in Colorado. He brings to us what this club needed, one with speed."[36]

Young commented: "I think I bring excitement. I'm the type of leadoff guy who can jumpstart the offense. That's my main thing. ... With (Baylor) you know what he wants. You can talk to (him) about anything. That is very important to a player."[37]

With two years remaining on the contract he signed with the Dodgers, Young became the sparkplug the Cubs were hoping for. In 2000 and 2001 he collected 348 hits and 105 walks. He scored 196 runs and stole 85 bases, including a career-high 54 in 2000.

After the 2001 season, Young again was granted free agency. Whether it was due to the Cubs not making the playoffs in either of Young's two years with them, or a fear that his performance would diminish as he got older, or simply that the Milwaukee Brewers offered him a two-year contract at $2 million per year, he did not re-sign with the Cubs.

Instead, Young signed a two-year agreement with the Brewers. Brewers general manager Dean Taylor said one of the team's goals "was getting some contact hitters to reduce the number of strikeouts, and we've done that with Eric Young."[38]

While there was some concern whether the Brewers would get their money's worth from the 34-year-old Young, Brewers manager Davey Lopes had no such concerns, saying, "When you have a guy at the top of your order who can do the things that 'EY' can, it sets a tone for your whole ballclub."[39]

Young, who had earlier promised GM Taylor that he would break the Brewers' stolen-base record of 54, said he was looking forward to working with Lopes and first-base coach Dave Collins, each a record-setting basestealer as a player. Young felt that with their insight and guidance he could continue to learn and use his basestealing abilities to an even greater extent.[40]

Instead of breaking the Brewers' stolen-base record, Young stole just 31 bases in 138 games for the 2002 Brewers. While apparently beginning to slow down, he continued to hit at a .280 pace with a .338 on-base percentage.

Toward the end of the season Young reflected on his rookie season with the Dodgers while discussing the help and coaching he was giving Brewers standout rookie Alex Sanchez. Young told Sanchez, "I made a lot of mistakes. Basically, you're so aggressive and you've got so much energy. ... Sometimes you try to be aggressive at the wrong time and it's something you hope a person will learn and adjust to. And become even better."[41] Perhaps a hint to his coaching future.

The 2003 season became another split season for Young: another trade. He played in 109 games for the Brewers before being sent to the San Francisco Giants for a minor leaguer on August 19. The Giants were in need of a replacement for the injured Ray Durham. Young said he was happy to be joining the Giants: "I just want to go over there and get to that playoff level again. I'd only experienced that one time in my career and that is what it is all about."[42] For the Brewers his batting average had slipped to .260 but he hit a career-high 15 home runs. However, he had only 25 stolen bases, far from the Brewers' record and his fewest since 1994.

While the Giants did make the playoffs in 2003, Young did not supply the spark they anticipated. Instead, in 26 games he hit just .197 with 3 stolen bases. Looking toward 2004, the Giants held a $3 million team option with a $1 million buyout if the option was not exercised.[43]

The Giants chose not to exercise their option, and Young became a free agent. In January 2004, he signed with the Texas Rangers, making the Rangers his sixth major-league team.

The 2004 season was a mixed success for Young. While he hit a strong .288 with an on-base percentage of .377, he had only 14 stolen bases in 104 games. Young was no longer a "terror on the bases." After the season, he was again granted free agency.

On December 9, 2004, Young agreed to a one-year, $850,000 deal with the San Diego Padres, with an $850,000 team option for the 2006 season or a $150,000 buyout.[44] Young's Padres career was doomed to fail. On April 7, 2005, during the Padres home opener, Young, then 37, was hurt making a leaping catch off the center-field wall. The Padres placed him on the 60-day disabled list with a dislocated right shoulder.[45] Young did not rejoin the Padres until three months later,[46] and played in just 56 games during the season. The Padres chose not to exercise their option and paid him the $150,000 buyout. Then, two weeks later, they re-signed him for one year at $700,000.[47]

On December 10, 2005, Young married Beyonka Jackson in Harris, Texas.[48] In spring training for what would turn out to be Young's final season, an emotional highlight occurred. The Padres were playing the Colorado Rockies. Young was selected to take the lineup card to the umpires before the game. When he got to the umpires, he found he knew the representative for the Rockies. It was a 21-year-old infielder in the Rockies' farm system by the name of Eric Young Jr., who had been brought up just to play that game against his father's team.[49]

"It was overwhelming," Young recalled. "He was wearing a Rockies uniform, a team I used to play for.

We were both on cloud nine." During the game, Eric Jr. hit a triple. Eric Sr. forgot he was on the opposing team and stood and cheered his son.[50]

Then came the real season. Young played in just 56 games for the Padres, batting just .203 with only 8 stolen bases. On August 1, the Padres waived Young for the purpose of giving him his unconditional release.[51]

On August 11, the Texas Rangers signed Young to a minor-league contract and assigned him to Triple-A Oklahoma.[52] On the 25th they called him up.[53] In his first game for the Rangers Young went 2-for-5 with a double and two RBIs. These were the last base hits of his major-league career. Young played in only four games for the Rangers and got just the two hits in 10 at-bats. After the season the Rangers released him.

Young did not sign another playing contract for the 2007 season. On September 12, 2008, he signed a one-day contract and officially retired as a member of the Colorado Rockies.[54]

In 1,730 games for seven teams in a 15-year career, Young had a .283/.359/.390 line with 1,731 hits and 465 stolen bases.

With his playing days behind him, Young embarked on the next phase of his career—first as an analyst on ESPN's *Baseball Tonight* from 2007 to 2009, and then in 2010 as minor-league outfield and baserunning coordinator for the Houston Astros. In 2011, Young was back in the major leagues when he was hired by the Arizona Diamondbacks to be their first-base coach. Young continued at first base for the Diamondbacks for the 2012 season.

It was also in 2012 that Young became eligible for the Baseball Hall of Fame. He received just one vote and was dropped from future ballots.

In 2014 Young returned to the Rockies, this time as their first-base coach with additional oversight of the outfield and baserunning instruction. He continued with the Rockies for the 2015 and 2016 seasons. He was let go after the 2016 season as part of a Rockies housecleaning after the resignation of manager Walt Weiss.[55]

Even after being fired by the Rockies, Young was considered in the Colorado Rockies' search for a manager to replace Weiss. He was noted for his development of both young and veteran players as well as having the "Colorado culture" as both a player and a coach.[56]

Young's career in baseball was prolonged when the Atlanta Braves hired him before the 2018 season as their first-base coach and outfield instructor.[57]

NOTES

1 youtube.com/watch?v=akvc44D-B6g.

2 Will Petersen, "Kingery's Role Reduced as Rox Announcer," *Denver Post*, July 14, 2009. neighbors.denverpost.com/view-topic.php?f=5&t=12834438&start=25 The words "goin" and "aint" are as rendered.

3 Thanks to Colorado Rockies team historian Paul Parker and Eric Young for providing this information.

4 Jimmy Greenfield, "Just Asking," *Chicago Tribune*, June 8, 2004: 33-20.

5 Jack Curry, "A Tough Decision for Rutgers Player," *New York Times*, August 23, 1988. nytimes.com/1988/08/22/sports/a-tough-decision-for-rutgers-player.html.

6 *Salina* (Kansas) *Journal Sun*, June 11, 2006: 51.

7 "Former Rutgers Player Eric Young to Be Inducted Into New Jersey Sports Writers' Hall of Fame," admin.scarletknights.com/news/2011/11/28/ Former_Rutgers_Baseball_Player_Eric_Young_to_be_ Inducted_into_New_Jersey_Sports_Writers_Hall_of_Fame. aspx?path=baseball.

8 Brian VanderBeek, "Local Tales Connect East, West Coasts," *Modesto* (California) *Bee*, April 17, 2007. modbee.com/lat-est-news/article3091478.html.

9 "Former Rutgers Player Eric Young."

10 Curry.

11 Ibid.

12 Ibid.

13 Ibid.

14 Ibid.

15 m.mlb.com/atl/roster/coach/124695/eric-young.

16 "Former Rutgers Player Eric Young."

17 livingstonalumni.org/rutgers-athletics-hall-fame.

18 "Former Rutgers Player Eric Young."

19 baseball-reference.com/players/y/younge01.shtml

20 Matt Romanoski, "Young, Rumer Honored," *Bridgewater* (New Jersey) *Courier-News,* September 9, 1991: 21. The newspaper incorrectly reported him as having 71 stolen bases.

21 Ibid.

22 Ibid.

23 Brian Kilpatrick, "Rockies Retro: Eric Young," purplerow. com/2009/2/28/775144/rockies-retro-eric-young.

24 John Bruns, "Young Makes History as First Rockie Batter," *Central New Jersey Home News* (New Brunswick), April 6, 1993: 19.

25 Ibid.

26 Kilpatrick.

27 Ibid.

28 Kilpatrick.

29 "Young: Comes Home Again," *Central New Jersey Home News,* August 20, 1997: 20.

30 "Colorado Rockies Manager Search: What About Eric Young Sr.?" foxsports.com/mlb/story/colorado-rockies-manager-search-what-about-eric-young-sr-100516.

31 Steve Springer, "Death of Former Teammate Hurts Young," *Los Angeles Times,* September 15, 1997: 47.

32 Associated Press, "Piazza's Blast Sparks L.A.," *South Florida Sun Sentinel* (Fort Lauderdale), September 27, 1997: 34.

33 Jim Murray, "E.Y. the Type of Player Teams Rally Around," *Los Angeles Times,* May 21, 1998: 130.

34 Ibid.

35 Ibid.

36 John Nadel, "Ricketts Involved in Five-Player Trade," *Jackson* (Tennessee) *Sun,* December 13, 1999: 19.

37 Phil Rogers, "Reunited (With Baylor) and It Feels So Good (to Young)," *Chicago Tribune,* December 13, 1999: 30.

38 Greg Giesen, "More Moves Brewing," *Racine* (Wisconsin) *Journal Times,* January 23, 2002: 25.

39 Drew Olson, "Young Has Feet Set on Steal Record," *Fond Du Lac* (Wisconsin) *Commonwealth Reporter,* February 22, 2002: 15.

40 Ibid. The article did not mention that Tommy Harper had 73 stolen bases for the Seattle Pilots, the Brewers' predecessors, in 1969.

41 "Crew has 2003 1—2 Punch Set," *Beaver Dam* (Wisconsin) *Daily Citizen,* September 11, 2002: 15.

42 "Brewers Send Eric Young to Giants," *Mattoon* (Illinois) *Journal Gazette,* August 20, 2003: 14.

43 Ibid.

44 Associated Press, "Baseball Notes," *Racine* (Wisconsin) *Journal Times,* November 22, 2005: 32.

45 "Shoulder Injury Puts Young Out 2 Months," *Indianapolis Star,* April 9, 2005: 49.

46 Associated Press, "Baseball Notes," *Racine* (Wisconsin) *Journal Times,* November 22, 2005: 32.

47 Ibid.

48 search.ancestry.com/search/collections/TXmarriageindex/13540126.

49 Tim Wendel, "As Father's Day Approaches ... ," *Salina* (Kansas) *Journal,* June 11, 2006: 51.

50 Ibid.

51 "Padres Release Young, Welcome Walker," *Honolulu Star-Bulletin,* August 2, 2006: 17.

52 "Rangers Sign Journeyman Eric Young," *Orlando Sentinel,* August 12, 2006: C5.

53 "Baseball Briefs," *Sioux City Journal,* Aug 26, 2006: 19.

54 Kilpatrick.

55 Patrick Saunders, "Rockies Don't Renew Contracts of 4 Coaches, Including Tom Runnells and Eric Young," *Denver Post.* October 8, 2016. denverpost.com/2016/10/8/rockies-dont-renew-contracts.

56 "Colorado Rockies Manager Search."

57 mlb.com/braves/news/braves-announce-2018-coaching-staff/c-261316796.

ROCKIES THUMBNAILS

BY ED MESERKO, GWEN MESERKO, AND CARM REALE

Nolan Arenado

Third baseman Nolan Arenado was a second-round pick of the Colorado Rockies in the June 2009 amateur draft. He is the only third basemen to win the Gold Glove Award in his first four major-league seasons, and in 2017 he won another in his fifth season. He is the active leader in fielding percentage and as of 2017 ranked fifth all-time in that category. In addition to his fielding, his accomplishments in hitting are just as impressive. In 2015 and 2016, he led the National League in home runs, runs batted in, and total bases. He also garnered Silver Slugger awards for both those seasons. In 2017, he hit a career-high .309 with 37 home runs and 130 RBIs.

Nolan Arenado

Charlie Blackmon

Outfielder Charlie Blackmon was born on July 1, 1986, in Dallas, Texas. This lefty attended Georgia Tech and was chosen by the Rockies in the second round of the June 2008 amateur draft. In 2017 he had his greatest season so far. He led the National League in runs scored, hits, triples, batting average (.331), and total bases. He hit a career-high 37 home runs. He set a major-league record for most RBIs by a leadoff batter with 103. He goes by the nickname of Chuck Nazty.

Jorge De La Rosa

Left-hander Jorge De La Rosa was born on April 5, 1981, in Monterrey, Mexico. He was signed on March 20, 1998, as an amateur free agent. He spent nine years with the Rockies and as of 2017 was the team's leader in career wins with 86. In 2003, as a Red Sox farmhand, he and three fellow farmhands were famously traded to Arizona for Curt Schilling. He saw his first career postseason action in 2017 as a member of the Arizona Diamondbacks. His career record through 2017 stood at 104 wins and 85 losses.

Dexter Fowler

Switch-hitting outfielder Dexter Fowler was born on March 22, 1986, in Atlanta. He was a 14th-round pick of the Colorado Rockies in the June 2004 amateur draft. As of 2017 he had spent 10 years in the major leagues, six of them as a member of the Rockies. As of 2017 he was the all-time Rockies leader in triples with 53. Fowler was a member of the 2016 World Series champion Chicago Cubs. On December 9, 2016, he signed a five-year, $82.5 million free-agent contract with the St. Louis Cardinals.

Carlos Gonzalez

Left-handed batting and throwing outfielder Carlos Gonzalez, 32, from Maracaibo, Venezuela, can be classified as one of the all-time greatest Rockies. He ranks in the team's top five in the following career hitting categories: runs, hits, doubles, triples, home runs, runs batted in, and stolen bases. He led the National League in batting in 2010 with a .336 average. He has also amassed three Gold Gloves for his fielding prowess. During spring training 2018, "Cargo" signed a 1 year, $8 million contract with the Rockies..

Matt Holliday

Matt Holliday was drafted in the seventh round by the Colorado Rockies in the June 1998 amateur draft. He played in 121 major-league games as a rookie in 2004. His best season with the Rockies and in his career was 2007, when he hit 36 home runs (highest in his career) and had a league-leading 137 runs batted in, 216 hits, 50 doubles, 386 total bases, and a .340 batting average. With his controversial slide into home plate in the one-game tiebreaker against the San Diego Padres, he paced the Rockies to the World Series against Boston, capturing the MVP award in the National League Championship Series. Holliday played for the Rockies through the 2008 season, then went on to play for the Oakland A's, eight years for the Cardinals, and then for the Yankees. As of 2017 he had made seven All-Star Game appearances, three with the Rockies. He has won four Silver Slugger awards, three wearing the purple, black, and silver.

Ubaldo Jimenez

Ubaldo Jimenez has spent 12 years in the major leagues as of 2017, mostly as a starting pitcher for the Colorado Rockies, Cleveland Indians, and Baltimore Orioles. He started one game for the Rockies in the 2007 Division Series and one in the NLCS (the Rockies won both games), and lost a close 2-1 Game Two of the World Series to the Red Sox. The pinnacle year of his career was with the Colorado Rockies in 2010. His fastball, reaching 100 mph, allowed him to post a 19-8 record, leading the National League in winning percentage (.704) with a 2.88 earned-run average. At Turner Field on April 17, 2010, Jimenez posted the only no-hitter in Colorado Rockies history with a 4-0 win over the Atlanta Braves. He started the 2010 All-Star Game for the National League, allowing no runs in two innings. His regular-season streak of pitching 33 consecutive scoreless innings in 2010 was still a franchise record as of 2017. With the Rockies seeking young starting pitching, Jimenez was traded to the Cleveland Indians in 2011. In 2014, Jimenez signed a free-agent contract with the Baltimore Orioles.

Trevor Story

Trevor Story was a first-round draft pick in 2011. He debuted with the Colorado Rockies on April 4, 2016, by smashing two home runs, tying a major-league record for Opening Day appearances, and set a major-league record by homering in each of his first four games. At 23 years old, the Texan shocked the majors by hitting 27 home runs and compiling a .272 batting average in an injury-shortened season of 97 games. His 10 home runs in April tied a major-league rookie record, previously set by Jose Abreu. His sophomore year, 2017, saw his power stroke continue with exceptional enhancement in his defensive abilities, ranking him second in double plays turned by a shortstop.

Troy Tulowitzki

Troy Tulowitzki was drafted by the Colorado Rockies in the first round, the seventh overall selection, in the June 2005 amateur draft. His 2007 debut saw him finish second in the Rookie of the Year voting, and helped propel the Colorado team to the World Series with 24 home runs, 99 RBIs, and dazzling defensive plays. No one present at Rockies games will ever forget the "TULO!" chants when he came to bat at pressure-packed moments. In his 10 seasons with the Rockies, his season highs included 32 home runs (2009), 105 RBIs (2011), a .340 batting average (2014), and a .603 slugging percentage (2014). Tulowitzki has won two Silver Slugger Awards and two Gold Gloves, and has been a five-time All-Star.

Troy Tulowitzki

Fans were shocked when Tulowitzki was traded to the Toronto Blue Jays in 2015 for pitching prospects and Jose Reyes.

The Arenado, Blackmon, De La Rosa, and Gonzalez thumbnails are written by Carmen Reale. The Holliday, Jimenez, Story, and Tulowitzki thumbnails are written by Ed and Gwen Meserko.

MILE HIGH STADIUM

BY CURT SMITH

IMAGINE TWO STRANGERS STRAND-ed on a South Sea island from Taos, New Mexico, and Butte, Montana. They differ in age, race, income, and religion. Their common denominator is the Colorado Rockies major-league baseball club that did not exist until a quarter-century ago. For a long time, however, the prospect of such a team in the Mountain Time Zone seemed described by the poet John Greenleaf Whittier, writing "For all sad words of tongue and pen, the saddest are these, 'It might have been!'"[1]

For almost a century after the region's first organized teams began in the 1860s, baseball treated most of the entire area as if it did not exist. Until 1958, St. Louis was the major leagues' Westernmost and Southernmost franchise. Even later, Mid-America remained "flyover country" to many living on each coast. The 14-state Mountain Time Zone's[2] first baseball beachhead of any size was 1948's construction of Bears Stadium at 2755 West 17th Avenue in Denver by native Bob Howsam, barely 30, Western League president, and owner of its then Class-A Denver Bears, dad Lee a businessman. Politically linked by marriage to the daughter of Edwin "Big Ed" Johnson, for 25 years a Colorado US senator or governor, Howsam crafted a Horatio Alger kind of life.[3]

Built at a former landfill, Bears Stadium, renamed Mile High Stadium in 1968, became the region's jerrybuilt baseball/football hub for the next half-century. The original 18,000-seat grandstand encircled the plate from one foul pole to another on the north and west sides, showing even then how thin air and the long ball mixed. Since the 1995 debut of nearby Coors Field, named for a beer sponsor synonymous with Denver and its regional market, upper deck row 20 has been painted team color purple to mark 5,280 feet, one mile above sea level. On Bears Stadium's August 14, 1948, Opening Day, Luther "Bud" Phillips slammed the future Mile High's first homer.[4] Denver led the league that year in attendance, next season

luring a minor-league high 463,069, more than the big-league St. Louis Browns.[5]

By then baseball had begun to worry about the growth of television. In 1946, Americans owned only 17,000 TV sets, buying 10,000 a day by 1950.[6] TV especially hurt minor-league attendance, keeping people at home, not flocking to a park. Denver's identity helped fight the trend: the cynosure of a region. In 1951, Howsam was named *The Sporting News* Single-A Executive of the Year. The 1952 and 1954 Bears won Western League titles. Bob then bought the Kansas City Blues of the American Association, moved them to Colorado, and birthed the Yankees' Triple-A affiliate Bears.[7] "To the country, this era introduced Denver as a baseball stronghold," said Jeff Kingery, its major-league Rockies' first radio Voice in 1993. "That pinstriped cachet made the difference."[8] It also fueled Denver's long and winding big-league road.

Howsam's junior Yankees featured future Bronx Bomber skipper Ralph Houk, outfielder Norm Siebern, bad-sighted fastballing reliever Ryne Duren, and the infield's legendary Tony Kubek and Bobby Richardson. In 1955, the Bears led the league in attendance for the first of three years; 1956, Howsam again was named *The Sporting News* Triple-A Executive of the Year; 1957, his Denver club won the Triple-A title and Little World Series.[9] As Mark S. Foster wrote in his book, *The Denver Bears: From Sandlots to Sellouts,* interest soared so strikingly that instead of "turning spectators away at Bears Stadium the club let latecomers stand in the outfield roped off on the warning track."[10] From there Howsam braved a near-miss for both Denver and himself which he rued even after forging as president and general manager the epochal 1975-76 world champion Big Red Machine.

In 1959, Branch Rickey and New York lawyer William Shea proposed a third major — Continental — league, to begin play in 1961. Its putative eight teams were Atlanta, Buffalo,

Dallas/Fort Worth, Houston, Minneapolis, New York, Toronto—and Denver, run by Howsam. Sadly, to undo the Continental, the National League announced in August 1960 that it would expand to Houston and back to New York in 1962, leaving big-league ball deserted on Pike's Peak.[11] At sea, Howsam founded the Denver Broncos of the American Football League, garbed his team in used uniforms, including infamous vertically striped socks, almost went belly-up, sold controlling 1960 first-year interest, and saw the Ponies become synonymous with Mile High as bleachers and temporary east stands upped capacity to 34,000—ironically, for baseball. It reached 76,037 by 1976, each Broncos home game sold out, a baseball crib turned football shrine.[12]

"The world's loudest outdoors insane asylum," Voice Chuck Thompson called Baltimore's Memorial Stadium during his 1949-83 football Colts' lovefest.[13] With Mile High's Broncos enjoying a like response, many, recalling Howsam, asked if a Denver big-league team franchise might climb its own Rocky Mountain High. In 1977 and 1979, oilman Marvin Davis vainly tried to move the A's from Oakland. Thereafter rumor had other clubs moving to the time zone's most populous city, using it as leverage to up local facilities or lower local rent.[14] Increasingly, Denver seemed a perpetual major-league franchise to be named (much) later, the tease not dimming local interest. In the 15 years before joining the NL, the 1978-92 Bears-turned-Zephyrs Triple-A outlet of five big-league teams drew more than half a million people four times, including 1980's best 565,214. After a century of neglect, the region waited for Lady Luck to belatedly change or common sense to finally touch the majors.

Soon a major-league expansion committee would inquire what had changed since Denver's early pioneer, sparse population, and as seen on TV Western age. One constant that *hadn't* was the air—"so thin, it made it [like] Little League," said Rockies 1993-98 manager Don Baylor.[15] Thus, liberal Mile High lengths lasted through the 1980s: left to right field, respectively: foul lines, 335 and 370 feet; gaping alleys, 375 and 400 feet; and center field, 423.[16] What did

change lay all around. Many more people, mostly young, were moving into than leaving Colorado and the region. The economy—high-tech, education, development—was moving up. By 1990, baseball had 26 teams, 14 in the American League. To gain parity, the NL scheduled 1993 expansion of two teams from six contenders: Buffalo, Denver, Miami, Orlando, Tampa-St. Petersburg, and Washington—for the Mountain Time Zone, the nearest big-league team, Kansas City, more than 600 miles away.[17]

Early planning to *become* big league seemed altogether sound. On August 14, 1990, the then six-county Denver area okayed by 54 percent to 46 percent a 0.1 percent sales-tax increase to build a new $138 million baseball park—Mile High being too old, large, and thin on amenities to be anything but transitional.[18] Had the referendum failed, Denver's franchise bid would have, too, contingent on a site to succeed Howsam's more than 40-year-old park. Instead, park financed, Governor Roy (Buddy) Romer fixed on finding investors to pay the NL's $95 million expansion fee.[19] No ownership group had stepped forth. Worse, the due date for the application fee was September 4—necessary for any hope to make the time zone's states from Arizona to Montana major-league in name.

Earlier supposed front-runner Denver had been shaken by the collapse of supposed owner-to-be John Dikeou, "who [suffered] the bottom [falling] out of … his real estate business," as the *Los Angeles Times* described the Triple-A Zephyrs owner. Tax increase passed, Romer three days later met new potential owners, "everybody sat around the table," he said, "and I just went around the room and said, 'Tell me who you are, how much you can put in, and what role you want to play.'"[20] The next week Romer put Paul Jacobs, senior partner at a large Denver legal firm, and third-generation Coloradan Steve Ehrhart, commissioner of the World Basketball League, in charge of ownership. Two potential moneymen whom Jacobs knew from Ohio, John Antonucci, a large beverage distributor, and Mickey Monus, Phar-Mor drug store chain CEO, became general partners. "By March 1991 [the final NL deadline]," wrote the *Denver Post*,

"Jacobs had commitments to meet the … expansion fee."[21]

One day the franchise group made Linda Alvarado baseball's first Hispanic would-be owner—diversity a key application issue.[22] Another, to show regional potential, it announced that in less than three *weeks* more than 18,000 people from Colorado, Montana, Wyoming, New Mexico, Nebraska, and Kansas had mailed deposits on season tickets two *years* before the 1993 season, as if denizens of Omaha and Abilene planned to spend 81 days that year in Denver.[23] Against such an arsenal—Colorado's booming commerce and youthful demographics were also decisive—fine baseball cities like Buffalo and Washington blew away. On March 26, 1991, the NL expansion committee visited Denver, 1,500 people greeting it at an atrium at 17th and Broadway by singing "Take Me Out to the Ball Game." Entering, members seemed surprised, many moved. Paul Jacobs walked in next to longtime league executive Phyllis Collins. "I looked over," he said, "and tears were streaming down her cheeks."[24]

Baseball's ancient anthem became Denver's expansion exclamation mark. That July 5, National League President Bill White announced to the shock of few that its (also South Florida's far shorter) big-league wait was over. Miami soon became a headache, still a baseball migraine a quarter-century later. By contrast, the only question about the newly named Colorado Rockies –accenting regional, not "Denver," and new, not "Bears"—was why it took so long. Few could have guessed it, but real worry *still* lay ahead. Three weeks later, Monus flew to Denver and, in a setback even worse than Dikeou's for baseball, told Jacobs he would need to sell his $20 million share in ownership. Given Tampa's rumored position as expansion runner-up, overnight the state of Florida seemed a possibility for two new 1993 NL teams, not one.

"We came closer to losing the franchise at that point than I thought at the time, and we hadn't even played a game," said Jacobs, then "nervous about everything." Looking back, he said, "so many serendipitous things happened that allowed us to put it together."[25] Eventually, Antonucci also exited as team owner, tied to Monus's conviction by a federal grand jury of embezzlement and fraud. Monus went to prison for 10 years. Antonucci went back to distributing beverages. The "serendipitous" began with limited partners, who began signing checks. Charlie Monfort, from family cattle and meat-packing, and Oren Benton, a uranium and banking billionaire, invested more heavily. The most crucial partner, trucker-rancher Jerry McMorris, became the key point-man, opening his own pockets and legally emptying others'.[26]

"The Rockies ownership there was strong enough, committed enough" to overcome the scandal, Antonucci told ESPN senior writer Gene Wojciechowski in 2007, the Rockies making the World Series in the franchise's 15th year.[27] Ultimately, McMorris's value lay above all in assembling a coalition of investors. By 1992, the now principal owner owned a controlling interest, serving as chairman, president, and chief executive officer until 2001 and part of ownership till 2005. The first challenge was to convert 21,000 movable seats at Mile High from football to baseball. Its grass field was heated to spur yearlong growth. A concert brochure hailed "the first fully distributed sound system" with "near stereo quality sound" of any US stadium." From the start, the new kid on the block ran scared. That, in turn, fueled the Rockies' riposte to their second challenge: at least partly unhorsing Mile High's chief tenant.

"Coming in, the Broncos owned the region," said McMorris. "How do you compete?" The Rockies tried straightaway in the November 1992 NL expansion draft. Atlanta pitcher David Nied became their number-one choice, a textbook case of peaking too soon. In 1992, Nied had compiled a 3-0 record with a 1.17 earned-run average. In 1993-96, the Rockies righty was 14-18, never had a single-season ERA less than 4.80, and braved more hits than innings pitched. Other imminent or eventual well-known names from their draft included Brad Ausmus, Vinny Castilla, Alex Cole, Joe Girardi, Charlie Hayes, Darren Holmes, Steven Reed, and Armando Reynoso. Andres Galarraga, Bruce Ruffin, and Bryn Smith were each signed as a Rockies free agent. Dante Bichette of the Brewers arrived in Denver by trade.[28]

That October, Canada won its first World Series: Toronto, in six games, over Atlanta. On December 16, 1992, George Bush feted the Blue Jays at the White House, gently ribbing US Trade Representative Carla Hills. "I thought she understood that our free-trade agreement with Canada did not mean that the United States would trade away the world's championship," the president said to laughter.[29] Some didn't like a Canadian team winning our Series. Actually, television's wildly successful *Hockey Night in Canada* taught the Rockies a lesson. Since 1931, by radio, and 1952, TV, the Saturday night series had fused a diffuse, largely rural Nation, listeners seduced hundreds of miles from a big-league site.[30] Might that be true of audio/video linking Mile High to farmhouses and sleepy small towns hundreds, even thousands, of miles away in New Mexico or Wyoming in Cubs or Cardinals Country?! Doubt didn't live, for long.

In early 1993, KWGN, Channel 2 in Denver, announced a 15-station, seven-state television network with itself as flagship. Outlets included Colorado's Colorado Springs, Durango, Glenwood Springs, Grand Junction, and Montrose; Nebraska's Scottsbluff; New Mexico's Las Cruces; South Dakota's Lead-Deadwood and Rapid City; Utah's Salt Lake City; and Wyoming's Casper, Cheyenne, and Sheridan.[31] The list evoked a lush film age of John Wayne and director John Ford and Monument Valley, the stunning backdrop of *Fort Apache* and *The Searchers* and other great cinema. Charlie Jones and partner Duane Kuiper, replaced by Dave Campbell in 1994, ferried the Rockies from Mike High and the road on Saturday, Sunday, and weekday nights. "Local TV mattered," said Jones, "because it touched the entire [*sic* much of the] region."[32] Unspoken was how *network* television belonged to the National Football League—the Broncos.

Meantime, the wireless became an even better way to mine the time zone's baseball gold, flagship News Radio 85/KOA Denver's Kingery and Wayne Hagin airing play-by-play over a giant first-year 12-state network of 42 affiliates.[33] In Colorado, 11 outlets

tied Cortez, Fort Collins, Greeley, Lamar, Pagosa Springs, Walsenburg, and TV's cited above. Arizona stations listed Coolidge and Tucson; Arkansas, Conway; Kansas, Garden City, and Goodland; Montana, Alliance and Chadron, beside Scottsbluff. In Wyoming, 11 affiliates included Buffalo, Evanston, Green River, Kemmerer, nationally known Laramie, Riverton, Thermopolis, and Worland, and TV's listed. Gallup, New Mexico, swelled the radio network, as did Bend, Oregon, and Blanding, Logan, and St. George, Utah, and Hot Springs and Belle Fourche, South Dakota. Other teams may have had more affiliates, but none rolled more grandly off the tongue.

Despite the time zone's interest, after the Rockies' first spring workout ended in 1993, the press session began, well, rockily. "Reporters from the region" cloistered around manager Baylor, said Kingery, only to have the first questioner ask, "Coach, how did it go?"—Jeff recalled, "so typical of a local media caring only for Broncos football."[34]

Baylor did a slow burn, trying not to light his noted fuse. "Let's get one thing straight," Baylor said. "I'm the manager." Later, Kingery laughed: "The education of a baseball-made area had begun."

According to his TV peer, Charlie Jones, former Commissioner Fay Vincent was a close friend of Baylor, an ex-American League star who had hoped to become a big-league skipper since his last playing season in 1988. "Don said that if he ever became a manager, he wanted Fay to be there," said Jones.[35] On April 5, 1993, Vincent arrived back from Europe at Shea Stadium to throw out the first ball of the Rockies' first year, Colorado losing, 3-0. The visiting lineup included five players culled from the expansion draft: Eric Young, leading off, at second base; Cole, center field; Bichette, right field; Galarraga, batting cleanup, first base; Jerald Clark, left field; Hayes, third base; Girardi, catcher; Freddie Benavides, shortstop, hitting eighth; and Nied, pitching. Mets win, 3-0. Two nights later Bichette had the Rockies' first homer and RBI, at Shea: New York again, 6-1.[36]

On Friday, April 9, Colorado played its inaugural game at Mile High against Montreal. Jones had called Wimbledon tennis, the Seoul and Barcelona

Olympics, and the 1986 World Cup final. Now, seeing baseball's largest-ever first-day crowd (80,227), he realized that "the Rockies' opener was as big as those combined," Charlie said.[37] "For [all these] years the Rocky Mountain region had been baseball's bridesmaid—and now the big leagues were here." If you were a child, a parent might take your hand, perhaps fumble for a ticket, and with an usher help find your seat. After a spring of groundskeepers planting and ushers cleaning and vendors prepping that for those who had despaired of ever seeing a big-game in this area was close to tear-provoking, finally, implausibly, major-league ball had *arrived*.

"Walking through the stands, into that great small [here, huge] old stadium, and there they were in the flesh," wrote the New Hampshire poet and former Poet Laureate of the United States Donald Hall. "I can see them now in their baggy old pants, the players that I had heard about, of whom I had seen photographs, but there they were, really walking about, live people, and the absolute enchantment, the enthrallment, the tension of starting the game. 'Play ball.'"[38] If you lived in the Rocky Mountain area, baseball's signature call to arms never meant more than when the home-plate umpire bellowed it that afternoon. Quickly, the Rockies made hash of the cliché that high altitude meant low result, Eric Young leading off the home half of the first inning by slamming a drive into the left-center-field stands.

To Jones, "You could hear the roar in California!" In center field, Montreal's Marquis Grissom said he felt the ground shake as the ball reached the seats. Left fielder John Vander Wal yelled to him, "This is not our day."[39] It *was* for those who clutched and grabbed at, then hoisted, the ball. Noise deafened, thousands stomping on the bleachers, the horseshoe becoming almost animate. Students and working men and housewives became a wave, bodies rocking, collectively and ecstatically. Young's was Opening Day's most memorable hit. Its first hit was Montreal's Mike Lansing's first-inning single off starting and winning pitcher Bryn Smith. The Rockies won, 11-4.[40] Young's only other day of homering in 1993 was Mile High's closing day. "Amazing bookends," said Charlie,

"but no more amazing than the entire opener—crisp, the sun out, and a region in love."

Mile High's next two games lured 65,261 and 66,987 to see, incidentally, the Expos, the park soon miming no experience as much as the 1958 seventh-place Dodgers at Los Angeles Memorial Coliseum: huge throngs nightly filling row upon row—a celebration, a sensation—not due to, but *despite*, the quality of the host. On the field, the Rockies, like number-one draft choice David Nied, peaked too soon, beating the Cubs, 14-13, on May 4 to come nearest .500 with a 10-15 record. Flush with (relative) success, they then lost five in a row, won once, braved a seven-set losing skein, won again, and lost *another* five, crashing to 12-32 by May 23. Colorado overlapped late July and early August with 13 straight defeats to reach a 36-74 nadir. By contrast, the Rockies were 26-20 in one-run games and 17-9 in September.[41] You recalled 1985-2012 Astros Voice Milo Hamilton saying, "Anyone who thinks he knows baseball is nuts."[42]

Ultimately, the Rockies settled closer to the '62 basement Amazin' Mets than the '69 champion Miracle Mets, placing sixth in the seven-team NL Western Division, something neither they nor any team would do again, since in 1994 each league segued to one division of four teams—the West—and two of five teams apiece, doubling playoff clubs to eight. On the one hand, the '93ers led the NL in triples (59), placed third in batting (.273), and topped the Mets and Padres with a 67-95 record, setting a league mark for first-year victories. On the other, they trailed every team in shutouts (zero), opponents' batting (.294), ERA (5.41), and fielding (.973). Armand Reynoso led in victories (12) and Bruce Ruffin in earned-run average (3.87). Galarraga, "The Big Cat," had a league-high .370 average and a team-best with Charlie Hayes' 98 RBIs, adding 22 homers to Hayes' 25 and Bichette's 21.[43] Like any "first"—love, car, child—that team remains special—had to be to compete with other 1993 baseball precincts, many of which gave *special* new connotation.

On April 5, 1993, a new president, Bill Clinton, threw out the year's first pitch at one-year-old Oriole Park at Camden Yards, its arched façade like old

Comiskey Park; ivy backdrop evocative of Wrigley Field, right-field scoreboard like Ebbets Field, and behind it the Eastern Seaboard's longest building. In the "The Last [True] Pennant Race," the NL Braves and Giants each won more than a hundred games: 104-58 Atlanta made postseason; 103-59 San Francisco did not. For the first time three mates—Toronto's John Olerud's .363, Paul Molitor's .332, and Roberto Alomar's .326—ranked 1-2-3 in league (AL) batting. The Blue Jays again made the Series. In Game Six, Toronto up, three sets to two, the visiting Phillies reversed a 5-1 hole to lead, 6-5, before reliever Mitch Williams began the Jays half of the ninth inning by putting two runners on base with one out. Joe Carter then lashed a would-be third strike down the left-field wall over the fence. Toronto wins! Carter leapt wildly around the bases of baseball's still capital. Retrieving how he said a year earlier that America didn't need to "trade away the world's championship" to Canada, former President Bush likely shook his head.[44]

In 1993, Toronto drew an AL record 4,057,947, many saying the affair wouldn't last. It didn't—surely not for as long as Colorado's still-standing major-league record set that season—4,483,350.[45] The mere number is astounding. What it cannot retrieve is the *feel* of a region that became addicted, of babies born and sermons given; of marriages begun and ended; of dinners grown cold and then reheated as Rocky Mountaineers joined Mile High's mammoth crowds and/or heard and viewed baseball's sound track on the air. From the distance of a quarter of a century, memory resurrects a river of handclapping flowing through a time zone. Leonard Bernstein said, "Music is something terribly special. It doesn't have to pass the censor of the brain before it can reach the heart." Like music, Mile High in 1993 disdained the finite.

Daily almost everyone came by car to Clay, West, Twentieth, and Elliott Streets, and Interstate 25. Charter buses imported parishioners from the far outposts of a far-flung diaspora, helping to temporarily depopulate one after another picture-perfect burg. Kingery recalled Don Baylor musing how "'rain,

show, cold, sun, they came from all over'"—a big-league record average of 56,751 in 79 home dates.[46] Jones joked that "it was an off night if we had 65,000. Duane [Kuiper] and I'd get Coors beer from viewers, food, an update on what family members were up to, as if *we* were members," a decade after that first season still terming it "unbelievable."[47] In a small town or city hundreds of miles away, play-by-play could erupt from a general store, as background music for a softball game, or from a traffic bottleneck, a Colorado victory prompting each driver to honk his horn, forging a sound wave of noise.

Watching from afar was a native Rocky Mountaineer whose father, Edward, a Union Pacific Railroad dispatcher, told him as a child, "Curtis, there's a big world out there. Someday I'd like to see a big-league game."[48] From 1966 to 1975, Wyoming-born Curt Gowdy telecast more network regular-season baseball than anyone had—*Game of the Week*, All-Star Game, World Series, and post-1968 League Championship Series—baseball's video face for a generation. In New England, they still know the avid hunter, fisherman, and conservationist as the 1951-65 Red Sox radio/TV man, knitting Canada to Connecticut as TV's Jones and radio's Jeff Kingery now did the Rockies. Gowdy was famed for telling Cape Cod, the Berkshires, and Bar Harbor "Hi, neighbor! Grab a 'Gansett!"—sponsor Narragansett beer, the Red Sox regional variant of Coors. Many parallels existed then and now between Curt's birthplace and his adopted place. Fenway Park was "New England's night club," he said. Mile High became its time zone's meeting club.

The Rockies readied for 1994 by ending their exhibition season in an April 1-3 tournament at BC Place in Vancouver also including Montreal, Seattle, and Toronto. On April 4, Opening Day, bats boomed—Phillies, 12-6—as 72,420 pilgrims packed baseball's Lourdes, the first of *twelve* times the year's Rockies topped *seventy* thousand. On April 24, America's Cubs lured 71,329, Colorado falling, 12-4, to fall below .500, a peak it reached again only once, May 3. In late May, 215,014 in three games saw Atlanta complete a Rockies' five-set losing streak.

On June 24-26, Mile High, teeming with Coastal expatriates, oozed more humanity: 73,957, 69,881, and 73,171 for the Giants. The All-Star Game came and went, and the counting that was big got bigger. Each of a 10-game post-break homestand drew between 58,613 and 70,493; six lured more than 60,000. On August 7-8 the Dodgers vaunted 70,283 and 70,372. Another two games that week against the Braves added 130,200. "Those games," Phillies skipper Danny Ozark once malapropped, "were beyond my apprehension."[49] At Mile High, series after series tested baseball's comprehension.

Four regulars at new or different positions gave the 1994 Rockies a partial if not extreme makeover: Nelson Liriano, second base; Mike Kingery, usually center field; Walt Weiss, shortstop; Eric Young, left field. The club scored 4.9 runs per game and yielded 5.45, tied the White Sox for most triples with 39, finished 53-64, and improved from 37 to 6½ behind. Starter Marvin Freeman anchored pitching with a 10-2 record and a 2.80 earned-run average. Another starter, Greg Harris, was a bust: 3-12 and 6.65, respectively. David Nied was 9-7 and tossed two franchise-first landmark or footnote shutouts, depending on your view: on April 14, 5-0 against Philadelphia (seven innings, relieved) and June 21, 8-0 against Houston (complete game).[50] Bichette led in runs batted in (95), hits (147), and consecutive games hit safely in (16), adding 27 homers. Galarraga broke his hand, but led in average (.319) and homers (31), adding 85 RBI. Projected over a full year, he and Bichette would have collected 43 and 37 homers, respectively. Reliever Bruce Ruffin had 16 saves.

In 1994, the 1991 top National League Rookie became MVP: Houston's Jeff Bagwell. The Dodgers' bumper crop reaped a third straight Rookie of the Year: outfielder Raul Mondesi. Atlanta's Greg Maddux snared a third straight Cy Young Award season. Colorado beat the Cardinals, Expos, and Mets and tied the Astros, Cubs, Padres, and Reds in its season series, losing to five other clubs. Each statistic rivaled throwing darts in the fog, though few knew so then. On August 11, the then-third-place Rockies lost their final Mile Highfest, 13-0, to

Atlanta, before 65,054, their record 53-64 and home attendance 3,281,511, a nonpareil 57,570 average. They were on pace to lure more than *4.6 million* spectators, more than any park had, or with smaller sites today, ever will—except that next day the season ended with a strike, actually a players lockout, which began August 12, lasted 234 days, canceled a World Series in 1994 for the first time since 1904, ended in late April 1995, and capsized each year's records.

In one sense, the season ending so abruptly meant that the Rockies never got to properly honor Mile High Stadium, said Jerry McMorris, the man whom upon his death in 2012 at 71 the *Denver Post* called "the savior of Major League Baseball in Colorado." In another sense, Mountain zoners salute Mile High yearly, packing successor Coors Field, the former site of an 1876 railroad depot, intended to seat 43,000 until Mile High's 1993-94 gate bonanza tossed that number off a peak. "We saw all those big crowds," McMorris said of what would have been some *nine million* paid admissions in two years sans lockout, "and we figured we'd better add some seats." Coors duplicated "The Rockpile"— 2,300 game-day bleachers seats — $1 for kids and seniors; $4, all else; everyone, bring a glove and binoculars. "We could sell them in advance," said an official. "But the spur-of-the-moment fans matter. So we sell 'em hours before the game, and you should see the jostling." The Rockpile made Coors capacity 50,200, becoming the first Mile High likeness.

Another was hitting. Like Mile High, Coors' alleys were deep, except that the ball "carries about 10 percent higher than the same ball high at sea level," Baylor said. Sharp angles turned gappers into triples. "That means we have to play deep," said right fielder Larry Walker, "which means hits fall in front of you." An eight-foot outfield fence trimmed a pitcher's Bellevue. Foul turf was baseball's smallest. Broadcaster Vin Scully told how offense was king by saying, memorably: "You don't need an official scorer at Coors Field, just a certified public accountant." A final parallel was a fondness for regional radio matched only by the Red Sox, Reds, and Braves and arguably topped only by the Cardinals. Colorado's website printed a "How to listen to Colorado Rockies radio and stream games live online"[51] in addition to hearing the old-fashioned way by plug-in or transistor.

In 1998, Denver hosted the All-Star Game: AL winning, 13-8. Mark McGwire went 510 feet in batting practice. A year later Walker became the first NLer to win a batting, slugging, and on-base percentage Triple Crown since Stan Musial in 1948. Meanwhile, the same task faces the Rockies as when Eric Young first went deep: As fine as hitting is, pitching might be finer. Not beautiful, to millions Mile High Stadium became beloved, which is even better, for being "Our House," sang Crosby, Stills, Nash, and Young.[52] Much of the region grieved its post-1994 baseball death as Brooklyn had Ebbets Field after the Dodgers' Westward-Ho. Before closing, the horseshoe housed a Billy Graham Crusade, the soccer Rapids, and such concerts as The Jacksons, Van Halen, and Bruce Springsteen. The Broncos played their final game in 2000, moving to Invesco (since 2011, Sports Authority) Field at Mile High next door.

In 2002, Denver tore the old joint down, having "paved paradise," as Joni Mitchell sang. A brick home plate recalled its location where, as she would rue, Coors Field "put up a parking lot."[53] The late baseball Commissioner A. Bartlett Giamatti often recalled entering Fenway Park for the first time at 10 in 1948. Leaving a tunnel, he saw "emerald grass and bases whiter than I'd ever seen. As I grew up, I knew that as a building it was on the level of Mount Olympus, the Pyramids at Giza, the nation's Capitol, the czar's Winter Palace, and the Louvre"—except, "of course, that [it] is better than all those inconsequential places."[54] For so many in the Rocky Mountain zone, Mile High Stadium still is.

SOURCES

In addition to the sources cited in the Notes, most especially the Society for American Baseball Research, the author also consulted Baseball-Reference.com and Retrosheet.org websites box scores, player, season, and team pages, batting and pitching logs, and other material relevant to this history. FanGraphs.com provided statistical information.

Books

Armour, Mark, ed. *The Great Eight: The 1975 Cincinnati Reds* (Lincoln: University of Nebraska Press, 2014).

Johnson, Boris. *The Churchill Factor: How One Man Made History* (New York: Riverhead Books, 2014).

Lowry, Philip L. *Green Cathedrals: The Ultimate Celebration of Major and Negro League Ballparks* (New York: Walker and Company, 2006).

Smith, Curt. *A Talk in the Park: Nine Decades of Baseball Tales from the Broadcast Booth* (Washington, D.C.: Potomac Books, 2011).

___. *Storied Stadiums: Baseball's History of Its Ballparks* (New York: Carroll & Graf, 2001).

___. *Voices of The Game: The Acclaimed History of Baseball Radio and Television*

Broadcasting (New York: Simon and Schuster, 1992).

___. *Voices of Summer: Ranking Baseball's 101 All-Time Best Announcers* (New York: Carroll & Graf, 2005).

Magazines

"The Great American Game," *Sports Illustrated*, April 12, 1956.

NOTES

1   "Maud Muller," written in 1856 by the American Quaker poet and abolitionist John Greenleaf Whittier (1807-92).

2   Six and eight states lie wholly or partly, respectively, in the Mountain State Zone. "Time Zones & Area Codes of the U.S. and Canada."

3   Mark Armour, "Bob Howsam," Society for American Baseball Research. Originally appearing in *Drama and Pride in the Gateway City: The 1964 St. Louis Cardinals,* edited by John Harry Stahl and Bill Nowlin.

4   National Baseball Hall of Fame and Museum, Giamatti Research Center, December 22, 2017.

5   Armour, "Bob Howsam."

6   Miller Presidential Center, Charlottesville, Virginia.

7   Armour, "Bob Howsam."

8   Jeff Kingery interview with author, July 28, 2003.

9   Armour, "Bob Howsam."

10   Mark S. Foster, *The Denver Bears: From Sandlots to Sellouts* (Boulder, Colorado.: Pruett Pub., 1983).

11   Matthew Silverman and Ken Samelson, *The Miracle Has Landed: The Amazin' Story of How the 1969 Mets Shocked the World* (Hanover, Massachusetts: Maple Street Press, 2009), 321.

12   National Football League Properties, *75 Seasons: The Complete Story of the National Football League, 1920-1995,* (Atlanta: Turner Pub., 1994), 194.

13   Chuck Thompson interview with author, May 15, 1987.

14   Kingery interview.

15   Ibid.

16   Irv Moss, "Jim Tolle, Mile High Stadium Stands Engineer," *Denver Post,* August 16, 2010.

17   Tom Verducci, "Analysis: Looking at National League Expansion," *Newsday,* June 10, 1991.

18   Irv Moss, "Jacobs Helped Find Way to Big Leagues," *Denver Post,* July 26, 2010.

19   Ibid.

20   Steve Berkowitz, "Denver Renews Expansion Bid," *Los Angeles Times,* February 22, 1991.

21   Moss, "Jacobs Helped Find Way to Big Leagues."

22   Irv Moss, "Linda Alvarado Satisfies Appetite for Baseball with Ties to Rockies," *Denver Post.* April 8, 2016.

23   Berkowitz.

24   Moss, "Jacobs Helped Find Way to Big Leagues."

25   Ibid.

26   Berkowitz.

27   Gene Wojciechowski, "Rockies' Born of Monus' Work, but He Never saw his Babies Grow Up." ESPN.com, October 23, 2007.

28   *Official Major League Baseball Fact Book 2000I Edition* (St. Louis: The Sporting News, 2001), 427.

29   *Public Papers of the Presidents of the United States: George Bush,* December 16, 1992, (Washington, D.C., Office of the Federal Register, National Archives and Records Administration), 2195.

30   Michael McKinley, *Etched In Ice: A Tribute to Hockey's Defining Moments* (Vancouver: Greystone Books, 1998), 62-66.

31   "Rockies on Radio and Television," *1993 Colorado Rockies Media Guide, Television,* 149.

32   Charlie Jones interview with author, October 14, 2002.

33   "Rockies on Radio and Television," *1993 Colorado Rockies Media Guide, Radio,* 149.

34   Kingery interview.

35   Jones interview.

36   *Official Major League Baseball Fact Book 2001 Edition,* 427.

37   Jones interview.

38   Donald Hall, from his extended poem "Baseball."

39   Jones interview.

40   *Official Major League Baseball Fact Book 2001 Edition,* 427.

41   Each statistic in this paragraph derived from Baseball-Reference.com.

42   Milo Hamilton interview with author in *A Discussion of America's Pastime* at the George H.W. Bush Presidential Library and Museum at Texas A&M University, October 28, 2011.

43   Unless otherwise indicated, baseball statistics in this and following paragraphs derived, as "Sources" notes, from Baseball-Reference.com and Retrosheet.org.

44   *Public Papers of the Presidents of the United States: George Bush,* 2195.

45   *Official Major League Baseball Fact Book 2001 Edition,* 424.

46   Kingery interview.

47   Jones interview.

48   Curt Smith, *Mercy! A Celebration of Fenway Park's Centennial Told Through Red Sox Radio and TV* (Washington, D.C.: Potomac Books, 2012), 57.

49   Bill Conlin, "Danny Ozark: In His Own Words," *Philadelphia Daily News.* May 8, 2009.

50   *Official Major League Baseball Fact Book, 2001 Edition,* 427.

51   "How to listen to Colorado Rockies radio and stream games live online," gotknowhow.com/articles/listen-to-colorado-rockies-radio.

52   "Our House," written, recorded, and released in 1970 on Crosby, Stills, Nash, and Young's album *Déjà vu.*

53   Excerpted from "Big Yellow Taxi," written, recorded, and released in 1970 by Joni Mitchell on her album *Ladies of the Canyon.*

54   Bruce Fellman, "Searching for a Whole, New Ballgame." *SRI* (Southern Rhode Island) *Newspapers,* May 4, 2017: 1.

COORS FIELD

BY THOMAS J. BROWN JR.

COORS FIELD OPENED FOR BASE-
ball on April 26, 1995. The Colorado Rockies had joined the National League two years earlier. They played their first two seasons in Mile High Stadium while Coors was being built.

When the National League got the OK in 1985 to expand by two teams, several cities, including Buffalo, Denver, Miami, Orlando, Tampa, and Washington, expressed interest in getting a franchise. One of the stipulations for being considered was having plans to build a ballpark. Denver and the state of Colorado showed that they were serious by forming the Denver Metropolitan Major League Baseball Stadium District in 1989.[1]

Voters in the six counties that made up metropolitan Denver approved a 0.01 percent sales tax for funding the new ballpark in 1990. This would eventually provide $168 million, or 78 percent of the cost of the ballpark. The remaining $47 million, or 22 percent, would come from the Rockies owners.[2] In June of 1991, franchises were awarded to Denver and Miami.

Construction of Coors Field began on October 16, 1992. While fans waited for the new ballpark to be completed, the Rockies played at Mile High Stadium. Fans were so excited about the arrival of baseball in the mile-high city that they played to packed houses most of the first season. The original plans for Coors Field called for a seating capacity of 43,000. But after 4,483,350 people poured through the Mile High turnstiles in the first season, the club announced in October 1993 that the Coors seating capacity would be increased to 50,000.[3]

When Coors Field was being built, it was the first baseball-only ballpark built for a National League team since Dodger Stadium was completed in 1962.[4] It was also the National League's first new ballpark since Montreal's Stade Olympique opened in 1977 upon the completion of the 1976 Olympics there.

Coors Field was designed by HOK Sports, later known as Populous. The company had sparked a re-surgence in ballpark design with the construction of Oriole Park at Camden Yards, which opened in 1992. Its design for Camden Yards incorporated the B&O warehouse building beyond the outfield and ended the generic "concrete doughnut" trend that had dominated baseball in the 1970s and 1980s.[5]

The design of the Coors Field recalls the same images evoked at Oriole Park. It is an industrial-strength steel and red-brick structure that incorporates an old brick building to enhance the overall atmosphere. The design provides a dramatic view of the Rockies in the distance, much as Camden Yards showcases the skyline waterfront of Baltimore.

HOK Sports wanted spectators to feel as if they were watching a game in one of the ballparks built in the 1920s and '30s. Hand-laid brick was used for the outer façade. A clock tower was built above the ballpark's main entrance. Adding to this "retro" feel are the asymmetrical dimensions of the outfield. These features along with the ballpark's location near the Union Pacific railroad tracks give it the feel of a 1920s ballpark. But once fans entered Coors Field, they could enjoy all the modern amenities and conveniences they were accustomed to.

Fans meet up below the clock tower. When they enter the ballpark, they notice that the ballpark sits below street level. This was done to help it blend in with the features of the surrounding neighborhood. Although most of the seats are green, a band of purple seats along the 20th row of the upper deck makes note of the one-mile location above sea level.

During the construction of Coors Field, crews found bones on the site. They were similar in size to the ribs of plant-eating dinosaurs like Triceratops, a dinosaur that was common in Colorado in the Cretaceous period, which ended 66 million years ago. Coloradans reveled in the find. A year later, when the Rockies revealed their mascot, it was a fuzzy Triceratops named Dinger.[6]

One of the distinctive features of Coors Field is the Rockpile. The name is meant to remind visitors of the Rocky Mountains, which are visible in the distance. The 2,300-seat section is located in deep center field, in the upper deck, about as far from home plate as you can get inside the ballpark. (Mile High Stadium also had a Rockpile.) At first Rockpile seats were priced at $1, but that price was later available only to youngsters and seniors, everyone else pays $4.

Ballpark designers had speculated that Coors Field would see a lot of home runs. Located at 5,200 feet above sea level, it is the highest-elevation park in majors-league baseball. Designers knew that the low air density at such a high elevation could result in balls traveling farther than in other parks. To compensate, they place the outfield fences farther from home plate. The deepest part of the field is right-center, which is 424 feet from home plate.

The first game at Coors Field was played on April 26, 1995. It also turned out to be the first extra-inning game in the new ballpark. The Rockies played the New York Mets. Brett Butler of the Mets was the first batter. Bill Swift was the Rockies pitcher. Butler hit Swift's first pitch for a single to right field for the first hit at Coors Field.

Naturally, the game was filled with other "firsts." The Mets' Rico Brogna hit the first home run at the ballpark when he powered a line drive over the fence against Swift in the fourth inning. The Mets' Todd Hundley hit the first grand slam two innings later. The Rockies' Dante Bichette eventually won the game, 11-9, with a three-run walk-off homer in the bottom of the 14th inning. These home runs were harbingers of the future.

Although the game took 4 hours and 49 minutes to complete, it was not the longest game at Coors Field. But there were other firsts that night. The first run scored (Walt Weiss in the first inning), the first batter to be hit by a pitch (Roberto Mejia in the sixth inning), the first strikeout (Swift striking out David Segui in the second inning), and more.

Other firsts occurred in rapid succession during the club's first month at Coors Field. The following night Eric Young had the first stolen base and Andres Galarraga hit the first triple. By the end of the inaugural season, most of the "firsts" had been accomplished. One had to wait until the ballpark's second season: On September 17, 1996, Hideo Nomo pitched the first no-hitter at Coors Field as the Dodgers beat the Rockies, 9-0. (On May 11 that season the Rockies were also the victims of the first Florida Marlins no-hitter when Al Leiter beat them 11-0.)

The last notable "first" at Coors came on April 29, 2007, when Troy Tulowitzki made the first unassisted triple play there. Tulowitzki caught a Chipper Jones line drive for the first out, then tagged Kelly Johnson out at second and caught Edgar Renteria near second after he had run on the pitch and could not get back to first in time.

In 1993 the Rockies named Don Baylor as the inaugural manager of the expansion team. He turned out to be a good choice; he led the Rockies to the postseason in just three years, faster than any previous expansion club. Baylor's teams had records of 67-95 in 1993 and 53-64 in 1994 before the Rockies turned things around in Coors Field's inaugural year. Their 77-67 record made them the National League wild-card team. It also earned Baylor Manager-of-the-Year honors.

The Rockies played the Atlanta Braves in the National League Division Series. In Game One, on October 3, before a crowd of 50,040, the Rockies led 3-1 after four innings, but eventually lost, 5-4, on Chipper Jones's ninth-inning solo home run.

Coors Field was packed the following night as the Rockies tried to even the series. After the Braves took a 1-0 lead in the first, the Rockies tied the game in the sixth when Larry Walker hit a three-run home run off starter Tom Glavine. But once again the Braves won in the ninth inning when they scored four runs off the Rockies bullpen to win, 7-4.

The Rockies won the third game but eventually lost the series, three games to one. It was the last time Coors Field hosted a postseason game until 2007, when the Rockies not won the NL pennant and brought the World Series to Coors Field.

In their march to the World Series the Rockies first swept the Philadelphia Phillies in three games in the Division Series. Coors Field hosted the clinching third game. Jeff Baker singled in the winning run in the bottom of the eighth inning and Manny Corpas earned his third save in as many games to help the Rockies move on to the Championship Series. They swept that series, too, against the Arizona Diamondbacks. Coors Field hosted the final two games. In Game Three, a packed ballpark watched the Rockies win 4-1. A three-run homer by Yorvit Torrealba in the sixth inning was the difference.

Coors Field was also filled to capacity the following night to watch the Rockies clinch the National League championship. A six-run fourth inning allowed the home team to hold off the Diamondbacks, who came close with three runs in the top of the eighth inning. The final score was 6-4. The Rockies were heading to the World Series for the first time in their short history.

Although the Rockies swept through the National League playoffs, they were not so fortunate in the World Series. When Coors Field hosted its first World Series game, on October 27, 2007, the Boston Red Sox had already taken a commanding 2-games-to-none lead in the Series. The temperature when the game started was a brisk 45 degrees. Almost 50,000 fans showed up hoping to see the Rockies rebound. But the Red Sox won, dominating the hometown team, 10-5.

With their backs to the wall, the Rockies took the field the following night with their hopes clinging to a thread. Although it was late October, temperatures at game time were a balmy 68 degrees and fans were not quite as bundled up as the night before. The Red Sox jumped out to a 3-0 lead before the Rockies were able to score a run in the bottom of the seventh inning.

After the Red Sox scored another run in the top of the eighth, the Rockies made one final attempt at a comeback. Garrett Atkins' two-run homer brought the Rockies to within one run. The hometown crowd finally had something to cheer about. With everyone on their feet and hoping for a miracle, Boston's Jonathon Papelbon shut down the Rockies in the ninth for his fourth save in as many games. The Red Sox had swept the Rockies and 50,041 fans quietly left Coors Field with their mile-high dreams vaporized into Denver's thin air.

After it opened, Coors Field quickly earned a reputation as a hitter-friendly ballpark. As early as the first season, people were talking about the number of home runs. After watching homer after homer in the Dodgers' first visit in 1995, broadcaster Vin Scully commented that any hitting record set by a Colorado player should automatically be accompanied by an asterisk.[7]

Early on, Coors Field earned the nickname "Coors Canaveral," a reference to the US astronauts' launching site.[8] This reputation as a launching pad for home runs was firmly planted in the public's mind in 1999 when the Rockies and their opponents hit a major-league-record 303 home runs.

The California Angels (then the Lost Angeles Angels) held the previous record, 248, set in 1961, their first year of existence, in their original home, Wrigley Field in Los Angeles.

In Coors Field's first year, the home run total fell just seven short of that mark, even though the team lost nine games from the home schedule due to the players strike, which forced a late start to the 1995 season. The next season, 1996, when the Rockies played a full schedule at the ballpark, the record fell when 271 home runs were hit at Coors Field. That mark was broken with 1999's total of 303, the record that still stood as of 2017.

No matter what index is used, Coors Field is recognized as a hitter's ballpark. Alan Nathan, a physicist, showed that a baseball would travel 5 percent farther at Coors Field than Fenway Park. Based on his analysis, baseballs that would travel 380 feet at Fenway Park would travel 400 feet at Coors Field.[9]

After several years of extraordinary home-run production, the Rockies installed a humidor to help bring production back to Earth. The idea came from Rockies employee Tony Cowell, who had observed that his leather boots dried faster at a high altitude and figured that baseballs would do the same. Cowell figured that the baseballs would not travel as far if they were slightly moist.

Cowell thought that if the baseballs were kept in a humidor, they would lose some of their bounce. He tried an experiment of sorts to see if he was correct, dropping baseballs off a third-deck ramp down to the concrete. "The results were pretty striking," Cowell said.[10]

With the permission of Major League Baseball,[11] the Rockies installed an $18,000 humidor, a giant version of the container that keeps cigars moist. It quickly made a difference when home-run production fell from 268 in 2001, the most in the major leagues, to 185 in 2007, ranking 10th. The Elias Sports Bureau also found that runs scored per game were down as well, from 13.4 in 2001 to 10.6 in 2007.[12]

The humidor at Coors Field keeps balls from drying out and shrinking. It is set at 40 percent humidity to compensate for Denver's low humidity. Rawlings, the manufacturer of baseballs, suggests humidity of about 50 percent and a 70-degree temperature.[13]

The longest measured home run at Coors was hit by Hall of Famer Mike Piazza on September 26, 1997, when he was with the Dodgers. Piazza's home run was measured at 496 feet. His home run beat out the 494-foot blast by Larry Walker of the Rockies a month earlier. Giancarlo Stanton tied Walker's mark when he hit one out of the ballpark on August 17, 2012.[14]

But these are just the ones that have been measured since they were hit during a game. Walt Weiss claimed he "saw Mark McGwire [hit one] off the facing of the Rock Pile. As we sit here (in the dugout) and look it doesn't seem possible, but I was there and I saw it."[15] McGwire also hit a ball that went 510 feet during the first round of the 1998 Home Run Derby. It was the longest of the 53 home runs hit in that round.[16]

In recent years, fewer home runs have been hit at Coors Field but it has remained the most hitter-friendly ballpark in the major leagues by a wide margin. From 2012 to 2015 the Rockies led the league in runs scored in home games.[17]

Two of the highest-scoring games in modern baseball history were played at Coors Field. On May 19, 1999, the Rockies and Cincinnati Reds engaged in a 36-run slugfest. Cincinnati led 6-4 after the first inning. The Rockies tied the game in the second, but the Reds went on a scoring spree starting in the fourth inning. Cincinnati scored 17 runs from the fourth to the seventh inning. The Reds' Sean Casey finished the game by going 4-for-4 with three walks while scoring five runs while his teammate Jeff Hammonds cleared the fences three times. The Rockies' 12 runs were enough to win most games, but not this one; Cincinnati got 24.

Nine years later, the Rockies got into another hitting contest and come out on top. On July 4, 2008, the Rockies and Florida Marlins celebrated Independence Day with plenty of fireworks. The two teams combined for 43 hits and 35 runs. Colorado's first four batters went a combined 16-for-22 with five homers and 13 runs. The Rockies entered the ninth inning trailing 17-16 but scored two runs on four singles in the ninth for a walk-off win.[18]

Over the years, many baseball players have knocked the ball out of Coors Field. The Rockies player with the most home runs there is Todd Helton. During his tenure with the Rockies, Helton hit 227 home runs at the ballpark. Barry Bonds hit 26 home runs at Coors Field and holds the record for the most home runs by an opposing player.[19]

Naturally, the accomplishments of pitchers at Coors Field tend to be overlooked. As of 2017, there has been just one no-hitter there, by Nomo in 1996. Nomo shut down the home team before 50,099 spectators, the largest crowd to watch a no-hitter in an existing ballpark as of 2017.[20]

The longest game in Coors Field history was not a high-scoring game. The Rockies beat the Giants, 4-3, on July 4, 2010. By the time the home team won in the bottom of the 15th inning, 5 hours and 24 minutes had passed. Jason Hammel started for the Rockies while Matt Cain took the mound for the Giants. Both pitchers threw seven strong innings.

The Rockies took the lead after Dexter Fowler tripled in the third inning and scored on Jonathan Herrera's sacrifice fly. The Giants' Travis Ishikawa singled home Pablo Sandoval to tie the game in the top of the eighth. From that point on both teams were scoreless for the next seven innings. Over those seven innings the Rockies left 15 runners on base. They left the bases loaded in the 10th, 13th, and 14th innings. Fowler hit his second triple of the night as he led off the 15th inning. Todd Helton then hit a fly ball deep down the left-field line and Fowler scored to end the game.[21]

It did not take long after the ballpark opened for a player to hit for the cycle. John Mabry of the Cardinals accomplished this feat on May 18, 1996. Mabry singled in the second inning, doubled the fourth, tripled and scored in the Cardinals' four-run fifth, and in the seventh, he launched the ball over the center-field wall for a home run to become just the 11th major leaguer to hit for a natural cycle (single, double, triple and homer in that order). Mabry's achievement came in a losing effort; the Rockies won, 10-7.

Two years after it opened, Coors Field hosted the All-Star Game on July 7, 1998. After the US Air Force was honored in pregame celebrities, the game literally took off. The American League beat the National League, 13-8, in a game that saw both teams collect 31 hits. Three home runs were hit during the game, including a solo shot by Roberto Alomar that cemented the American League's lead and earned Alomar MVP honors.

Coors Field's location has allowed it to host some interesting events. The coldest baseball game since baseball began recording such things in 1991 took place on April 23, 2013. The day started ominously for a baseball game. Grounds crews began clearing several inches of snow from the playing surface at 6 A.M. Although the field was clear when the game started, some parts of the ballpark remained closed, including the Rock Pile section. Workers made sure the batters eye background in center field was green by hosing off the snow on the stand of evergreen trees behind the wall.

The temperature at game time was 23 degrees. Although most players bundled up, Atlanta pitcher

Mike Minor chose to wear short sleeves. He told reporters after the game that he felt restricted with long sleeves. But that doesn't mean that he didn't notice the temperature. He said: "The biggest thing was grip, just being cold and dry. I pretty much just battled through it." At one point, Minor said, he got so cold that he had a trainer rub his back, arms, and thighs with a heating ointment.[22]

The Braves won, 4-3. Some 19,124 fans showed up for the game but there is no record of how many stayed for the entire 2 hours and 37 minutes that it took to finish it.

Although Coors Field is the most hitter-friendly ballpark in the major leagues, there have been a few moments when the pitchers took command of the game. On July 9, 2005, in its 10th year, the ballpark finally had its first 1-0 game. Before that the ballpark had witnessed three 2-0 games. The 1-0 game (won by the Rockies) came in Coors Field's 847th regular-season game, the most games played at any major-league ballpark before its first 1-0 game.[23]

Jason Jennings pitched seven scoreless innings before getting a little help from his bullpen. Brian Fuentes, the Rockies closer, escaped a bases-loaded jam in the ninth to earn a save. Colorado got its run in the sixth when Aaron Miles beat out a bunt and scored on a double by Luis Gonzalez.

When he was asked about the win after the game, Rockies manager Clint Hurdle laughed and reminded reporters that his pitching staff had allowed 12 runs the night before. "What a difference 22 hours makes," Hurdle said.[24]

In subsequent years, there were eight more 1-0 games at Coors Field. The last time (as of the end of the 2017 season) that fans witnessed one was on June 12, 2010. On that day, Jason Hammel pitched eight scoreless innings and scored the lone run of the game in the sixth inning. He walked to lead off the inning, went to third base on a single by Todd Helton, and scored on a sacrifice fly by Carlos Gonzalez. After the game, Hammel joked with reporters, "I've got to do everything here."[25]

Although low-hitting games are rare at Coors Field, the Rockies have been successful in such contests. They are 6-3 in the nine 1-0 games at the ballpark.

Another interesting game at Coors Field took place on August 22, 2000, against Atlanta. With the game tied, 3-3, in the 11th inning, John Wasdin came into the game as the Rockies' seventh pitcher. He was the last man out of the bullpen but manager Buddy Bell figured that Wasdin would be good for a few innings since he had not pitched for a few days. Wasdin confounded Bell's strategy by hitting hit the first batter he faced and was ejected.[26]

Bell was forced to bring in a starting pitcher, Brian Bohanon, who retired the Braves, throwing 10 pitches. Bohanon had thrown 99 pitches the night before and was spent. After the Rockies failed to score in their half of the inning, Bell turned to backup catcher Brent Mayne. "Can you pitch?" Bell asked. "Yeah, I can pitch," Mayne replied.[27]

Mayne retired the first two batters, Tom Glavine on a grounder and Weiss on a fly ball. But Rafael Furcal singled and went to second on a wild pitch as Mayne worried that "I didn't want to balk. I was thinking what is the balk (rule)? Can I go into the glove and take the ball out of my glove? That was probably the most nerve-wracking thing."[28] But Mayne recovered and got Chipper Jones to ground out.

The Rockies hit back-to-back singles in the bottom of the 12th inning. Suddenly it was Mayne's turn to bat but he had an injured wrist. Bell pinch-hit Adam Melhuse, who singled in the winning run. Mayne was credited with the win, the first time a catcher was credited with a win at Coors Field.[29]

The ballpark has witnessed several other notable achievements. On August 7, 2016, Ichiro Suzuki, playing for the Marlins, got his 3,000th major-league hit, a triple in the seventh inning to become the 30th player to reach that milestone. As Suzuki arrived at third, third-base coach Lorenzo Bundy hugged him and the Marlins streamed out of the dugout to congratulate him. Always modest, he waved his helmet to acknowledge the cheers at Coors Field.

Rockies pitcher Chris Rusin said after the game that he was fine with being a part of history.

"Congratulations to him. All I ask for is a signed bat in return. It's crazy to be a part of."[30]

At 42 years and 290 days, Suzuki was the second oldest player by three days over Rickey Henderson to reach the milestone. Only Cap Anson, who was 45 when he got his 3,000th hit in 1897, was older.

As of 2018 only one Rockies player has had his number retired, Todd Helton. Helton played for the Rockies from 1997 to 2013 and his number 17 was retired on August 17, 2014. Helton was the Rockies' first-round pick in the 1995 first-year player draft. He debuted with the Rockies on August 2, 1997, and played the next 17 years in a Rockies uniform.

Rockies owner Dick Montfort explained the decision to hang Helton's number from Coors Field's rafters: "Seventeen years is the first thing. No one else has been here that long and for his whole career. He was one of our earliest top draft picks. He holds a lot of team records. With his play and his leadership, it was just natural [to retire his number]."[31]

Coors Field hosted its first concert on July 3, 2015. More than 42,000 people packed the ballpark to hear the Zac Brown Band. Seats and a dance floor were placed on the field. A large stage was placed against the center-field wall to allow the sound from the band to echo throughout the ballpark.

"This is a very, very special night to be the first band to play in this stadium. Thank you. Thank you. Thank you," said Brown as he returned to the stage for an encore.[32] The crowd cheered and Brown didn't even bother to sing the chorus to his final song, "Chicken Fried." Instead he just watched from the stage as thousands roared out the words in unison. The band returned to Coors Field on July 29, 2017, for another concert.

Coors Field hosted several hockey games in 2016. The first was played on February 20. A hockey rink was set up to allow the University of Denver to play Colorado College. The two teams had played each other for 66 years but this was the first time that they played in a ballpark.[33]

Denver University coach Jim Montgomery lined up for television interviews in front of a large photo of a Larry Walker, a former hockey player. "I want to stand by Larry Walker. He's Canadian. He's the pride of Canadian baseball," Montgomery said.[34] A crowd of more than 35,000 watched Denver University win 4-1 in balmy 50-degree weather.

A week later, the National Hockey League held its annual Winter Classic hockey game at the ballpark. The Colorado Avalanche lost to the Detroit Red Wings, 5-3.

Coors Field is sure to continue as a focal point for the Denver sports fans in years to come. The ballpark is located in the "LoDo" area of downtown Denver. This part of town is Denver's answer to New York's Soho. It is a rejuvenated area containing art galleries, small shops, and artists' lofts.[35] With so much excitement surrounding it, Coors Field brings even more excitement as the home team plays for the opportunity to bring another World Series to the city.

SOURCES

In addition to the sources cited in the Notes, the author also utilized the Baseball-Reference.com and Retrosheet.org websites for box scores, player, team, and season pages, pitching and batting game logs, and other material pertinent to this biography. FanGraphs.com provided some statistical information.

NOTES

1   "Coors Field," BallparksofBaseball.com, accessed August, 22, 2017.

2   Paul Munsey, "Coors Field," Ballparks.com, June 2007.

3   Ibid.

4   Ibid.

5   Allison Mast and Kevin D. Murphy, "The Rebirth of the Ballpark Could Be Baseball's Saving Grace," BaseballInsider.com, April 9, 2017.

6   James Hagadorn, "Fossils Underfoot," *Front Porch* (Northeast Denver), June 1, 2014.

7   Mike Downey, "Nursing a Denver Hangover," *Los Angeles Times*, May 10, 1995.

8   Patrick Saunders, "Tony Cowell's Humidor Brought Rockies Baseball at Coors Field Back Down to Earth," *Denver Post*, May 13, 2017.

9   Alan Nathan, "Baseball at High Altitude," *Physics of Baseball*, accessed August 24, 2017.

10 Saunders, "Tony Cowell's humidor."

11 Hal Bodley, "Baseball Gives Rockies' Humidor Its OK," *USA Today*, June 14, 2002. MLB said, "We're satisfied with what

(Cowell) saw and feel the matter in which the balls are stored is consistent with what would probably be recommended if we were to make such a recommendation."

12   Saunders, "Tony Cowell's Humidor."

13   Ibid.

14   "Coors Field Home Runs: Who Hit the Longest, and Who Hit the Most," Denver.CBSLocal.com, June 10, 2015.

15   Ibid.

16   Jayson Stark, "25 Greatest Home Run Derby Moments," ESPN.com, July 12, 2010.

17   "How Do Ballpark Factors Affect Batters for MLB DFS?," DFS Strategy.com, March 24, 2016.

18   Ibid.

19   "Coors Field Home Runs."

20   Graham Night, "No Hitters Thrown by Ballpark," Baseball Pilgrimages.com, accessed September 4, 2017.

21   Ryan Freemyer, "A Look at the 3 Longest Games the Colorado Rockies Have Ever Played," Purplerow.com, September 16, 2015.

22   Ibid.

23   "Rockies' 1-0 Victory a First in 11-Year History of Ballpark," ESPN.com, July 10, 2005.

24   Ibid.

25   "Rockies' Hammel Tosses 8 Shutout Innings, Scores Game's Only Run," ESPN.com, July 13, 2010.

26   Grant Brisbee, "The Time a Catcher Pitched at Coors Field and Won," SB Nation.com, August 21, 2015.

27   Ibid.

28   Ibid.

29   Ibid.

30   "Rusin Gives Up Ichiro's 3,000th Hit; Rockies Lose to Marlins," USA Today.com, August 7, 2016.

31   Thomas Harding, "Helton Calls No. 17 Jersey Retirement 'Very Special,'" MLB.com, February 6, 2014.

32   Evan Semón, "Zac Brown Band Plays the First Major Concert at Coors Field," *Denver Post*, July 4, 2015.

33   Nick Groke, "Big Hockey Crowd at Coors Field Sees Denver Play Like Kids vs Colorado College," *Denver Post*, February 20, 2015.

34   Ibid.

35   Herbert Muschamp, "A Wonder World in the Mile High City," *New York Times*, May 7, 1995.

A ROCKY MOUNTAIN HIGH ON OPENING DAY

APRIL 9, 1993: COLORADO ROCKIES 11, MONTREAL EXPOS 4, AT MILE HIGH STADIUM

BY JOHN BAUER

AFTER DECADES OF WAITING, Denver would finally have a major-league Opening Day of its own. The expansion Colorado Rockies, along with the Florida Marlins, joined the National League for the 1993 season. Expectations for on-field success were appropriately tempered, but the excitement for big-league baseball was palpable. Five thousand spectators showed up at Mile High Stadium, the Rockies' temporary home while Coors Field was being built, for the team's workout on Thursday, April 8. That same day, 20,000 people lined the streets of downtown Denver for a parade. The club also announced season-ticket sales totaling 28,250 and advance purchases of 2.8 million tickets.[1] Further, the 80,227 who jammed Mile High Stadium comprised the largest home opener in baseball history, surpassing the crowd that greeted the Dodgers' arrival at the Los Angeles Coliseum in 1958.

The excitement, however, was no assurance that everything would go smoothly. For one, the Rockies lost their first two games, at Shea Stadium against the New York Mets, scoring a single run in both games; to be fair, Colorado had faced Dwight Gooden and Bret Saberhagen, but the output was less than optimal. During Thursday's workout, the condition of the patchy turf became an issue. Manager Don Baylor gave his verdict: "Not real good."[2] He added, "To just be opening a baseball season in Denver and you have grass that's not even growing in certain spots, it's a little strange."[3] After the game, Rockies owner Jerry McMorris noted that the club offered to pay to resod parts of the field 10 days before the opener.[4] Nothing happened, and McMorris grumbled, "I'm not at all happy about it."[5]

The visiting Montreal Expos faced concerns about which players would actually take the field. Right fielder Larry Walker strained his lower right hamstring in the previous game in Cincinnati, and second baseman Delino DeShields became the latest player in the Expos organization to be felled by chicken pox.[6]

To face Montreal, Baylor called upon veteran right-hander and former Expo Bryn Smith. Possessing a fastball that barely registered at 80 mph and having started only one game the prior season, the 37-year-old Smith seemed an unlikely candidate to take the mound in the inaugural home game.[7] Baylor, however, wanted a veteran presence on the mound and Smith would deliver. The first two Expos batters, Mike Lansing and Moises Alou, grounded out to second baseman Eric Young. Marquis Grissom and Frank Bolick singled to place runners at the corners, but Young earned his third assist of the inning by collecting John Vander Wal's grounder for the final out.

Expos manager Felipe Alou had managed previously in Denver with the American Association's Bears and he was familiar with baseball at Mile High. His starting pitcher, Kent Bottenfield, was one of 16 players on Montreal's roster with fewer than two years of major-league service time, but he had pitched at Mile High Stadium in the minors.[8] That experience would mean nothing, however. Young led off the for the Rockies and worked the count full. He deposited Bottenfield's sixth pitch, a fastball, over the left-field fence, 380 feet away. Crediting the thin mountain air, Young said, "The altitude carried it. I was just hoping I had a double."[9]

Alex Cole walked on five pitches, and then swiped second and third with Dante Bichette at the plate. Cole said after the game, "We knew we still had to apply the pressure. If we started to sit back and relax, we're in trouble."[10] Cole's aggressiveness positioned him to score easily when Bichette singled to left-center field. Bichette applied the same tactics in stealing second base before Andres Galarraga's at-bat ended with a fly out to Moises Alou in short right field. But Charlie Hayes swatted Bottenfield's slider 390 feet into the left-field stands for a 4-0 Rockies lead. For Hayes, unlike Young, there was no doubt about the result. „When I hit it, I knew it was a home run," he said.[11] Jerald Clark doubled to left, but Joe Girardi grounded out and Freddie Benavides struck out to end Bottenfield's miserable inning.

Two Expos hitters reached in the top of the second—Tim Laker on an error by Benavides at shortstop and Bottenfield on an infield single—but Smith held Montreal scoreless. Smith led off the Rockies' second with a groundout to Bottenfield. Young walked on five pitches, then Cole's ball found a gap in the right side of the infield for a single. As Young raced toward third on the play, Alou's throw to third bounced away from Bolick for an error, allowing Young to race home. Bichette popped up and Galarraga flied out, but the Rockies led, 5-0.

Smith continued to control the Expos from the mound. Alou's double to start the third inning amounted to nothing when he tried to stretch it to a triple and was thrown out. Grissom grounded out and Bolick popped up. In the Expos' fourth, Laker reached first with two outs when he was struck by a pitch from Smith, but Archi Cianfrocco's grounder ended the inning. On the defensive side, Bolick was having a game to forget. In the third, Bolick committed errors on consecutive at-bats, first by making a bad throw from Girardi's ball and then booting Benavides's grounder, but the Rockies failed to capitalize. Young singled to open the Colorado fourth and Cole bunted. Fielding Cole's ball, Bolick threw wildly to put Rockies at second and third. Young scored on Bichette's fly, and Cole plated when Galarraga singled through the hole between Bolick and shortstop Wil Cordero. Hayes's double-play ball ended the inning with the Rockies now ahead, 7-0.[12] Felipe Alou made known his displeasure with Bolick's

three-error performance, stating tersely, "We're going to have to make some changes."[13]

In the Expos' fifth, Smith allowed one-out singles to Lansing and Alou, but Grissom's liner and Bolick's grounder ended the inning. The Rockies added to their advantage in the bottom half. Against Mike Gardiner, Clark singled over second base and Girardi doubled to deep right-center. With Clark at third, Benavides singled for an 8-0 lead. After Smith struck out on a foul bunt, Girardi scored on Young's single to center. Cole's line drive started an inning-ending double play, but the Rockies had stretched the lead to 9-0. That advantage held through a scoreless sixth inning.

Smith maintained his shutout by setting down the Expos in order in the top of the seventh. Baylor sent Daryl Boston to hit for Smith in the bottom of the inning, ended his pitcher's afternoon. Smith was clearly satisfied with his performance. He said, "This is the biggest win I've ever had, and there's been a lot of them."[14] Gardiner gave way to Bruce Walton, whom the Rockies abused for four hits and two runs. Boston lined a single to center field, and Young singled with a groundball through the left side of the infield. Cole lined out to Alou, and Dale Murphy came to the plate. Murphy had replaced Bichette in the sixth, and Rockies fans greeted the longtime Atlanta Brave with a standing ovation. An impressed Baylor said, "I thought it was one of the classiest moves I've seen in a long time."[15] Murphy repaid the gesture with a line-drive single that scored Boston. Galarraga followed with another single, scoring Young and extending the lead to 11-0.

After a scoreless eighth inning, Steve Reed took the mound in the ninth with the goal of preserving the Rockies shutout. He would not, however. Vander Wal delivered a shot to center field for a double, and Cordero followed with a single. Tim Spehr, who replaced from Laker behind the plate in the sixth, lofted a fly ball to Clark in left field that scored Vander Wal and broke the shutout. After pinch-hitter Darrin Fletcher lined out to Murphy, Reed walked Lou Frazier. Lansing, who would not have been playing but for DeShields's illness, launched Reed's pitch into the left-field stands for a three-run homer.[16] Although the Rockies still led, 11-4, some fans began booing. Bichette joked, „Isn't that something? They're spoiled already, huh?"[17] Reed retired Alou for the final out, but his performance was no joking matter. He said, "I came out for one inning and couldn't get the job done, so that's disappointing."[18]

While the ninth inning had not gone according to plan, the other eight innings could not have been scripted any better for the Rockies. After decades of waiting for a major-league team of their own, Rockies fans received a fantastic reward. While 1993 would witness many more losses than wins for the Rockies, Denver's first big-league Opening Day provided plenty of thrills. Murphy observed, "These people are hungry for baseball. When you play in front of people as excited as they were, that makes it fun."[19]

SOURCES

In addition to the articles cited in the Notes, the author also referred to baseball-reference.com.

NOTES

1 Tracy Ringolsby and Jack Etkin, "Rockies Report," *Rocky Mountain News* (Denver), April 10, 1993: 14R.

2 Irv Moss, "A Cut Below Expectations," *Denver Post*, April 9, 1993: 1D.

3 Ibid.

4 B.G. Brooks, "Reed Regrets Losing Shutout After Smith's Strong Effort," *Rocky Mountain News*, April 10, 1993: 15R.

5 Ibid.

6 Jeff Blair, "Montreal Expos," *The Sporting News*, April 19, 1993: 17.

7 Joseph Sanchez, "Smith Calls Victory Sweetest of Career," *Denver Post*, April 10, 1993: 1C.

8 David Fleming, "Expos Rookie Unfazed About Historic Start," *Rocky Mountain News*, April 9, 1993: 12R.

9 Woody Paige, "Homers Flying at Mile High," *Denver Post*, April 10, 1993: 3C.

10 Tracy Ringolsby, "Baseball, Victory Barge Into Denver," *Rocky Mountain News*, April 10, 1993: 3R.

11 Paige.

12 Hayes exited the game, having injured his hamstring coming out the batter's box. The incident was partly blamed on field conditions.

13 Blair.

14 Sanchez.

15 Brooks.

16 It was the first home run of Lansing's young major-league career.

17 Jim Armstrong, "Rockies Roar for 80,227," *Denver Post*, April 10, 1993: 1C.

18 Brooks.

19 Ringolsby.

THE OPENING OF COORS FIELD AND THE BIRTH OF THE BLAKE STREET BOMBERS

APRIL 26, 1995: COLORADO ROCKIES 11, NEW YORK METS 9 (14 INNINGS), AT COORS FIELD

BY ERIEL F. BARCENAS

FANS TEND TO EXPECT EXPANSION baseball teams to endure several years of subpar ball, but meanwhile enjoy a brand-new ballpark. Rockies fans had to wait two years while a new ballpark was being built. Finally, on April 26, 1995, public-address announcer Alan Roach said, "Welcome to Coors Field, home of the Colorado Rockies," and 47,228 fans, along with the ESPN Wednesday Night audience, saw the new ballpark open with a game to remember.

After the players strike was settled, Opening Day was delayed.[1] But at 5:38 P.M. on the 26th, the Rockies and the New York Mets got baseball underway at Coors Field, in an early moment foreshadowing the "chicks dig the long ball" era.[2]

On this cold, mid-30s evening, managers Don Baylor of the Rockies and Dallas Green of the Mets turned over lineup cards to a crew of replacement umpires.[3] Only Terry Bovey had experienced working in a major-league game (17 of them).[4] High-profile free-agent pitcher Bill Swift was the Rockies' starter. Things started quickly, as the Mets' speedy center fielder Brett Butler didn't give history a moment. He took a swing at the first pitch and beat out a close play from shortstop Walt Weiss for the first base hit at Coors Field. Two pitches later, Mets shortstop Jose Vizcaino hit into a 5-4-3 double play. Rico Brogna grounded out to end the inning.

Bobby Jones, the first visiting pitcher to experience Coors Field, quickly received an inkling of the experience. Weiss led off the bottom of the first with a single to right and the first home hit at the new park. Catcher Joe Girardi singled, Weiss going to third. Things were now set for the eminent free-agent right fielder of the Rockies. Larry Walker, eventually

identified with Ozzy Osbourne's "Crazy Train" as his walk-up song, and hereafter seen as the locomotive of the Rockies, doubled to left, scoring Weiss and sending Girardi to third. Original Rockie and fan favorite left-fielder Dante Bichette drove Girardi in with a fly ball to right field. Colorado had a 2-0 lead.

Colorado controlled the game throughout the first five innings, and Walker added another RBI when he doubled Girardi in from first base in the third. The Rockies entered the fourth inning with everything going their way, but Swift allowed a leadoff home run to first baseman Brogna. Swift himself led the fifth with a base on balls, and Weiss sacrificed him to second. Girardi doubled him in and scored himself on a single by first baseman Andres Galarraga. With Swift at 56 pitches entering the sixth and with a 5-1 Rockies lead, fans may have believed fate planned an easy victory.

The sixth inning saw the Mets shift that narrative quickly. The Mets loaded the bases on Swift, with singles by Brogna, left fielder David Segui, and right fielder Carl Everett. With two outs, switch-hitting catcher Todd Hundley, poised for a career peak year, stepped up, already 2-for-2. He made it 3-for-3 with a grand slam that tied the game, 5-5, and chased Swift after the inning. It was a game again; the Mets would not be relegated to history without a fight.

Once in the Rockies' hands, the game now began to oscillate. The Rockies loaded the bases in the bottom of the sixth after Jerry DiPoto hit Roberto Mejia with a pitch. Dallas Green let lefty hitter John Vander Wal be announced to bat for Swift, then summoned lefty Eric Gunderson. Baylor countered with righty Eric Young, Vander Wal never hitting. Young's sacrifice fly scored a run, but also led to a 9-6-5-2 double play. The Rockies had a 6-5 lead. The Mets countered in the top of the seventh, with Butler getting to third via a walk, a bunt, and a wild pitch, then scored on a double to center field by third baseman Bobby Bonilla off Mike Munoz. The resulting six-run tie would hold until the ninth inning.

In the top of the ninth, Brett Butler drew a walk from lefty Bruce Ruffin, Colorado's fifth pitcher of the game. Butler reached third on a sacrifice and a groundout, then scored on a single by Bonilla, a liner to short left.

In the bottom of the inning, Mets closer John Franco walked Weiss with one out. After Girardi struck out, Walker's third RBI double of the night sent the game into extra innings.

Hundley doubled to right field with one out in the Mets' 10th and Butler again walked, but Ruffin's strikeout of Vizcaino ended the threat. In the 11th, after being called out on strikes, Bonilla threw his bat and helmet at the plate.[5] Home-plate umpire Terry Bovey ejected Bonilla, and manager Green, too, when he popped out to defend Bonilla. The *New York Times* reported that Bonilla "was obviously attempting to show up the replacement umpire."[6]

Butler doubled to center in the 13th for his second hit in four at-bats, with three walks. With one out, Vizcaino's hit scored Butler, but Vizcaino was thrown out by Bichette trying to advance to second base.

In the Rockies' 13th, center fielder Mike Kingery singled off Mike Remlinger and Jim Tatum doubled him home, yielding another tie, now 8-8.

Ricky Otero made his major-league debut, coming in to play left field in the 11th; he started things in the top of the 14th with a single to left. Hard-hitting second baseman Jeff Kent was asked to forgo his stroke for a sacrifice bunt. The strategy worked when Joe Orsulak doubled to left to score Otero for a 9-8 Mets lead.

The Rockies came storming back. Joe Girardi led off the bottom of the 14th with a single. Walker struck out swinging. Galarraga reached on an error by third baseman Tim Bogar. Dante Bichette was up next and Kingery was on deck. Twenty years later he confided that while waiting he had wondered why, with a base

open, the Mets didn't walk Bichette. "I can't believe they are pitching to him," Kingery thought.[7]

As for Bichette, "I went to the plate for one thing, that was to hit a home run and win that game."[8] Taking a whack at a 2-and-1 pitch from Remlinger, Bichette smote a high fly into left center, out of the ballpark, and provided the final entry for all the evening's scorecards.[9] Forty-three players had been used, 33 hits, three home runs and only one of those home runs by the Rockies. However, there's no doubt that one home run forged the Blake Street Bombers.[10]

SOURCES

In addition to the sources cited in the Notes, the author consulted Retrosheet.org, Baseball-Reference.com. and the following:

Associated Press. "Colorado Rrrrrrockies' Stadium Announcer Roach Steps Down," *Denver Post*, February 26, 2007. denverpost.com/2007/02/26/colorado-rrrrrrockies-stadium-announcer-roach-steps-down.

Chass, Murray. "Rockies Open Their Wallet for Two Stars." *New York Times*, April 9, 1995.

Colorado Rockies, *Coors Field*, n.d. colorado.rockies.mlb.com/col/ballpark/.

Costello, Rory. "John Franco," sabr.org/bioproj/person/2966ede2.

Rockies: 20 Seasons of History. youtu.be/670CZAyCfyk. Produced by MLB.com.

Silverberg, Evan. "Greatest Mets—Edgardo Alfonzo," NYSportsDay, November 5, 2003. nysportsday.com/news/memories/1068092180.html.

Weiss, Noah M. *The Republican Revolution? The Transformation and Maturation of the House Republican Party, 1980-1995.* Undergraduate Research Fellows, Philadelphia: University of Pennsylvania ScholarlyCommons, 2009.

Zimniuch, Fran. *Baseball's New Frontier* (Lincoln: University of Nebraska Press, 2013).

NOTES

1   Paul D. Staudohar, "The Baseball Strike of 1994-95," *Monthly Labor Review*, March 1997. bls.gov/opub/mlr/1997/article/baseball-strike-of-1994-95.htm.

2   Ted Berg, "Tom Glavine Explains How He and Greg Maddux Came Up With 'Chicks Dig the Longball,'" *USA Today*, August 8, 2014. usatoday.com/2014/08/greg-maddux-and-tom-glavine-came-up-with-chicks-dig-the-longball.

3   The umpires had also been embroiled in a dispute with Major League Baseball, and had been locked out since January 1. The umpires didn't return to work until May 3.

4   Chris Spears, "Rockies Opening Day Weather 'Luck' Almost as Hot as Story's Bat News," CBS Denver 4, April 7, 2016. denver. cbslocal.com/2016/04/07/rockies-opening-day-weather-luck-almost-as-hot-as-storys-bat/

5   Jennifer Frey, "This One Has It All, Except Met Victory," *New York Times*, April 27, 1995.

6   Ibid.

7   "Memories by Rockies Players From the First Game at Coors Field," CBS Denver 4, May 4, 2015. denver.cbslocal. com/2015/05/04/top-15-memories-by-rockies-players-from-the-first-game-at-coors-field/.

8   *Baseball's Seasons: 1995. "Baseball Returns,"* MLB Network, 2009.

9   ESPN, "Bichette Hits a Walk-Off in Coors Opener," MLB. com, 1995. youtu.be/TVFO_BhUOHk.

10 Patrick Saunders, "Blake Street Bombers Left Unforgettable Impression in Rockies' First 25 Years," *Denver Post*, July 22, 2017.

THE MOST CONSEQUENTIAL COMEBACK

OCTOBER 1, 1995: COLORADO ROCKIES 10, SAN FRANCISCO GIANTS 9, AT COORS FIELD

BY JOHN BAUER

THE REQUIRED RESULT WAS SIMPLE: Win and they're in. In their third season as a major-league franchise, the Colorado Rockies stood on the brink of qualifying for the baseball postseason faster than any previous expansion team. To be sure, the Rockies' postseason quest was aided by the introduction of the wild card, an innovation that would have been implemented in 1994 but for the season-ending strike and subsequent cancellation of the postseason. It is doubtful the Rockies cared. All that mattered was that defeating the San Francisco Giants would lead to a National League Division Series date with the Atlanta Braves. A Rockies loss, combined with a win by the Houston Astros at Wrigley Field, would promise nothing more than a one-game playoff to determine the NL wild-card team.

To secure the win, Rockies manager Don Baylor turned to two-time Cy Young Award winner Bret Saberhagen. Acquired from the New York Mets in a July 31 trade, Saberhagen was intended to be the final piece in assembling a playoff-caliber roster. The Rockies had signed outfielder Larry Walker and pitcher Bill Swift through free agency before the season. Battling a sore shoulder that would necessitate offseason surgery, Saberhagen aspired for 85 pitches and a lead through five or six innings.[1] The Giants, on the other hand, had nothing to play for aside from pride. Winding up a last-place season, manager Dusty Baker started Joe Rosselli for the first time since July 7.

Marvin Benard opened the game for the Giants with a single through the gap between second baseman Eric Young and first baseman Andres Galarraga. Mike Benjamin advanced Benard to second base with a sacrifice bunt before Barry Bonds struck out looking. With two out, Matt Williams launched the ball over the left-field fence and through the front door of Buckaroos restaurant for a 2-0 Giants lead.[2] Saberhagen earned his second strikeout of the inning against Mark Carreon to end the Giants first. Leading off the Rockies' half of the inning, Young lofted a fly ball into center field for a triple. Joe Girardi popped up, but Dante Bichette sent a fly ball to deep right field. While Carreon made the catch, Bichette's fly had enough distance to bring home Young. Walker's grounder to first baseman J.R. Phillips ended the inning, but the Rockies had halved the deficit to 2-1.

In the second inning, Phillips restored the Giants' two-run advantage by slamming Saberhagen's pitch against the upper-deck facing in right-center field.[3] Rich Aurilia doubled to center field in the next at-bat, but the Giants could not add to the 3-1 lead. The Rockies gained a run back in the bottom of the inning. Following Galarraga's leadoff fly to Benard in center field, Ellis Burks lined a triple into left. Burks scored on Vinny Castilla's long fly ball to Bonds in left-center field, and Walt Weiss ended the inning with a short fly to Carreon.

The Giants offense continued to attack Saberhagen in the third and brought his afternoon to an early conclusion. Benjamin lined the ball to left-center for a leadoff single. With Bonds at the plate, the Giants second baseman swiped second base. The steal set up Benjamin to score when Bonds doubled to right field. Weiss's error on Williams's groundball put runners at the corners for Carreon. His double to left field scored Bonds and Williams for a 6-2 lead. After Saberhagen walked Phillips—the fifth Giant to reach base with none out—Baylor summoned Mark Thompson from the bullpen. Saberhagen's day ended well short of the goal he established for himself. The Colorado starter commented, "I just didn't have very good stuff today."[4] Saberhagen's pitching line worsened after his exit as Aurilia and Kirt Manwaring hit sacrifice flies that plated Carreon and Phillips, respectively. The wild-card-chasing Rockies trailed, 8-2.

Assuming Saberhagen's spot in the batting order, Thompson hit a short fly ball to the left-field line for a leadoff single in the Rockies' third. Although hobbled by a sore hamstring just days earlier,[5] Young walloped the ball over the center-right fence to cut the deficit to 8-4. Three batters later, Walker homered with Girardi (infield single) on second for an 8-6 score. The home run was Walker's 36th of the campaign and put his RBI tally into triple digits, more than justifying the expense in bringing him from Montreal to Denver. „It wasn't my money (that signed Walker)," Baylor said. „But money well spent is right."[6] Baker replaced the faltering Rosselli with Mark Leiter. (Rosselli would never pitch again in the majors.) Leiter had started and pitched into the seventh inning of Friday night's game, making the switch seem a bit curious. With Leiter's record at 10-11, Baker admitted the move was done to get him to .500.[7] Although Leiter got out of the inning on grounders from Burks and Castilla, the move would not work as Baker intended.

Neither team scored in the fourth inning, and the Giants left two on base in the top of the fifth. Girardi opened the Rockies' fifth by doubling to left field; he held second base on Bichette's infield single to third baseman Williams. Walker's single through the right side of the Giants' infield scored Girardi and advanced Bichette to third. Bichette scored easily on Galarraga's groundball double to left field, tying the game at 8-8. Leiter struck out Burks for the first out, but surrendered the lead on the second out as Walker scored from third base on Castilla's grounder to Aurilia. Weiss's fly ball dropped in short right field for a run-scoring double as Galarraga crossed the plate for a 10-8 Rockies lead. Leiter intentionally walked pinch-hitter John Vander Wal to set up the force, but Young's fly to Bonds actually provided the final out. As the inning ended with the Rockies ahead, the right-field scoreboard announced the

Astros' 8-7 win over the Cubs. Weiss conceded later that the team was following events at Wrigley Field: „We were all watching what was going on."[8] Thus, the Rockies knew they had to win to avoid a playoff with Houston.

Since being chased from the game in the third, Saberhagen had become the Rockies' biggest cheerleader. „When I came in after I gave up that bunch of runs, I said, ‚There's a lot of game left. Don't give up. Keep battling like you have all year.'"[9] The Rockies had battled to the lead; now the bullpen needed to hold on to it. From his perspective behind the plate, Girardi had confidence in the relief corps. „I'll put our bullpen up against anybody's," he said.[10] In the sixth, Bryan Rekar allowed only a two-out single to Matt Williams. Phillips started the Giants' seventh with a double, which was converted into a run on another Manwaring sacrifice fly. After pinch-hitter Dave McCarty hit a two-out double, Bruce Ruffin closed the door on the rally, getting Benard to ground out, keeping the score at 10-9. Darren Holmes pitched a three-up, three-down eighth inning, setting up Curt Leskanic to seal the win.

Leskanic's previous save opportunity had ended disastrously. Tasked with closing out a 7-5 lead in Friday's game, he coughed up four runs before being pulled by Baylor. He recovered, however, to pitch a scoreless ninth in Saturday's 9-3 win. Leskanic struck out pinch-hitter Tom Lampkin for the first out, and Phillips stared at strike three for the second out. Down to his last out, Baker opted for pinch-hitter Glenallen Hill, who slapped Leskanic's 2-and-1 pitch over the left side of the infield for a single. That left it for Jeff Reed, batting for Manwaring. Reed's grounder was scooped up by Galarraga, who completed the Rockies' 36th come-from-behind win of the season by stepping on first base for the final out. Playoff baseball would be coming to Denver.

The manner of the win, even though it was the biggest comeback of the season, had a familiar feel for the Rockies. Darren Holmes said, "That's the way we have done it all year. We get up against the wall and seem to pull it out somehow."[11] With champagne being sprayed in the clubhouse, Walker commented, „This is the first year for this, so I don't know how we're supposed to react."[12] Baylor was especially happy for those players who had been with the club since its inception. Twelve Rockies players, including Bichette, Galarraga, Castilla, and Young, were selected in the November 1992 expansion draft or signed as free agents shortly afterward.[13] Walker, who never experienced playoff baseball in seven seasons in Montreal, was determined to enjoy the moment. The right fielder said, „We're going to enjoy this for now. We're going to take a day off and then worry about the Braves. This is celebrating time."[14]

SOURCES

In addition to the sources cited in the Notes, the author also referred to baseball-reference.com and the *San Francisco Chronicle*.

NOTES

1 Joseph Sanchez, "Bullpen Bails Saberhagen Out of Mess," *Denver Post*, October 2, 1995: C-05.

2 Ibid.

3 Ibid.

4 Ibid.

5 Jack Etkin, "Win Has Special Meaning for Original Rockies," *Rocky Mountain News* (Denver), October 2, 1995: 19B.

6 Jeff Hamrick, "Walker Gives Rockies Lift They Needed," *Rocky Mountain News*, October 2, 1995: 19B.

7 Joe Roderick, "Bay Teams Help Angels, Rockies," *Contra Costa Times* Walnut Creek, California), October 2, 1995: D01.

8 Irv Moss, "Walker Swats Away the Doubts," *Denver Post*, October 2, 1995: C-02.

9 Tracy Ringolsby, "Wild Ride to Wild Card," *Rocky Mountain News*, October 2, 1995: 1B.

10 Ibid.

11 Ibid.

12 Ibid.

13 Etkin.

14 Hamrick.

DENVER BALLPARK HOSTS HIGHEST SCORING ALL-STAR GAME - EVER!

JULY 7, 1998: AMERICAN LEAGUE 13, NATIONAL LEAGUE 8, AT COORS FIELD

BY ALAN COHEN

"I'm going to give it (the All-Star MVP trophy) *to my mom. I think she's the one who deserves it. When we* (he and his brother Sandy Alomar Jr. the 1997 MVP) *were young, she used to take us to the ballpark. Without her, we wouldn't be here."*

— Roberto Alomar, *who earned MVP honors at the 69th All-Star Game.*[1]

TO NOBODY'S GREAT SURPRISE, THE 1998 All-Star Game played in the high altitude of Denver was the highest-scoring midseason classic ever. A ballpark-record crowd of 51,267 looked on as the teams combined for a record 31 hits, only three of which were home runs. American League batters had 19 hits (including two homers), and their runners combined for six stolen bases in a come-from-behind 13-8 win. It was the second consecutive win for the AL and the eighth in 11 years. The 21 runs broke an All-Star Game record that had stood since 1954.

The scoring barrage did not start immediately. David Wells of the Yankees, who had pitched a no-hitter earlier in the season, was named to start the game by Indians manager Mike Hargrove, and Greg Maddux of the Braves was the National League starter, selected by his Marlins manager Jim Leyland. The first two innings were scoreless, although the American League threatened in the opening inning. Kenny Lofton singled and stole second base. He advanced to third on a bunt single by Roberto Alomar, but with runners on the corners and none

out, Maddux got out of the jam striking out Alex Rodriguez with the bases loaded and two out to end the threat. In the second inning, Pudge Rodriguez singled off Maddux but was eliminated on a double play. Tom Glavine relieved Maddux in the third inning and pitched a scoreless frame.

The NL jumped to a 2-0 lead on a third-inning two-run single by Tony Gwynn off Roger Clemens. Denver favorite Larry Walker led off the inning with a walk and advanced to second on a single by Atlanta's Walt Weiss, who was in his first All-Star Game, at age 34, in his 12th major-league season. Glavine's bunt advanced the runners to second and third, and the bases became loaded when Clemens hit Craig Biggio of Houston with a pitch. Gwynn's run-scoring single to right went off the glove of second baseman Roberto Alomar.

As Weiss, who had spent four seasons with the Rockies, stood at first base after his single, AL first baseman Jim Thome came over and tapped Weiss on his chest, near the heart, with his gloved hand. The tap had more than a bit of significance.[2] It had been an eventful couple of weeks for Weiss. His 3-year-old son, Brody, contracted an illness related to a deadly form of E. coli bacteria. Weiss rushed home to be with his family. Brody was released from the hospital and was at the game. By the start of the game, the Weiss story was well known, and the fans gave Weiss the loudest cheers as the players were being introduced. By the time Weiss signed on as manager with the Rockies in 2013, Brody was a star high-school shortstop, and that year he was drafted by the Rockies in the 22nd round. He chose to go to college.

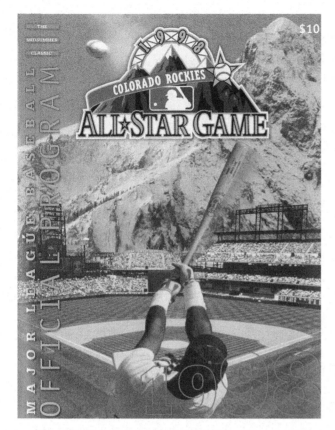

The AL, held scoreless for the first three innings, broke through in the top of the fourth, and proceeded to score in each of the game's final six stanzas.

In the fourth inning, Tom Glavine was in his second inning of work. The American League batted around, scoring four runs. Keying the rally were Pudge Rodriguez's second consecutive single, a two-run double by the starting AL shortstop, Cal Ripken Jr. (scoring both Pudge and Alex Rodriguez), a bases-loaded walk to Ken Griffey Jr., and a sacrifice fly by the Rangers' Juan Gonzalez, who at the time led the majors in RBIs with 101.

Walt Weiss's second single brought the NL to within a run of the lead in the bottom of the fourth, but the AL responded with a run of its own when Alex Rodriguez homered in the top of the fifth.

Young Bartolo Colon of the Indians, in his first All-Star Game appearance, came on to protect the two-run lead, but yielded a triple to Devon White and walked Mark McGwire of the Cardinals. The next batter was Barry Bonds, to whom Colon fed four straight fastballs that resulted in two balls and two strikes. The next pitch was an off-speed pitch that

went out much more quickly than it came in, sailing 451 feet off the façade just below the ballpark's upper deck in right field. The National League led 6-5, and Colon's family watching the game on television in the Dominican Republic saw the pride of the family on the verge of being tagged with the loss after blowing the lead. (Bonds and his father, Bobby Bonds, are one of the two father-son combos to homer in All-Star competition, the other being the Griffeys.)

The American League went ahead to stay with three sixth-inning runs, highlighted by defensive lapses by the National League and singles and stolen bases by both Pudge Rodriguez and Baltimore second baseman Roberto Alomar. With the bases loaded, NL catcher Javy Lopez was unable to handle a pitch by reliever Ugueth Urbina, and Roberto Alomar, who had singled to lead off the inning, scored on the passed ball. Ken Griffey Jr., who had reached on an infield hit, scored on an Urbina wild pitch. Pudge Rodriguez's single sent Jim Thome home with the inning's final run. It was the last of three hits in the game for the Texas Rangers catcher, who was making his sixth consecutive All-Star Game start and his seventh appearance overall. His three hits made him the first catcher to achieve the feat in an All-Star Game.

It looked as if the seesaw would swing back in the National League's favor in the bottom of the sixth inning when Andres Galarraga, who had played five great seasons with the Rockies before moving on to the Braves, sent a long fly ball to center field with two runners on. However, the ball did not clear the fence and was gloved by center fielder Darin Erstad. AL reliever Rolando Arrojo put a zero on the board and the AL took an 8-6 lead to the seventh inning.

Roberto Alomar's second hit of the game, a seventh-inning homer, put the AL up 9-6 and the American Leaguers tacked on another run in the eighth inning, thanks to singles by Alomar and Omar Vizquel, to extend their lead to four runs.

The American League took a 10-6 lead into the bottom of the eighth inning. The National League was down to its last six outs and loaded the bases off Boston's Tom Gordon. Moises Alou singled and advanced to second when Edgar Renteria reached on an error by Scott Brosius. A walk to Fernando Vina loaded the bases for pinch-hitter Greg Vaughn. Vaughn singled to left and when two runners scored, the lead was cut to two.

That brought up Devon White and resulted in a game-saving defensive play. With runners on first and second, White singled to left field. Paul O'Neill fielded the ball and gunned down Vina trying to score from second on the play. That was the inning's first out. The NL was still in business, however, with runners on first and second.

On the subsequent play, Cleveland's brilliant shortstop, Vizquel, who had replaced Ripken at the position, grabbed a groundball up the middle by Andres Galarraga, forced White at second and threw to first base to complete the double play and the inning. For Vizquel, who was in the midst of his sixth consecutive Gold Glove season, it was his first All-Star Game in 10 major-league seasons. He had spent his time videotaping the festivities on the Monday before the game.[3]

The game advanced to the ninth inning with the score 10-8 in favor of the American League, and the AL scored three runs in their half of the inning. Scott Brosius of the Yankees singled and stole second base. He scored on a single by Ray Durham. Erstad reached on an error by second baseman Fernando Vina and scored on a fly ball by Manny Ramirez. The final run came home on a single off the bat of Rafael Palmeiro.

Troy Percival of the Angels came on in relief to get the final three outs for the American League. The game ended in 3:38, the longest nine-inning All-Star Game to that point.

Cal Ripken Jr. started his 15th consecutive All-Star Game, breaking the all-time record, and Pudge Rodriguez's three singles tied an All-Star record. Ripken was inducted into the Hall of Fame in 2007 and Rodriguez in 2017.

Roberto Alomar was named the game's MVP for his three hits, each of which factored in the scoring. He became part of the Cooperstown induction class of 2011.

SOURCES

In addition to the sources shown in the notes and Baseball-Reference.com, the author used:

Doyle, Paul. "MVP Alomar Enjoys Bright Side, *Hartford Courant*, July 8, 1998: C-4.

Lonnquist, Kevin. "Pudge Pounds 3 Singles; Rodriguez Crucial in AL's 13-8 win," *Arlington* (Texas) *Morning News*, July 8, 1998: 1B.

Massarotti, Tony. "Baseball—The All-Star Game—AL Tops All-Star Bash—Slugs It Out with NL for 13-8 Victory," *Boston Herald*, July 8, 1998: 92.

Reid, Jason. "Scoring Mark Disappears in Thin Air, 13-8," *Los Angeles Times*, July 8, 1998.

Weinreb, Michael. "AL Goes on Offensive; Tribe's Colon Is Winner in 13-8 Victory Over NL Stars," *Akron Beacon Journal*, July 8, 1998: C1.

NOTES

1   Associated Press, "Baseball Today," July 8, 1998.

2   Ross Newhan, "Stricken Son Tested All-Star Weiss's Faith," *Los Angeles Times*, July 8, 1998: C1.

3   Michael Weinreb. "Lights, Camera, Action! Omar Goes Hollywood; Tribe Shortstop Gets First All-Star Game on Tape," *Akron Beacon Journal*, July 8, 1998: C4.

ROCKIES' TODD HELTON HITS FOR THE CYCLE WITH FOUR LEAD-OFF AT-BATS

JUNE 19, 1999: COLORADO ROCKIES 10, FLORIDA MARLINS 2, AT COORS FIELD

BY MIKE HUBER

ON JUNE 19, 1999, TODD HELTON became the third person in the Colorado Rockies' seven-season history to hit for the cycle. Helton had just four at-bats, but he had four different hits — a single, double, triple and home run — and he became the first batter to hit for the cycle while leading off an inning in every at-bat.

Helton wasn't even supposed to play. He had injured his left wrist the night before when Florida Marlins catcher Jorge Fabregas stepped on it during a rundown. Helton was convinced he was spending the Saturday night game on the bench saying, "the trainers worked some magic because when I woke up this morning, there was no way I was going to play." For Colorado fans, it's a good thing he was in the lineup.

The Rockies came into the game having won five of their last six. Florida, meanwhile, had lost four straight and seven of eight. The setting for this game was definitely one-sided: Colorado had been scoring a lot of runs lately, and Florida had been giving them up.

Right-hander Bobby Jones got the nod for the Rockies, opposed by fellow righty Alex Fernandez of the Marlins. Both pitchers were in search of their third win of the season. Jones retired the Marlins in order to start the game, and Darryl Hamilton singled short left field to start the bottom half of the first. Florida's left fielder Cliff Floyd booted the ball and Hamilton advanced to second. Neifi Perez bunted the ball to third and beat it out for a single, with Hamilton going to third. Larry Walker sent a fly ball to right for a sacrifice, bringing in Hamilton for the game's first run.

In the bottom of the 2nd, Helton led off with a double to right field. He scooted to third on a Fernandez wild pitch, but the Marlins hurler got the next three batters to hit ground balls to the infield for outs, and Helton was stranded at third.

Two innings later, Helton again led off and this time the lefty drove Fernandez' first offering into right field for a single. An out later, Henry Blanco lashed a double to right. Jones helped his own cause with a single, driving in Helton and sending Blanco to third. Hamilton reached on a fielder's choice to second baseman Luis Castillo; everyone was safe and Blanco scored. Perez reached on an error by shortstop Alex Gonzalez, scoring Jones. Walker drove a two-RBI double to center as Hamilton and Perez crossed the plate. Fernandez retired Dante Bichette and Vinny Castilla, but the Rockies had scored five runs (four earned) and built a 6-0 lead.

Colorado had batted around in the fifth, which meant that Helton led off the sixth. On a 2-1 count, he sent a fly ball deep down the left field line, over the fence for a home run. He was 3-for-3 off of Fernandez. Kurt Abbott tripled into center and scored when Blanco lined a single up the middle. Fernandez retired the next three Rockies hitters on ground outs, but his club was trailing, 8-0.

Florida manager John Boles inserted Mike Lowell as a pinch-hitter to start the sixth, sending Fernandez to the showers. Lowell flied out to left. Jones was in a groove, and although Castillo singled (only Florida's third hit of the game), Jones kept his shutout alive. Braden Looper came on to pitch for the Marlins and retired the Rockies in order. In the top of the seventh, Jones tired, as hit pitch count crept into the 90s. He allowed three straight two-out hits, a single to Kevin

Orie, a double to Kevin Millar and a two-RBI single to Mike Redmond. Dave Berg entered as a pinch hitter for Looper and flied out to center, ending the inning and Jones' night on the mound.

Brian Edmondson became the third Marlins hurler in the bottom half. Of course, the leadoff batter was Helton, and he was looking for a ball to drive between the outfielders. Helton smacked the ball into the right-field gap and starting running. He said after the game, "I knew what I had to get. I was going to run until they tagged me. Once I hit the ball into the gap, I just took off and put my head down and didn't stop until I got to third."[1] After Helton slid safely into third base, the Coors Field crowd of 47,051 gave him a standing ovation. Edmondson retired the next three in order. It didn't matter that Helton was stranded at third with no outs for the second time in the game, as his teammates failed to bring him home. He had hit for the cycle.

The Rockies added two more runs in the eighth on a home run by Walker, giving him five runs batted in for the game. The final score was 10-2. As this was a home game, Colorado did not bat in the 9th. However, Castilla, the Rockies third baseman and the player just before Helton in the lineup, did make the last out in the bottom of the 8th, so Helton would have led off the 9th inning, had the Rockies not been ahead.

In earning his third win in eight decisions, Jones did not walk a batter and retired 15 of 16 batters between the second and seventh innings, getting 11 in a row at one point. He scattered seven hits in seven innings pitched, telling the press, "The only thing working was my fastball. For the most part, every slider and changeup I threw early got hit hard or for a base hit, so I just pretty much bagged it and went after it."[2] The Florida Marlins lost their fifth game in a row. The first five batters in the lineup combined to go 2-for-20.

The Colorado victory brought them to .500 (32-32) for the first time since April. They won the next day to complete a series sweep against the Marlins, but then the Rockies dropped 10 of their next 11 games and finished the season at 72-90. They didn't record a single winning month all season. Florida, meanwhile, lost its fifth consecutive game. They continued to lose another five games after that and finished 1999 with a 64-98 mark.

Helton's line score was four hits in four at-bats with two runs scored and only one run batted in. Helton, runner-up for the 1998 National League Rookie of the Year Award, continued his hot hitting in 1999. He fell short of hitting a second cycle on four different occasions during the 1999 season (getting three of the four different hits needed), which would have made him only the second player since 1900 to hit for the cycle twice in the same season (Babe Herman was the first to do so in 1931).[3]

Rockies hitting coach Clint Hurdle's father had recently given a little toy spaceship to Walker "for no apparent reason,"[4] and Walker then started a tradition of passing the toy around to the player of the game. On this day that player was Helton. John Henderson of the *Denver Post* wrote, "The way Helton is hitting, the Rockies could ride him to the moon."[5] In fact, Helton might have put the rocket ship on permanent display in his locker, as Walker told reporters, "He's hogged it the last four days."[6] In his last seven games, Helton went 13-for-26 (.500) at the plate with four home runs and 17 runs batted in. He raised his batting average 20 points. Walker, who went 3-for-4 with five RBI, further explained, "As long as we have got Todd in the lineup, it seems like we are going to score runs. Todd is clicking right now."[7] The duo of Walker and Helton combined to hit .667 (12-for-18) in the two games so far in the Marlins series. According to Helton, "When you're in the situation I'm in, you don't think about it. Once you think, it's over."[8]

Since Helton's rare feat, five more Colorado players have hit for the cycle.[9] Amazingly, all eight of the cycles in Rockies history have taken place at Coors Field. Helton was the second of three players in 1999 to hit for the cycle, coming after San Francisco's Jeff Kent (May 3) and before Chicago White Sox' Chris Singleton (July 6).

SOURCES

In addition to the sources mentioned in the notes, the author consulted baseball-reference.com, mlb.com and retrosheet.org.

NOTES

1   "Rockies ride Helton's cycle," *Baltimore Sun*, June 20, 1999: 187.

2   "Helton Hits For Cycle," *cbsnews.com/news/helton-hits-for-cycle/*, June 20, 1999.

3   As of the end of the 2017 regular season, Babe Herman (1931) and Aaron Hill (2012) are the only two batters in history to have hit for the cycle twice in the same season.

4   John Henderson, "Rockies win brings team to .500," *Denver Post*, found online at *extras.denverpost.com/rock/game0620.htm*. Accessed October 2017.

5   Ibid.

6   Ibid.

7   "Helton Hits For Cycle," *cbsnews.com*.

8   Henderson.

9   They are: Mike Lansing (June 18, 2000, against the Arizona Diamondbacks), Troy Tulowitzki (August 10, 2009, against the Chicago Cubs), Carlos Gonzalez (July 31, 2010, against the Chicago Cubs), Michael Cuddyer (August 17, 2014, against the Cincinnati Reds, his second career cycle), and Nolan Arenado (June 18, 2017, against the San Francisco Giants).

KEN GRIFFEY JR. YOUNGEST PLAYER TO HIT 400TH HOME RUN

APRIL 10, 2000: COLORADO ROCKIES 7, CINCINNATI REDS 5, AT COORS FIELD

BY RICHARD CUICCHI

WHAT DO YOU GIVE AS A BIRTHDAY present to a person who already has everything? Well, in Ken Griffey Jr.'s case on the occasion of his father's 50th birthday on April 10, 2000, the 30-year-old Cincinnati Reds outfielder delivered his 400th career home run. Ken Griffey Sr. was a former major leaguer himself, a three-time All-Star who had a productive 19-year career that included 12 seasons with the Reds. What made the present even more extraordinary was that Griffey Jr. became the youngest player in history to reach that milestone. The home run also had special meaning for Griffey's father, since he was in the dugout that day as the bench coach with the Reds.

Griffey Jr.'s major-league career started when he was a 19-year-old in 1989 with the Seattle Mariners, and he immediately made his mark in the sport as a gifted athlete. After finishing third in the American League Rookie of the Year voting, he ran off a string of 10 All-Star seasons that included an American League MVP Award in 1997 as well as four other top five finishes.

Griffey's performance peaked with an average of 52 home runs and 142 RBIs per year from 1996 to 1999. He had accumulated 398 career home runs by age 29 and was arguably the best player in baseball.

The 2000 season was Griffey's first with the Reds. His acquisition had been one of the top stories during the offseason. In early November 1999, he let it be known that he wanted to be traded from Seattle after rejecting the Mariners' offer of $135 million over eight years. Because he had been in the major leagues for 10 years and with the same team for five years, he had the right to reject any trade. He initially gave the Mariners a list of four clubs (Braves, Mets, Astros,

and Reds) he would consider going to. Mariners GM Pat Gillick was able to put together a deal with the Mets, which Griffey vetoed.[1]

Griffey suddenly narrowed down the list to only the Reds, which left Gillick in an untenable situation with regard to getting comparable value in return. Through no fault of Gillick, the Mariners wound up trading Griffey to the Reds for Mike Cameron, Brett Tomko, Antonio Perez, and Jake Meyer on February 10, 2000, in what was deemed one of the most lopsided baseball deals ever.[2] However, Griffey was literally going home to Cincinnati, where his father had started his career as a member of the Big Red Machine in the 1970s and where Junior spent his childhood.

The game on April 10 was Opening Day at Coors Field in Denver, pitting the Colorado Rockies against Griffey's Reds. The Rockies had gone 2-4 on the road, while the Reds had three wins in their first seven contests of the season.

The Rockies were coming off a 72-90 season and fifth-place finish in the National League West Division in 1999 under manager Jim Leyland. Leyland had been replaced by Buddy Bell.

The Rockies' Opening Day roster contained only six players from the Rockies' roster on Opening Day in 1999. At the time, the 19-player turnover was believed to be the most in major-league history. The 1997-98 Florida Marlins had seven players remaining.[3]

The Reds were managed by Jack McKeon, who had led the team to a second-place finish (96-67) in the National League Central Division the year before. Griffey was being counted on to lead them to their first division title since 1995.

The Rockies having led the National League in attendance every year since their inaugural season in 1993, the huge crowd of 48,094 at the Monday afternoon game at Coors Field came as no surprise. Bell gave the starting pitcher's job to Rolando Arrojo, who had been in the baseball headlines in 1997 when he defected from Cuba, eventually signing with the Tampa Bay Rays. The 6-foot-4 righty was in his first season with the Rockies and had pitched 5⅔ innings in a no-decision game against the Atlanta Braves on April 4.

Right-hander Steve Parris drew the starting assignment for the Reds. The four-year major-league veteran was coming off his best season in 1999 when he posted an 11-4 record and 3.50 ERA for the Reds. He had taken the loss against the Milwaukee Brewers in the April 5 game in Cincinnati.

The Rockies got on the scoreboard first in the bottom of the second inning when Darren Bragg doubled in Jeff Cirillo, who had led off with a double.

The Reds tied the score in the top of the fourth inning with Griffey's historic 400th home run, with the bases empty. It was his fourth career home run off Arrojo.

In the bottom of the fifth, the Rockies broke the tie with four runs. Arrojo led off the inning with a single in only his third major-league game as a batter. Tom Goodwin followed with a line drive triple to deep center field that scored Arrojo. Mike Lansing then hit a home run to make the score 3-1.

After a single by 1998-99 National League batting champion Larry Walker and a walk to Cirillo, Reds pitcher Parris was replaced by Hector Mercado. Todd Helton flied out for the first out, and then Walker was caught trying to steal home. Bragg singled in Cirillo for his second RBI of the game and the Reds' fourth run of the inning.

In the top of the sixth, the Reds recorded three straight singles by Alex Ochoa, Chris Stynes, and Barry Larkin. Griffey hit a sacrifice fly to center that scored Ochoa, but the rally was killed when Dante Bichette, who had been traded from the Rockies in the offseason, grounded into a double play to end the inning.

Helton added to the 5-2 Rockies lead with a homer off Reds reliever Scott Sullivan with Cirillo on base in the bottom of the seventh.

Trailing 7-2, the Reds tried to mount a comeback in the top of the ninth, but fell short. Rockies reliever David Lee started the inning. With two outs, rookie D.T. Cromer hit a home run with Ed Taubensee and Aaron Boone on base. It was Cromer's first major-league home run after he spent the previous eight seasons in the minors.

Ochoa reached base on an error by Lee, who was then replaced by former Reds reliever Stan Belinda. Belinda struck out Stynes to record a save in the Rockies' 7-5 win.

Arrojo, who gave up two earned runs on six hits in six innings pitched, got credit for the win. Parris took his second loss in as many games by yielding five earned runs on eight hits in four innings.

Cirillo hit two doubles and scored three of the Rockies' runs. He and Helton would become the first pair of National League teammates to hit 50 or more doubles in the same season.[4]

After the game, Griffey retrieved the home-run ball from the spectator who caught it by swapping his fielder's glove for it. Griffey wanted the ball so much he was prepared to also give up an autographed bat and a warm-up jacket. He said, "I can get another glove. I can't get another 400." He presented the ball to his father, who proudly displayed it while strolling through the clubhouse after the game.[5]

The previous record holder for youngest player to reach 400 career home runs was Jimmie Foxx, who was 30 years and 248 days old, while Griffey was 30 years and 141 days old.[6] Griffey's home run moved him into 30th place on the career home-run list, passing Detroit Tigers Hall of Famer Al Kaline.[7]

Griffey finished the season with 40 home runs. His career was on a trajectory to potentially surpass Hank Aaron as the all-time home-run leader. However, he suffered several injury-plagued seasons that affected his power output during the second half of his career. Consequently, he fell considerably short of Aaron, finishing his career in 2010 with 630 home runs.[8]

Griffey hit home runs on his father's birthday on three other occasions, including the first one of his career in his 1989 major-league debut.[9] The father-son duo shared another memorable home-run moment when they both hit round-trippers in the same game as teammates with the Seattle Mariners in 1990. But the historic one in 2000 also had to rank among the most unforgettable for the family.

SOURCES

In addition to the sources cited in the Notes, the author also consulted:

Baseball-Reference.com.

Hawks, Emily. "Ken Griffey Jr.," SABR BioProject, sabr.org/bioproj/person/3e8e7034.

2000 Colorado Rockies Information Guide.

NOTES

1   Michael Knisley, "Griffey Leaves Seattle Red-Faced," *The Sporting News*, February 21, 2000: 44.

2   Ibid.

3   *2001 Colorado Rockies Information Guide*, 199.

4   *2001 Colorado Rockies Information Guide*, 198.

5   Chris Haft, "A Birthday Gift for Dad," *Cincinnati Enquirer*, April 11, 2000: A4.

6   Haft: A1.

7   Haft: A4.

8   As of 2018, Griffey is sixth on the all-time list of home-run leaders behind Barry Bonds (762), Aaron (755), Babe Ruth (714), Alex Rodriguez (696), and Willie Mays (660). At the end of the 2017 season, Albert Pujols trailed Griffey by only 16 home runs.

9   Haft: A1.

THE WINNING PITCHER WAS THE CATCHER

AUGUST 22, 2000: COLORADO ROCKIES 7, ATLANTA BRAVES 6, AT COORS FIELD

BY PAUL HOFMANN

THE GAME BETWEEN THE ATLANTA Braves and Colorado Rockies was one of the most exciting games of the year at Coors Field. The Braves entered the game with a 76-48 record, 2½ games ahead of the second-place New York Mets in the National League East Division. The Rockies were 62-63, good enough for fourth place, 10 games behind the NL West-leading San Francisco Giants. The game also produced a rare feat that had not been accomplished in than 30 years.

An announced crowd of 41,707 witnessed a pitching matchup of two struggling right-handers. John Burkett started for the Braves and entered the game with an 8-5 record and a 4.77 ERA. The Rockies countered with Masato Yoshii. A veteran of 13 seasons in Japan before coming to the United States in 1998, Yoshii was 5-13 with 5.94 ERA. The matchup, coupled with the high altitude of Coors Field, suggested that the bullpens might be busy that night. They were and when the dust settled, the two teams used 17 pitchers in a 12-inning affair that included an 11th-inning melee.

Yoshii, who delivered the first pitch at 7:05 P.M. under cloudy skies with a game time temperature of 78 degrees, started the game by walking Rafael Furcal. With one out, Furcal stole second and advanced to third when catcher Ben Petrick sailed his throw to second into center field. After retiring Chipper Jones on a comebacker and walking B.J. Surhoff, Yoshii escaped by getting Andres Galarraga to ground into an inning-ending fielder's choice.

The Rockies opened the scoring with two runs in the bottom of the first. Juan Pierre led off with a single. With two outs the Rockies' speedy center fielder stole second. After a walk to Jeffrey Hammonds, Todd Walker drilled a triple to deep right-center to score Pierre and Hammonds. Burkett struck out Jeff Cirillo to end the inning.

Yoshii escaped unscathed again after two Braves reached base in the top of the second. Burkett was not as lucky in the bottom of the inning. Todd Hollandsworth led off with a single and advanced to third on Petrick's single to right. Hollandsworth scored when Pierre lifted a fly ball to right. The Rockies led, 3-0.

The Braves broke through in the top of the third when Andruw Jones singled to start the inning. Going on the first pitch, the center fielder swiped second. Two batters later, Jones scored when Surhoff sent a fly ball to deep left-center to cut the Rockies lead to 3-1. Burkett retired the Rockies in order in the bottom of the inning.

After the Braves failed to score in the top of the fourth, the Rockies went back to work. Cirillo led off with a groundball double to short left field and moved to third when Hollandsworth followed with his second consecutive single. Petrick singled to drive in Cirillo and move Hollandsworth up 90 feet. Yoshii's sacrifice bunt set the table for Pierre, who failed to drive in a run when he was caught looking at strike three. Just when it appeared that Burkett might wiggle off the hook, Neifi Perez delivered a two-out, two-run double to deep right-center to give the Rockies what appeared to be a comfortable 6-1 lead.

The Braves responded with three runs of their own in the top of the fifth. Andruw Jones hit a one-out solo home run to right-center, which was followed by a Chipper Jones single, an RBI double by Surhoff, and a run-scoring single to center by Galarraga. In a matter of minutes, the Braves had cut the Rockies' lead to 6-4.

Burkett held the Rockies in check in the bottom of the fifth before the parade of pitchers began. Mike DeJean pitched a scoreless sixth for the Rockies and left-hander Terry Mulholland came on in relief of Burkett to get the final out of the sixth for the Braves.

The Braves tied the game in the top of the seventh. Chipper Jones hit a one-out home run to cut the lead to 6-5. Surhoff walked and moved into scoring position when he stole second. Galarraga's single advanced Surhoff to third. Trying to preserve the once comfortable lead, Rockies manager Buddy Bell summoned Jose Jimenez from the bullpen. Javy Lopez greeted Jimenez with an RBI single to tie the score. From there it was a war of attrition.

Mulholland pitched a scoreless seventh for the Braves and was followed by Mike Remlinger in the eighth, Kerry Ligtenberg in the ninth, and Scott Kamieniecki in the 10th and 11th innings. Jimenez finished the seventh and pitched a scoreless eighth for the Rockies. He was followed by Gabe White, Craig House, Bobby Chouinard, and Mike Myers, who kept the game tied.

With two outs in the top of the 11th inning, Bell called on his last available reliever, right-hander John Wasdin, to presumably pitch the rest of the way. On a 3-and-2 pitch, Wasdin hit Galarraga with an off-speed pitch that was up and in. Galarraga, who made no attempt to get out of the way of the pitch, began making his way toward first base before charging the mound and inciting a bench-clearing brawl (despite the hit batter being the first of the game … in extra innings … on a full count … with two outs).[1]

Galarraga defended his reaction, saying, "He started talking (garbage), that's why I had to jump on him. I have to fight. I don't know why he started talking. I don't know what the guy's thinking."[2] The last Rockies reliever was ejected along with Galarraga and Rockies manager Bell.

The Rockies called on the previous night's starter, Brian Bohanon, to get them through the 10th inning. Left-hander Bohanon, who had thrown 99 pitches the night before, walked Brian Jordan before retiring Lopez on a fly ball to deep left. Despite throwing only 10 pitches, Bohanon had nothing more to give.

While Scott Kamieniecki was retiring the Rockies in the bottom of the 11th, Bell, managing from the clubhouse, had no idea which of his position players could pitch. Recalling the situation, Rockies catcher Brent Mayne speculated that perhaps Bell was thinking, "[C]atchers usually have strong arms, or whatever, hell, I don't know." When Bell asked Mayne, who was nursing a sore left wrist, if he could pitch, Mayne slightly fibbed. "Yeah, I can pitch."[3] Mayne later admitted he had never pitched at any level.[4]

Entering the game in the top of the 12th inning with the score tied at 6-6, Mayne stood on the mound fulfilling a lifelong dream.[5] First up was Tom Glavine, the Braves' All-Star starting pitcher, who was called on to pinch-hit for Kamieniecki. After getting ahead with a 1-and-2 count, Mayne sailed an off-speed pitch five feet behind the left-handed-hitting Glavine. Two pitches later, Glavine hit a little nubber between the mound and first base, which Mayne fielded cleanly and tossed to first for the inning's first out. Walt Weiss flied out to center for the second out. Things then turned a bit tense when Furcal singled and moved to second on a wild pitch. Mayne then walked Andruw Jones on five pitches to set the stage for Chipper Jones, who chopped a weak, checked-swing grounder to third to end the Braves half of the inning.

Controversial left-handed reliever John Rocker started the Rockies 12th inning for the Braves. Perez singled to center and raced to third when Todd Helton singled to right. When Hammonds lined out to center, Perez played it safe and stayed at third. Braves manager Bobby Cox called on right-hander Stan Belinda to extinguish the fire and keep the game tied. After striking out Terry Shumpert, Belinda intentionally walked Cirillo to pitch to Mayne. However, Mayne was lifted for pinch-hitter Adam Melhuse. On Belinda's first pitch, Melhuse made catcher-turned-pitcher Mayne the winning pitcher with a line-drive single to left that scored Perez. Rocker was tagged with the loss.

Mayne's victory marked the first time a position player picked up a win since Rocky Colavito relieved Steve Barber and pitched 2⅔ shutout innings in the first game of doubleheader against the Detroit Tigers at Yankee Stadium on August 25, 1968.[6] As of 2018, Mayne was one of only eight position players who earned a win in their only pitching appearance.[7]

Since Mayne's historic night, three other position players have recorded victories (as of 2018): Philadelphia's Wilson Valdez (2011), Baltimore's Chris Davis (2012), and the Chicago Cubs' John Baker (2014), who beat the Rockies.[8]

SOURCES

In addition to the sources cited in the Notes, the author also relied on Baseball-reference.com and Retrosheet.org.

NOTES

1   Kevin Henry, "Colorado Rockies History: Brent Mayne Makes History on The Mound," *Fandsided*. roxpile.com/2017/08/22/colorado-rockies-history-brent-mayne-makes-history-mound/.

2   Grant Brisbee, "The Time a Catcher Pitched at Coors Field and Won," SBNation.com, August 21, 2015. sbnation.com/2015/8/21/9188267/brent-mayne-pitching-rockies-braves.

3   Ibid.

4   "Winning Pitcher Is a Catcher," *New York Times*, August 24, 2000. nytimes.com/2000/08/24/sports/national-league-winning-pitcher-is-a-catcher.html.

5   Brisbee.

6   Ibid.

7   Zachary Rymer, "Chris Davis and Top 10 Position-Player Pitching Performances of All-Time," May 7, 2012, bleacherreport.com/articles/1175094-chris-davis-and-top-10-position-player-pitching-performances-of-all-time.

8   Joe Nguyen, "That Time Rockies Catcher Brent Mayne Pitched a Scoreless 12th Inning for the Win," *Denver Post*, August 22, 2017, denverpost.com/2017/08/22/rockies-catcher-brent-mayne-pitches-scoreless-inning-for-win/.

JASON JENNINGS HOMERS, SHUTS OUT THE METS IN DEBUT GAME

AUGUST 23, 2001: COLORADO ROCKIES 10, NEW YORK METS 0, AT SHEA STADIUM

BY JOSEPH WANCHO

IT SEEMS SIMPLE, BUT EVERY PLAYER who has stepped onto the diamond at a major-league ballpark had a debut game in the big leagues. But it would be hard to find one as auspicious as the game Jason Jennings had on August 23, 2001, at Shea Stadium.

The 1999 number-one draft pick of the Colorado Rockies was as celebrated a pick as there was. The Texas native was a two-sport star (football and baseball) at Ralph H. Poteet High School in Mesquite. He excelled as a punter and placekicker in football, but it was his impressive numbers in baseball that brought the most attention. In his senior season at Poteet, Jennings batted .410 with seven home runs and posted a 10-3 record with a 0.92 ERA and 132 strikeouts.[1]

Jennings was selected by the Arizona Diamondbacks in the 54th round of the free-agent draft on June 4, 1996. He bypassed the invitation to enter professional baseball and instead enrolled at Baylor University.

His decision was sound, as he had a banner career at Baylor. In his junior year, Jennings hit .386 with 17 home runs and 68 RBIs. As a pitcher, he won 13 games and totaled 172 strikeouts with a 2.58 ERA. He was named the National Player of the Year in 1999.[2] As a result, his stock skyrocketed and the Colorado Rockies selected Jennings with their first pick (16th overall) in the free-agent draft on June 2, 1999.

Jennings ascended through the Rockies farm system with mixed results. Even though his record in 2000 was 8-13, he had a 3.47 ERA and showed tremendous control. Jennings struck out 166 and walked 53 between Class-A Salem and Double-A Carolina. He followed that up with a 7-8 record at Triple-A

Colorado Springs. His ERA was 4.72, but he struck out 110 batters in 131⅔ innings pitched.

The 2001 Colorado Rockies were in the basement of the National League West. On August 23 they had a 53-72 record, 20 games behind division leader Arizona. Veteran Mike Hampton was the leader of a rather abysmal pitching staff, posting a 12-10 record with a 5.26 ERA before Jennings made his first start.

The Rockies, seeking a spark, recalled Jennings and inserted him as the starting pitcher in the third game of a series against the New York Mets. The Mets had won the first two games of the series and were riding a four-game winning streak. New York was also the reigning National League champion. But the Mets were experiencing a bit of a hangover from the previous year's success, and they were 11½ games back in the NL East with a 58-68 record. Despite their precarious position, it was a daunting assignment for the young hurler to debut in the Big Apple.

To add to the 23-year-old's anxiety, a one-hour rain delay made the waiting seem interminable. But Jennings received the gift that many starting pitchers would treasure. On the strength of singles by Juan Pierre and Terry Shumpert and a sacrifice fly by Larry Walker, his teammates gave him a 1-0 lead. But the parade to home plate continued. Mets starter Glendon Rusch issued walks to Jeff Cirillo and Alex Ochoa, which were followed by a two-run single by Juan Uribe.

Jennings took the mound with a 3-0 lead. The Mets were able to get baserunners aboard in the first two innings, but they were unable to score. The 3-0 advantage was intact until the top of the fifth inning, when the Rockies scored two more runs. A single by Cirillo was followed by a bunt attempt by Todd

Helton. A throwing error on the play by third base-man Desi Relaford put baserunners at the corners. Ochoa followed with a sacrifice fly to score Ochoa and advance Helton to second. Helton moved to third on a passed ball charged to catcher Mike Piazza. Sal Fasano followed with a single to plate Helton.

In the top of the fourth inning, Jennings singled to left field for his first big-league hit but was forced at second base on a grounder to short by Pierre. Having just been called up from the minors, Jennings needed a bat. He used one of Uribe's bats, and showed off the hitting ability he had demonstrated in high school and college.

The Mets' Rusch was lifted after pitching five in-nings and giving up five runs (three earned). Grant Roberts emerged from the bullpen to take his place. Meanwhile, Jennings worked around a two-out double by Matt Lawton in the bottom of the fifth and struck out two batters in the sixth to keep the Mets off the scoreboard.

Colorado scored three runs in the top of the sev-enth inning to increase its lead to 8-0. The Rockies totaled five hits in the frame, with singles by Cirillo, Ochoa, Uribe, and Jennings and a double by Pierre that spelled the end of the day for Roberts. Jennings's single scored Ochoa and gave him his first ma-jor-league RBI.

Donne Wall entered the game for the Mets. Helton doubled and scored on Ochoa's single. The Rockies' final run came in the top of the ninth inning, when Jennings slugged his first career home run, over the right-field fence, to make the score 10-0. He set down the Mets in the ninth inning to post the shut-out. He was the first major-league pitcher to throw a shutout and also hit a home run in his debut game. Jennings, who threw a mix of breaking balls and two-seam fastballs, whiffed eight Mets batters and walked four. "I guess you can't get better than that," he said. "It's going to be hard to top that one."[3] On the day,

Jennings scattered five hits, striking out eight and walking four. At the plate, he was 3-for-5 with two RBIs and a run scored.

"I tip my hat to him," said New York manager Bobby Valentine. "You don't expect that. I don't know if I saw a hitting debut like that."[4] Added Relaford, "He pitched a great game, not to mention those three hits. It was kind of fun to watch, if you look at the positive. He's probably thinking it's pretty easy at this level now."[5]

The National Baseball Hall of Fame in Cooperstown requested some items from the historic game. "It's my picture and hat and Juan Uribe's bat," said Jennings. "It's a cool thing to be recognized in Cooperstown. It's something I can tell my grandkids. It's extra-special."[6]

As a team, the Rockies didn't escape the cellar in their division, finishing with a 73-89 record. The Mets finished the season strong with an 82-80 record, good for third place in the East.

As for Jennings, he finished the season with a 4-1 slate and a 4.58 ERA. He was one of 26 pitchers used by Rockies manager Buddy Bell. Jennings was the leader of the Rockies staff in 2002. He went 16-8 with a 4.52 ERA and totaled 127 strikeouts. He was named NL Rookie of the Year by the Baseball Writers Association of America and *The Sporting News*.

NOTES

1   Jerry Hill, "Hall of Fame Profile: Jason Jennings," *Baylor Bear Insider, Baylorbears.com*, October 11, 2009.

2   Ibid.

3   Liz Robbins, "Punchless Mets Surrender to Rockies' Rookie Pitcher," *New York Times*, August 24, 2001: D3.

4   Ibid.

5   Ibid.

6   Irv Moss, "Colorado Classics: Jason Jennings Former Rockies Pitcher," *Denver Post*, June 18, 2013.

ROCKIES RESILIENT ROOKIES LEAD COMEBACK

APRIL 4, 2005: COLORADO ROCKIES 12, SAN DIEGO PADRES 10, AT COORS FIELD

BY PAUL HOFMANN

Baseball can be the most agonizing of games because blame is so clear and individual failures are so carefully quantified. Yet for those players with tough minds and resilient talents, it is also among the most forgiving fields of endeavor.[1]

The 2005 Opening Day matchup between the San Diego Padres and Colorado Rockies stands as a clear reminder of the dichotomy of quantifiable failures of and the need for a determined, unrelenting resilience. The game itself was a microcosm of a baseball season, complete with the ebbs and flows marked by disappointments and triumphs that characterize the American pastime. Right down to the last at bat.

The Padres were coming off an 87-75 season in 2004, good for third place in the NL West, six games behind the division champion Los Angeles Dodgers. The Padres entered the new season optimistic that they could improve upon their previous year's finish. The Rockies finished 2004 with a record of 68-94, 25 games off the pace. While little was expected of the club in 2005, there was a newfound enthusiasm that accompanied the club's youth movement. The Rockies' Opening Day lineup included three rookies.

Woody Williams was the Opening Day pitcher for the Padres. The 38-year-old right-hander signed a two-year, $8 million contract during the offseason to return to San Diego after a successful 3½-year stint with the St. Louis Cardinals in which he compiled a 45-22 record. The Padres were hoping the veteran's presence would be enough to put them over the top. Left-hander Joe Kennedy was given the Opening Day start for the Rockies. Kennedy was coming off the best year of his career (9-7 with a 3.66 ERA) in 2004. Both pitchers were making their second Opening Day start. Williams started and lost the Padres opener in 2001 against the San Francisco Giants and Kennedy earned a no-decision as the Opening Day pitcher for the Tampa Bay Devil Rays in 2003.

Kennedy delivered the first pitch just after 2:00 P.M. The game was played under cloudy skies with a balmy game-time temperature of 68 degrees and barely the hint of a breeze blowing out to center field. The southpaw hurler struck out Khalil Greene and Mark Loretta to start the game before loading the bases. He walked Brian Giles, yielded a single to Phil Nevin, and walked Ryan Klesko before escaping by getting Padres catcher Ramon Hernandez to pop out to second.

Williams's second stint with the Padres got off to a tough start. Second baseman Aaron Miles led off the home half of the first with a double to right. He immediately came around score when rookie Clint Barmes doubled to center. Todd Helton followed with a walk and Preston Wilson smacked a three-run home run. Four batters in and the Rockies were up 4-0! Following a Matt Holliday single, Williams settled down and retired the next three Rockies to avoid an even more catastrophic start to the season.

Both pitchers had uneventful second innings before the Padres answered in the top of the third. Loretta started the inning by beating out a groundball to short and Giles cut the Rockies' lead in half with a line-drive, two-run homer. On the very next pitch, Nevin hit a solo shot to right-center. Just like that, the Padres were back in the game, trailing only 4-3.

It didn't take long for the Rockies to respond in the bottom of the frame. Holliday reached on a one-out single to center and scored when third baseman Jeff Baker, who was making his major-league debut, recorded his first major-league hit, a two-run homer that increased the Rockies' lead to 6-3.

Kennedy followed by striking out the side on the top of the fourth before the Rockies mounted another threat in the bottom of the inning. After retiring Kennedy on a groundball to short, Williams yielded singles to Miles and Barmes before being lifted by manager Bruce Bochy in favor of left-handed journeyman Dennys Reyes.[2] Despite balking the runners to second and third, Reyes was able to escape further damage when he struck out Helton and retired Wilson on a foul pop to first base. It was not the return that Williams or the Padres had hoped for. In 3⅓ innings, he yielded nine hits and six runs, all earned.

Again, Kennedy retired the Padres in order in the top of the fifth before the Rockies added a run in the bottom of the inning. Holliday led off with a triple to deep left-center and scored when right fielder Dustan Mohr singled to left. With the Rockies now leading 7-3, it appeared they were on their way to an easy Opening Day victory. However, as demonstrated by the ballpark's first decade of operation, no lead is ever safe at hitter-friendly Coors Field.

Klesko, the Padres' left-handed-hitting left fielder, led off the top of the sixth with a line single to center. Hernandez followed with a walk before Xavier Nady drilled a three-run homer to cut the Rockies' lead to 7-6 and send Kennedy to the showers. Left-hander Javier Lopez was summoned from the bullpen and promptly gave up a single to Sean Burroughs. Burroughs was forced at second on Eric Young's grounder. Young stole second and scored when Greene doubled to right field. The Rockies called upon right-hander Allan Simpson to extinguish the flames, but he was immediately greeted by Loretta's single to right that advanced Greene to third. Next up was Giles, who plated the Padres' fifth run of the inning with a fly to center that scored the Padres' shortstop. The inning came to a merciful end when Simpson retired Nevin on a groundball that ricocheted off him to short. However, the damage was done. The Padres had batted around and taken an 8-7 lead.

The Rockies quickly countered in the bottom of the sixth. Miles collected his fourth hit and third double of the game when he shot a groundball down the right-field line off right-handed reliever Rudy Seanez. The Rockies second baseman advanced to third when Barmes grounded out to the right side of the infield and he scored when Helton singled to center. After six eventful innings the game was tied at 8 runs apiece.

Right-hander Scott Dohmann came on in relief for the Rockies in the seventh. After Klesko struck out to start the inning, Hernandez homered to right center to put the Padres back in front. Two pitches later, Nady followed with his second homer of the game to put the Padres up 10-8.

Things calmed down a bit during the next inning and a half. Unheralded right-hander Scott Linebrink, who had a career year in 2005, pitched a scoreless seventh for the Padres, as did Rockies left-hander Brian Fuentes. Akinori Otsuka, the Padres' setup man, took the ball in the eighth and was able to navigate around a one-out single and two-out walk to hold the two-run lead.

The Padres loaded the bases in the top of the ninth but failed to add insurance runs. Hernandez reached on an error to lead off the inning and stole second with one out. Burroughs walked, and Rockies manager Clint Hurdle called upon right-hander Ryan Speier to face Adam Hyzdu, who had replaced Klesko in left. The right-handed-hitting Hyzdu popped out to second. Greene followed with a walk to load the bases, but the threat died when Loretta grounded into an inning-ending fielder's choice.

Down by two entering the bottom of the ninth, the Rockies had the unenviable task of facing the Padres' Trevor Hoffman. The All-Star closer entered the campaign with 393 saves[3] to his credit. After Mohr started the inning by flying out to left, Hoffman appeared well on his way to recording his first save of the 2005 season. But this group of Rockies had no quit.

Baker started the rally with a double to left, bringing the tying run the plate in catcher JD Closser. The rookie backstop grounded out to second, advancing

Mohr to third. Hoffman was still working with a two-run lead when Cory Sullivan, who was also making his major-league debut, sliced a run-scoring double into the left-field corner. The switch-hitting Miles, batting left-handed, then tied it, 10-10, with his career-high fifth hit of the game, a run-scoring single up the middle.[4] Barmes followed with the climactic blow, a two-run homer to left that gave the Rockies a 12-10 victory and sent the near-capacity crowd of 47,661 into a frenzy.

What made the Rockies' comeback so surprising, if not improbable, was that most of the damage was done by youngsters. Three of the four hits Hoffman allowed—two doubles and Barmes' first-pitch, walk-off homer—were the work of their resilient rookies.[5]

NOTES

1   Tim Sullivan, "Dusted Hoffman Reacts With Class," *San Diego Union Tribune*, May 5, 2005. Retrieved from legacy. sandiegouniontribune.com/uniontrib/20050405/news_1s5sullivan.html.

2   Reyes was appearing with his eighth club in nine seasons.

3   Sullivan.

4   John Marshall, What an Opening …," *Summit Daily* (Summit County, Colorado), May 5, 2005. Retrieved from summitdaily. com/news/sports/what-an-opening-day/.

5   Sullivan.

GAME 163

OCTOBER 1, 2007: COLORADO ROCKIES 9, SAN DIEGO PADRES 8, AT COORS FIELD

BY LAUREN CRONIN

AFTER THE FULL 162-GAME SCHED-
ule had been played, the Colorado Rockies and
San Diego Padres were tied for second place in the
National League West at 89-73. That was better than
any other wild-card contender, so a 163rd-game tiebreaker was required to determine the wild-card
team. On both September 29 and 30, the Padres had
lost potentially clinching games in Milwaukee. The
Rockies had won 13 of their last 14 games, to squeeze
into the tie on the scheduled last day of the season.

The Rockies had won the season series, going 5-4
in Denver and 5-4 in San Diego. Josh Fogg took the
mound for the Rockies in front of a raucous Coors
Field crowd of 48,404. He quickly dispatched Brian
Giles and Scott Hairston, but after getting ahead
0-and-2 to Kevin Kouzmanoff gave up a bloop single
to right. Fogg then got Adrian Gonzalez swinging on
a full count to end the inning.

Jake Peavy took the mound for the Padres. Peavy
led the league in wins, ERA, and strikeouts that
season, and won the Cy Young Award.[1] Rockies
manager Clint Hurdle had told the media that his
team would be aggressive against the Padres ace, and
the truth of that statement showed in the bottom of
the first.

Second baseman Kazuo Matsui led off by lacing a
ball to right-center, sprinting around first, and taking
second. Rookie shortstop Troy Tulowitzki, who would
finish two points behind the Brewers' Ryan Braun in
NL Rookie of the Year voting, slapped a grounder up
the middle from his deep crouch. Padres shortstop
Khalil Greene knocked the ball down, but Tulowitzki
reached and Matsui moved to third. Matt Holliday
approached the plate to deafening "M-V-P!" chants
from the crowd, and worked a walk to load the bases.
The Rockies then got on the board with a sacrifice

fly from Todd Helton. Third baseman Garrett Atkins
then dropped a single into shallow right that drove
in Tulowitzki and made the score 2-0. Brad Hawpe's
pop fly in foul territory and Ryan Spilborghs' fly to
center ended the inning.

Rockies catcher Yorvit Torrealba's leadoff home
run in the bottom of the second extended the
Rockies' lead to 3-0. But Fogg ran into trouble quickly
in the top of the third. Peavy smacked a single up
the middle past a diving Tulowitzki, and then Fogg
walked Giles and allowed a broken-bat single to
Hairston to load the bases with nobody out. After
Kouzmanoff flied to left, Gonzalez furthered his
reputation as a Rockies killer by taking Fogg's first
pitch, a sinker that didn't sink, into the stands in
right field for a grand slam that gave the Padres a
4-3 lead and silenced the crowd. Greene's single, Josh
Bard's double, and an intentional walk to Geoff Blum
loaded the bases again. On Brady Clark's groundball
to shortstop, Tulowitzki fired to Matsui at second
for the out, but the throw to first skipped in front of
Helton, allowing Clark to reach and Greene to score,
and giving the Padres a 5-3 lead.

In the Rockies' third, Helton smashed a low pitch
into the right-field seats, bringing the Rockies to
within one run.[2] The game settled for a bit after that,
as Peavy retired the side and both teams went down
1-2-3 in the fourth inning.

After a leadoff double by Gonzalez in the fifth,
Taylor Buchholz took over for Fogg and retired
the side.

In the Rockies' fifth, Tulowitzki doubled and
Holliday singled him home with the tying run. This
locked up the batting title for Holliday, and tied him
with Ryan Howard for the NL RBI lead. A combination of Buchholz, Jeremy Affeldt, and Ryan Speier

held the Padres scoreless in the top of the sixth. In the bottom of the inning, the Rockies grabbed the lead again when September call-up Seth Smith tripled to center and Matsui brought him home with a sacrifice fly.

Blum began the Padres' eighth with a single off new pitcher Brian Fuentes, the ball reaching Cory Sullivan, who had replaced Spilborghs in center. Clark hit a foul pop to the right side, where Helton, who led all NL first basemen in 2007 with a .999 fielding percentage, made an over-the-shoulder Willie Mays-style catch for the first out. Michael Barrett struck out swinging, but a wild pitch on the third strike allowed Blum to make it to second. On a 1-and-1 count, Giles hit a fly ball to left field, where a misplay by Holliday allowed Blum to score and tie the game, 6-6.

Neither team scored in the ninth, 10th, 11th, or 12th, though each had runners in scoring position in the 11th and the Padres did again in the 12th.

In the 13th inning, Rockies manager Hurdle called on Jorge Julio to pitch to the Padres. Julio walked Giles on five pitches, and San Diego had its leadoff batter on base for the third straight inning. Hairston then drove a ball to left-center. Like a ball Atkins hit in the seventh, the ball appeared to hit the top of the wall. Hairston's bounced into the stands for a two-run homer. After Chase Headley's pinch-hit single, Ramon Ortiz came on to pitch for the Rockies—their 10th pitcher of the night—and retired the next three batters.

The Rockies' predicted win percentage for the game had dropped to 8%.[3]

As the Rockies came to bat in the bottom of the 13th down by two runs, the fans at Coors Field cheered as loudly as they had all night, donning their rally caps in hopes of swaying the baseball gods. Coming off their stretch drive, the Rockies had cultivated a reputation as a team that wouldn't give up.

This time they had to overcome Trevor Hoffman, who was at the time baseball's all-time saves leader.[4] First to face him was Matsui, who after two quick balls watched a ball go by him for the first strike, then slapped two fouls down the third-base line.

Finally, he smacked a ball into right-center, where it rolled to the wall before Jason Lane, who had come into the game the previous inning, could track it down and fire it to second; Matsui was already there. Tulowitzki, at this point just a home run short of the cycle, worked a full count, then lined a pitch high in the strike zone to left-center, Lane once again firing in to second, where Tulowitzki got in just before the tag, popped up and pounded his fists in elation.[5] The Rockies now had the tying run in scoring position with nobody out.

Holliday, who had misplayed the ball in the eighth that allowed the Padres to tie the game, strode to the plate. He went after Hoffman's first pitch, driving it to right field where it hit the bottom of the manual scoreboard, bounced over the head of right fielder Giles, and ricocheted back toward the infield. Tulowitzki, who held at second until the ball hit the wall, scored easily and Holliday slid headfirst into third with a triple. Padres manager Bud Black then called for Hoffman to intentionally walk Helton, leading to derisive boos from the home crowd. Black and catcher Michael Barrett went to the mound to chat with Hoffman, and Black motioned for the outfielders to come in as shallow as they dared to fend off the winning run on a sacrifice fly.

Jamey Carroll approached the plate, kicked at the dirt, and adjusted his batting gloves. He then swung his bat toward Hoffman a few times, glanced back at third for the briefest of moments, and settled the bat above his shoulder. Connecting on Hoffman's first pitch, Carroll drove the ball to right field. "I was just trying to get a ball up in the zone," he said after the game.[6] Giles reached over his head to catch it, and at that moment Holliday, who had tagged up as soon as the ball was in the air, put his head down and ran. "The ball appeared to beat Holliday to the plate," wrote the *New York Times*.[7] Holliday slid headfirst, and his head bounced off the ground as Barrett reached back to tag him. The ball popped loose. Dazed, and with blood dripping down his chin, Holliday lay on the ground for what seemed like an eternity until home-plate umpire Tim McClelland finally called Holliday safe, ending the game and sending the Rockies to their first playoff berth since 1995.[8]

SOURCES

In addition to the sources cited in the Notes, the author consulted Baseball-Reference.com.

NOTES

1   Against the Rockies, however, his record coming into the game was only middling. He'd gone 4-4 lifetime against them, including a 3-3 record at Coors Field.

2   It was only the second time all season that Peavy had allowed more than one home run in a game.

3   baseball-reference.com/boxes/COL/COL200710010.shtml.

4   Hoffman was elected to the Hall of Fame in 2018.

5   Adrian Gonzalez also finished one hit short of a cycle, lacking only a triple.

6   Associated Press, "Rockies Score Three in 13th to Beat Padres," *Baton Rouge Advocate,* October 2, 2007: 34.

7   Pat Borzi, "Rockies Have One Last Rally in Them, Scoring 3 Off Hoffman in 13th," *New York Times,* October 2, 2007: D2.

8   Holliday admitted he didn't know if he'd been safe or out, blocked by Barrett's foot. "I don't know. He hit me pretty good. I got stepped on and banged my chin. I'm all right." Padres manager Bud Black allowed that Holliday was probably safe, "It looked to me like he did get it." Associated Press. Ortiz got the win, and the Padres had lost their third consecutive opportunity to clinch.

ROCKIES OUT-BLAST MARLINS IN FIREWORKS NIGHT GAME

JULY 4, 2008: COLORADO ROCKIES 18, FLORIDA MARLINS 17, AT COORS FIELD

BY MIKE HUBER

THE COLORADO ROCKIES AND Florida Marlins celebrated the Fourth of July in 2008 "with plenty of fireworks, combining for 43 hits and 35 runs."[1] Colorado overcame a nine-run deficit and defeated the Marlins, "their expansion brethren,"[2] with a bases-loaded, walk-off single in the bottom of the ninth inning. And then the commercial fireworks began.

From the first batter of the game, who drove in a run, to the last batter, who drove in the winning run, an Independence Day crowd of 48,691 fans watched all those runners cross the plate in an epic battle. Coors Field, known as "the happiest place on Earth for runs,"[3] became home to the biggest comeback in Rockies history.[4] Colorado batters launched six home runs. Florida added two. After seeing the baseballs fly out of the ballpark like bottle rockets in a pyrotechnic display, the crowd stuck around for the Fireworks Night promotion.

Coming into the game, the Rockies had won three in a row, including an 11-inning 6-5 walk-off win over the Marlins the night before. Before that, however, they had lost eight in a row and were stuck in fourth place in the National League's West Division, with a 35-51 record. Florida (44-41), meanwhile, was 4-7 in its last 11 games but was still only 2½ games out of first place in the East.

Rockies rookie Greg Reynolds made his 11th start of the season, bringing a 5.75 ERA to the mound. He was opposed by Scott Olsen (4-4, 3.47), who had pitched seven innings in each of his previous two starts.

The Marlins set the tone early by plating five runs in the first inning. Hanley Ramirez led off with a home run. Jeremy Hermida walked and advanced when Jorge Cantu was hit by a pitch. One out later, Mike Jacobs doubled to right, scoring Hermida. After Cody Ross popped out, Matt Treanor capped off the inning with a three-run firecracker bomb to deep left. An inning later, the Marlins added two more tallies on singles by Ramirez and Cantu, who both scored when Josh Willingham doubled on a play involving fan interference. When Jacobs walked, Colorado manager Clint Hurdle made the call to the bullpen, bringing in Cedrick Bowers to relieve Reynolds.

After Colorado scored one, then two, then one run in the first three innings, the "Marlins took the plate in the fourth inning and exploded."[5] The first three batters reached on two singles and a walk, and then Ross cleared the bases with a double to center. Treanor was called out on strikes but Alfredo Amezaga doubled to center, sending Bowers to the showers. The next hurler, Luis Vizcaino, struck out Olsen but then allowed a double to Ramirez and a single to Hermida, and Florida had scored six runs in the inning. With three hits in the Marlins' first four innings, Ramirez was a triple shy of the cycle.

After the top of the fourth inning, Florida's 13-4 lead gave the Marlins a 98.3 percent chance of winning, according to FanGraphs.[6] But the Rockies had some aerial effects of their own. In the bottom of the fourth, Ryan Spilborghs sent a solo homer over the left-field wall. In the fifth, Matt Holliday led off with a blast to the seats in right-center. Garrett Atkins singled, Jeff Baker doubled to left, and Chris Iannetta slugged a three-run shot deep down the left-field line and over the barrier, trimming the Marlins' advantage to 13-9. Florida's Taylor Tankersley replaced Olsen to begin the bottom of the sixth, and Spilborghs sent a 3-and-1 offering to the left-center bleachers for his second home run of the game. Clint Barmes followed with a single, Holliday struck out, and then Barmes moved to second on a wild pitch. Atkins worked a 10-pitch full count before crushing the ball to deep left. After allowing two round-trippers and retiring only one batter, Tankersley was lifted, in favor of Joe Nelson. With the score now 13-12, the Marlins' chances to win had dropped to 67.9 percent.[7]

In the sixth inning Jason Grilli became the fourth Rockies pitcher, and an inning later, he let the Marlins grab back some runs. Cantu and Willingham led off the seventh with back-to-back doubles, but Cantu stopped at third. Grilli intentionally walked Jacobs to load the bases with no outs. Ross slapped a single into short left-center and two runners came home. Manuel Corpas strode in from the bullpen and retired the next two batters, but Florida had two runners in scoring position. When pinch-hitter Luis Gonzalez hit a line drive up the middle, Ross and Amezaga both scored. Suddenly, after building a 17-12 lead, Florida's winning chances had grown to 95.3 percent.[8]

Justin Miller's name was added to the box score as Florida's fourth hurler of the evening. He lasted two batters, yielding a double to Omar Quintanilla and a walk to Spilborghs. Miller's ball four was in the dirt and got away from the catcher, allowing Quintanilla to advance to third. Logan Kensing came on in relief, walked Barmes, and then battled Holliday to a full count. Holliday rocketed a home run to left. His third career grand slam pulled the Rockies within one run, 17-16. According to FanGraphs, the Marlins still had a 73 percent chance to come away with a W, with only two innings to play.[9] But it was not to be.

Both teams were held scoreless in the eighth — a rare accomplishment — and then Taylor Buchholz came on to pitch a scoreless ninth inning for Colorado. Florida's skipper, Fredi Gonzalez, countered with Kevin Gregg to hold onto the one-run lead, but the Rockies greeted him with a barrage of singles. Barmes grounded a 1-and-2 pitch up the middle for a leadoff hit. Holliday moved Barmes to second with a single into short right field. Atkins

followed with an RBI single to left, tying the score. Gregg had blown his second straight save. Baker hit a ball to second baseman Amezaga, who threw to shortstop Ramirez for a possible double play, but Hanley could not safely make the catch, and all three runners were safe. Ramirez was charged with an error. Iannetta took a strike and then hit a weak groundball past third base and Holliday scored. The fans exploded in cheers, making their own fireworks, as Colorado had won, 18-17. Buchholz earned his third victory while Gregg picked up his fourth loss and second in two days in a walk-off fashion.

The Marlins confined their scoring outbursts to only four different innings, while Rockies crossed the plate in every inning except the eighth. Colorado batters sent six souvenirs into the stands for homers. Atkins had a career-best five hits in his six at-bats, and he scored three runs and batted in three more. Spilborghs and Holliday each had two home runs. The first four batters in the Rockies' lineup (Spilborghs, Barmes, Holliday, and Atkins) combined for 16 hits, 2 walks, 13 runs scored, and 13 runs batted in. Ten different Florida batters registered hits. Ross drove in five runs, while teammate Cantu scored four runs. Jacobs was 4-for-4 with two walks, increasing his on-base percentage by 16 points. Yet the 17 Florida runs proved to not be enough. A combined 14 pitchers from both squads made their way to the mound, and yet the game was completed in one minute under four hours.

Two seasons had passed since a team had come back from nine runs down.[10] In addition it had been over nine years since two teams combined for more than 35 runs in the major leagues.[11] The Marlins won six of their next eight games, but they could not gain any ground and first place eluded them. The Rockies continued to be streaky, losing six of their next nine before winning nine of ten, but they, too, finished in third place in their division.

SOURCES

In addition to the sources mentioned in the Notes, the author consulted baseball-reference.com and retrosheet.org.

NOTES

1   Andrew Gould, "The Top 15 Highest Scoring MLB Games in
    History," bleacherreport.com/articles/2698031-the-top-15-high-
    est-scoring-mlb-games-in-history, accessed July 2017.

2   Michael Jong, "This Day in Marlins History: Marlins, Rockies
    Play to Wild 18-17 Defeat," fishstripes.com/2012/7/4/3131214/
    this-day-in-marlins-history-marlins-rockies-play-to-wild-18-
    17-defeat, accessed July 2017.

3   Ibid.

4   Associated Press, "Rockies Outlast Marlins 18-17," denverpost.
    com/2008/07/04/rockies-outlast-marlins-18-17/, accessed
    July 2017.

5   Jong.

6   Ibid.

7   Ibid.

8   Ibid.

9   Ibid.

10 "Rockies Outlast Marlins 18-17."

11 On May 19, 1999, Cincinnati doubled up Colorado, 24-12, in a
    game also contested at Coors Field.

ROCKIES' TROY TULOWITZKI HAS 5-FOR-5, 7-RBI NIGHT AS HE HITS FOR THE CYCLE

AUGUST 10, 2009: COLORADO ROCKIES 11, CHICAGO CUBS 5, AT COORS FIELD

BY MIKE HUBER

TROY TULOWITZKI COLLECTS RARE event achievements. On August 10, 2009, he smashed his way into the rare feat record books, hitting for the cycle in a Colorado 11-5 victory over the Chicago Cubs. He also became just the second Major League player to have hit for the cycle and to have turned an unassisted triple play, joining former Boston Red Sox shortstop John Valentin.[1] There were 34,485 fans on hand to witness history.

On the mound for the home team Rockies was Jorge de la Rosa, making his 22nd start of the season, with a 5.00 ERA. Opposite de la Rosa was Tom Gorzelanny, whom the Cubs had acquired from Pittsburgh with John Grabow in a July 30, 2009, trade in exchange for Kevin Hart, Josh Harrison, and Jose Ascanio. Gorzelanny was making his second start for the Cubs.

The Cubs had notions of a rally, loading the bases with two outs in the top of the first, but Alfonso Soriano forced Derrek Lee at third base for the third out. In their half, the Rockies got on the board. Todd Helton hit a two-out single to left field. Tulowitzki then smashed a home run to deep left, and Colorado had a lead it would not relinquish.

In the second inning, the Cubs again loaded the bases and again failed to score. The Rockies kept the hot bats going. With one out, Clint Barmes homered well beyond the left field fence. Yorvit Torrealba doubled to left and de la Rosa singled to left. Dexter Fowler lined a shot off of Gorzelanny's foot, and the pitcher fell while trying to field the ball. Torrealba scored and de la Rosa advanced to second. Chicago skipper Lou Piniella was forced to make a pitching change, and he brought in Esmailin Caridad from the bullpen. Caridad was making his major league debut,

as he had just been called up from the Iowa farm team that day. Ryan Spilborghs flied out and Helton walked. Batting with the bases loaded, Tulowitzki swung at the first pitch and crushed a very high fly ball down the left field line, over the foul pole. It was so high that "not even the television cameras could capture it."[2] Third base umpire Bill Welke called the ball foul and Colorado manager Jim Tracy asked the umpire crew for a review. This made the distinction of being the first video review at Coors Field. The homer was denied. Two pitches later, Tulowitzki "lashed a two-run single to left to give Colorado a 6-0 lead."[3]

In the fourth, Colorado added two runs when Spilborghs and Helton each singled with two outs. With Tulowitzki batting, Helton was picked off first base but was safe on an error by Caridad. Spilborghs scored on the throwing miscue and Helton wound up at third. Tulowitzki then doubled to center field, driving in Helton.

Chicago managed a tally when Geovany Soto led off the sixth with a homer deep beyond the left field wall. The score was now 8-1. In the seventh inning, needing a triple, Tulowitzki had been secretly discussing the idea of a cycle with right fielder Brad Hawpe, saying, "I probably wouldn't have done it if Hawpe had not said something. I'd have felt selfish, going for a cycle. I was like, 'What if I'm on second and the ball's coming?' He was like, 'You've still got to go.'"[4] It was as if Hawpe was ordering Tulowitzki to stretch any hit into a triple. Hawpe confirmed the conversation, saying, "What happens all the time is people think they're not going, then they rush it and make a bad throw."[5]

Sure enough, the Rockies shortstop led off the inning by driving a 3-2 pitch into the left field corner, and Alfonso Soriano bobbled the ball as it caromed off the wall. As Tulowitzki raced to second base, Soriano had the ball. The relay throw to shortstop Ryan Theriot was not a good one, and third baseman Jake Fox could not handle the second relay throw. Tulowitzki's gamble had paid off and he now owned a cycle, despite an awkward slide into the bag. "I thought I was out," said Tulowitzki. "I felt like I slid at shortstop. I felt like I crawled there."[6] The crowd roared their approval. Hawpe followed with a double and Tulowitzki scored his second run of the game.

The Cubs loaded the bases for a third time in the eighth, and for a third time, came up empty. Rafael Betancourt replaced de la Rosa and retired pinch-hitter Aaron Miles to end the inning. In the bottom of the eighth, Tulowitzki singled and drove in two more runs as Colorado turned a walk and three singles into two runs.

With the score 11-1, Huston Street came on to pitch the ninth for Colorado. He faced six Chicago batters and gave up a walk, two singles and two doubles, which led to four runs. Joe Beimel had to come on to clean things up and retire the last two Cubs outs. The final score was 11-5. De la Rosa earned his tenth victory, while Gorzelanny's record fell to 4-2. The Cubs had left 13 men on base, nine in three innings.

Tulowitzki's cycle was the fifth in Rockies history, and it had been nine years since Mike Lansing had cycled for Colorado. All eight cycles to this point which involved the Rockies had occurred at Coors Field.[7] Chicago's manager Piniella was duly impressed with Tulowitzki's performance, saying, "What did he have, five hits? Seven RBIs? And he just missed that one around the flagpole. I've never seen a guy drive in nine runs in a game. Thank God I didn't."[8] His own skipper Tracy said, "What you saw offensively from our shortstop, that's a pretty good career for some guys."[9] And Tulowitzki himself mused, "When the other team is coming up to you, congratulating you, you know you've done something special."[10]

SOURCES

In addition to the sources mentioned in the notes, the author consulted baseball-reference.com, mlb.com, and retrosheet.org.

NOTES

1   Tulowitzki turned the unassisted triple play for the Rockies on April 29, 2007, against the Atlanta Braves. Boston's Valentin hit for the cycle on June 6, 1996, against the Chicago White Sox, and he turned the unassisted triple play on July 8, 1994, against the Seattle Mariners. Valentin and Tulowitzki each accomplished both rare feats in front of their home crowds. Further, Tulowitzki was Colorado's starting shortstop and drove in a run when Ubaldo Jimenez pitched a no-hitter against the Atlanta Braves on April 17, 2010.

2   Thomas Harding, "Tulo hits for fifth cycle in Rockies history," *m.mlb.com/news/article/6359942//*, August 11, 2009.

3   "Tulowitzki becomes fifth Colorado player to hit for cycle," http://cbssports.com/mlb/gametracker/recap/MLB_20090810_CHC@COL, August 11, 2009.

4   Harding.

5   Ibid.

6   Ibid.

7   The previous Colorado batters to hit for the cycle are Dante Bichette (June 10, 1998), Neifi Perez (July 25, 1998), Todd Helton (June 19, 1999), and Mike Lansing (June 19, 2000).

8   Harding.

9   Ibid.

10   Ibid.

SPILBORGHS' WALK-OFF SLAM BOOSTS PLAYOFFS DRIVE

AUGUST 24, 2009: COLORADO ROCKIES 6, SAN FRANCISCO GIANTS 4 (14 INNINGS), AT COORS FIELD, DENVER

BY JACK ZERBY

CLINT HURDLE WAS THE LON-gest-tenured manager in Colorado Rockies history as the team entered the 2009 season. In 2007 he'd led the franchise, which debuted with major-league baseball's 1993 expansion, to its greatest success — two series sweeps in the National League playoffs and a World Series matchup in which a not-to-be-denied Boston Red Sox team turned the tables and swept them. The Rockies then slipped to 74-88 and third in the 2008 NL West and despite a 2009 spring training in which Hurdle tried to take the team "back to basics,"[1] little went right in the early part of the season.

After an 8-6 home loss to the first-place Los Angeles Dodgers on May 27 that capped a three-game sweep by the visitors, Colorado was a dismal 18-28 and already 14 games back in the National League West. Although Rockies general manager Dan O'Dowd "had long been Hurdle's strongest ally," he admitted: "Our execution of fundamentals has been terrible. It's been hard to watch. We have to get better at that regardless of who the manager or general manager is."[2]

With that, Hurdle was out. O'Dowd installed first-year bench coach Jim Tracy as manager. Tracy, with prior National League managerial experience in Los Angeles and Pittsburgh, debuted on May 29 as Jason Marquis and closer Huston Street combined for a six-hit, 3-0 win over the visiting San Diego Padres. And in what would be a portent for the rest of the season, Colorado notched its first walk-off win of 2009 the next night.[3]

Tracy's 2-0 record as manager slipped to 2-4 as the Rockies then suffered four straight losses. But on June 4 they erupted for 10 runs in a blowout win at Houston and were on their way to winning 11 games in a row and 17 of their next 18 through June 22. The streak took them past .500 to a 37-33 record and lifted them to third place in the NL West. By July 20 the Rockies were 51-42 and had reached second place, still eight games behind Los Angeles. But Colorado's record was good for third best in the overall National League standings used for playoffs wild-card determination,[4] a marked improvement over their 14th-place standing when Tracy took over.

Colorado continued to chop games off the Dodgers' lead, and on Monday morning, August 24, stood 70-54, just 3½ games back both in the division and overall, good enough for the National League wild-card lead as that race began to take on greater significance. The prior Friday the Rockies had opened a homestand against San Francisco. The Giants came in two games behind Colorado in the wild-card race. After losing 6-3 on Friday night, they nipped the Giants 14-11 in a typical Coors Field slugfest on Saturday and won 4-2 on Sunday.

A Monday-night crowd of 27,670[5] settled in to watch right-hander Marquis, who had gotten Tracy's tenure off to a positive start back in late May, match up with Giants' lefty Barry Zito. At 30, Marquis had a workmanlike National League career behind him with a 14-8 record and 3.58 ERA thus far in 2009.[6] Zito, the American League Cy Young Award winner seven years earlier with the Oakland A's, had signed with the Giants as a free agent before the 2007 season. He was 8-11, 4.26 as he faced Colorado with a two-game swing in the National League wild-card race on the line.

The Giants got on the scoreboard in the top of the first inning. Leadoff batter Eugenio Velez singled to right-center on Marquis's third pitch of the night, then stole second with Randy Winn at the plate. Velez advanced to third as Winn lined to deep left-center. Pablo Sandoval then delivered a sacrifice fly to score Velez before Bengie Molina bounced out to end the half-inning.

Colorado posed no threat to Zito until the fourth, when Todd Helton walked and advanced to third on a two-out single by Brad Hawpe. That brought the number-6 hitter, outfield swingman Ryan Spilborghs, to the plate. The 29-year-old fifth-year man battled Zito to a 3-and-2 count but went down on a swinging strikeout.

The Rockies managed to break through with the tying run in the fifth, though, and might have had more. Ian Stewart walked to open the half-inning and reached second base when Giants third baseman Juan Uribe, who had replaced an injured Sandoval in the third, couldn't handle Yorvit Torrealba's groundball. Marquis delivered a sacrifice bunt to advance Stewart to third and Torrealba to second. Dexter Fowler rapped a ball deep in the short-third hole; Stewart hesitated long enough to be caught in a rundown between third and home for the second out. But Clint Barmes then worked Zito for an eight-pitch walk to load the bases. Helton did the same on five pitches to score Torrealba and tie the game before slugger Troy Tulowitzki roused, then disappointed, the crowd with a bases-loaded fly ball to deep right field that Nate Schierholtz tracked down.[7]

The score held at 1-1 for another eight innings. Zito was gone after 105 pitches through six; Marquis threw 122 through eight. For what amounted to offense, Stewart reached third again in the Rockies' ninth, but Brian Wilson struck out Barmes. Colorado posed another mild threat in the 10th but after a leadoff single by Helton, "Tulowitzki rounded first base too aggressively and was trapped in a rundown, setting up an intentional walk [to Hawpe] and a double play groundball [by Spilborghs, with Wilson still pitching]."[8]

San Francisco broke through in the 14th against Adam Eaton, Colorado's seventh pitcher. Triples by Edgar Renteria and Velez on either side of a walk scored two runs, and Uribe's single plated another to bump the score to 4-1.

Leading off the Rockies' last-chance half, Fowler fouled a ball off his knee and took several minutes to recover.[9] With the Rockies down to one remaining position player, catcher Chris Iannetta, Fowler stayed in the game although "limping badly,"[10] and managed to work a walk off Brandon Medders, San Francisco's sixth pitcher. After a popfly out, Iannetta[11] greeted new pitcher Justin Miller with a pinch-hit single; Tulowitzki then walked on a 3-and-2 count to load the bases. With no bench left, pitcher Eaton faced Miller as Tracy, the Rockies, and the fans watched with crossed fingers.[12] The veteran Eaton, though, less fearful of striking out than hitting into a double play, kept the bat on his shoulder and waited out the erratic Miller for a five-pitch walk, bringing Fowler limping home to make it 4-2.[13]

That brought up Spilborghs. He'd managed a single in the sixth but was quickly erased from the bases by Stewart's double-play ball. Otherwise, he had failed to deliver in the fourth with Helton on third base and two outs, and again by hitting into a double play with one out and the potential winning run on third base in the 10th. Giants manager Bruce Bochy went to right-hander Merkin Valdez, the seventh man out of his bullpen in the game, to face the righty-swinging Spilborghs. This time, with the game nearing its fifth hour,[14] Spilborghs came through in the most dramatic way possible. He launched Valdez's 0-and-1 pitch to deep right-center—the first walk-off grand slam in Rockies history.[15]

The marathon ended 6-4 Colorado, the Rockies' longest game of 2009 in terms of innings played and time elapsed.

"I went from zero to hero," an ecstatic Spilborghs said after the game. "I just wanted to go home at that point. It was surreal."[16]

The Rockies engineered another walk-off the next night against the Dodgers on Tulowitzki's single in the 10th inning, narrowing the division lead to two games. But they then lost five straight and six of eight before reeling off eight straight wins, including another walk-off[17] against Cincinnati on September 9.

Colorado closed to within one game of the division lead with a 4-3 win in Los Angeles on October 2 to open a season-ending series that would decide the NL West. The Dodgers, though, regrouped to win the remaining two games of that series to relegate Colorado to the wild card with a 92-70 record. In the divisional series against Philadelphia, the Rockies eked out a 5-4 road win in Game Two and returned to Coors Field with the series tied 1-1 and the opportunity for more walk-off magic.

But it wasn't to be—Philadelphia closed out the Rockies' season with, ironically, two top-of-the-ninth-inning wins that Colorado couldn't counter.

SOURCES

In addition to the sources cited in the Notes, the author used the Baseball-Reference.com and Retrosheet.org websites for the excellent detail in their box scores, player, team, and season pages, pitching and batting logs, and play-by-play summaries.

NOTES

1   Troy E. Renck, "Hurdle Out as Rockies Manager," DenverPost.com, May 29, 2009, accessed July 11, 2017.

2   Ibid.

3   Merriam-Webster defines "walk-off" as an event ending a baseball game immediately by causing the winning run to score in the bottom of the final inning. Merriam-Webster.com/dictionary/walk-off, accessed July 17, 2017. Prior to the May 30 walk-off win, the Rockies had lost walk-off games on May 3 and 5, at San Francisco and San Diego respectively.

4   Major League Baseball introduced the wild-card element to its playoffs in 1994, when both leagues realigned from two to three divisions. The first use of the wild card, however, was in 1995, due to 1994 labor issues that cost the playoffs and World Series. Through 2011, the non-division-winning team with the best record in each league became the wild card—the fourth playoff team—and played a five-game series with one of the divisional winners. (In 2012, Major League Baseball added a

second wild-card team in each league, again determined by best non-division-winning records. These two teams play each other in a one-game elimination, with the winner advancing to the divisional playoffs.)

5   The Rockies had drawn 48,704 on Sunday and 47,178 on Saturday to see their wins over the Giants.

6   Marquis's 3.58 ERA included 11 home starts at Coors Field, notorious for offensive output.

7   Tulowitzki had 23 home runs at that point in the season. He finished the 2009 season with 32 homers.

8   Troy E. Renck, "Rox Jolt Giants With Grand Slam in 14th Inning," DenverPost.com, August 24, 2009, accessed July 14, 2017.

9   Ibid.

10 Ibid.

11 Iannetta, the last nonpitcher Tracy had available, hit for Carlos Gonzalez. "Two days earlier [Gonzalez] cut himself trying to catch a steak knife as it fell off his plate." He had entered the game as a pinch-runner for Helton in the 10th inning. "The Rockies determined that [Gonzalez] was healthy enough to run the bases, which he did in the tenth, healthy enough to bunt, which he did [as the leadoff hitter, making an out] in the twelfth, and healthy enough to play defense, which he did in between. However, [Tracy] did not want him swinging a bat full force in fear it would slice his hand open." Matt Gross, "Thank You, Ryan Spilborghs," Purple Row blog, August 25, 2015, purplerow.com, accessed July 17, 2017. Gonzalez was first able to start and complete a game six days later, on August 30.

12 The Rockies acquired Adam Eaton, age 31, as a free agent on June 6, 2009, after he was released by the Baltimore Orioles. He appeared in only four games with Colorado. This August 24 plate appearance was his only one in the 2009 season, and the game, in which he was the winning pitcher, was his last one in the major leagues.

13 Fowler's knee injury was sufficiently severe that he missed the next 14 games and didn't appear in the lineup again until September 9.

14 The official game time was 4 hours 57 minutes.

15 Renck, "Rox Jolt."

16 Ibid.

17 The 2009 Rockies had eight walk-off wins against five walk-off losses. All eight wins came during Tracy's managerial tenure.

UBALDO JIMENEZ'S BIG NIGHT

APRIL 17, 2010: COLORADO ROCKIES 4, ATLANTA BRAVES 0, AT TURNER FIELD

BY MICHAEL T. ROBERTS

THROUGH THE 2017 SEASON, ONLY one pitcher wearing a Colorado Rockies uniform has thrown a no-hit game. It happened in Atlanta on Saturday evening, April 17, 2010, the Rockies 18th season of National League play. The Braves came into the contest having won their last three games, including a 9-5 win over the Rockies the night before. They would go on to win 91 games that year and earn the National League wild-card playoff spot.

The Rockies were the defending NL wild-card team, coming off an incredible season the year before to claim the postseason spot. More success was anticipated again in 2010. Likewise, 26-year-old right-hander Ubaldo Jimenez was expected to do big things. This was Jimenez's third full season in the majors. He had earned the Opening Day start, going six innings in Milwaukee while striking out six and walking one to get the win in a 5-3 decision over the Brewers. He won again at home in his second start, against San Diego, again going six innings, with seven strikeouts and three walks while throwing 115 pitches.

This night would be the 6-foot-5 Jimenez's third start of the young season. Before the game, catcher Miguel Olivo approached pitching coach Bob Apodaca to say, "What will you do if I catch a no-hitter?"[1] Apodaca responded that he would give Olivo $1,000, to which he replied, "Get ready to pay."[2]

As the game got underway, the Rockies gave the big righty an early lead with a run in the top of the first when Troy Tulowitzki's sacrifice fly plated Carlos Gonzalez, who had doubled and advanced to third on a groundout. Jimenez gave up a one-out walk in the bottom of the first, but got Chipper Jones on a double-play grounder to end the inning. Pitching for the Braves was right-hander Kenshin Kawakami, in his second year of major-league baseball.

Jimenez, a native of the Dominican Republic, walked another batter in the second inning and two in the third, struggling with his command early. But his stuff was so good he was able to pitch around the wildness without incurring any further damage. Jimenez and Olivo both showed some good defense in the bottom of the third. After Jimenez walked leadoff batter Melky Cabrera, Kawakami tried to bunt Cabrera to second base but Jimenez fielded the ball and threw Cabrera out at second. After a strikeout and another walk that pushed Kawakami into scoring position at second base, Olivo fired the ball to shortstop Tulowitzki, picking Kawakami off the base.

In the top of the fourth, the Rockies scored three more times. Brad Hawpe led off with a single to left. After Olivo struck out, third baseman Ian Stewart also singled to left, with Hawpe taking second. Clint Barmes popped to second, then Jimenez helped his own cause by hitting a single to center field, Hawpe scoring, then taking second base on the throw home. Gonzalez doubled, scoring both Stewart and Jimenez, before Dexter Fowler grounded out to end the inning. It was Rockies 4, Braves 0.

The fourth and fifth innings both started with Jimenez walking the leadoff man. Still he pitched through the location problems. After 83 pitches the imposing right-hander had thrown more balls than strikes, 42-41.

When Jimenez went to the mound to pitch the bottom of the sixth, pitching coach Apodaca, trying to help him gain better control of his exploding fastball and secondary pitches, suggested that he pitch from the stretch. It looked to be the answer as Jimenez retired the Braves in order on 10 pitches. He was even better in the seventh, using only 12 pitches to retire the side. But it did not come without some drama.

Troy Glaus led off the Braves seventh with a towering drive to left-center field. At first it looked as if the ball might land in the bleachers, but a brisk wind was blowing in and held the ball up. Center fielder Dexter Fowler made an all-out sprint toward the gap. Racing 40 yards, he dove for the ball and gloved it just before tumbling to the ground. ("Play of the year, given the circumstances," Rockies first baseman Jason Giambi said after the game.[3])

The next batter, Yunel Escobar, hit a looping liner to shallow center. Again it was Fowler stepping up on defense, charging in and making a basket catch at his knees to record the out. After the game, Jimenez enthused, "That was unbelievable. The way he dove, I was, like, unbelievable."[4] He then struck out rookie Jason Heyward for the final out of the inning. Jimenez was well aware he had a no-hitter doing. "After the seventh inning I was like 'Whoa, there's only two innings left. I have a chance to do this.'"[5]

Rockies fans and players breathed easier in the eighth inning, as the Braves went down 1-2-3 in routine fashion on two groundouts and a popup behind home plate.

By the ninth inning the Rockies still held their 4-0 lead. The game's outcome was in little doubt — all of the drama was focused on Ubaldo Jimenez and whether or not history would be made. The closest a Rockies pitcher had come to a no-hitter up to this time was in 2002 when Jason Jennings threw 6⅔ hitless innings against the Pittsburgh Pirates.[6]

The bottom of the ninth started harmlessly enough, with Martin Prado hitting a 2-and-1 pitch for a short fly to second baseman Barmes. Due up next was future Hall of Famer Chipper Jones, followed by All-Star catcher Brian McCann. In talking about this moment after the game, Jimenez com-

mented, "I was like, 'Why does it have to be them? Can't you guys give me a break?' But Jones flied out to left field, then McCann could not square up an inside pitch and grounded to second for the last out, setting off a Rockies celebration.

Ubaldo Jimenez was at the top of his game that night, in what has been his best major-league season to date. Three times he hit 100 miles an hour on the gun, and his last pitch of the game was 97. He threw 128 pitches, striking out seven. He walked one batter in each of the first five innings, two in the third, to end the game with six. In McCann's postgame comments he said, "After my first at-bat, I knew it was going to be one of those nights. His stuff was so good. We couldn't find the barrel on anything."

Reserve infielder Melvin Mora was the first player off the bench to greet Jimenez after the final out. "Before the last inning, I told him to go forward into the spotlight, to grab it," Mora said. "It was his night and now he's going to remember it forever."

SOURCES

In addition to the sources cited in the Notes, the author consulted Baseball-Reference.com.

NOTES

1   Troy E Renck, "Fowler's Catch Saves the Day—Center Fielder's Long, Speedy Run, Then Dive, Robs Braves' Glaus of Hit," *Denver Post*, April 18, 2010: CC-05.

2   Ibid.

3   Troy E Renck, "No-No Ubaldo!—Jimenez Becomes First Rockies Pitcher to Throw a No-Hitter," *Denver Post*, April 18, 2010: CC-01.

4   Associated Press, "No-Hitter Is the First One for the Rockies," *New York Times*, April 18, 2010: SP1.

5   Charles Odum, Associated Press, "Jimenez No-Hits Braves," *The Advocate* (Baton Rouge), April 18, 2010: 37. All subsequent quotations in this article come from this article.

6   Ibid.

A RECORD, THE ROOFTOP, AND A ROUT: OPENING DAY 2014 AT COORS FIELD

APRIL 4, 2014: COLORADO ROCKIES 12, ARIZONA DIAMONDBACKS 2, AT COORS FIELD

BY JOHN BAUER

CHARLIE BLACKMON HADN'T EXPECT-ed to be in Denver. After a difficult spring, the Rockies outfielder expected to open the season in Colorado Springs with the Triple-A SkySox.[1] Instead, Blackmon stayed with the Rockies when they broke camp to form an outfield platoon with Drew Stubbs and Corey Dickerson.[2] He started two games and pitch-hit in two more during Colorado's season-opening series in Miami, in which the Rockies lost three of four. Blackmon would announce himself forcefully in front of the home fans at Coors Field.

Arriving home to meet the Arizona Diamondbacks, the Rockies found changes to the physical structure of Coors Field that seemed to generate more excitement for Opening Day than the players on the field. To provide space for fans who prefer to move around the ballpark during games or meet up with friends, the Rockies spent approximately $10 million creating The Rooftop in the upper deck of right field. After consecutive last-place finishes, the 3,500 seats that were removed to make way for the party deck had been largely unused in recent seasons. Rockies owner Dick Monfort hoped the new adult playground would prove an attractive option for fans. Monfort said, "The sightlines are truly incredible, and I think the food and amenities are top of the line."[3] The capital investment did not necessarily deter those critical of Monfort's investment in the on-field product, something disputed by the owner. Monfort countered, "I live and die by games. ... I care more about winning than anybody. I worry about it more than anybody."[4] To be sure, Monfort also invested in the on-field product when he signed Justin Morneau on a two-year, $12.5 million deal to assume first base responsibilities from the recently retired Todd Helton.

Juan Nicasio made his first start of the season for Colorado. The Rockies pitching staff had collectively struggled in Miami: No starter made it past the sixth inning and the bullpen surrendered 11 earned runs in 12 innings. After posting a 5.14 ERA in 2013, Nicasio used the offseason to develop a hard slider and a split-finger fastball.[5] The effort would show. In the first inning, Nicasio allowed only a two-out walk in a scoreless frame. Nicasio's counterpart on the mound, Arizona's Randall Delgado, was also making his first start of the season.[6] In a sign of things to come, Blackmon ripped a pitch from Delgado to center field for a leadoff double. He scored when Michael Cuddyer, facing a full count, singled with a groundball to right field. Carlos Gonzalez hit into a 4-6-3 double play and Troy Tulowitzki grounded out to third baseman Martin Prado, but the Rockies had grabbed an early 1-0 advantage.

After a scoreless second, Nicasio struck out A.J. Pollock and Delgado to start the third inning and got Gerardo Parra to tap an 0-and-2 pitch to Morneau. Nicasio grounded out to open the Rockies third, but his teammates extended Colorado's lead. Blackmon and Cuddyer hit back-to-back singles to put runners at the corners for Gonzalez,[7] who plated both runners when he drove the ball against the right-field wall for a triple. Tulowitzki singled to center, scoring Gonzalez and putting the Rockies ahead, 4-0. Pollock snared Morneau's line drive to center for the second out. Wilin Rosario singled to keep the inning alive but Nolan Arenado struck out to end the frame.

The Rockies padded the lead in the bottom of the fourth. D.J. LeMahieu rapped a leadoff single to left field. Nicasio's attempted two-strike bunt went foul for the strikeout, bringing Blackmon to the plate. Blackmon blasted Delgado's 0-and-1 pitch over the right-field wall for a 6-0 Rockies lead. Cuddyer stared at the third strike on a full-count delivery from Delgado and Gonzalez's fly to Parra in right field ended the inning. Mark Trumbo blemished Nicasio's line with a solo home run to start the Diamondbacks fifth, but his teammates failed to follow up. Chris Owings grounded out to second basemen LeMahieu and Pollock struck out on three pitches. Morneau proved his value in the field when he scooped an offline throw from third baseman Arenado on Delgado's grounder.[8] When Delgado allowed Tulowitzki and Morneau to reach base to open the home fifth, manager Kirk Gibson brought in J.J. Putz. The change ended a rough outing for Delgado. Gibson seemed to know the reason for his starter's undoing, "Fastball command is essential to everybody. Randall couldn't do it."[9] Rosario's grounder to shortstop Owings forced Morneau at second before Arenado struck out. Putz intentionally walked LeMahieu to pitch to Nicasio, a move that worked when Nicasio grounded to second baseman Aaron Hill for the third out.

Nicasio continued to pitch well into the later innings, a result he credited to his off-speed pitches. "The slider. It was important," said Nicasio afterward.[10] His pitching coach, Jim Wright, praised Nicasio's work, "He's definitely matured. It's a big step for him."[11] Hill reached base for Arizona in the sixth on a ground-rule double following fan interference. Colorado made the plays in the field to keep the score at 6-1, including another rescue by Morneau of an errant throw (this time by LeMahieu) for the third out. In the home half of the inning, reliever Joe Thatcher resembled Delgado more than Putz to the Diamondbacks' detriment. Blackmon led off with a double, but was thrown out by catcher Miguel Montero attempting to steal third. On the play, third baseman Prado was spiked when his glove was caught between the base and Blackmon's spikes. Bleeding, Prado exited the game, but did not require stitches. „Fortunately for me, it just took a little skin off," he

said.[12] An Owings error allowed Cuddyer to claim first base ahead of Gonzalez's bomb to deep right field for an 8-1 advantage. In the top of the seventh, Owings recovered to line a two-out single to center field but that was all Nicasio allowed. Although it could be argued that Nicasio might have continued, having only thrown 88 pitches, manager Walt Weiss lifted his starter after seven innings. „Pretty much what the doctor ordered," said Weiss of Nicasio's performance.[13]

Brad Ziegler continued the pattern of struggle for Diamondbacks pitchers in the bottom of the seventh. Although Ziegler began his stint with a groundout by Arenado and a fly out by LeMahieu, Ziegler would face six more batters before achieving the third out. Hitting for Nicasio, Brandon Barnes tripled on a liner to deep right-center. Blackmon singled through the gap between first and second to score Barnes. Cuddyer singled to left field and Gonzalez walked on four pitches to load the bases. Bereft of his command, Ziegler hit pinch-hitter Charlie Culberson with his first pitch. Blackmon trotted home, allowing Culberson to collect an RBI without swinging his bat. Morneau could not add to the 10-1 lead as Ziegler cleanly fielded his groundball for the third out.

The Rockies made a series of changes to start the eighth inning, which included bringing in Chad Bettis to pitch. With one out, Bettis struck out Parra but strike three was a wild pitch that sent Parra to first base. That play proved costly—relatively speaking in a 10-1 game—when Parra scored two batters later on Goldschmidt's infield single. Oliver Perez started positively against the Rockies in the eighth, inducing a groundout from Rosario and a fly out from Arenado. Consecutive walks to LeMahieu and Barnes brought Blackmon to the plate. Blackmon rapped a 2-and-2 pitch down the left-field line, scoring both baserunners and extending the Rockies' lead to 12-2. With that hit—his sixth of the game—Blackmon tied a club record established by Andres Galarraga in 1995.[14] Blackmon joked later about his performance: "It's like something you get when you are 12 when you hit a home run. Sure I have had six hits before. I remember one game in Whiffle (sic) Ball in 1989."[15]

The Rockies closed out the win in the ninth, as Wilton Lopez allowed singles by Trumbo and Pollock without permitting either to cross the plate. With the loss, the Diamondbacks fell to 1-6, equaling the worst start in club history. For the Rockies, there were a number of contributors to the home-opening rout but Nicasio and Blackmon stood out. Nicasio provided Weiss with a sorely needed quality start to ease the pressure on the struggling bullpen. About Blackmon, Weiss announced his plans to continue platooning his young outfielder but added, "He'll be in there tomorrow."[16]

SOURCES

In addition to the articles cited in the Notes, the author also referenced baseball-reference.com.

NOTES

1   Troy E. Renck, "Deep Sixed," *Denver Post*, April 5, 2014: 1B.

2   "Charlie Blackmon Ties Rockies' Record With Six Hits in 12-2 Rout," espn.com, April 4, 2014, accessed at: espn.com/mlb/recap/_/id/340404127.

3   Patrick Saunders, "Rooftop Stunning Addition," *Denver Post*, April 3, 2014: 1B.

4   Saunders, "Time to Play Ball Arrives With Guarded Optimism," *Denver Post*, April 4, 2014: 1B.

5   Nick Groke, "Weiss: Strong Start by Nicasio 'Pretty Much What the Doctor Ordered' for Bullpen Breather," *Denver Post*, April 5, 2014: 11B.

6   Delgado had made a short relief stint during the Diamondbacks' season-opening series against the Los Angeles Dodgers in Australia.

7   With his second hit, Cuddyer secured his fourth multihit game out of the campaign's five games to date.

8   Saunders, "Justin Fitting in Just Fine," *Denver Post*, April, 5, 2014: 9B.

9   Nick Piecoro, "D-Backs Aren't Pushing Panic Button Yet," *Arizona Republic* (Phoenix), April 5, 2014: C7.

10   Renck.

11   Ibid.

12   "Charlie Blackmon Ties."

13   Groke.

14   Renck.

15   Ibid.

16   "Charlie Blackmon Ties."

ROCKIES AND DODGERS COMBINE FOR A RECORD 24 PITCHERS, 58 TOTAL PLAYERS, IN 16-INNING GAME

SEPTEMBER 15, 2015: COLORADO ROCKIES 5, LOS ANGELES DODGERS 4, AT DODGER STADIUM

BY MIKE HUBER

THE LONGEST GAME OF THE 2015 season for either the Colorado Rockies or the Los Angeles Dodgers started with consecutive bunt base hits and ended after an extra-inning home run. A crowd of 45,311 came out to Dodger Stadium to see their team creep closer to clinching the National League West Division for the third consecutive year. They witnessed a game in which, thanks to end-of-season roster expansion, more players saw action than ever before.

Dodgers starting pitcher Brett Anderson had been on the Rockies' roster in 2014, but he signed with LA as a free agent in the offseason. Making his 28th start of the season, he was seeking his 10th win for the 83-60 Dodgers. For the visiting Rockies, Chris Rusin was making his 19th start, coming into the game with a 5.14 earned run average, having lost six of his last eight decisions for the last-place Rockies.

Charlie Blackmon led off the game by bunting the first pitch toward second base, legging out a single. Jose Reyes then squared to bunt the second pitch of the game. The ball died in front of the catcher, and Reyes was safe, too. Anderson retired the next three batters without incident. In the bottom half, Justin Ruggiano doubled to left and advanced to third when Chase Utley grounded out to first. Justin Turner singled into the hole at short and Ruggiano scored. Both pitchers then settled down for a few innings.

Anderson lasted six innings, allowing three runs (two earned). He struck out seven Colorado batters, but three consecutive singles to start the fourth inning, coupled with a key error by Dodgers shortstop Corey Seager, led to the runs. Anderson then retired nine in a row before Dodgers manager Don Mattingly called for J.P. Howell to start the seventh, with the Dodgers holding a 3-1 lead.

Rusin pitched six solid frames but seemed to run out of gas in the seventh. The left-hander allowed a double to Adrian Gonzalez and walked A.J. Ellis (who gave way to pinch-runner Jimmy Rollins). Boone Logan replaced Rusin on the mound and Seager walked on a full count, loading the bases. Chris Heisey then lined out to right field, deep enough to bring Gonzalez home and send Rollins to third. Austin Barnes followed with a single into short left-center, and Rollins scored the game-tying run. Justin Miller was called from the bullpen to retire the next two batters.

With the game tied in the seventh, both managers started making roster changes, and then made more roster changes. For the next nine innings, only the bottom of the 13th saw no replacements.

The Dodgers had a chance to make this a non-historic game in the bottom of the ninth. With Rex Brothers now pitching for Colorado, Scott Schebler led off with a walk. Seager hit into a fielder's choice, but Rockies second baseman D.J. LeMahieu dropped the ball. With runners on first and second, Scott Oberg replaced Brothers on the mound. On the first pitch to Heisey, Schebler and Seager attempted a double steal and Schebler was caught between short and third for the first out (C-SS-3B). Seager advanced to second on the play. Two strikes later, Oberg uncorked a wild pitch, allowing Seager to get to third. Oberg then walked Heisey, but he did retire Yasmani Grandal on a popout into foul territory near third base. Rockies manager Walt Weiss then yanked Oberg in favor of Christian Friedrich, the third pitcher of the inning. Friedrich retired Andre Ethier on a lineout to left-center, and the game entered extra innings.

In the 11th inning, in the span of about 20 minutes, Heisey "blew the game when he slipped on a leaping attempt at the wall in center field, then saved the game with a swinging bunt that scored the tying run."[1] Justin Morneau drove a ball to the wall and Heisey did not make the play, allowing Morneau to motor to third for a triple. Then LeMahieu drove in the go-ahead run with a single, only to be picked off at first by Dodgers reliever Juan Nicasio. This brought a challenge from the Rockies dugout, and after review, the call was upheld. The tag had hit LeMahieu's arm before he was back on the base. In the bottom half, Schebler walked and went to third on Seager's single. Heisey hit an infield dribbler that brought in Schebler to knot the score again.

When the 13th inning had concluded, the game was still tied, 4-4, and both squads had used exactly 50 players. According to the *Los Angeles Times*, "More fans than that remained, but not by much."[2]

And then came the 16th inning. It was Mat Latos's first career relief appearance. He struck out Colorado's Carlos Gonzalez to start the inning. Gonzalez had fouled a ball off his foot, stayed in the batter's box to strike out swinging, but did not return. Nolan Arenado swung at the first pitch he saw from Latos, a 95-mph fastball, and launched the ball beyond the fence in right-center field, where it landed 431 feet from home plate.

The Rockies listed 14 active relievers on their roster. In this game, they used 13 — working 12 on the mound and inserting Jason Gurka as a right fielder in the bottom of the 16th. When Gonzalez went down, the Rockies were out of outfielders. "I was nervous," Gurka said. "The whole time I was out there, I was saying, 'Please don't hit it to me.'"[3] Gonzalez Germen was now the 13th pitcher for the Rockies. Seager, batting with one out, stroked a single into right, but Gurka fielded it cleanly. Heisey walked, and the Dodgers tried to create a rally. However,

Grandal hit a first-pitch grounder to second, and Heisey was forced out, Ronald Torreyes struck out on three pitches and the game ended with the Rockies' 5-4 victory.

The 30 players used by Colorado set a club record and tied the major-league record for most players used in a game.[4] Los Angeles also set franchise records with 11 pitchers and 28 players total. The total of 58 players combined by two teams established a new major-league record. This was only possible because the rules for the final month of the season allow teams to expand their rosters from 25 to 40 players, which "fundamentally alters the way the game is played at the time of the year when the results matter most."[5] After each starter pitched six innings and allowed three runs (giving both Anderson and Rusin a quality start), 20 of the 22 relievers pitched one inning or less. Only Brooks Brown for the Rockies and Pedro Baez for the Dodgers went out to the mound for a second inning.

After the game, which lasted for 5 hours, 23 minutes, Mattingly said, "We had a few chances. This time of year, you don't expect to run out of guys but we pretty much ran out of guys."[6] Colorado skipper Weiss said, "We had a little bit of everything tonight. It was weird all around. A pitcher ends up in right field at the end and it rains in LA. I don't even know how many players we used. It was a strange game."[7]

Arenado's 39th home run of the season tied him with the Washington Nationals' Bryce Harper for the National League lead. Arenado commented that his homer was "a relief more than anything. We battled. It was a long game. Obviously that home run was great, but our pitchers kept us in the game so I could do that."[8]

Even with the loss, the Dodgers' magic number dropped to 11, as the San Francisco Giants lost to the Cincinnati Reds. The Dodgers went on to capture the National League West Division crown.

Perhaps putting things into perspective, Los Angeles reliever Ian Thomas entered the game in the top of the 10th inning with two outs. Thomas had been recalled by the Dodgers from Triple-A Oklahoma on September 1.[9] The lefty retired the only batter he faced, Gonzalez, on a grounder to short. Ironically, Thomas wore Number 58 for the Dodgers.

SOURCES

In addition to the sources mentioned in the Notes, the author consulted Baseball-Reference.com, MLB.com, and Retrosheet.org.

NOTES

1 Zach Helfand, "Anderson Shows He Can Hang in There," *Los Angeles Times*, September 16, 2015: 8.

2 Ibid.

3 Bill Shaikin, "A Play-In Game," *Los Angeles Times*, September 17, 2015: 13.

4 The Oakland Athletics set the record by using 30 players in a 15-inning game against the Chicago White Sox on September 19, 1972. The White Sox used *only* 21 players, and each team used seven pitchers, as Chicago defeated Oakland 8-7.

5 "58 Players, 24 Pitchers, One Game? Baseball Needs to Adjust," foxsports.com, September 16, 2015. Found online at foxsports.com/mlb/just-a-bit-outside/story/58-players-24-pitchers-one-game-baseball-needs-to-adjust-091615.

6 Ken Gurnick and Thomas Harding, "Arenado's 39th homer dooms Dodgers in 16th," *MLB.com*, September 16, 2015. Found online at *mlb.com/news/nolan-arenado-homers-in-16th-to-beat-dodgers/c-149751534/*.

7 Thomas Harding, "CarGo's injury sends rookie pitcher into right field," *MLB.com*, September 16, 2015. Found online at *mlb.com/rockies/news/gonzalez-injury-sends-pitcher-gurka-in-to-right/c-149882602*.

8 Gurnick and Harding.

9 Thomas had five call-ups in 2015 between the Dodgers and Braves, as he was traded earlier in the season as part of a Juan Uribe-Alberto Callaspo deal.

ROCKIES' NOLAN ARENADO COMPLETES "CYCLE FOR THE AGES"[1] WITH WALK-OFF HOMER

JUNE 18, 2017: COLORADO ROCKIES 7, SAN FRANCISCO GIANTS 5, AT COORS FIELD

BY MIKE HUBER

ON A BEAUTIFUL, SUNNY SUNDAY AF-ternoon, the Colorado Rockies and San Francisco Giants finished a four-game series in front of a sellout Father's Day crowd at Coors Field. The game-time temperature was 78 degrees, and the there was a slight wind blowing out to left field. The first 15,000 fans received a Rockies BBQ spatula as part of the Father's Day promotional schedule, and they joined another 33,341 spectators to witness Rockies history, as Nolan Arenado became the first major leaguer to hit for the cycle and bring his team to victory with a come-from-behind, walk-off home run.

Rockies skipper Bud Black called for Tyler Chatwood to make the start. The right-hander had won his two previous decisions. San Francisco countered with Ty Blach, a Denver native, to try to stop the hot Colorado bats, as the Rockies were winners of 11 of their last 14 games. The Giants were struggling to find wins. Although they had scored eight or more runs in three of their previous eight games, they had managed only two or fewer in the others, and had a 1-7 record to show for that stretch.

Opportunities knocked, with the Giants putting their leadoff batter aboard in each of the first four innings, but they could not push a run across against Chatwood. The Rockies had no luck, either, despite a two-out triple by Arenado in the first and back-to-back singles by Arenado and Mark Reynolds to start the fourth.

In the top of the fifth, however, the leadoff-batter-getting-on-base streak ended. Chatwood struck out Blach to start the frame. Denard Span worked a full count and then drew a walk, his third free pass

of the game. Joe Panik lined out to left fielder Ian Desmond. With Brandon Crawford batting, Span stole second base, and two pitches later, Crawford smashed a ball deep down the left-field line for an opposite-field two-run homer. It was Crawford's sixth round-tripper of the season.

That 2-0 score lasted until the bottom of the sixth. D.J. LeMahieu walked to start the inning for the Rockies. He scored when the next batter, Arenado, stroked a double that went to the wall in left-center. San Francisco's lead was cut in half. In the bottom of the seventh, Colorado's Trevor Story led off with a home run into the left-field bleachers. Tom Murphy followed with a fly to deep right, which Gorkys Hernandez tracked down for the inning's first out. On the very next pitch from Blach, Pat Valaika crushed a ball to deep left, giving Colorado a 3-2 advantage. Three batters, three deep fly balls. After a Charlie Blackmon groundout, Giants manager Bruce Bochy summoned George Kontos from the bullpen to relieve Blach. Kontos struck out Arenado to end the seventh and also kept the Rockies off the score-board in the eighth inning.

Colorado was trying to keep its one-run lead as the ninth inning began. Jake McGee came in from the bullpen to relieve Jordan Lyles, who had pitched the eighth inning for Colorado. McGee retired Aaron Hill on a groundout to third. Hernandez then walked on four pitches. Hunter Pence hit for Kontos and launched an 0-and-1 offering over the left-center-field wall, giving San Francisco back the lead. It was Pence's first career pinch-hit home run and his fourth round-tripper of the 2017 campaign.

After retiring Span, McGee gave up a single to Panik, who stole second base. Crawford then drove the ball into deep right field for a double and Panik raced around the bases, upping the score to 5-3 in favor of the Giants. Carlos Estevez trotted in from the bullpen and threw five pitches, striking out Buster Posey to end the inning.

In their final at-bat in regulation, Arenado was due up fifth for the Rockies, who "would need something spectacular to keep from losing for the first time in 44 games in which they led after seven innings."[2] Arenado told reporters that he "wanted that last at-bat."[3] Somehow, he must have felt that the game rested on his shoulders.

The bottom-of-the-ninth rally began with a one-out bloop single into center field by Raimel Tapia off Mark Melancon, who entered in the ninth to save the game for San Francisco. Blackmon followed with another single, advancing Tapia to third. LeMahieu rolled the third single of the inning past second base. Tapia scored and Blackmon scampered to third. That set the stage for Arenado. "I was fired up," Arenado said, describing his emotions as he entered the batter's box. "I heard the crowd. But I just said a little prayer. 'Calm down, give me strength to be able to slow this game down.'"[4] He said that although he knew he had the possibility of completing a cycle, he was more concerned about hitting "something to drive in a run."[5] When Melancon delivered the first pitch of the at-bat, a fastball inside, Arenado swung and connected. "I thought it had a chance. I put some backspin on the baseball and I was hoping it would go out."[6] The ball sailed over the Jimmy Johns sign in left-center, just beyond the reach of San Francisco's Austin Slater, and a fan caught it about three feet above the wall's yellow line. Most of the Giants were already walking off the field by the time Arenado rounded first base with his arms raised high in the air.

The fans showed their appreciation with "an earth-shaking response,"[7] rocking Coors Field. As Arenado was mobbed at home plate by his teammates, the frenzied crowd shouted, "MVP! MVP!"[8] Jack Corrigan was calling the game for the Rockies on radio station KOA. As the blast sailed over the fence, Corrigan told listeners that this was "a cycle for the ages!"[9] In the crazy celebration at home, Blackmon's helmet caught Arenado just above his left eye, creating a gash that bled down his uniform. Arenado was not concerned, stating, "It's blood and it's not coming off."[10] He vowed not to wash the jersey.

After the game Colorado manager Black told reporters that Arenado was "one of the best players in the game. He's capable of doing these things, no doubt about that."[11] By going 4-for-5, two-time All-Star[12] Arenado had raised his batting average to .299, his slugging percentage to .573, and his OPS to .925. His four runs batted in kept him in the National League lead, with 55. In fact, the two-time ML-defending RBI leader was tied for the most runs batted in at the 2017 All-Star break with 70.

This was the eighth cycle in Colorado Rockies history.[13] Said Arenado, "Obviously, it's one of the best moments of my career. I've had some big homers, but this is by far the best."[14] Estevez, who pitched to only one batter, earned the win, raising his record to 4-0.

According to the Elias Sports Bureau, Arenado's achievement was "the first walk-off, cycle-completing home run with the batter's team trailing in Major League history."[15] It was only the 10th come-from-behind walk-off hit of any type when a batter has hit for the cycle. Four of those previous nine walk-off hits were home runs, but in every one of those games, the score had been tied.[16]

The Giants, stuck in last place in the National League's West Division, suffered their sixth consecutive loss, a season high. Melancon remarked to reporters, "My performance has been absolutely terrible." The only bright spots for the Giants were Pence's home run and Crawford's 3-for-5, 3-RBI day. The Rockies had now won five straight games. The victory also capped the first time that the Rockies had swept the San Francisco Giants in a four-game series in their 25-season history. Arenado's 15th home run of the 2017 season cemented his place in Colorado history.

Fans can watch mlb.com's recap of Arenado hitting for the cycle at mlb.com/video/must-c-arenado-hits-for-cycle/c-1514007183.

SOURCES

In addition to the sources mentioned in the Notes, the author consulted baseball-reference.com, mlb.com and retrosheet.org.

NOTES

1   Thomas Harding, "'Cycle for the Ages!' Rockies, Nolan Rollin'," m.mlb.com/news/article/237315934/rockies-nolan-arenado-hits-for-cycle/, accessed July 2017.

2   Ibid.

3   Ibid.

4   Ibid.

5   Patrick Saunders, "Nolan Arenado's Walk-Off Homer Completes Cycle in Rockies Win Over Giants," denverpost.com/2017/06/18/Nolan-arenado-completes-cycle-rockies-win-giants/, accessed July 2017.

6   Ibid.

7   Harding.

8   Michael Kelly, "Nolan Arenado Completes Cycle With Walk-Off Homer in Rockies' 7-5 Win Over Giants," chicagotribune.com/sports/baseball/ct-nolan-arenado-hits-cycle-20170618-story.html, accessed July 2017.

9   Harding.

10 Ibid.

11 Ibid.

12 Arenado was elected to his third consecutive All-Star Game in 2017.

13 Michael Cuddyer was the seventh Rockies batter to hit for the cycle, on August 17, 2014. It was the second time in his career that he had hit for the cycle (the first occurred on May 22, 2009, when he was with the Minnesota Twins).

14 Harding.

15 Ibid.

16 The four other players to hit walk-off home runs in completing a cycle were Ken Boyer (St. Louis Cardinals, September 14, 1961, second game), Cesar Tovar (Minnesota Twins, September 19, 1972), Dwight Evans (Boston Red Sox, June 28, 1984), and Carlos Gonzalez (Colorado Rockies, July 31, 2010). All four came with the score tied.

CHAD BETTIS COMES HOME

AUGUST 14, 2017: COLORADO ROCKIES 3, ATLANTA BRAVES 0, AT COORS FIELD

BY BILL NOWLIN

Tho' much is taken, much abides… that which
we are, we are;
One equal temper of heroic hearts,
Made weak by time and fate,
but strong in will
To strive, to seek, to find, and not to yield.

Alfred Lord Tennyson, *Ulysses*

THE NIGHT WAS PERFECT FOR BASE-
ball, as so many nights are at Coors Field; the temperature hovered around 70 degrees and the wind blew around 8 miles per hour. This night was perfect, however, because the 2018 honoree of the Tony Conigliaro Award, Chad Bettis returned to the mound for the first time in 2017.

This was no ordinary game. The Rockies were tied for second place in the NL West. It was mid-August and there were thoughts of a possible return to the postseason. Bettis had led the Rockies in wins the year before (14-8), in starts (32), and in innings pitched (186). At age 28, he was older than any other starter on the 2017 team. But he hadn't pitched all year. The night of August 14 was his first start. He'd been battling cancer.

In November 2016, just a few days before his first wedding anniversary and with his first child due in March, Bettis learned he had testicular cancer. After surgery, no more disease was evident. But in March he learned that cancer had spread to his lymph nodes. Intensive chemotherapy began on March 20. Treatment for his recurrence was nine weeks of chemotherapy which left him weakened. Bettis lost his hair as well, and concern for his condition was widespread. Despite his immune system being suppressed, he was able to be present with his wife, Kristina, for

the birth of their daughter, Everleigh Rae, who was born nine days later. "Everleigh's birth completely took the attention off me, which was really nice," he said later. "It's what I needed."[1] Reflecting nearly six months later, Bettis said, "I never wanted that kind of attention on me. It wasn't like, 'How are you feeling today?' It went straight to Kristina and Everleigh, and it was like 'How's she doing? How are they doing?'"[2]

There followed the process of regaining strength to his core and especially to his arm. He rejoined the Rockies in early June to begin training.[3]

As he approached the mound in the top of the first, he was greeted by a standing ovation from the fans at Coors Field and high-fived by his teammates. The game was already overshadowed by the reminder of what cancer can do. The first manager in Colorado Rockies history, Don Baylor, had died exactly one week earlier—after a 14-year battle with multiple myeloma—and Baylor's jersey was hung in the Rockies' dugout in his honor.

Bettis had done the best he could to approach the game in a businesslike fashion. It was back to work. That morning, however, the magnitude of the moment hit him. "It crept in when I woke up. Just thinking about everything that happened, everything my family went through. I was holding back tears until the game started."[4]

The first batter he faced was Braves center fielder Ender Inciarte, who pounced on an 0-and-2 pitch and tripled down the left-field line. Gerardo Parra valiantly dove for the ball but it got by him. He quickly recovered the ball, threw a strike to Trevor Story at short, and then watched Story fire the ball to Jonathan Lucroy at the plate, cutting down Inciarte, who'd been going for an inside-the-park home run. One out, but a dramatic one. Bettis admitted his heart had sunk for a moment. "I went from incredibly high to 'Oh, no, we're about to be down 1-0.' I've never had a problem with guys laying out, Parra tried to make a spectacular play and ended up still making a spectacular play."[5] Two groundouts sandwiched around a single got Bettis through the first.

Defense played a big role one more time. In the top of the fourth, with two outs and Nick Markakis on second base, Atlanta left fielder Danny Santana shot the ball toward right field but second baseman DJ LeMahieu "slid on his knees" to snare the ball and throw out Santana at first base.

In the top of the seventh, Kurt Suzuki doubled to lead off the inning. He advanced to third base on a sacrifice bunt by Santana, Bettis fielding it cleanly and throwing to Mark Reynolds at first base. A fly ball to center field by Ozzie Albies wasn't deep enough to allow Suzuki to score, and another fly ball to deep center field by Dansby Swanson was also tracked down and caught by Charlie Blackmon.

Rockies manager Bud Black was in his first year running the team. He had seen Bettis pitch two innings in spring training but was now watching him pitch in his first regular-season game during Black's tenure. During the bottom of the sixth, as the Rockies batted, Black sat with his pitcher in the dugout. Bettis said, "He came and sat by me and said, 'How do you feel? Be honest with me. We're kind of in uncharted territory,' which is true. And I looked him in the eyes and said, 'I feel great. And, to be honest with you, we're going to get through this.'"[6]

In the bottom of the seventh, Black said, "You're done. We couldn't ask for much more from you right now."[7] With a runner on second and one out, Nolan Arenado pinch-hit for Trevor Story and fouled out. Then Bettis was removed for a pinch-hitter, whom Braves starter Julio Teheran retired on a swinging strikeout. Bettis's evening was done.

Teheran was as stingy with hits as Bettis and the two battled each other for seven full innings. Bettis gave up six hits and walked no one; Teheran allowed four hits and walked three (one of them Bettis[8]). Bettis had thrown 90 pitches.

The game was still scoreless.

Mike Dunn pitched a scoreless eighth inning. Charlie Blackmon led off with a triple to center field off Atlanta's Rex Brothers in the bottom of the eighth. After an intentional walk, a single to left by Parra drove in Blackmon. Jason Motte replaced Brothers and walked Reynolds to load the bases. A single into center field by Carlos Gonzales drove in two more runs.

Greg Holland held the Braves in the ninth, and the Rockies scored a 3-0 win over the Braves, bringing them to 66-52 for the season.

The Rockies were in the race for the postseason and Chad Bettis had come home to help try to get them there.

After the game, Bettis admitted, "I don't think I was really in tune with what was going on until the fifth. Just so many emotions and I was trying to get them under control, but it was taking longer than I expected."[9]

He also said, "[Kristina] doesn't know how big of a façade I was putting on. As strong as I was trying to be, I was more leaning more on her and our families and our teammates and everybody that was lending support, whether it was via social media, letters, prayers, everything."[10]

Bettis received a no-decision. Dunn got the win. Bettis was 2-4 for the rest of the season, but he got 46⅓ innings under his belt. The two wins were both over the NL champion Los Angeles Dodgers, with a 3.00 ERA in 12 innings. He saw the Rockies reach the wild-card game with the Diamondbacks, and started to set his sights on 2018.

In December, it was announced that Chad Bettis would be the recipient of the Tony Conigliaro Award, to be presented in Boston in January. On January 11 and 12, he hosted the Chad Bettis Charity Classic at Talking Stick Resort in Scottsdale, teaming with the Testicular Cancer Society.[11]

Of the experience he had gone through, he said, "That was a very big teaching. We don't get to control everything that happens to us; we have to just roll with what's going on. Without my family and my support system and my wife, with Everleigh coming along, it would have been a completely different experience."[12] He added, "Having gone through it and being on the other side now [in remission], I feel extremely blessed in the sense that everything went as smoothly as it did. There are some potential side effects that are essentially irreversible. Your livelihood, your profession is at stake and some of those side effects can affect your profession. To have gone through it and to go as smoothly as it did was remarkable."

SOURCES

In addition to the sources cited in the Notes, the author also consulted Baseball-Reference.com, and replay of the game highlights on MLB TV. Thanks to Nicolette Cavallaro for the Tennyson quotation and important assistance with this article. Thanks as well to Gordon Edes of the Boston Red Sox, and to Chad and Kristina Bettis.

NOTES

1   Patrick Saunders, "Chad Bettis' Return to Rockies Is a Story of Love, Not a Story of Cancer," *Denver Post*, August 14, 2017.

2   Author interview with Chad Bettis on January 18, 2018.

3   Ibid. "If it was up to me, I probably would have wanted to come back sooner, but it wouldn't have been in the best interest of my health," Bettis said. Kristina added, during the discussion, "He wanted to play through chemo."

4   Nick Groke, "Chad Bettis Returns to the Rockies With Flair in a Commanding Outing Against the Braves at Coors Field," *Denver Post*, August 15, 2017.

5   Associated Press, "Bettis Back from Cancer Treatment, Rockies Blank Braves 3-0," August 15, 2017.

6   Thomas Harding, "Smile High! Bettis Awes in Return from Cancer," MLB.com, August 14, 2017.

7   Ibid.

8   "Which was remarkable in itself!" Bettis added in the author interview.

9   Groke.

10   Harding, "Smile High!" In the October 18, 2018, interview, Bettis said that former major leaguer John Kruk reached out personally to him, and Mike Lowell (also a testicular cancer survivor, and a fellow Tony Conigliaro Award recipient) sent his condolences through Kruk. Bettis said, "It was very surprising to me how the whole baseball community in general responded and offered support—not just to me, but to my wife and my family. It was unbelievable."

11   Photographs from the event, and information on how to support the Testicular Cancer Society's efforts in increasing awareness, access and quality of care may be found at: cbccevent.org/?utm_source=tcs-page&utm_content=button.

12   Thomas Harding, "Bettis Ready to Block Noise, Rediscover Calm," MLB.com, January 5, 2018. He added, "Having gone through it and being on the other side now [in remission], I feel extremely blessed in the sense that everything went as smoothly as it did. There are some potential side effects that are essentially irreversible. Your livelihood, your profession is at stake and some of those side effects can affect your profession. To have gone through it and to go as smoothly as it did was remarkable." Author interview.

2009, JIM TRACY, AND THE MIRACLE AT 20TH & BLAKE

BY MICHAEL T. ROBERTS

AS IS THE CASE WITH MOST EXPAN-sion teams, the Colorado Rockies did not experience much on-field success in the early years of their existence. In the first 14 years, 1993 through 2006, they had only four winning seasons. The high point had come in their third year, 1995, when they finished 10 games over .500 in a strike-shortened year to earn the National League wild-card playoff berth. They were subsequently eliminated by the eventual World Series champion Atlanta Braves three games to one in the National League Division Series.

Three more modest winning seasons, 1996, 1997, and 2000, followed. The Rockies then lost at least 86 games every year over the next six seasons. The club had replaced manager Buddy Bell with Clint Hurdle early in the 2002 season, and stuck with Hurdle as manager going into the 2007 season despite the lack of success. Loyal, affable, and popular within the organization, Hurdle was kept as a stabilizing influence.

The team improved in 2007 with the continual development of Matt Holliday into a star and rookie shortstop Troy Tulowitzki showing All-Star potential. Still the Rockies were a modest 76-72 in mid-September, before going on a tear and winning 13 of their final 14 games to force a tie with San Diego for the National League wild-card playoff spot. In a wild and crazy one-game tiebreaker at Coors Field against the Padres, the Rockies won, 9-8 in 13 innings, and kept winning all the way to capturing their first National League pennant.

It took the American League's Boston Red Sox to slow down the 2007 Rockies express, sweeping them in the World Series. That did not diminish the enthusiasm surrounding the Rockies. They looked to be an up-and-coming team that could consistently win in the foreseeable future.

But injuries and the regression of some key players sent the Rockies back down the standings in 2008. At the end of July they were 12 games under .500, and never got untracked, finishing with a 74-88 record. Hurdle was retained as the manager for 2009 despite criticisms about his tendency to overmanage and constant lineup changes. Still the amazing 2007 season was fresh in the minds of Rockies management and fans.

The onset of the 2009 season brought with it the hope that 2008 was an aberration. Todd Helton had missed half of that season, and Tulowitzki missed 61 games. Having these two healthy again would, it was hoped, offset the loss of slugger Holliday, traded to Oakland after he could not come to terms on a contract with the Rockies. But as is often the case, any chance of getting back to a winning record was pinned to the pitching staff. "With just mediocre starting pitching, this team has hope," the *Denver Post* opined in its preseason forecast of the National League West.[1]

As the season progressed into May, it was more of the same poor baseball. While the Rockies still had some good players, including athletic rookies Dexter Fowler and Ian Stewart, the team was uninspiring under Hurdle. By mid-May rumors circulated that Hurdle would be replaced. Lack of executing the fundamentals and Hurdle's unwillingness to be a stronger disciplinarian magnified prior perceived shortcomings to turn up the heat on his job. On the morning of May 29, with the Rockies' record a dismal 18-28, general manager Dan O'Dowd replaced Hurdle with first-year bench coach Jim Tracy.

James Edwin Tracy was born on December 31, 1955, to Jim and Virginia Tracy in Hamilton, Ohio. Jim Sr. was a minor-league pitcher in the Giants and Phillies organizations from 1948 to 1951. Jim Jr. starred in basketball, baseball, and football at Badin High School in Hamilton, and was named to the school's athletic Hall of Fame in 1995. An outfielder, he was drafted by the Chicago Cubs in 1977, eventually making it to the majors in 1980. He played 87 games with the Cubs across the 1980 and 1981 seasons.

Tracy's managerial career started in 1987 as pilot of the Peoria Chiefs of the Class-A Midwest League. He managed seven seasons in the minors before becoming the bench coach under Felipe Alou with Montreal in 1995. He was the Expos' bench coach for three years, and credited Alou with influencing him on the nuances of leading a major-league ballclub. "He embraced his players in a manner which I try to do now," Tracy said in 2009. "That is, he was not invasive toward them. He did not invade their space, but he tried to keep them informed on where they stood with the team."[2]

Tracy's major-league managerial career began in 2001 when he was hired by the Los Angeles Dodgers, replacing Davey Johnson. A relative unknown at the time, his teams had winning records the first three

Jim Tracy.

years he was at the helm in Los Angeles, culminating in an NL West Division title in 2004. The Dodgers lost the division playoff series to the eventual NL champion St. Louis Cardinals that year, three games to one. In 2005 the Dodgers lost 22 more games than the previous year, and Tracy was fired after the season. He was hired by the Pirates in 2006, but the franchise was in the midst of 20 consecutive losing seasons. Success was not something any Pirates manager had experienced for a while. Tracy fared no better than his recent predecessors, as the Pirates lost 95 and 94 games in '06 and '07.

The Rockies front office viewed Tracy's hiring in 2009 as an audition over the remainder of the season, after which the manager position would be assessed. Upon the hiring Tracy said, "What we need to do is re-establish our identity. And to do that we need to recall the past. We don't have to look far, just two years back. The players have to realize that their performance to this point has been subpar. And we are not going to pretend that we are OK with that."[3]

Tracy's audition was a success from the start. From his first game as manager, on May 29, through the end of June the team went 23-8. Statistically and philosophically, the primary difference in the Rockies under Hurdle and Tracy was pitching. Starting on June 4, the Rockies went on an 11-game winning streak. The pitching staff allowed two fewer earned runs per game during the streak than they had in games before it. While Hurdle tended to make a lot of pitching changes, Tracy stuck with his starters longer. He tried to keep them in the game to get the win, and get them out before they would lose a game. That instilled confidence in the starters, which led to a staff on which each man worked to hold up his end of things. A good start by one guy meant the next guy wanted to pitch well, and so on.

In comparing the poor start in the first third of the season to the final two-thirds, hitting stayed consistent. The offense scored 4.86 runs per game in April and May, and increased its production slightly the remainder of the year to 5.01 runs per game. Defensively, the improvement was over a run per game, from 5.20 runs allowed during the first two months, to 4.07 from June through October. Overall the Rockies scored 89 more runs than allowed in 2009, which as of 2018 was the second best all-time run differential in franchise history, exceeded only by the +102 mark put up by the 2007 pennant winners. (The 715 runs allowed in 2009 still stood as of 2018 as the best mark in Rockies history.

The results of those statistics is predictable. In April and May, they never won more than three straight games, and that happened only once. In June they had the 11-game winning streak, lost a game, then won the next six. In September they won eight in row. The biggest win of the season may have been a September 16 game in San Francisco. The Rockies had lost some momentum, and ballgames—four in a row heading into the contest. In this game Jorge De La Rosa had shut out the Giants on three hits through eight innings, and the Rockies carried a 4-0 lead into the bottom of the ninth. But reliever Franklin Morales gave up three singles to start the inning, resulting in a run scoring and runners on first and second. Tracy turned to Rafael Betancourt, acquired from Cleveland in July, who induced a groundball from the first batter he faced, former Rockies player Juan Uribe. Tulowitzki's throwing error resulted in another run scoring and left runners at first and third. A popup and groundout stabilized the situation, with a run scoring on the grounder. The tying run was on third, with power-hitting Nate Schierholtz at bat and two out. Betancourt struck out Schierholtz to seal the win. The *Denver Post* commented on that moment in a late-season article about the Rockies' surge, "(Ryan) Spilborghs said later it was the most nervous he's ever been in baseball, while other Rockies admitted they couldn't even spit in the ninth inning because of pressure's vise-grip."[4]

It was an amazing turn of events for Jim Tracy and the Rockies in 2009. On June 3, the team was in last place in the NL West, 15½ games behind the first-place Dodgers and 9½ behind in the wild-card chase. Playing at a furious pace over the final four months brought them to within a game of the division lead with two to play when Ubaldo Jimenez and Huston Street combined to beat the Dodgers 4-3 on October

2. The Rockies had clinched a postseason appearance the day before, and with two games remaining against LA had a chance to win their first Western Division title. But the Dodgers won the final two games to secure the division championship. The Rockies finished 92-70, third best in the National League, topping the Central Division-winning Cardinals by one game.

Some numbers put the 2009 turnaround orchestrated by Tracy in historical perspective. For one, no team in history that switched managers in midseason had been 10 games under .500 and rose to 20 games over (the Rockies were 85-65 at the 150-game mark). Tracy was the first manager since Bob Lemon in 1978 to win 50 of his team's first 75 games after a midseason managerial change.[5] He brought stability to the lineup, and a quiet confidence that resonated with the players.

After the October 1 postseason clincher, Tracy commented in a loud and raucous Rockies clubhouse, "This is my most special moment in 33 years in baseball. Nothing can match it. No way."[6]

Neither Jim Tracy nor the Rockies have experienced the success of 2009. With the franchise's resurgence in 2017 under Bud Black, perhaps the near future holds more joys and highlights that will be reminiscent of that magical season, and 2007.

As for Jim Tracy, he remained the Rockies manager for three more seasons but the team looked like an escalator going down with the number of wins steadily declining to 83, 73, and 64. With a year remaining on his contract, Tracy resigned after the 2012 season, in part due to differences in philosophy with management concerning the pitching staff. He is one of four people to have managed the Rockies for at least 600 games, Hurdle, Don Baylor, and Walt Weiss being the other three. Tracy's .488 winning percentage is the best of four.

He made a brief return to managing in 2015, piloting TeamUSA to a silver medal in the Pan Am games. As of 2018 he was retired and living in Florida with his wife, Debra. The Tracys' three sons, Brian, Chad, and Mark, who like their grandfather and father have baseball in their blood and played in the minor leagues, were still involved in the game in some capacity.

SOURCES

In addition to the sources cited in the Notes, the author consulted Baseball-Reference.com, and Retrosheet.org.

NOTES

1   Troy E. Renck, "Can Rox Mimic Rays?—Fowler, Stewart May Help, but Team a Longshot in Flawed Division," *Denver Post*, April 5, 2009: C-12.

2   Patrick Saunders, "Tracy Discusses the Man Behind the Manager," *denverpost.com*, June 20, 2009—update May 6, 2016.

3   Troy E. Renck, "Tracy's Turn—Bench Coach Replaces Hurdle, Who Is Let Go After Seven Seasons," *Denver Post*, May 30, 2009: CC-01.

4   Troy E. Renck, "Clinch a Cinch—Rockies Broom Brewers 9-2 to Earn a Spot in Playoffs, West Division Title Within Grasp With Sweep of Dodgers," *Denver Post*, October 2, 2009: CC-01.

5   Jason Stark, "Unassuming Tracy Ideal Fit for Rockies," espn.com, September 21, 2009.

6   Troy E. Renck, "Clinch a Cinch."

CONTRIBUTORS

MALCOLM ALLEN co-edited SABR's *Pitching, Defense and Three-Run Homers* about the 1970 Baltimore Orioles. He manages a production warehouse in Brooklyn, New York, where he lives with his wife, Sara, and daughters Ruth and Martina. Keep an eye out for his upcoming book about Joaquin Andujar.

ERIEL F. BARCENAS is the proud husband of wife Lisa, and Cuban-American son of Marta Rego proudly raised on the urban streets of New Jersey, and the punk rock world surrounding it. He is a longtime musician and audio engineer educated at the Institute of Audio Research. He continues to work producing and engineering music, including his nephew Chris Cioce's musical venture. He has completed a Business Liberal Arts Associate's degree at Hudson County Community College in Jersey City, with plans to attend Xavier University in Cincinnati, Ohio. He has merged his place in audio and baseball with a SABR venture recreating 19th century games in broadcast format with author William Ryczek and historian John Thorn. Eriel's passion for reading was nurtured by his late brother Noel. His unique brand of writing and commitment to history was inspired by the encouragement of Professors Bradley Philbert and Dorothy Anderson. Eriel's drive into his education and the world of sports is motivated everyday by his friend Danny Correa-Gutierrez, lost on September 11, 2001 at the age of 25.

JOHN BAUER resides with his wife and two children in Parkville, Missouri, just outside of Kansas City. By day, he is an attorney specializing in insurance regulatory law and corporate law. By night, he spends many spring and summer evenings cheering for the San Francisco Giants and many fall and winter evenings reading history. He is a past and ongoing contributor to other SABR projects.

THOMAS J. BROWN JR. is a lifelong Mets fan who became a Durham Bulls fan after moving to North Carolina in the early 1980s. He was a national board certified high school science teacher for 34 years before retiring in 2016. Tom sill volunteers with the ELL students at his former high school, serving as a mentor to those students and the teachers who are now working with them. He also provides support and guidance for his former ELL students when they embark on different career paths after graduation. Tom has been a member of SABR since 1995 when he learned about the organization during a visit to Cooperstown on his honeymoon. He has become active in the organization since his retirement. He has written numerous biographies and game stories, mostly about the NY Mets. Tom also enjoys traveling as much as possible with his wife and has visited major-league and minor-league baseball parks across the country on his many trips.

ROBERT BRUSTAD is a professor in the School of Sport and Exercise Science at the University of Northern Colorado with a focus in the social, psychological and cultural aspects of sport. He had the good fortune of growing up in Southern California where Vin Scully's radio broadcasts provided him with an advanced appreciation of the game during his impressionable youth. He has also presented research at the SABR Analytics Conference.

ALAN COHEN has been a SABR member since 2011, serves as Vice President-Treasurer of the Connecticut Smoky Joe Wood Chapter, and is the datacaster (stringer) for the Hartford Yard Goats, the Double-A affiliate of the Colorado Rockies. He has written more than 40 biographies for SABR's BioProject, and more than 30 games for SABR's Games Project. He has expanded his research into the Hearst Sandlot Classic (1946-1965), an annual youth All-Star game which launched the careers of

88 major-league players. He has four children and six grandchildren and resides in West Hartford, Connecticut with his wife Frances, one cat (Morty) and two dogs (Sam and Sheba).

MIKE COONEY has been a SABR member since 1999. Retired for a third time, Mike, his wife Jade, and their two rescue German Shepherds live on a bluff overlooking the Ohio River. Since his first retirement, Mike has written over 500 newspaper columns which he titles *A Stones Throw*.

Born and raised in Colorado, **LAUREN CRONIN** had the misfortune to be raised a Red Sox fan when it wasn't a pleasant thing to be. Currently residing in Wheat Ridge, Colorado, she roots for the Rockies and Rays and fits in studying art conservation around her busy baseball-watching schedule.

RICHARD CUICCHI joined SABR in 1983 and is an active member of the Schott-Pelican Chapter. Since his retirement as an information technology executive, Richard authored *Family Ties: A Comprehensive Collection of Facts and Trivia about Baseball's Relatives*. He has contributed to numerous SABR BioProject and Games Project publications. He does freelance writing and blogging about a variety of baseball topics on his website TheTenthInning.com. Richard lives in New Orleans with his wife, Mary.

KYLE EATON, a lifelong Atlanta Braves fan, is a nonprofit professional residing in Germantown, Tennessee with his wife, young son, and two dogs. He holds a Bachelor of Arts Degree and a Master of Public Administration degree from the University of Memphis, and spends his free time running, watching baseball, and faking this whole fatherhood thing until he can hopefully figure it out. He currently serves on the board of a local animal rescue and Germantown's Historic Commission. He admittedly owns more bobbleheads than any grown man should own, but he is at peace with this, for now. He previously authored the biography of Javy López for SABR's *Puerto Rico and Baseball: 60 Biographies*.

BRIAN ENGELHARDT is a native of Reading, Pennsylvania where he resides with his wife, Suzanne, a good sport about any number of things. The author of *Reading's Big League Exhibition Games*, he has written a number of biographies for SABR, several articles appearing in other SABR publications and also is a regular contributor to the *Berks County Historical Review*. The collapse of the 1964 Phillies along with his mother throwing out his baseball cards that same year resulted in his emotional growth being stunted at age 13. Although Suzanne and he raised their three daughters as Phillies fans, his daughter living in Pittsburgh with her husband and son, seem to now also favor the Pirates (as evidenced by the painting of Bill Mazeroski in their family room) resulting in Brian, as a loving father and grandfather, developing a warm spot for the Buccos as well as the Phils.

JOY HACKENMUELLER is a healer/writer. She holds a Master of Science degree in Acupuncture and a Bachelor of Arts degree in Photography and African Studies. Joy credits her father Gary for her ability to strategize for the win, especially when the game runs long; because of him the thread of continuity between sport and spirituality was always a clearly presented package for human betterment. Joy encourages us all to tell it like it is, and never ever allow an edit in favor of a Hollywood ending. Her first book, *When At War The Soldier Never Sleeps*, published by Endless Press Publications in 1994, included her favorite interview of all time with former Black House of David African-American Semi-League "barnstorming" team member, Wilbert Lamar, who always told her like it was.

THOMAS HARDING has covered the Colorado Rockies since 2000 — for *The Gazette* in Colorado Springs and for MLB.com since 2002. He brings a different catalogue experience to the beat. That›s because on his way to the major leagues he hit each step of the minors. After his senior year at Bluefield (West Virginia) High School in 1981, he began covering the Bluefield Orioles of the Rookie-level Appalachian League, then the Myrtle Beach Blue Jays of the Class-A South Atlantic League for the

Sun News in Myrtle Beach, the Memphis Chicks of the Double-A Southern League, and the Memphis Redbirds of the Triple-A Pacific Coast League — while mixing in some St. Louis Cardinals coverage — for the *Commercial Appeal* in Memphis.

PAUL HOFMANN is the Associate Vice President for International Programs at Sacramento State University. He is a native of Detroit, Michigan and lifelong Detroit sports fan. His research interests include 19th century and pre-World War II Japanese baseball. He is also an avid baseball card collector. Paul currently resides in Folsom, California.

SABR member **MIKE HUBER** is Professor of Mathematics at Muhlenberg College in Allentown, Pennsylvania, where he routinely sponsors undergraduate research in sabermetrics. He frequently contributes to SABR's Baseball Games Project and enjoys studying rare events, including players who pitch no-hitters or hit for the cycle.

RYAN KEELER has been a member of SABR for one year. He is a Grand Junction native and a graduate of Colorado Mesa University. He currently resides in Denver and is entering his fifth season as a Colorado Rockies front office employee. He enjoys playing golf and other recreational activities such as hiking and biking. Ryan is a big family man that tries to spend as much time with his parents and sister as possible.

ROGER KINNEY retired from the Colorado Rockies in 2004 and now lives in Colorado where he enjoys coaching, writing, playing catch with his grandchildren, and rooting for the Rockies.

BOB LEMOINE is a high school librarian and adjunct professor in New Hampshire. While visiting Colorado only a handful of times, he enjoys researching and writing on just about any baseball history topic. He has contributed to several SABR book projects since joining in 2013, including co-editing with Bill Nowlin on 2016's *Boston's First Nine: The 1871-75 Boston Red Stockings*.

LEN LEVIN has been the copy editor for many SABR publications, including this one. A SABR member since 1977, he lives with his wife in Providence, Rhode Island, and is a retired newspaper editor. Besides editing for SABR, he has a part-time gig editing the decisions of the Rhode Island Supreme Court. Having two daughters living in Seattle and in the Washington, D.C., area gives him the chance to see games other than those of his beloved Red Sox.

ALEX MARKS has been a SABR member since 2013, and most recently was elected to be the Secretary for the Rocky Mountain SABR Chapter. He has a great passion for baseball, based on his lifelong affiliation with the sport, from playing in high school, to coaching multiple levels of Little League youth teams, to today being an advocate for Rocky Mountain SABR and Colorado Rockies baseball.

ED MESERKO is a retired salesperson. He enjoys traveling, music, reading, and baseball. SABR has been a recent enjoyment, allowing him to share stories with other baseball enthusiasts. Ed grew up a Cleveland Indians fan, bearing a lot of losing seasons. Being a resident of Colorado since 1983 has naturally allowed him to become a Rockies fan. Corporate sponsorship allowed Ed to sponsor promotional days at the ballpark and on two different occasions to throw out the ceremonial first pitch. Ed graduated from Rutgers and received his MBA from the University of Phoenix.

GWEN MESERKO is a retired travel agent and now volunteers for the Dumb Friends League. Gwen grew up in the shadow of Forbes Field and was a staunch Pittsburgh Pirates fan. Now, she has been a Colorado Rockies supporter for 25 years. She says, "Nolan Arenado is the only player who should be given the keys to the Rockies for the next 10 years." Gwen graduated from Kent State University. She enjoys traveling, reading, and playing card games.

CHAD MOODY is a nearly lifelong resident of suburban Detroit, where he has been a fan of the Detroit Tigers from birth. An alumnus of both the University of Michigan and Michigan State University, he has spent 25 years working in the automotive industry. Chad's first foray into baseball research occurred as a teenager, when he had a letter published in *Baseball Digest*. From that humble beginning, he has since frequently contributed to SABR's BioProject and Games Project. Chad and his wife, Lisa, live in Northville, Michigan, with their children, Jacob and Jessica, and dog, Daisy.

BILL NOWLIN has something of a Rockies connection through family, his mother being born in Denver in 1919 and some extended family in the area. His sister Joyce went to college at D.U. and stayed, living in Centennial. In 2007, though, there was no hesitation. He himself has been a lifelong Red Sox fan, and author of a couple of dozen Red Sox-related books. Co-founder of Rounder Records and a former political science professor, he spends most of his time now to helping edit books for SABR.

PAUL PARKER has been Club Historian of the Colorado Rockies for 25 years. He is also Manager of Community Affairs for the team. He has been a member of SABR since 1995, and is the long-time president of the Rocky Mountain chapter, based in Denver. Paul has attended the last 18 national conventions in a row. He holds a Bachelor's Degree in History from Southern Connecticut State University. A native of Brooklyn, New York, Paul's first major-league game was Game Three of the 1960 World Series at Yankee Stadium. Paul lives in Boulder, Colorado with his wife Ruth, and is the father of three adult children: Michelle, Rebecca, and Marcus.

JOHN W. PAUL JR. holds a CPPA from the National Property Management Association. He retired from Ball Aerospace & Technologies Corporation after a 32-year career with the United States Air Force and the Air National Guard as a Logistics/Supply Systems Analyst. Currently a Guest Relations Supervisor with Event Services of the Colorado Rockies. He is a lifelong Milwaukee Braves, St. Louis Cardinals, and Colorado Rockies fan and a member of SABR since 2001. He resides in the Denver area with his wife.

MANNY RANDHAWA is a baseball writer and member of the Statcast research team at MLB.com. He has covered Major League Baseball since 2013, with his work being featured or cited by MLB Network, Sports on Earth, CBS Sports, FanGraphs.com, the *St. Louis Post-Dispatch,* the *Seattle Times,* the *Indianapolis Star,* and other outlets. He lives in Denver, Colorado, and serves as a board member for the Rocky Mountain Chapter of the Society for American Baseball Research (SABR). He received his Bachelor of Arts degree in political science from the University of California, Berkeley, and his Master of Arts degree in sports journalism from Indiana University.

CARMEN REALE is a retired Air Traffic Control Specialist with 25 years of experience. Born and raised in Syracuse, New York, he is a graduate of Niagara University. He became a Red Sox fan in 1967 thanks to Call Yastrzemski and The Impossible Dream season. He now resides in Denver, Colorado when he is an adjunct professor of Air Traffic Control at Metro State University of Denver. He became a SABR member in 2017 and this is his first written contribution.

KEN REED is sports policy director for League of Fans, a sports reform project started by Ralph Nader. Reed is a long-time sports industry consultant, sports studies instructor, sports columnist and author. He holds a doctorate in sport administration with an emphasis in sport policy. His writings have appeared in a variety of publications, including the *New York Times, USA Today, Chicago Tribune,* and *Denver Post.* Reed regularly blogs on sports issues for the *Huffington Post.* He is the author of the books *How We Can Save Sports: A Game Plan, Ego vs. Soul in Sports, Game Changer,* and *Sara's Big Challenge.* Reed played baseball and basketball at the University of Denver. He continues to believe that the Oakland A's of the 1970's would've been the best baseball dynasty in the history of the game if one Charles O. Finley hadn't neglected to make an insurance annuity payment to Catfish Hunter, per a stipulation in Hunter's contract. As a result of Finley's blunder, Hunter's contract was terminated and he became a free agent. Finley then proceeded to conduct a wholesale dismantling of a great team still in its prime. A SABR member, Reed lives in Littleton, Colorado.

CARL RIECHERS retired from United Parcel Service in 2012 after 35 years of service. With more free time, he became a SABR member that same year. Born and raised in the suburbs of St. Louis, he became a big fan of the Cardinals. He and his wife Janet have three children and he is the proud grandpa of two.

MICHAEL T. ROBERTS has been a SABR member since 1981. This is his first published article. A diehard St. Louis Cardinals fan, Mike plans to contribute more SABR BioProject articles, focusing on mostly forgotten Cardinal players. A member of the Colorado Vintage Base Ball Association since its inception in 1993, "Bicycle Mike" was the primary shortstop for the Denver Blue Stockings and renditions of other 1860s and 1870s teams in the Rocky Mountain area. "Bike Mike" is a corporate accountant by day, and is now in a semi-retirement phase of his career hoping to spend more time studying baseball history, travelling, and enjoying time with his wife Cathy at their vacation property in the Big Horn mountains of Wyoming.

CURT SMITH's 17th book will be released in 2018: *The Presidents and the Pastime: The History of Baseball and the White House*, from University of Nebraska Press, the first book to chronicle in-depth the historical relationship between two American institutions— baseball and the Presidency. Red Sox radio Voice Joe Castiglione calls it "a masterpiece. His anecdotes and research are remarkable." Smith's prior books include *Voices of The Game, Pull Up a Chair: The Vin Scully Story*, and *The Voice: Mel Allen's Untold Story*. From 1989-93, he wrote more speeches than anyone else for President George H.W. Bush. Smith is a GateHouse Media and mlbblog.com columnist, Associated Press award-winning commentator, and senior lecturer at the University of Rochester. He has hosted or key-noted the Great Fenway Writers Series, numerous Smithsonian Institution series, and the Cooperstown Symposium on Baseball and American Culture. The former *The* Saturday *Evening Post* senior editor has written ESPN TV's *Voices of The Game* series, created the Franklin Roosevelt Award in Communication at the National Radio Hall of Fame, and been named to the Judson Welliver Society of former Presidential speechwriters.

ALFONSO L. TUSA C. is a writer who was born in Cumaná, Venezuela and now writes a lot about baseball from Los Teques, Venezuela. He's the author *Una Temporada Mágica* (A magical season), *El Látigo del Beisbol. Una biografía de Isaías Látigo Chávez.* (The Whip of Baseball. An Isaías Látigo Chávez biography), *Pensando en ti Venezuela. Una biografía de Dámaso Blanco.* (Thinking about you Venezuela. A Dámaso Blanco biography) and *Voces de Beisbol y Ecología (*Voices of Baseball and Ecology). He contributes to some websites, books, and newspapers. He shares many moments with his boy Miguelin.

JOSEPH WANCHO has been a SABR member since 2005. He has made occasional contributions to both the BioProject and the Games Project. Currently he is working on a BioProject book for SABR featuring the 1995 Cleveland Indians entitled *The Sleeping Giant Awakes.*

KURT WELLS is on the Board of Directors of SABR's Rocky Mountain chapter. He has spent many years as Finance Director for several government contracting firms. In the late 1980's, he co-hosted a radio sports talk show, promoting bringing major-league baseball to Denver and was subsequently a loaned executive to the Colorado Baseball Commission to support the efforts in the award of the Colorado Rockies franchise. Mr. Wells hosted Rockies players in his home from 2001 to 2013 as part of the teams' Winter Development Program that brought top prospects to Denver in January to prepare for the upcoming season.

BRIAN WERNER has been a SABR member since 1986. Although he grew up a Pittsburgh Pirate fan, he became a full-fledged Rockies fan on their creation in his home state. Brian has been a Rockies season ticket holder since day 1, attended the Rockies' first-ever game in New York City, followed by their first home opener against the Expos and Eric Young's leadoff HR later that same week in April 1993. He has attended every Rockies home opener. In real life he is a public information officer for a water agency.

CHRIS WILLIAMSON joined the Rocky Mountain Chapter of SABR in 2017. He works in software implementation but writes about prospects for dynasty fantasy baseball owners on his website—makeprospectsgreatagain.com and will be a contributor for baseball-farm.com during the upcoming 2018 season and beyond. His loyalty lies with the White Sox but he has become an adopted Rockies fan since moving to Denver in 2015.

A lifelong Pirates fan, **GREGORY H. WOLF** was born in Pittsburgh, but now resides in the Chicagoland area with his wife, Margaret, and daughter, Gabriela. A professor of German studies and holder of the Dennis and Jean Bauman Endowed Chair in the Humanities at North Central College in Naperville, Illinois, he has edited eight books for SABR. He is currently working on projects about Wrigley Field and Comiskey Park in Chicago, and the 1982 Milwaukee Brewers. As of January 2017, he serves as co-director of SABR's BioProject, which you can follow on Facebook and Twitter.

JACK ZERBY counts it just one of the many benefits of SABR membership that he was able to enjoy a ballgame in Coors Field with SABR 33 in Denver. He now follows Rockies prospects through their longtime South Atlantic League affiliate, the Asheville Tourists. Jack, a member of SABR since 1994, is a retired attorney and estates administrator. He lives in Brevard, North Carolina, with his wife Diana, a professional violinist. He has been a member since inception (2002) of the BioProject and continues to write, edit, and do fact checks for it and the newer Games Project. While living in southwest Florida Jack co-founded the Seymour-Mills regional chapter with SABR colleague Mel Poplock.

THANKS AND ACKNOWLEDGMENTS

A special thanks to Kurt Wells and Bill Achbach, who participated in the selection of the biographical subjects and memorable moments and games that went into this publication.

Thanks to Colorado Rockies team photographer Matt Dirksen, who provided many of the images that appear in this book.

As this literary effort goes to print, I am completing 25 years as Club Historian and Manager of Community Affairs, among other responsibilities, and retiring as of February 9, 2018. I wish to express my gratitude to my Rockies family, to all of my colleagues in the Front Office who have been so forthcoming with their support and friendship.

Also worthy of kudos are the great folks of the Rocky Mountain chapter of SABR, who have given freely of their time and enthusiasm to bring this publication to fruition.

And finally, a heartfelt thanks to my family for tolerating my baseball habit for so many years: my wife, Ruth, my daughters Michelle and Rebecca and my son Marcus.

Paul T. Parker
Denver, Colorado
February 8, 2018

Thanks, as always, to the great community that is SABR. Thanks to Carl Riechers for detailed fact-checking and to Len Levin for final copy editing. Both are really quick and help all of us writers with the errors and oversights we all have.

Particular thanks to the "pinch-writers" who stepped in and wrote up a bio or a game story when a couple of the original volunteers went incommunicado.

Thanks to Jill Campbell and Brian Gaffney of the Colorado Rockies, and to John Horne of the National Baseball Hall of Fame for supplying all of the photographs for this book.

Bill Nowlin
Cambridge, Massachusetts
February 8, 2018

SABR BioProject Team Books

In 2002, the Society for American Baseball Research launched an effort to write and publish biographies of every player, manager, and individual who has made a contribution to baseball. Over the past decade, the BioProject Committee has produced over 6,000 biographical articles. Many have been part of efforts to create theme- or team-oriented books, spearheaded by chapters or other committees of SABR.

THE 1986 BOSTON RED SOX:
THERE WAS MORE THAN GAME SIX
One of a two-book series on the rivals that met in the 1986 World Series, the Boston Red Sox and the New York Mets, including biographies of every player, coach, broadcaster, and other important figures in the top organizations in baseball that year. .
Edited by Leslie Heaphy and Bill Nowlin
$19.95 paperback (ISBN 978-1-943816-19-4)
$9.99 ebook (ISBN 978-1-943816-18-7)
8.5"X11", 420 pages, over 200 photos

THE 1986 NEW YORK METS:
THERE WAS MORE THAN GAME SIX
The other book in the "rivalry" set from the 1986 World Series. This book re-tells the story of that year's classic World Series and this is the story of each of the players, coaches, managers, and broadcasters, their lives in baseball and the way the 1986 season fit into their lives.
Edited by Leslie Heaphy and Bill Nowlin
$19.95 paperback (ISBN 978-1-943816-13-2)
$9.99 ebook (ISBN 978-1-943816-12-5)
8.5"X11", 392 pages, over 100 photos

SCANDAL ON THE SOUTH SIDE:
THE 1919 CHICAGO WHITE SOX
The Black Sox Scandal isn't the only story worth telling about the 1919 Chicago White Sox. The team roster included three future Hall of Famers, a 20-year-old spitballer who would win 300 games in the minors, and even a batboy who later became a celebrity with the "Murderers' Row" New York Yankees. All of their stories are included in Scandal on the South Side with a timeline of the 1919 season.
Edited by Jacob Pomrenke
$19.95 paperback (ISBN 978-1-933599-95-3)
$9.99 ebook (ISBN 978-1-933599-94-6)
8.5"x11", 324 pages, 55 historic photos

WINNING ON THE NORTH SIDE
THE 1929 CHICAGO CUBS
Celebrate the 1929 Chicago Cubs, one of the most exciting teams in baseball history. Future Hall of Famers Hack Wilson, '29 NL MVP Rogers Hornsby, and Kiki Cuyler, along with Riggs Stephenson formed one of the most potent quartets in baseball history. The magical season came to an ignominious end in the World Series and helped craft the future "lovable loser" image of the team.
Edited by Gregory H. Wolf
$19.95 paperback (ISBN 978-1-933599-89-2)
$9.99 ebook (ISBN 978-1-933599-88-5)
8.5"x11", 314 pages, 59 photos

DETROIT THE UNCONQUERABLE:
THE 1935 WORLD CHAMPION TIGERS
Biographies of every player, coach, and broadcaster involved with the 1935 World Champion Detroit Tigers baseball team, written by members of the Society for American Baseball Research. Also includes a season in review and other articles about the 1935 team. Hank Greenberg, Mickey Cochrane, Charlie Gehringer, Schoolboy Rowe, and more.
Edited by Scott Ferkovich
$19.95 paperback (ISBN 9978-1-933599-78-6)
$9.99 ebook (ISBN 978-1-933599-79-3)
8.5"X11", 230 pages, 52 photos

THE TEAM THAT TIME WON'T FORGET:
THE 1951 NEW YORK GIANTS
Because of Bobby Thomson's dramatic "Shot Heard 'Round the World" in the bottom of the ninth of the decisive playoff game against the Brooklyn Dodgers, the team will forever be in baseball public's consciousness. Includes a foreword by Giants outfielder Monte Irvin.
Edited by Bill Nowlin and C. Paul Rogers III
$19.95 paperback (ISBN 978-1-933599-99-1)
$9.99 ebook (ISBN 978-1-933599-98-4)
8.5"X11", 282 pages, 47 photos

A PENNANT FOR THE TWIN CITIES:
THE 1965 MINNESOTA TWINS
This volume celebrates the 1965 Minnesota Twins, who captured the American League pennant in just their fifth season in the Twin Cities. Led by an All-Star cast, from Harmon Killebrew, Tony Oliva, Zoilo Versalles, and Mudcat Grant to Bob Allison, Jim Kaat, Earl Battey, and Jim Perry, the Twins won 102 games, but bowed to the Los Angeles Dodgers and Sandy Koufax in Game Seven
Edited by Gregory H. Wolf
$19.95 paperback (ISBN 978-1-943816-09-5)
$9.99 ebook (ISBN 978-1-943816-08-8)
8.5"X11", 405 pages, over 80 photos

MUSTACHES AND MAYHEM: CHARLIE O'S THREE TIME CHAMPIONS:
THE OAKLAND ATHLETICS: 1972-74
The Oakland Athletics captured major league baseball's crown each year from 1972 through 1974. Led by future Hall of Famers Reggie Jackson, Catfish Hunter and Rollie Fingers, the Athletics were a largely homegrown group who came of age together. Biographies of every player, coach, manager, and broadcaster (and mascot) from 1972 through 1974 are included, along with season recaps.
Edited by Chip Greene
$29.95 paperback (ISBN 978-1-943816-07-1)
$9.99 ebook (ISBN 978-1-943816-06-4)
8.5"X11", 600 pages, almost 100 photos

SABR Members can purchase each book at a significant discount (often 50% off) and receive the ebook edtions free as a member benefit. Each book is available in a trade paperback edition as well as ebooks suitable for reading on a home computer or Nook, Kindle, or iPad/tablet.
To learn more about becoming a member of SABR, visit the website: sabr.org/join

THE SABR DIGITAL LIBRARY

The Society for American Baseball Research, the top baseball research organization in the world, disseminates some of the best in baseball history, analysis, and biography through our publishing programs. The SABR Digital Library contains a mix of books old and new, and focuses on a tandem program of paperback and ebook publication, making these materials widely available for both on digital devices and as traditional printed books.

GREATEST GAMES BOOKS

TIGERS BY THE TALE:
GREAT GAMES AT MICHIGAN AND TRUMBULL
For over 100 years, Michigan and Trumbull was the scene of some of the most exciting baseball ever. This book portrays 50 classic games at the corner, spanning the earliest days of Bennett Park until Tiger Stadium's final closing act. From Ty Cobb to Mickey Cochrane, Hank Greenberg to Al Kaline, and Willie Horton to Alan Trammell.
Edited by Scott Ferkovich
$12.95 paperback (ISBN 978-1-943816-21-7)
$6.99 ebook (ISBN 978-1-943816-20-0)
8.5"x11", 160 pages, 22 photos

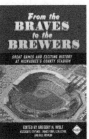

FROM THE BRAVES TO THE BREWERS: GREAT GAMES AND HISTORY AT MILWAUKEE'S COUNTY STADIUM
The National Pastime provides in-depth articles focused on the geographic region where the national SABR convention is taking place annually. The SABR 45 convention took place in Chicago, and here are 45 articles on baseball in and around the bat-and-ball crazed Windy City: 25 that appeared in the souvenir book of the convention plus another 20 articles available in ebook only.
Edited by Gregory H. Wolf
$19.95 paperback (ISBN 978-1-943816-23-1)
$9.99 ebook (ISBN 978-1-943816-22-4)
8.5"X11", 290 pages, 58 photos

BRAVES FIELD:
MEMORABLE MOMENTS AT BOSTON'S LOST DIAMOND
From its opening on August 18, 1915, to the sudden departure of the Boston Braves to Milwaukee before the 1953 baseball season, Braves Field was home to Boston's National League baseball club and also hosted many other events: from NFL football to championship boxing. The most memorable moments to occur in Braves Field history are portrayed here.
Edited by Bill Nowlin and Bob Brady
$19.95 paperback (ISBN 978-1-933599-93-9)
$9.99 ebook (ISBN 978-1-933599-92-2)
8.5"X11", 282 pages, 182 photos

AU JEU/PLAY BALL: THE 50 GREATEST GAMES IN THE HISTORY OF THE MONTREAL EXPOS
The 50 greatest games in Montreal Expos history. The games described here recount the exploits of the many great players who wore Expos uniforms over the years—Bill Stoneman, Gary Carter, Andre Dawson, Steve Rogers, Pedro Martinez, from the earliest days of the franchise, to the glory years of 1979-1981, the what-might-have-been years of the early 1990s, and the sad, final days.and others.
Edited by Norm King
$12.95 paperback (ISBN 978-1-943816-15-6)
$5.99 ebook (ISBN978-1-943816-14-9)
8.5"x11", 162 pages, 50 photos

ORIGINAL SABR RESEARCH

CALLING THE GAME:
BASEBALL BROADCASTING FROM 1920 TO THE PRESENT
An exhaustive, meticulously researched history of bringing the national pastime out of the ballparks and into living rooms via the airwaves. Every play-by-play announcer, color commentator, and ex-ballplayer, every broadcast deal, radio station, and TV network. Plus a foreword by "Voice of the Chicago Cubs" Pat Hughes, and an afterword by Jacques Doucet, the "Voice of the Montreal Expos" 1972-2004.
by Stuart Shea
$24.95 paperback (ISBN 978-1-933599-40-3)
$9.99 ebook (ISBN 978-1-933599-41-0)
7"X10", 712 pages, 40 photos

BIOPROJECT BOOKS

WHO'S ON FIRST:
REPLACEMENT PLAYERS IN WORLD WAR II
During World War II, 533 players made the major league debuts. More than 60% of the players in the 1941 Opening Day lineups departed for the service and were replaced by first-times and oldsters. Hod Lisenbee was 46. POW Bert Shepard had an artificial leg, and Pete Gray had only one arm. The 1944 St. Louis Browns had 13 players classified 4-F. These are their stories.
Edited by Marc Z Aaron and Bill Nowlin
$19.95 paperback (ISBN 978-1-933599-91-5)
$9.99 ebook (ISBN 978-1-933599-90-8)
8.5"X11", 422 pages, 67 photos

VAN LINGLE MUNGO:
THE MAN, THE SONG, THE PLAYERS
40 baseball players with intriguing names have been named in renditions of Dave Frishberg's classic 1969 song, Van Lingle Mungo. This book presents biographies of all 40 players and additional information about one of the greatest baseball novelty songs of all time.
Edited by Bill Nowlin
$19.95 paperback (ISBN 978-1-933599-76-2)
$9.99 ebook (ISBN 978-1-933599-77-9)
8.5"X11", 278 pages, 46 photos

NUCLEAR POWERED BASEBALL
Nuclear Powered Baseball tells the stories of each player—past and present—featured in the classic Simpsons episode "Homer at the Bat." Wade Boggs, Ken Griffey Jr., Ozzie Smith, Nap Lajoie, Don Mattingly, and many more. We've also included a few very entertaining takes on the now-famous episode from prominent baseball writers Jonah Keri, Joe Posnanski, Erik Malinowski, and Bradley Woodrum
Edited by Emily Hawks and Bill Nowlin
$19.95 paperback (ISBN 978-1-943816-11-8)
$9.99 ebook (ISBN 978-1-943816-10-1)
8.5"X11", 250 pages

SABR Members can purchase each book at a significant discount (often 50% off) and receive the ebook edtions free as a member benefit. Each book is available in a trade paperback edition as well as ebooks suitable for reading on a home computer or Nook, Kindle, or iPad/tablet.
To learn more about becoming a member of SABR, visit the website: sabr.org/join

SABR BioProject Books

In 2002, the Society for American Baseball Research launched an effort to write and publish biographies of every player, manager, and individual who has made a contribution to baseball. Over the past decade, the BioProject Committee has produced over 2,200 biographical articles. Many have been part of efforts to create theme- or team-oriented books, spearheaded by chapters or other committees of SABR.

THE YEAR OF THE BLUE SNOW:
THE 1964 PHILADELPHIA PHILLIES
Catcher Gus Triandos dubbed the Philadelphia Phillies' 1964 season "the year of the blue snow," a rare thing that happens once in a great while. This book sheds light on lingering questions about the 1964 season—but any book about a team is really about the players. This work offers life stories of all the players and others (managers, coaches, owners, and broadcasters) associated with this star-crossed team, as well as essays of analysis and history.
Edited by Mel Marmer and Bill Nowlin
$19.95 paperback (ISBN 978-1-933599-51-9)
$9.99 ebook (ISBN 978-1-933599-52-6)
8.5"X11", 356 PAGES, over 70 photos

DETROIT TIGERS 1984:
WHAT A START! WHAT A FINISH!
The 1984 Detroit tigers roared out of the gate, winning their first nine games of the season and compiling an eye-popping 35-5 record after the campaign's first 40 games—still the best start ever for any team in major league history. This book brings together biographical profiles of every Tiger from that magical season, plus those of field management, top executives, the broadcasters—even venerable Tiger Stadium and the city itself.
Edited by Mark Pattison and David Raglin
$19.95 paperback (ISBN 978-1-933599-44-1)
$9.99 ebook (ISBN 978-1-933599-45-8)
8.5"x11", 250 pages (Over 230,000 words!)

SWEET '60: THE 1960 PITTSBURGH PIRATES
A portrait of the 1960 team which pulled off one of the biggest upsets of the last 60 years. When Bill Mazeroski's home run left the park to win in Game Seven of the World Series, beating the New York Yankees, David had toppled Goliath. It was a blow that awakened a generation, one that millions of people saw on television, one of TV's first iconic World Series moments.
Edited by Clifton Blue Parker and Bill Nowlin
$19.95 paperback (ISBN 978-1-933599-48-9)
$9.99 ebook (ISBN 978-1-933599-49-6)
8.5"X11", 340 pages, 75 photos

RED SOX BASEBALL IN THE DAYS OF IKE AND ELVIS: THE RED SOX OF THE 1950s
Although the Red Sox spent most of the 1950s far out of contention, the team was filled with fascinating players who captured the heart of their fans. In *Red Sox Baseball*, members of SABR present 46 biographies on players such as Ted Williams and Pumpsie Green as well as season-by-season recaps.
Edited by Mark Armour and Bill Nowlin
$19.95 paperback (ISBN 978-1-933599-24-3)
$9.99 ebook (ISBN 978-1-933599-34-2)
8.5"X11", 372 PAGES, over 100 photos

THE MIRACLE BRAVES OF 1914
BOSTON'S ORIGINAL WORST-TO-FIRST CHAMPIONS
Long before the Red Sox "Impossible Dream" season, Boston's now nearly forgotten "other" team, the 1914 Boston Braves, performed a baseball "miracle" that resounds to this very day. The "Miracle Braves" were Boston's first "worst-to-first" winners of the World Series. Refusing to throw in the towel at the midseason mark, George Stallings engineered a remarkable second-half climb in the standings all the way to first place.
Edited by Bill Nowlin
$19.95 paperback (ISBN 978-1-933599-69-4)
$9.99 ebook (ISBN 978-1-933599-70-0)
8.5"X11", 392 PAGES, over 100 photos

THAR'S JOY IN BRAVELAND!
THE 1957 MILWAUKEE BRAVES
Few teams in baseball history have captured the hearts of their fans like the Milwaukee Braves of the 1950s. During the Braves' 13-year tenure in Milwaukee (1953-1965), they had a winning record every season, won two consecutive NL pennants (1957 and 1958), lost two more in the final week of the season (1956 and 1959), and set big-league attendance records along the way.
Edited by Gregory H. Wolf
$19.95 paperback (ISBN 978-1-933599-71-7)
$9.99 ebook (ISBN 978-1-933599-72-4)
8.5"x11", 330 pages, over 60 photos

NEW CENTURY, NEW TEAM:
THE 1901 BOSTON AMERICANS
The team now known as the Boston Red Sox played its first season in 1901. Boston had a well-established National League team, but the American League went head-to-head with the N.L. in Chicago, Philadelphia, and Boston. Chicago won the American League pennant and Boston finished second, only four games behind.
Edited by Bill Nowlin
$19.95 paperback (ISBN 978-1-933599-58-8)
$9.99 ebook (ISBN 978-1-933599-59-5)
8.5"X11", 268 pages, over 125 photos

CAN HE PLAY?
A LOOK AT BASEBALL SCOUTS AND THEIR PROFESSION
They dig through tons of coal to find a single diamond. Here in the world of scouts, we meet the "King of Weeds," a Ph.D. we call "Baseball's Renaissance Man," a husband-and-wife team, pioneering Latin scouts, and a Japanese-American interned during World War II who became a successful scout—and many, many more.
Edited by Jim Sandoval and Bill Nowlin
$19.95 paperback (ISBN 978-1-933599-23-6)
$9.99 ebook (ISBN 978-1-933599-25-0)
8.5"X11", 200 PAGES, over 100 photos

SABR Members can purchase each book at a significant discount (often 50% off) and receive the ebook editions free as a member benefit. Each book is available in a trade paperback edition as well as ebooks suitable for reading on a home computer or Nook, Kindle, or iPad/tablet.
To learn more about becoming a member of SABR, visit the website: sabr.org/join

THE SABR DIGITAL LIBRARY

The Society for American Baseball Research, the top baseball research organization in the world, disseminates some of the best in baseball history, analysis, and biography through our publishing programs. The SABR Digital Library contains a mix of books old and new, and focuses on a tandem program of paperback and ebook publication, making these materials widely available for both on digital devices and as traditional printed books.

CLASSIC REPRINTS

BASE-BALL: HOW TO BECOME A PLAYER
by John Montgomery Ward
John Montgomery Ward (1860-1925) tossed the second perfect game in major league history and later became the game's best shortstop and a great, inventive manager. His classic handbook on baseball skills and strategy was published in 1888. Illustrated with woodcuts, the book is divided into chapters for each position on the field as well as chapters on the origin of the game, theory and strategy, training, base-running, and batting.
$4.99 ebook (ISBN 978-1-933599-47-2)
$9.95 paperback (ISBN 978-0910137539)
156 PAGES, 4.5"X7" replica edition

BATTING by F. C. Lane
First published in 1925, *Batting* collects the wisdom and insights of over 250 hitters and baseball figures. Lane interviewed extensively and compiled tips and advice on everything from batting stances to beanballs. Legendary baseball figures such as Ty Cobb, Casey Stengel, Cy Young, Walter Johnson, Rogers Hornsby, and Babe Ruth reveal the secrets of such integral and interesting parts of the game as how to choose a bat, the ways to beat a slump, and how to outguess the pitcher.
$14.95 paperback (ISBN 978-0-910137-86-7)
$7.99 ebook (ISBN 978-1-933599-46-5)
240 PAGES, 5"X7"

RUN, RABBIT, RUN
by Walter "Rabbit" Maranville
"Rabbit" Maranville was the Joe Garagiola of Grandpa's day, the baseball comedian of the times. In a twenty-four-year career that began in 1912, Rabbit found a lot of funny situations to laugh at, and no wonder: he caused most of them! The book also includes an introduction by the late Harold Seymour and a historical account of Maranville's life and Hall-of-Fame career by Bob Carroll.
$9.95 paperback (ISBN 978-1-933599-26-7)
$5.99 ebook (ISBN 978-1-933599-27-4)
100 PAGES, 5.5"X8.5", 15 rare photos

MEMORIES OF A BALLPLAYER
by Bill Werber and C. Paul Rogers III
Bill Werber's claim to fame is unique: he was the last living person to have a direct connection to the 1927 Yankees, "Murderers' Row," a team hailed by many as the best of all time. Rich in anecdotes and humor, Memories of a Ballplayer is a clear-eyed memoir of the world of big-league baseball in the 1930s. Werber played with or against some of the most productive hitters of all time, including Babe Ruth, Ted Williams, Lou Gehrig, and Joe DiMaggio.
$14.95 paperback (ISNB 978-0-910137-84-3)
$6.99 ebook (ISBN 978-1-933599-47-2)
250 PAGES, 6"X9"

ORIGINAL SABR RESEARCH

INVENTING BASEBALL: THE 100 GREATEST GAMES OF THE NINETEENTH CENTURY
SABR's Nineteenth Century Committee brings to life the greatest games from the game's early years. From the "prisoner of war" game that took place among captive Union soldiers during the Civil War (immortalized in a famous lithograph), to the first intercollegiate game (Amherst versus Williams), to the first professional no-hitter, the games in this volume span 1833–1900 and detail the athletic exploits of such players as Cap Anson, Moses "Fleetwood" Walker, Charlie Comiskey, and Mike "King" Kelly.
Edited by Bill Felber
$19.95 paperback (ISBN 978-1-933599-42-7)
$9.99 ebook (ISBN 978-1-933599-43-4)
302 PAGES, 8"x10", 200 photos

NINETEENTH CENTURY STARS: 2012 EDITION
First published in 1989, *Nineteenth Century Stars* was SABR's initial attempt to capture the stories of baseball players from before 1900. With a collection of 136 fascinating biographies, SABR has re-released *Nineteenth Century Stars* for 2012 with revised statistics and new form. The 2012 version also includes a preface by **John Thorn**.
Edited by Robert L. Tiemann and Mark Rucker
$19.95 paperback (ISBN 978-1-933599-28-1)
$9.99 ebook (ISBN 978-1-933599-29-8)
300 PAGES, 6"X9"

GREAT HITTING PITCHERS
Published in 1979, *Great Hitting Pitchers* was one of SABR's early publications. Edited by SABR founder Bob Davids, the book compiles stories and records about pitchers excelling in the batter's box. Newly updated in 2012 by Mike Cook, *Great Hitting Pitchers* contain tables including data from 1979-2011, corrections to reflect recent records, and a new chapter on recent new members in the club of "great hitting pitchers" like Tom Glavine and Mike Hampton.
Edited by L. Robert Davids
$9.95 paperback (ISBN 978-1-933599-30-4)
$5.99 ebook (ISBN 978-1-933599-31-1)
102 PAGES, 5.5"x8.5"

THE FENWAY PROJECT
Sixty-four SABR members—avid fans, historians, statisticians, and game enthusiasts—recorded their experiences of a single game. Some wrote from inside the Green Monster's manual scoreboard, the Braves clubhouse, or the broadcast booth, while others took in the essence of Fenway from the grandstand or bleachers. The result is a fascinating look at the charms and challenges of Fenway Park, and the allure of being a baseball fan.
Edited by Bill Nowlin and Cecilia Tan
$9.99 ebook (ISBN 978-1-933599-50-2)
175 pages, 100 photos

SABR Members can purchase each book at a significant discount (often 50% off) and receive the ebook editions free as a member benefit. Each book is available in a trade paperback edition as well as ebooks suitable for reading on a home computer or Nook, Kindle, or iPad/tablet.
To learn more about becoming a member of SABR, visit the website: sabr.org/join

Society for American Baseball Research

Cronkite School at ASU
555 N. Central Ave. #416, Phoenix, AZ 85004
602.496.1460 (phone)
SABR.org

Become a SABR member today!

If you're interested in baseball — writing about it, reading about it, talking about it — there's a place for you in the Society for American Baseball Research. Our members include everyone from academics to professional sportswriters to amateur historians and statisticians to students and casual fans who enjoy reading about baseball and occasionally gathering with other members to talk baseball. What unites all SABR members is an interest in the game and joy in learning more about it.

SABR membership is open to any baseball fan; we offer 1-year and 3-year memberships. Here's a list of some of the key benefits you'll receive as a SABR member:

* Receive two editions (spring and fall) of the *Baseball Research Journal*, our flagship publication
* Receive expanded e-book edition of *The National Pastime*, our annual convention journal
* 8-10 new e-books published by the SABR Digital Library, all FREE to members
* "This Week in SABR" e-newsletter, sent to members every Friday
* Join dozens of research committees, from Statistical Analysis to Women in Baseball.
* Join one of 70 regional chapters in the U.S., Canada, Latin America, and abroad
* Participate in online discussion groups
* Ask and answer baseball research questions on the SABR-L e-mail listserv
* Complete archives of *The Sporting News* dating back to 1886 and other research resources
* Promote your research in "This Week in SABR"
* Diamond Dollars Case Competition
* Yoseloff Scholarships

* Discounts on SABR national conferences, including the SABR National Convention, the SABR Analytics Conference, Jerry Malloy Negro League Conference, Frederick Ivor-Campbell 19th Century Conference, and the Arizona Fall League Experience
* Publish your research in peer-reviewed SABR journals
* Collaborate with SABR researchers and experts
* Contribute to Baseball Biography Project or the SABR Games Project
* List your new book in the SABR Bookshelf
* Lead a SABR research committee or chapter
* Networking opportunities at SABR Analytics Conference
* Meet baseball authors and historians at SABR events and chapter meetings
* 50% discounts on paperback versions of SABR e-books
* Discounts with other partners in the baseball community
* SABR research awards

We hope you'll join the most passionate international community of baseball fans at SABR! Check us out online at SABR.org/join.

- -

SABR MEMBERSHIP FORM

	Annual	3-year	Senior	3-yr Sr.	Under 30
Standard:	❏ $65	❏ $175	❏ $45	❏ $129	❏ $45
(International members wishing to be mailed the Baseball Research Journal should add $10/yr for Canada/Mexico or $19/yr for overseas locations.)					
Canada/Mexico:	❏ $75	❏ $205	❏ $55	❏ $159	❏ $55
Overseas:	❏ $84	❏ $232	❏ $64	❏ $186	❏ $55
Senior = 65 or older before Dec. 31 of the current year					

Participate in Our Donor Program!

Support the preservation of baseball research. Designate your gift toward:
❏General Fund   ❏Endowment Fund   ❏Research Resources   ❏_____
❏ I want to maximize the impact of my gift; do not send any donor premiums
❏ I would like this gift to remain anonymous.
Note: Any donation not designated will be placed in the General Fund.
SABR is a 501 (c) (3) not-for-profit organization & donations are tax-deductible to the extent allowed by law.

Name _____

E-mail* _____

Address _____

City _____ ST_____ ZIP_____

Phone _____ Birthday _____

* **Your e-mail address on file ensures you will receive the most recent SABR news.**

Dues $_____

Donation $_____

Amount Enclosed $_____

Do you work for a matching grant corporation? Call (602) 496-1460 for details.

If you wish to pay by credit card, please contact the SABR office at (602) 496-1460 or visit the SABR Store online at SABR.org/join. We accept Visa, Mastercard & Discover.

Do you wish to receive the *Baseball Research Journal* electronically? ❏ Yes   ❏ No
Our e-books are available in PDF, Kindle, or EPUB (iBooks, iPad, Nook) formats.

Mail to: SABR, Cronkite School at ASU, 555 N. Central Ave. #416, Phoenix, AZ 85004

Made in the USA
Las Vegas, NV
25 April 2022